STRATEGIC PLANNING
FOR UNIVERSITY RESEARCH

SERIES TITLES

STRATEGIC PLANNING
FOR
UNIVERSITY RESEARCH

Edited by
Oliver D. Hensley

Texas Tech University Press
Lubbock, Texas

SRA MONOGRAPHS NO. 4

Published in cooperation with the Society of
Research Administrators, Chicago, Illinois

Copyright 1992 Texas Tech University Press

Library of Congress Catagloging-in-Publication Data
Strategic planning for university research / edited by Oliver D.
  Hensley
       p. cm. — (SRA monographs ; no. 4)
    Includes bibliographical references.
    ISBN 0-89672-239-2
    1. Research—United States—Management. 2. Universities and
colleges—United States—Research. I. Hensley, Oliver D.
II. Series.
Q180.U5S77 1992
001.4'068'4—dc20   92-18227
                                                CIP

92 93 94 95 96 97 98 99 00 / 9 8 7 6 5 4 3 2 1

Texas Tech University Press
Lubbock, Texas 79409-1037 USA

CONTENTS

FOREWORD

For a quarter-century, the Society of Research Administrators has promoted the exchange of information related to research administration by holding annual meetings predominantly devoted to the presentation of information from major research sponsors, to individual professional development, and to institutional advancement. To advance research administration information, the research committee was given the charge of exploring the field of research administration. The SRA Research Symposia and SRA Monographs grew from this primary charge and are structured to promote the study of topics that are fundamental to the field of research administration.

In 1990, SRA committees developed and/or updated action plans to advance the work of the Society. The SRA Research Committee's action plan established the following broad goals for the committee: (1) To improve and enhance the competence and effectiveness of professional research administrators. (2) To coordinate SRA Study Groups in the pursuit of knowledge related to research administration or the research phenomena. (3) To improve and enhance the role, stature, and influence of the profession of research administration through the study of critical issues related to the research enterprise. (4) To facilitate professional information exchange among members of the profession. (5) To provide information that will influence state or national policies, which have an impact on the research or sponsored programs environments. (6) To develop knowledge of those factors that create a facilitative environment for research to occur by studying those personnel and organizational variables that are conducive to research. The SRA Research Committee recommended a restructuring of their committee and an SRA Board of Directors' commitment to long-term development of the SRA Symposia and Monographs. The SRA Research Committee Action Plan was studied for two years.

This year, I asked the SRA Board of Directors to separate the SRA Symposia and Monograph activities from the research committee and make a long-term commitment to support the development of the symposia and monographs which long have been a labor of love of Oliver Hensley, currently a professor at Texas Tech University. Marcia Zuzolo, chair of the SRA Publications Committee, and Jack Mandel and Paul Saenger, co-chairs of the newly formed Marketing Task Force, focused their attention on developing a marketing program for the monographs. The SRA Board of Directors recognized the importance of these activities to society advancement and supported the reorganization plan and budget recommendations. With a new task force for monographs/special publications, the strong commitment from the board, and the completion of the fourth monograph, I believe that SRA has established the foundations for sustained study of critical issues in research administration. Such a sustained study required the participation of many; I hope that an increasing number of researchers and research administrators will attend the SRA Symposia and contribute to the monographs.

The symposia and monographs were conceived to complement the existing array of workshops, annual and section meeting programs, journal articles, and professional development sessions. They have the purpose of focusing the intellectual resources of the society and its partners on the imperatives of the field. The symposia are designed to bring together small groups of leading scholars to discuss the findings of preliminary studies and to chart the future exploration of subjects that have major importance to research administration. Distinguished members of the research community with a particular expertise are chosen by the society to study indepth one segment of the major problem chosen by the study group. Later, select members of that group are invited to present their preliminary findings to a larger study group for critique and additional study. After the study group's critique and the principal investigators' revision, the invited papers are published in an SRA Monograph and disseminated within and outside the society.

I am pleased to see the completion of the most recent work of this group of distinguished scholars. On behalf of the society and the profession, I thank them for their sharing of ideas related to strategic planning for research. Special acknowledgments and appreciation goes to Oliver Hensley and Texas Tech University. For many years, Ollie has generously given of his time and expertise to lead this effort. I wish the task force well as they continue to share ideas and prepare the foundation for building our knowlege of the planning process in the research enterprise. This topic is of great value to all of us in research administration as we reassess our organization's mission for relevancy in this threshold decade. Strategic planning, which is the base for the future scientific and educational policy and for rational daily decision-making, deserves our on-going attention. The SRA Board of Directors has authorized the publication of the SRA Monograph Number 4, *Strategic Planning for University Research,* and encourages the membership to assist this and other study groups with future studies of research administration. The society is proud to make the release of this research administration manuscript.

Claudette D. Beyer
President SRA 1991-92
President and CEO
Heat Transfer Research, Inc.

PREFACE

Strategic planning for university research is a process of establishing the future purposes of a unit considering common understandings for developing its research with its chief partners and major constituencies. A strategic plan for university research is an outline of the intended future of an institution. Strategic planning is about the work of moving the whole institution, its partners, and its constituencies in a certain direction for particular purposes. It operates on the assumption that people with similar motivations can agree on what their mutual purpose should be and can form beneficial partnerships that will advance a shared interest. Strategic planning promotes an ordered development as opposed to the incremental growth from uncoordinated, individual initiatives. It requires considered and innovative thought about the future, which will impose a discipline and direction on the research efforts of all who come under its purview.

Research administrators are the architects of the nation's future. Strategic plans are their blue prints. They design the organizational structures and select the leaders to guide the research planning, coordinate the activities of numerous principals within an expanding research enterprise, and set the research development agenda for institutions and agencies. It is research administrators who initiate and nurture the strategic planning processes and who project their visions and use their persuasive powers to lead research activities in certain directions. Teaching programs later follow the research. Since university research and education form the foundation for our technological civilization, it is imperative that the research community study strategic planning with the intent of improving it as it is becoming the preferred tool for the advancement of research and higher education.

Stategic planning is the newest, most powerful, and most effective technology for institutional development. It is a radical departure from traditional university modes of university growth. Currently, about one-fourth of the American research universities acknowledge using formal strategic planning. Approximately, one-twelfth are beginning such planning. Others are seriously considering its adoption.

Strategic planning for university research has become the base for state, federal, and institutional resource allocation, policy-making and policy-analysis. Currently, there is within the research enterprise a strong demand for greater standardization of information and improved joint planning. During the many decades that research universities have been partners with the federal and state governments, various methods of planning and several national information exchanges have evolved. Many established data bases and planning formats are obsolete or incompatible with new sys-

1

tems. Several new systems for conducting research strategic-planning have been proposed or implemented in recent years. Prior to the SRA Annual Program devoted to The New Research Environment—Responding with Plans and Strategies held in St. Louis in the fall of 1985, there had been no opportunity to hear comprehensive explanations of the existing planning systems and to learn about new systems scheduled for implementation in the next few years by the Congress, the National Science Foundation, pioneering states and university associations. The 1987 SRA Symposium—Strategic Planning for Academic Research—made a basic identification of the types of planning protocols currently in existence in the enterprise. The speakers at the Symposium were the leaders in the field and the innovators or current administrators of the new systems.

SRA's fourth monograph, *Strategic Planning for University Research* grew out of the SRA 1987 Symposium and was written for the research administrator with the intent of displaying the work of key planners in the research enterprise, discussing their planning technologies, and analyzing the final products of their labor. It is a description of the planning process from the perception of several administrators who have been involved in the daily planning of university research. The volume as a whole tries to give the reader a feeling for the intricacy of a planning technology that attempts to guide and coordinate multiple activities under a common purpose in an enterprise of incredible complexity. Also, it was the intent of the editor to present a comprehensive description of the current planning process that would help strategists to know the planning requirements of the performers and sponsors of research. Hopefully, this knowledge will lead to more efficient research administration planning, thus facilitating practice and increasing the productivity of the research university and its partners.

Chapter One introduces the reader to strategic planning for university research by providing a series of definitions, theories and models critical to modern planning for the research university. It identifies problems and issues that research administrators encounter as they try to model the research planning activities of a university. The first chapter is based on the editor's beliefs in the primacy of the researcher's ideas for the advancement of our technological society, in the unique value of the research university, and in the importance of strategic planning for accurately modeling the researcher's ideas so decision makers can make appropriate choices in an age of complexity.

This chapter discusses the value of Killoren's Impact Model for university scans of the research environment. It identifies the major sectors impacting university research and the influence paths inside the impact areas. It identifies in each sector essential planning mechanisms and documents, critiques the planning efficacy of extant research indicators, and analyzes the processes and products of university strategic planning in the major research sectors.

It introduces the companion concepts of the Theory of Project Incrementalism and the Performer/Sponsor Partnership Thesis to explain the development of university research in the last-half of the twentieth century.

The authors of Chapter Two take the position that the philosophical foundations for a research university are much different than those in other post-secondary education institutions and that sponsored research is the major influence in creating this difference. It identifies a number of academic philosophical assumptions and considers their influence on strategic planning. This chapter deals with the traditional concepts of research and discusses the reasons for universities vastly expanding the scope and types of research during the past five decades. It considers the functional differences among institutions in the higher education enterprise and presents three conceptual models for studying colleges and universities. The authors introduce "A Complexity Index" to provide a method of quantifying the increasing complexity of planning and performing university research that has occurred during the past half-century.

The authors of Chapter Three make the case that at this time 200 universities have been altered profoundly by five great waves of external and internal changes that have slowly transformed teaching institutions into research universities. The Historical Foundations point out that significant institutional changes occurred during several transitional stages when new research partners or organizational changes were adopted. Within these transitional stages, the effects of a steady accretion of sponsored projects on the traditional values and priorities of the institution are shown and the evolution of university planning is discussed as a response to organizational demands for better management within the institution.

This chapter recalls that since the beginning of the government/university partnership, faculty and administrators have been concerned about their lack of input into shaping the destiny of their institutions. It also recalls that sponsors, especially Congressmen and state legislators, were concerned about their lack of control over recurrent funding for "separately budgeted" research and research appropriations made according to formula. Chapter Three traces the evolution of research planning and points out that the research enterprise has arrived at a stage where strategic planning is seen as a way of controlling the direction of development of an institution and its research activities rather than letting it grow like Topsy. Most importantly, it stresses that strategic planning in now seen as a means of achieving research excellence in certain areas by directing the institutions' and sponsors' resources to targeted areas.

Chapter Four was written in response to an imperative in research policy making and analysis that requires the gathering of baseline information related to institutional planning. This chapter is built upon the data gathered from the 1989 Survey to identify and characterize existing strategic-planning protocols for university research. The Survey data allows the authors to present and discuss actual models from the present strategic plans for research in U.S. universities. It describes the physical characteristics of existing university strategic plans, the current planning and review processes, and the planning assumptions of the sample-institutions.

Chapter Five discusses specific technologies and the modalities associated with research planning. It models the strategic planning process. A Model of the Strategic Planning Processes for University Research provides a frame of reference for discussing planning activities. The authors explain how they have used the Model to assist planners in checking their progress toward the development of agreed upon outcomes. This chapter introduces a goal hierarchy and explains the importance of using standard terms in formulating many individual unit plans. It discusses methods of designing unit plans and then incorporating them into the institution's strategic plan.

Chapter Six is devoted to showing (1) how strategic planning was carried on in one institution; (2) the value of organizing the institution in a requisite fashion for planning; (3) the importance of selecting research-development oriented people to perform the planning; and (4) the merit of setting an institutional agenda and sticking to it. Darling and the editor employ a total-systems model to show the complexity of research development and an academic orientation grid to demonstrate their views on organizing planning teams within the institution.

They direct their thoughts to vice-presidents for research who have the responsibility for developing strategic research plans for the institution. They provide informational materials related to the structure, functions, and outputs of the major research planning teams. They discuss the current relationships between their offices and the rest of academe, suggest ways of improving the liaison mechanisms, and assess the adequacy of extant data-gathering instruments, their validity, and their use. They stress that the value of strategic planning is that it encourages people who are busy with routine procedures to step out of their daily activities and to consider where they want to be at some period in the future.

In Chapter Seven, Harlan L. Watson discusses academic research planning from the perspective of a coordinator and consultant to the U. S. House of Representatives' Committee on Science, Space, and Technology. His insightful description of the Congress's multiple points of access and input into policy, their comprehensive information gathering systems, and their joint drafting of legislation show their individual influence and sharing of power in shaping federal programs for research. His liberal use of government planning documents and his insider account of the Congressional planning process present a clear picture of how the government moves the Nation toward certain science and technology goals.

Jerold Roschwalb, Director, Governmental Relations, National Association of State Universities and Land Grant Colleges, as usual interjects a bit of mirth into his work. His chapter on research planning in national university associations takes a humorous approach to discussing the serious business of representing the universities' positions in the development of national plans. He points out that national associations have a role in strategic planning because they have the numbers, facts and details that are essential in the generally rational activities that occur in national planning for university research development. He also lets his readers know that in planning with Congress, the national associations do not call the shots and that anything can change at any time. While he exaggerates a form of political reasoning and interaction that must be followed in Washington, he makes the point that the most important rules are not put down and that all the planning in the world will not replace respect for people serving the interests of their principals. He leaves us remembering several valuable lessons and smiling.

F. Roger Tellefsen, former Deputy Secretary and Director of the Office of Technology Development, Pennsylvania Department of Commerce, provides a brief history of the development of state research and technology transfer programs and delivers insights into the motivations of politicians using research to strengthen their economic development plans. He discusses in some detail the strategic planning process initiated by Governor Dick Thornburgh of Pennsylvania. Tellefsen, the acknowledged master of bringing together politicians, scientists and business leaders for the development of technology, discusses in his modest manner how a series of inducements were used in the very successful pioneering experience in performing state strategic planning and in developing the Pennsylvania Ben Franklin Partnerships. He emphasizes the importance of using the media to help the development staff tell the public about state plans. He shares with us how the Ben Franklin Partnership Program and its place in the economic revitalization plans of the State were placed before the people of Pennsylvania and later adopted by the Legislature.

William A. Webb, Deputy Commissioner, Financial Planning Division, Texas Higher Education Coordinating Board, discusses the Texas Formula System for Public Senior Colleges and Universities. The Texas Formula System provides the framework for university and legislative strategic planning in the State of Texas. Dr. Webb, drawing on his many years of professional experience as a coordinating board staff member, explains the evolution of university funding from the political maneuverings of regents and presidents in the 1950s to the present systematic approach used in determining the financial requirements of institutions of higher education. He provides a rare description of the lengthy planning process used in the construction of a state's higher education budget. He recounts the elaborate nature of the study and testing used to develop the present fourteen formulas. Everywhere in this chapter Webb helps the reader see the complexity of a modern state's higher education planning system.

This volume was designed to present a comprehensive picture of strategic planning for university research in the closing decades of the twentieth century. It explains the evolution of the strategic planning process in universities, presents the perspectives of several key strategists, and models the current strategic planning processes. The book intends to bring to the reader a better understanding of the complexity of the process, of the development of partnerships, and of the importance of planning to research development. It should help the reader appreciate the multiple, planning activities performed by the research administrator and the indispensable roles played by researchers at all levels of university planning.

Oliver D. Hensley

CHAPTER ONE

THE CHARACTERISTICS OF STRATEGIC PLANNING FOR UNIVERSITY RESEARCH

Oliver D. Hensley

This chapter defines strategic planning for university research, discusses its value to the research enterprise, and presents a mosaic of strategic planning documents. The problems and issues that research administrators encounter as they try to model the research activities of a university are identified. Killoren's Impact Model for university scans of the research environment is used to identify the major sectors impacting university research. This chapter traces the influence paths inside the impact areas. It considers select planning mechanisms and documents, critiques the planning efficacy of extant research indicators, and analyzes the components that make up university strategic planning.

University research plans are designed very carefully to achieve certain purposes. Once designed, these plans are directed toward certain areas where they will have a particular impact. Conversely, an impact area may have a profound influence on a particular university. This chapter discusses the interaction that strategic planning creates when the university and its sponsors begin joint planning for research.

A Definition of Strategic Planning for Research in Universities

Strategic planning for university research is a process of establishing the future purposes of a unit considering common understanding for developing its research with its chief partners and major constituencies. Strategic planning requires the arranging of mutual work among a series of partners over the long-term. It is different from other types of planning. This book discusses three types of planning: Operational Planning, Tactical Planning, and Strategic Planning. The chapters are concerned mostly with the latter, although it is impossible to uncouple the planning activities and documents of the three types as they complement one another. Strategic planning requires a total systems approach to long- and short-term university planning for research. The strategic planning process produces a number of planning documents that are discussed in some detail in later chapters.

The term "strategic" comes from the Greek word "strategia" meaning generalship. The principles of strategic planning come directly or indirectly from military science. However, the concept has been adopted by all very large organizations as the management of complexity requires such planning to keep the organization abreast of a rapidly changing technological society.

Traditionally, armies have relied on their generals to see the long-term outcomes of present plans and actions, to see the composite structure for the war effort, to understand the various functions of the different branches of the military, and to focus the resources of the entire nation on key objectives at critical times.

Generalship is why the president of the United States is commander in chief of the armed forces, and why he is given mobilization authority over both the public and private sectors during war. Generalship assumes the ability of the president to subordinate all units within a common plan and to subordinate current activities for the long-term common good. Otherwise, each unit operates autonomously for individual benefit. Independent operation of units does not assure the preservation and advancement of the whole.

Subordination is risky business in a democracy and strategic planning is an extremely dangerous political activity nationally or on a campus. Nevertheless, it is the chief-executive officer's responsibility to see the general picture and to present a plan for future action. The CEO must recognize the good ideas that will give the nation a long-term advantage. The president of the United States has to establish the national purpose in terms of specific goals that can be carried out by individual agencies. He has to formulate policy within a strategic plan and then make decisions and direct resources according to that plan. The ultimate in national planning is creating the policy that will direct world resources to meet national purposes. Although this planning process is guided by the chief-executive, the positioning of ideas of reliable subordinates is the key to successful planning and achievement of purpose.

Vannevar Bush, director of the United States Office of Scientific Research and Development and a pioneer research administrator, put together the Roosevelt/Truman national plan for the long-term cooperative development of post-war science. This research administrator's splendid little book, *Science—The Endless Frontier* (1945), was the strategic plan that guided national science philosophy, policy, and practice for almost a half-century.

The strategic planning concept is no different in a university; it is the responsibility of the university central administration to provide a common vision, common data, and common purpose for decision makers. It is the university research administrator's responsibility to see that the best research ideas are incorporated into the plan and that the needs of the university's constituencies are addressed. The strategic plan lets everyone know the general ideas for the future development of the institution.

The Value of Strategic Research Planning

Prior to World War II, most higher education institutions were too small, research was an individual concern, and society was stable enough that strategic planning was not as necessary as it is now. Today, many of our large, complex universities have adopted strategic planning so they can better meet the rapidly changing needs of society while preserving the mission of the institution. University research has become an essential part of national defense strategies, general welfare plans, and the keystone of state economic development strategies. As research is now the dominant function in research universities, the growth of the entire institution depends upon the development of research.

The strategic plan becomes the blue print for the growth of the university for an extended period (1-50 years). It is the modern mechanism that is essential to faculty governance of the research activities in the university and to long-term support from university partners. These plans are of great value as they assess the mission of the institution in the light of past service, of present status, and of the dreams for the future. They require considerable faculty and administrative development time and financial resources. Strategic planning is a very practical exercise for the institution will be judged by the vision and the acumen of their plans.

In this modern world, an institution is advanced by the proposals it puts forward, not just by the scholars it has trained. More important, proposals attract funds for the support of future research and this research becomes the seed for economic growth, modern defense, and improved health.

For example, the Texas National Research Laboratory Commission proposal application for the superconducting supercollider weighed more than a ton. This plan required over thirty file boxes to contain the technical proposal and contract boiler-plate. The planning process involved several Texas universities and many scientists and engineers in writing the technical portion. This research plan required a special appropriation of two million dollars to cover development costs. This multivolume proposal was successful and has become the national plan for the next half-century of high-energy physics investigation.

The odds for Texas obtaining the award were low, for many states were competing. In Texas at least two million dollars of development funds were ventured and many thousands of new ideas proferred in this proposal, but the stakes were a thousand times larger than the development capital. If Congress appropriates the money, the winner of the Department of Energy competition could receive more than four billion dollars for the construction of a 52-mile tunnel of magnets where protons will be accelerated to almost the speed of light and then smashed together to reveal the basic building blocks of the universe.

The grantee institution or consortium will become the world center for high-energy physics during the last of the twentieth century and should maintain a dominant position far into the twenty-first century. Research opportunities for Texas universities will increase tremendously. It has great immediate economic implications. Once completed, it will employ over two thousand research support personnel and is expected to have an annual operating budget in excess of 200 million dollars. The spin-off industries that will grow from this center are inestimable. The Texas National Research Laboratory Commission Proposal shows the complexity of modern research and points out the need for strategic planning by research universities and their sponsors.

The Strategic Plan for University Research is a Mosaic Composed of Many Brilliant Smaller Plans

About one-third of American research universities concede that they plan strategically for their research advancement. These plans are quite diverse in length and format. However, at the beginning of every strategic plan is an overview. The overview may be as simple as a contents page. It may be an executive summary in a single, slender volume that introduces a multivolume work. Whatever its form, there should be a single document that succinctly explains the purpose of the whole work and guides the reader to the major components of the plan.

The strategic plan *sets the direction of the university for an extended period of time* and serves as a guide to thousands of supporting plans. Ultimately, the strategic plan for the university should incorporate all acceptable plans coming from within the university and acceptable external plans that require delivery of university services. For purposes of explanation, the author lists several planning-document covers to show the diversity of documents and the complexity of the strategic planning process for university research. In the Texas Tech University Mosaic for Strategic Planning, prominence is given to the following documents: (A) The University Strategic Plan, (B) The 1984 Institutional Self Study, (C) Unit Plans and Reports, (D) The University Research Budgets, (E) The College Five-Year Planning and Achievement Reports, (F) White Papers on Research Development and Administration, (G) Accreditation Reports, (H) Commonground Research Development Plans, (I) The Texas Charter, (J) Past Generations of University Strategic Planning, (K) Proposals for the Development of Organized Research Units, (L) Project Proposals, (M) HEAF Plan.

The Scan of the Research Environment

Environmental scanning for strategic planning requires an identification of the major sectors performing and conducting research and an identification of the areas that will be impacted by the plan. Within the impact areas, the research strategists will want to acquire all the documents and have their staff attend all the meetings that have relevancy to the strategic planning goals of their institution.

Four acronyms, MORE, HAT, RAP, and SWOT serve to guide the research planning of an institution. MORE is concerned with an analysis of the Mission of the organizations within the impact areas, with a determination of the Organization's structure and functions used to accomplish the organizations' missions, with an assessment of Resources of the organizations, and with an Evaluation of the past, current, and future operations of relevant organizations. HAT stands for a Historical understanding of the research environment, an Analysis of current plans and policies in the research environment related to the plans of the strategists, and a knowledge of the Traditions within the research environment. RAP stands for the acquisition of Reports, Agenda, and Plans of partners and competitors in the research arena. SWOT guides the assessment of the strengths, weakness, opportunities and threats of partners and competitors.

Several models will be used to explain the environmental scan. Chapter Five Figure 5.4 shows the technology for identifying the research principals and their planning assumptions. The following sections of this chapter provide a general model and general information about an environmental scan for strategic planning for university research.

The Killoren Impact Model

The first model we shall consider is shown in Figure 1.1—The Strategic Plan Impact Areas. This model was designed by Killoren (1979), who suggested that it be used in a holistic approach to planning for research. Successful planners recognize that their strategies will be influenced by individuals and institutions from certain quarters and in turn, that their plans will impact significantly certain areas. These quarters of influence were appropriately called "impact areas" by Killoren. With the minor modifications that have been made in this model, the author advocates its use as it identifies the major impact areas and guides strategic-planning activities for university research. Killoren's impact model has been a valuable tool in the author's strategic-planning conference presentations as it shows the scanning process on one transparency and leads the viewer to the correct conclusion that a great number of areas will be impacted by the plan and that these areas also should contribute in an active way to the planning.

STRATEGIC PLANNING FOR UNIVERSITY RESEARCH

The Strategic Plan Impact Areas

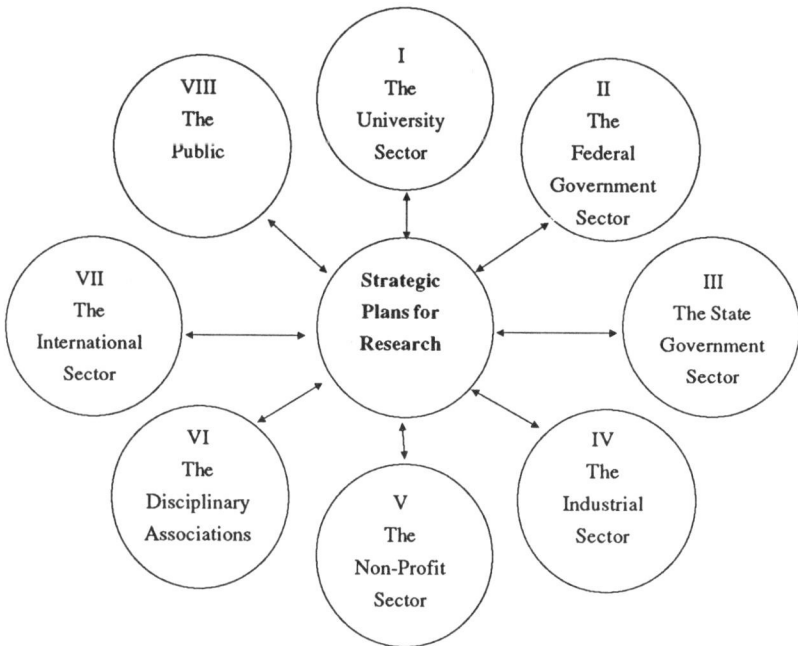

Figure 1.1. A Model of the Strategic Plan Impact Areas

An impact model allows planners to identify areas currently contributing to the research of the university, to identify existing competitors, and to target areas for future development. It should be constructed at the outset of any strategic plan as it provides an opportunity to all who assist in the development of the model to have their input. As specific plans are discussed, the number of impact areas will grow. That is an indicator that the strategic-planning process is working. Strategic plans are only as good as their input; consequently, the more impact areas that are initially identified the more congruence there will be between strategic plans and later operations.

General Responsibilities of the Major Impact Areas

In assessing the impact of plans on the major impact areas, the functions of the major sectors should be well understood. Your author identifies five sectors in Figure 1.1 that have direct responsibility for the development of research: (1) The University Sector, (2) The Federal Government Sector, (3) The State Government Sector, (4) The Industrial Sector, (5) The Nonprofit Sector, and he identifies the following three areas that contribute directly or indirectly to the advancement of research: (6) The Disciplinary Associations, (7) The International Sector, (8) The Public.

The sectors must be considered carefully according to specific functions and responsibilities as each performs a distinctive mission and provides unique services to the research enterprise. Together, their diversity, decentralized locations, and independent efforts make for a broadly responsive and effective enterprise.

THE UNIVERSITY SECTOR

The University Sector serves as the beginning link in a chain of important sectors and complementary systems that produces the foundation knowledge for the nation's science and technology and prepares its researchers. The *work* of the University Sector must be well understood and its outputs reliably measured. In the University Sector, the faculty and students are the principals who have the responsibility for doing original thinking in a disciplined manner, for organizing knowledge within disciplinary structures, and for disseminating knowledge according to professional standards. The Research University is the principal institution in the research enterprise that has the responsibility of providing an environment conducive to research. Their major role is to encourage and further the development and dissemination of new ideas.

It is the sponsoring sectors'—the federal and state governments, industry, and the non-profit organizations—responsibility to explain in some detail in their reports, program announcements, and their requests for proposals (RFPs) exactly what problems they want investigated or solved. The sponsoring sectors must plan to give full support to their projects for the duration of the partnership with the university.

The research administrator's role is to facilitate research development throughout the research enterprise. They must help the public understand the critical nature of and need for research in a modern technological society. This requires responsibility for directing information on research to the news media and ensuring that selected information is channeled to the principal groups in the impact areas.

Also, the research administrator must assist the professional associations as editors and meeting chairpersons to organize the ideas and knowledge necessary for the advancement of disciplinary research. The research administrator must help the faculty in their efforts to organize research into the existing bodies of knowledge—the disciplines.

Part of the research administrators planning function is to develop faculty interest inventories and institutional capabilities statements for institutional, state, and national information systems. Organizations such as

Strategic Alliances at the national level and the Texas Innovation Information Network System (TIINS) at the state level acquire massive amounts of information about the principal players in the research enterprise. In return for supplying faculty information to these professional and institutional associations, their systems provide even greater amounts of information about the total systems. This expanded data base allows the university strategists to determine areas of research strengths and resources and to query the system when they need to put together a team of experts. It is important that research administrators link their university to state and national information systems as these systems are necessary for the strategist to engage in very sophisticated planning for research financing, technology licensing, research expansions, and international technology transfer.

The Value of Elegant Education to American Students

If our students, their parents, and the patrons of higher education are to appreciate the value of an education earned at the research universities, they must know the intellectual power and the comparative advantage that are gained from following the regimen demanded by the faculty in a research university. Although graduates of research universities are much sought after and receive premium salaries, one cannot value a degree by merely assessing the increased earning of its graduates. Education at a research university is exceptionally advanced and most rigorous. No college program in the past is like it. For the value of today's education to be appreciated, it must be analyzed and compared to conventional types of programs.

Because traditional terms such as *quality education* and *big science* do not explain the nature of modern education at the research universities, Hensley (1987) coined two new words—*elegant education* and *sophisticated science* to clearly differentiate them from traditional education and conventional scientific activities that occur in most other institutions of higher education. There are tremendous differences in the quality of education and science in America's post-secondary education institutions. In looking at the impact of strategic plans on the University Sector, these difference must be distinguished immediately and taken into account in every strategy.

If our patrons are to support adequately the higher costs of research universities, they must know that elegant education is an exclusive educational process lately created by the nation's research universities for preparing highly motivated students to be researchers, not just practitioners, in the professional fields of our technological society. It is certainly not the classical educational process that is imagined as a student on one end of a log and a master on the other end; to the contrary, the real image shows many students sitting in front of computer monitors interacting with elaborate systems that are strategically positioned around the world.

Elegant education places a strong emphasis on the utilitarian purpose of teaching the student to search for creative solutions to real problems derived from regional needs and industrial mandates, as well as the conventional disciplinary imperatives. Today, it is advisable for universities and local communities to plan with industry to meet the demands for skilled professionals who have been trained on state-of-the-art equipment and by the best faculty and staffs in a particular professional field.

The strategic plans of most research universities include a recruiting component that is aimed at attracting the best minds of the world to their institutions. Here, a three- to six-year mentoring process focuses on the use of *Advanced Technology* and sophisticated science and helps the student to move easily between academe and industry. This new linkage is vital for maintaining local industrial competitiveness and for the continued development of advanced technology in this country. On the university side of the partnership, the industrial connection greatly enhances faculty and student research opportunities and promotes the currency and relevancy of the curriculum. Maintaining the industrial connection requires university research administrators to form influence paths in the Industrial Sector. University research administrators spend considerable time with their industrial counterparts in joint planning for arranging a visiting scientist and engineer exchange program, for establishing summer student work and cooperative education programs with individual companies, and for initiating cooperative research programs.

Similarly, sophisticated science is not *bench science* nor *big science*. It has gone far beyond these two forms. It is distinguished from other forms of science by its selection of problems of incredible complexity, by its enormous range of investigation, and by its reliance upon multidisciplinary modes of inquiry. Sophisticated science, like elegant education, uses expanding professional networks and rapid exchange of information to advance science. Also, it depends greatly upon an elaborate and expensive infrastructure. Most importantly, science has been changed by the heightened expectations of society for immediate scientific solutions to all of man's problems. During World War II, American government-industry-university partnerships built the greatest military machine the world has ever seen. The atomic bomb, the Salk vaccine, and lunar landings by NASA have convinced the public that science's frontiers are endless and that science will not just tell us how far away the moon is—it will put a man on it. Today, social expectations and government-industry-university partnerships are the driving forces of sophisticated science and advanced technology that require strategic planning within the University Sector to assure that the performers and sponsors meet their respective responsibilities according to agreed upon conditions.

The two processes, elegant education and sophisticated science, advance hand-in-hand, each, dependent upon the other. Although many practicing scientists and faculty recognize the uniqueness of these new processes, the public and many of our leaders do not always understand the peerless nature of elegant education and sophisticated science, their inextricability, and the reasonableness of present costs for such rare and essential commodities.

Too often, the public gets the wrong view of the University Sector by listening to popular education leaders discount the value of these national resources. Bloom (1987) made blanket accusations that universities have closed the minds of our students, and Bennett (1986) charged that institutions of higher education are sumptuously supported. Both charges are patently wrong; nevertheless, they are much quoted in the news media and legislative halls. It is my personal view that the central argument behind these sustained attacks on universities has been generated less by political motivations than by misunderstanding of the differences among the three types of educational institutions and their differing missions. The U. S. Congress, state legislators, the electorate, parents, and students are no longer convinced by the arguments that poetry and philosophy are the foundations from which the individual and our technological society advances. If the public judges from the titles of best selling books, *The Closing of the American Mind* and *A Nation at Risk* (1983), they would believe that the American university is decaying. That is not the case, to the contrary, they are performing exceedingly well. Influential public figures, both inside and outside the university still do not understand the essential scientific and technological role that research universities play in our advanced technological society. They do not comprehend the need for the United States—federal government, state government, nonprofit sector, and industry—to support these centers of excellence and to provide the proper tribute to the faculty who do the work. Research universities are not just an intellectual frill, they are the foundation for the nation's technological infrastructure that is at least as significant to the national interest as the interstate highway system.

It is necessary to continuously inform the public of the value that the University Sector has for the economy, the health of our citizens, and the defense of the nation. With our top educational leaders projecting such poor images of the research university, it is very difficult for university administrators to appeal for new monies that will allow the faculty to take the next steps in preparing the future generation of scientists, engineers, and health professionals and in finding super-conducting materials, in acquiring a high-resolution linkage map of the human genome, and in finding new energy sources. Without strategic planning, the future support for our research universities would be slowed considerably and the United States would have to give up the race for finding scientific explanations of the unknown and would surely forfeit the early production of goods related to the aforementioned research areas.

Research Universities Are the Stewards of the World's Knowledge

The University Sector is charged with preserving, disseminating, and creating knowledge. To accomplish this vital mission, research universities build over the decades the critical mass of faculty, students, facilities, equipment, and the infrastructure essential to compete internationally. These knowledge centers are located strategically across the country to serve the many needs of the nation.

To perform the essential knowledge-preservation role for West Texas, Texas Tech University's central library has for general use over 1,310,000 volumes and 900,000 microform units on its shelves, conserves in special collections 16,479,000 rare books and original documents, maintains thousands of oral history units, and can access through reciprocal agreements several-hundred-million volumes in other research libraries. The central library is designated by the federal government as the regional depository for 600,000 current government documents. Most important for this region and time, the library daily accesses hundreds of on-line databases through its elaborate computer networking and it subscribes to over 12,000 scientific journals and periodicals. The Tech Law Library and the Health Sciences Center libraries could present an additional set of impressive statistics on holdings and services rendered to two professional fields.

Tech disseminates knowledge by offering each semester 5,000 undergraduate, graduate, and professional classes. It broadcasts via KTXT-TV and radio, hundreds of quality-education and specialized-information programs to the West Texas public. It keeps the professional in this region up-to-date by providing post-graduate and continuing education. The Texas Tech University Press publishes and distributes hundreds of very specialized scholarly works. Tech's faculty and students write thousands of research articles and technical reports every year. They deliver hundreds of professional papers and conduct professional seminars in all parts of the world. In doing this the faculty builds in the Public Sector a favorable image for Tech, Texas, and the nation. Other research universities provide similar critical services to their regions.

The most important element in the research university is the community of scholars who discover new knowledge. Research universities act like intellectual magnets. They attract the most distinguished scholars and the best students. These institutions employ rigorous selection processes that winnows-out all those who are not capable or are not willing to dedicate themselves to advancing the knowledge of their disciplines (mathematics, chemistry, physics, law, medicine, etc.) and to serving their sponsors (students, nations, states, foundations, industries). Once in this enriched environment and research-charged atmosphere, tremendous institutional pressure is applied to scholars to not only stay abreast of the latest information and techniques, but to produce new knowledge. Moreover, they are obligated to organize it into disciplinary structures so the rest of the higher education enterprise and all practicing professionals can have easy access to the latest knowledge. They are the people in our society who write most of the research articles, textbooks, and technical reports that keep this nation's industry on the leading edge of technology. Almost all of the scientific research conducted in American institutions of higher education occurs in this tier of institutions. The American government and industry are very dependent upon the University Sector for most of their basic research and their scientific and technological manpower.

While their faculty and student body make a research university an international community of scholars and while their distinguished reputations put the faculty onto the globe-trotting circuit, these institutions are tremendous regional assets. Stanford University's and the University of California's research spin-offs started Silicon Valley, and MIT and Harvard spin-offs began the multibillion dollar high technology industries along Boston's Route 128. These cultural and intellectual oases are not maintained without cost. The greater the social expectations become for the universities, the larger they will grow and the more expensive they will become. The alternative to keeping the research and graduate students flowing into our economy is to dry-up the research university. That would lead quickly to a withering of the entire region. It is always telling, in arguing the regional value of the research university, to present the total amount of research dollars that comes into a region through research contracts. In some regions, that figure exceeds a billion dollars annually.

An audit of much of our present technology would show that the wonder medicines, the new materials, automated processes, electronic technology, and new plant and animal forms had their beginning in the laboratories of the University Sector. The public does not always remember where the basic research was done and they certainly have little understanding of the costs of supporting these uniquely valuable institutions. It is an on-going responsibility of the strategic planner to let the public know the present value of our research universities as they are rapidly appreciating national and regional assets.

The research universities with their special mission, unique organization, extensive infrastructure, and vast resources are the only institutions capable of producing elegant education, sophisticated science, advanced technology, and a broad spectrum of creative activities that advance our technological society. Their wide mission and enormous capabilities allow them to grant baccalaureate, professional, masters, and doctoral degrees. As Hensley, Clarke, and Peterson (1986, 1987) studies have shown within the last decade, many states have made research universities centers for their regional economic development. The recent assumption of economic development responsibilities increases greatly the need for strategic research planning in the university sector. The following sections and chapters provide fuller explanations of how strategic planning for university research occurs in other sectors and in the university.

THE FEDERAL GOVERNMENT: A KEY IMPACT AREA

The research university was created and is sustained by funding from the federal government through a number of legislative initiatives. The federal-government–university partnership means much more to universities than just funding—the government identifies in its hearings and reports the problems of the nation and then prioritizes them through the amount of funding allocated to agency programs. Without the political determination of national needs, universities could not react as effectively to the needs of the nation. The merging of political knowledge with academic expertise creates a stream of research plans that are designed to meet national needs and that are affordable by the people.

The complex process of setting national agenda is at the heart of all government planning for research and is the original source of knowledge for government–university planning. It is a marvelous process that typically meets the research needs of the nation.

Knowing who the principal planners are in the federal government, acquiring their plans and interpreting the national agenda, knowing how to make a meaningful input into the political process, and knowing how to couple government plans with university priorities is the essence of university strategic planning for research.

Mutual Planning in the Federal-Government–University Partnership.

It is essential for university research administrators to remember that for a half-century the Congress and the president have made universities partners with the federal government in meeting the needs of the nation. This partnership is expected to continue for it is essential to executing the missions of both parties. Figure 1.2 shows the influence paths of principal individuals and groups within the federal impact area. With a little imagination one can see that Figure 1.2 resembles a crude boat. With a bit more imagination, one can consider that model as the ship-of-state with its major groups aligned in a manner that carries the entire nation in one direction. As the figure indicates the president steers the nation into the future.

If one uses a longitudinal analysis to discern federal strategies, the funding trends of government programs as described in congressional testimony, statutes, and appropriations show the high-water marks for past swells in government support, and are good indicators for predicting future funding areas within the federal government. The continuing stream of research acts of Congress form the plans for the nation. It is instructive to the research administrator to study federal statutes, to read the testimony to and the special reports from the Congress and to understand the legislative process which ultimately forms an act.

The Executive Offices' Influence on Research Planning

The president of the United States is a principal research planner for university research. The presidents' initiatives for identifying missing resources in the nation and their setting of plans for influencing decision-makers to accept a national research and development agenda have long-term impacts on future national welfare. The president's budget message and his State of the Union Message should always be monitored to detect immediate policy related to basic research and to determine what the next term holds for the fate of nationally sponsored research.

In his first inaugural address, President George Washington set the course of the United States government to support science and literature. The first president spoke as follows: "The advancement of agriculture, commerce and manufacturing, by all proper means, will not I trust, need recommendation; but I cannot forbear intimating to you the expediency of giving effectual encouragement as well to the introduction of new and useful inventions from abroad as to the skill and genius in producing them at home . . . nor am I less persuaded that you will agree with me in opinion that there is nothing which can better deserve your patronage than the promotion of science and literature."

Since Washington, the presidents have continued to urge government moral support of science and education. President Thomas Jefferson, the architect of our government and the founder of the University of Virginia, was a particularly staunch advocate and planner for government support of science and higher education. Although most presidents have generally

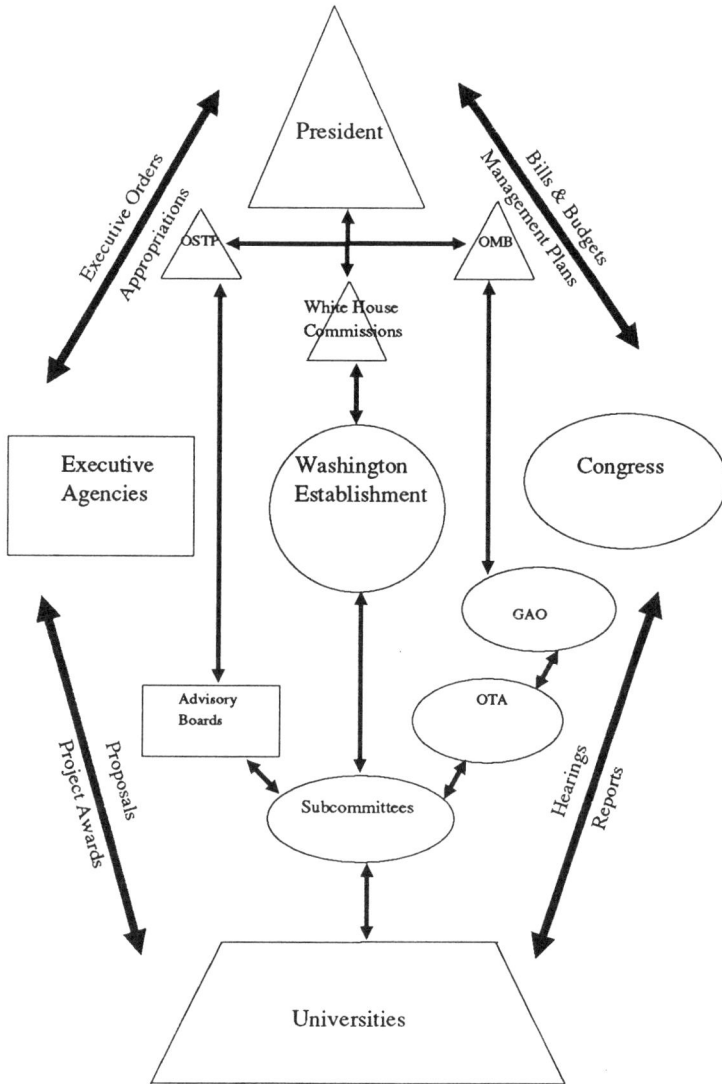

Figure 1.2 The Influence Paths of Principal Groups Within the Federal Impact Area.

urged the promotion of science and literature, prior to Franklin D. Roosevelt there are few examples of presidents planning working partnership between the federal government and the universities.

Presidents Roosevelt and Truman set the plans for an on-going partnership between the federal government and the universities. Vannevar Bush's (1945) research administration classic, *Science—The Endless Frontier*, prepared at the behest of President Roosevelt, set the roles for the partners in the early research enterprise and outlined a strategy for national research development that governs the partners to this day. In the Bush Model, the independence of the partners was stressed and separate planning among the sectors was strongly encouraged.

President Kennedy in 1957 triggered a national debate on the nation's fundamental mission in space. Initially, there was considerable resistance to mounting an American space program. However, after several orbits of a beeping Sputnik, the President and the Congress decided that the United States should be the first nation to land a man on the moon. Once President Kennedy had public opinion behind him, he called for massive budgets to support space research and installed the National Aeronautics and Space Administration (NASA). His administration, lead by Thomas Glennan, transferred the military strategic planning system to NASA and brought the universities in as a major component of NASA's first Ten-Year Plan in 1960.

President Nixon's establishment of Research Applied to National Needs (RANN) brought industry into the government-industry-university partnership. With the RANN initiative President Nixon held the expectation that industry would assist government in supporting basic research in universities and that universities would be motivated to find ways of applying their research resources to national needs. It was the Nixon administration's strategy to forge stronger links among the government agencies, industry, and universities through joint planning and joint research ventures.

Nixon (1971) in his State of the Union Speech and Health Message called for an intensified attack on the Nations' problems by asking the Congress to recommend additional funds for expanded research and development efforts. In particular, he wanted to influence the conquest of cancer by calling for long-term and comprehensive commitment to a national cancer program. He asked the National Institutes of Health (NIH) for a strategic plan to present to the Congress.

The strategic planning process that evolved from the Nixon administration is now considered a model for science agencies. Rauscher (1973) describes in detail how he and others in the National Cancer Institute incorporated into *The Strategic Plan* of the National Cancer Program the ideas of the president's cancer panel; the National Cancer Advisory Board, the advisory committee to the director of NIH; the Institute of Medicine of the National Academy of Sciences; the Office of Science and Technology Policy; Office of Management and Budget; two ad hoc groups of distinguished scientists and science administrators; and members of the Association of American Cancer Institutes. Rauscher (1973,v) comments, "Two hundred and fifty laboratory and clinical scientists, representing a broad spectrum of biomedical and clinical disciplines, met in a series of forty planning sessions and two major review sessions between October 1971 and March 1972 to develop a scientific and operational foundation for a National Cancer Program." Although there have been many addenda to the *1973 Edition*, The Strategic Plan continues to provide a hierarchical structure of program goals focusing on constant, disease-oriented objectives.

President Carter added a new direction for the government-industry-university partnership by insisting that the government should also address American industrial needs. Early in his administration, he asked the secretary of commerce to lead the government in a review to determine the status of the national economy and to suggest what actions the federal government should take to encourage industrial innovation. The *White House Fact Sheets* on the *President's Industrial Innovation Initiatives*, October 31, 1979 and the *Economic Program for the Eighties*, August 28, 1980 expressed a policy that grew out of President Carter's early instructions to his cabinet to design a carefully targeted series of initiatives to reduce unemployment in the short-term and to address the long-term needs of the economy. Most important to our study, President Carter's *Industrial Innovation Initiatives*, *White House Fact Sheet* of October 31, 1979 is a turning point in government policy as it established a federal strategy for industrial revitalization that relied heavily on university research.

President Carter demanded that federal departments and agencies plan their research and development programs to assure an appropriate balance between basic or long-term research and shorter-term applied research and development. The Executive Office became very much involved in strategic planning for university research when President Carter generally directed the mission agencies to begin strategic planning for technology transfer within their agencies. Later, the Office of Management and Budget Director, Bert Lance, in his *Memorandum of August 15, 1977* to the heads of executive departments and agencies specified how the agencies were to identify specific problems in the agency's impact areas and how they should take a careful view in developing their R&D programs in relation to other sponsors during the long-term.

Although the Carter initiatives have different names now, the philosophy undergirding his 1979 initiatives motivates planning in most agencies, today. For many years in the future, university research administrators can expect to see the following Carter plans surface in federal legislation and agency programs:

1. Amending the Internal Revenue Codes to promote research;
2. Enhancing the transfer of technical information;
3. Increasing technical information;
4. Improving the Patent System to promote the commercialization of research;
5. Clarifying Antitrust Policy to promote joint research and to speed its commercialization;
6. Fostering the development of smaller innovative firms; and
7. Maintaining a supportive attitude toward innovation.

Reports from the executive offices must be constantly monitored for the president's strategic research plans and for national updates such as *The Report of the White House Science Council Panel on the Health of U. S. Colleges and Universities.* In 1986, the Panel warned that the higher education enterprise was at a transition point after a decade of belt tightening and retrenchment and could no longer be taken for granted. They noted that the aging facilities, obsolete equipment and growing shortages of both faculty and students in many important areas could seriously reduce the Nation's effectiveness in producing new knowledge and in training the young minds needed to use this knowledge in innovative ways. The Panel concluded that although increased support is important, "What is most needed is a re-examination and restructuring of the relationships that have evolved among the federal government, the universities, and U. S. industries." University strategic planning for research is, of course, an excellent way of re-examining and initiating a restructuring program while considering presidential and congressional initiatives and existing areas of federal support for research. A strategic plan will show which federal agency programs significantly impact university research and in turn which university research impacts federal areas of responsibility.

The Reagan administration recognized the needs expressed by his Science Council Panel and made considerable improvements in upgrading the university stock of research equipment. He made an important first step in addressing the facilities problem by approving in the NSF reauthorization, P. L. 100-570, a modest $80 million for university research facilities in 1989. That funding is expected to rise to $250 million in 1992.

President Reagan supported the Panel recommendations, and science R&D enjoyed a renaissance, as federal funding for university research increased by more than a third during his tenure. The Reagan proposal, to double the budget of the research agencies, came at a time when several super-science programs were under serious consideration. The superconducting supercollider, the Strategic Defense Initiative (SDI), AIDS research, the mapping and sequencing of the human genome and the understanding and controlling the effects of industrial pollutants on the environment involve strategic planning and great human and financial resources from the research enterprise. Each of the major federal research agencies were involved in these super programs and many universities determined which of the Reagan initiatives coincided with their long-term plans and put forth from their areas of strength their best proposals.

In addition to being financially supportive of research, the Reagan administration introduced a number of new research programs and brought in the concept of reducing paperwork in dealing with the federal government. This lead to the establishment of the federal Demonstration Projects (FDP), which has brought about an entirely new level of joint planning and testing designed to improve operational efficiency in the federal-government–university partnership and to increase university research productivity.

If these federal programs are to succeed, and if the university is to strengthen its capabilities of doing basic science and training the nation's researchers, there must be a joint development of plans between the government-university partners.

The Office of Science and Technology Policy (OSTP). In establishing the Office of Science and Technology Policy by the Science Policy Act, May 1976, the Congress intended that the OSTP would be an advisory group to the president. The office was expected to prepare reports indicating what the national investment should be in the areas of science and research. Senator Ted Kennedy thought these advisors should suggest what might be some goals for the Congress to establish in certain areas and how funds should be allocated to these areas over five years periods. The Congress expected OSTP to provide some planning guideposts for the whole area of developing science and research. Vice-President Rockefeller thought that OSTP should provide plans and reports for a conceptual approach to the whole of science and technology, should provide information on how science and technology fits into the whole of our society, should explain the role of science and technology in world affairs, should show how S&T affects our daily lives, and should project the future of science and technology.

There was a mixed reaction to the time and effort that would be required to produce such products. The scope of the work was obviously too much for the small staff of the first office.

A number of witnesses advocated long-range planning as an essential function of the science advisory office. Several witnesses discussed the necessity of OSTP performing long-range planning in conjunction with current S&T programs. H. Guyford Stever, the then presidential science advisor, talked about the long-range or "horizontal scanning" function of OSTP and the necessity of OSTP having listeners in the Oval Office, executive agencies, and the Congress. After weighing many considerations, the Congress saw the OSTP as bringing a focus to the overall S&T policies of the nation.

The director of the Office of Science and Technology Policy is a principal in national research planning. As the president's chief science advisor, he has great influence on the White House planning operations. The stature of the individual serving in the office is very high as the director must have the respect of both the scientific community and the government bureaucracy. These advisors are expected to make their plans known in the White House and exercise considerable clout in the presidents' inner circle. Their influence comes from the director having an opportunity to recommend a plan of action on a broad range of science policy issues.

Initially, OSTP was required by Congress to prepare a national vision of future science and technology in a report designed to provide a "Five Year Outlook" on science and technology issues of national significance. The five-year report was to be followed by annual revisions keeping the five year perspective current. Also, OSTP was expected to include in the "Science and Technology Report" reviews of past developments of national significance. President Carter transferred much of OSTP planning and reporting functions to the NSF in his Reorganization Plan No. 1 of 1977. From 1977 to 1983, both of these reports were prepared by NSF. They have been extremely useful to the university research administrator, but they are bound by the conservative thinking and the outmoded conceptual model of the NSF bureaucracy, which restricts the thinking of research planners.

The Office of Management and Budget publishes the *Catalog of Federal Domestic Assistance*, which provides a year-by-year explanation of government program planning and spending. Collectively, they provide a detailed history of the ebb and flow of the federal government's programmatic support to university research.

The National Science Foundation. The National Science Foundation has the important responsibility for reporting on the state of science to the nation in addition to their responsibility for promoting basic research and education in the sciences. Their Division of Science Resource Studies publishes an extensive series of reports on science and engineering personnel, R&D expenditures, and a detailed statistical table on science that are very useful for strategic planning. In July of 1982, Charles E. Falk, director, Divison of Science Resources Studies, NSF noted, "Over the past several years, projections of scientific and engineering manpower and R&D expenditures have been issued. This publication presents projections of R&D expenditures for the year 1990." The NSF current reports and projections are widely used in the government and in universities for strategic planning purposes.

In response to the Reagan administration proposal to double the NSF budget in five years, the *NSF Long-Range Plan FY1989-1993* sets forth its role and future programs for operating in the context of an enormous national education enterprise, and for spending twice its 1987 appropriation. NSF (1989,9) notes in their long-range plan, "The NSF will significantly expand its effort to develop educational and human resources over the next five years. Among the key NSF themes and strategies, this will be the top priority. The rate of growth in support of education and human resources will be maintained at a level at least 50% higher than that in other strategic areas." This plan will impact positively those institutions that have research administrators who know how to compete for the money. The university science and engineering undergraduate curricula, graduate student support, and senior scientist opportunities for cross-disciplinary training should be substantially enhanced through the infusion of government money into these program areas.

The NSF Division of Policy Research and Analysis (PRA) has recently initiated a source book, *The State of Academic Science and Engineering*, which provides the information necessary for an empirical elaboration of the relationship of the government to fundamental research in academe. This first edition by the PRA staff concentrates on the last three decades, covering a period of U. S. history with very different demographic and economic characteristics on both the national and world level. It examines this period of change very closely and provides quantitative data and comprehensive analyses that were not available in current literature. It provides the university research strategists with an excellent overview of what has happened in academic science in the last generation.

Congressional Influence on Research Planning

Since the inception of the federal-government–university partnership, the Congress has been a principal planner for university research.

The statutes of the United States Congress are the most potent sponsor plans for development of university research as they place the resources of the nation behind the intent of Congress. Typically, when the Congress drafts legislation they set forth in the preamble of the statute their intent. That intent is in response to the needs expressed by a particular constituency. The statutes of the United State Congress are the plan for the federal government's contribution to the federal-government–university partnership. The statute identifies the executive agency to administer a clearly defined program conceived by the Congress. The act prescribes the objectives of the program, the organizational structure, the level of funding, and the reports that must be submitted to assure accountability to the taxpayer.

The strategic planning of the Congress is clearly stated in the statutes of the United States. Despite the general cynicism of the public who constantly complain of the flip-flopping of politicians on particular issues, the direction of Congress is seldom changed once the needs of the nation are identified and the course of the government is set by statute. Of course, there are always great debates on the issue of government entrance into a particular area and the yearly squabbles over the amount of the appropriation for a program, but once an agency or program is established the long-term planning of the United States government is easy to follow. Agreed, there is no specific plan, with specific authorizations for the next twenty years. There is however, in the enabling acts the intent of Congress, the plan for the government organization, and the prescription for methods of planning and for rendering accountability for those plans. The enabling act is the plan. Subsequent statutes and amendments only modify the plan as needed. That is as it should be in strategic planning. Despite the many criticisms to the contrary, the Congress does do strategic planning. We shall see the efficacy of Congressional strategic planning in a brief look at the government's founding and continuance of the National Science Foundation. The planning process is never pretty. Powerful ideas vie for attention, strong personalities clash with one another, and interest groups attack their opponents. Nowhere is the carnage of planning more apparent than in the Congress as they draft legislation.

The intent of Congress for the long-term, general development of university research is seen in general legislation establishing the National Science Foundation. England (1982) in *A Patron for Pure Science The National Science Foundation's Formative Years, 1945–57* provided an accurately written and a very detailed account of the role of legislation in planning and developing university research. England's work describes the many testimonies to Congress, the drafting of numerous bills, the letter writing and proposal submissions by various constituency groups, and the floor debates that went into the planning of the National Science Foundation. It is informative to read England's explanation of the drafting of the Senate Bill 247 (the final Senate bill) reported by the Senate Committee on Labor and Public Welfare on March 18, 1949 and of the maneuvering of the Commerce Committee of the House of Representative's to report Bill 4846 to the nation on June 14, 1949. England described a summer, fall, and winter of intensive debate over H. R. 4846 and its many amendments. The bill finally passed the House, 247–126 on March 1, 1950 paving the way for a conference to resolve the considerable differences between two versions of S247. On May 10, 1950, President Harry S. Truman signed the National Science Foundation Act of 1950. President Truman recalled on the day of signing that five years earlier Vannevar Bush had submitted to him *Science—The Endless Frontier.* It had taken Bush and his colleagues almost a year to draft the original plan for a science foundation and the first strategic plan for the federal government's development of national research. It then took five years of planning by politicians and scientists to draft the statutes necessary to establish the National Science Foundation.

The Science Policy Task Force (1990,2) noted that Congress receives periodic reports, one-time research related reports, letters, and verbal testimony to stimulate plans and obtain accountability information from the executive departments of the government. The Congress mandates 2,078 periodic reports on all subjects. Two-hundred and forty of these reports relate to science issues. Periodic Science Reports can be categorized under the following three headings:

1. Research Activities and Programs Reports are from science advisory committees and science facilities. About 55 percent or over 130 science reports fall in this category.
2. Science Administration and Funding Reports are from agencies and programs. These 70 reports makeup about 33 percent of the Congressionally mandated science reports.
3. Man Power and Education Reports come from many areas. There are 30 such reports, comprising about 12 percent of the total science reports.

These science reports mandated by statute are excellent research planning documents and are easy to find. The statutes specify one or more committees in each house to which the report is to be submitted. The Science, Space, and Technology Committee and the Energy and Commerce Committee are the principal recipients of periodic reports containing government plans. The Appropriations, Agriculture, Armed Services, Government Operations, and Veteran Affairs committees also receive large numbers of science reports and they become intimately involved in university research planning.

One-Time Reports are generally mandated through the vehicle of legislative report language. These reports are very useful in planning as they come generally from the research agencies and are most helpful in the debates over resource allocation and policy preferences.

The Science Policy Reports show the repeated efforts by the Congress to continue long-term planning and to look at longer-term trends in relation to the needs in federal policy for the support of research. These reports approach the problems and issues of individual disciplines, government-industry-university relations, and science and engineering manpower.

This author believes that the influence of congressional hearings and special reports on university strategic planning has been largely neglected in the literature. Consequently, he has selected two examples of congressional hearings and reporting series that supported the previously referenced Carter initiatives for revitalizing American industry through the use of university research.

Since 1970, the Congress has held a large number of hearings on federal-government research policy and economic revitalization. These hearings resulted in more than forty major studies on the commercialization of research. The distribution of thousands of copies of congressional reports has a great influence that reaches far beyond the federal government. These reports advance the formation of a national research philosophy that is the *sine qua non* for public support of a federal government strategy that will include appropriations for specific agency budgets for university research.

In the early seventies, the Senate Committee on Commerce, Science, and Transportation held a series of hearings on the problems and issues of trade between the United States and the rest of the industrialized world. Out of these hearing came reports warning that American industry would soon meet intense competition from foreign companies, particularly from the Japanese in industries targeted by the Ministry of International Trade and Industry (MITI).

These congressional reports usually came from a team of experts on a particular technology. University research and the transfer of research from the laboratory to industry were the center piece for congressional fact finding and national policy recommendations. Although most of these reports were printed originally for information purposes only, their recommendations soon became the philosophical foundations for congressional and national policy.

The House of Representatives' Committee on Science and Technology is probably the most influential of government bodies in planning national research strategy. Congressman Olin E. Teague, Texas and then Congressman Don Fuqua, Florida chaired this very important committee. The work of the committee as a whole and the work of the subcommittees have a profound impact on university strategic planning. In turn, testimony from university representative had a major impact on congressional legislation.

The Subcommittee on Domestic and International Scientific Planning and Analysis (DISPA), chaired by Congressman Thornton of Arkansas began in 1975 a series of hearing pursuant to its new Special Oversight function of the country's scientific and technological enterprise. Congressman Thornton (1976,1) noted its function was "to bring longer-range planning, coordination, and responsible oversight to its (congressional) activities." The reports prepared by DISPA ranged from mechanisms for the intergovernmental exchange of R&D results to international cooperation in energy research and development.

DISPA's 1,360 page report on *Government Patent Policy* (the Ownership of Inventions Resulting from Federally Funded Research and Development) caught the attention of many university research administrators as the federal government historically had developed patent policies primarily on an agency-by-agency basis. This meant the universities had to deal with several different approaches to developing patents derived from an agency interpretation of what should be allowed. Within agencies, several interpretations could be found for a course of action. From the university viewpoint, there was an obvious need for Congress to develop a long-range, integrated patent policy to end the nightmare of ambiguity that was paralyzing the transfer of university research to use in American industry.

The universities had a considerable impact on these hearing as Raymond J. Woodrow, president, the Society of University Patent Administrators provided many pages of cogent testimony regarding the problems of patenting under existing federal-government–university partnership arrangements. Representatives from industry, aerospace associations, departments for Commerce, Navy, Health, Education, and Welfare, and NASA discussed at some length the many difficulties of patenting inventions resulting from federally funded research and development projects.

The subcommittee's reports formed the basis for a patent bill which became Public Law 96-517, *The Patent and Trademark Amendments of 1980*. This law gave universities a right of first refusal to title in inventions made in performance of federal grants and contracts, subject to some limited exceptions. With this law the government dramatically reversed its previous policy and abolished twenty-six conflicting statutory and administrative policies. Later in 1982, OMB was given the responsibility for establishing a uniform and equitable series of patent regulations for universities. Responsibilities and opportunities for holding title to inventions that had previously resided with the federal agency were turned over to the universities. Public Law 96-517 and subsequent amendments put into place a national strategy to further technology transfer and to enhance the commercialization of university research.

The reports prepared by the Subcommittee on Science, Research, and Technology of the Committee on Science and Technology of the House of Representatives provide good examples of the comprehensive analyses the federal government gives to national research problems and the integration of its legislation. Again, in the late seventies Congressman George E.

Brown, Jr., chairman of the Subcommittee on Science, Research, and Technology conducted hundreds of days of hearings and published a number of reports on the role of universities in the revitalization of American industry. The *Analyses of President Carter's Initiatives in Industrial Innovation and Economic Revitalization* was most prominent. This report contained a variety of studies on innovation and economic productivity during the late seventies. The subcommittee reports usually extracted innovation and productivity information from legislative activities, oversight hearings, testimony to the Congress, and the speeches of members of Congress. The subcommittee pursued three basic strategies during this analysis: (1) they studied the problems of innovation and productivity in the economy of the United States very broadly; (2) they drafted bills on innovation and productivity legislation which fell within their jurisdiction; (3) they shared their information with other congressional groups and with university partners interested in innovation and productivity issues.

In other House chambers during the seventies, the Subcommittee on Trade of the Committee on Ways and Means, conducted numerous hearing on trade between Japan and the United States. The subcommittee examined the difficulties in the semiconductors, computers, and telecommunication industries from a broad perspective. Their hearings provided a stream of testimony from experts on solid state microelectronics, trade and investment, and United States–Japan relations. Their most provocative report was *High Technology and Japanese Industrial Policy: A Strategy for U. S. Policymakers* (1980).

The principal bills to emerge from the many congressional hearing and reports of the 1970s was the *Stevenson-Wydler Technology Innovation Act of 1980*. This act became Public Law 96-480, which provided a legislative base for several of President Carter's October 1979 Industrial Innovation Initiatives and his Economic Program for the Eighties. The *Stevenson-Wydler Act* and the *Research Revitalization Act of 1981* became the congressional strategy for using university research to revitalize the American economy. The university that did not consider these congressional strategies in their long-range planning missed excellent opportunities to develop at their institution a sophisticated science with federal dollars.

Congressional staff members such as John Holmfeld, Harold Hanson, and Harlan Watson are principal planners of university research. Their native intelligence, professional training, and many years in Washington give them a set of competencies that command respect from both academicians and government representatives. Their careful scanning and selecting from the world's literature topics of interest to the Congress give them great influence in the initial stages of federal government planning. For more than two decades, John Holmfeld has provided for the Society of Research

Administrators (SRA), National Council of University Research Administrators (NCURA), and other interested organizations progress reports on the initiatives of Congress. More importantly, he has dutifully listened to university needs and has arranged to have these needs reported directly to the Congress.

Hanson (1985), executive director, Committee on Science and Technology, U. S. House of Representatives reviewed for the Society of Research Administrators the key role that Congress plays in the support of research in this country. In his address on *Federal Strategies on Research*, he repeatedly made the point that the budget is a policy statement and that the historical analysis of the United States budget and its projections form a research strategy for the nation. He noted that during 1985, the Committee on Science and Technology conducted a comprehensive review of American science and science policy with the intent of reversing the growing trend in budget deficits. The purpose of this particular review was to examine the rationale and mechanisms for the support of scientific research by the federal government. The 18 member task force organized their study to look beyond the annual budget cycle to explore the direction that the government–science relationship should take in the future. He provided to the Society of Research Administrators a progress report on this very important investigation and discussed its significance to university strategic research planning. The draft copy of the congressional report, which appeared in January 1990, confirmed many of the policies discussed by Hanson in the 1985 annual meeting. The SRA meetings have proven to be an excellent source of early information on emerging national plans.

In Chapter 6, Watson, drawing on his many years of experience as a consultant to Congress, provides a general explanation of how the Congress plans strategically and how their influence works.

The Influence of the Federal Agencies

The research administrator should know the plans of the principal agencies in the executive departments. These government units are often termed mission agencies. They include the Departments of Agriculture, Commerce, Defense, Education, Energy, Health and Human Services, Housing and Urban Development, Interior, Justice, Labor, and State; and the Environmental Protection Agency, the National Aeronautics and Space Administration, the National Science Foundation, the Smithsonian Institution, and the Veterans Administration.

The U. S. Department of Agriculture conducted or funded research in the last quarter of the twentieth century through the following agencies: the Agricultural Research Service, the Economic Research Service, Farmer Cooperative Service, Forest Service, Statistical Reporting Service, and the

Cooperative State Research Service. These and other agencies report to the National Science Board (1978) on their policies concerning basic research, list their most significant projects of the last ten years, and outline their priorities for the future.

It is vital that university strategists know the strategic plans of the principal federal agencies as they will have specific impacts on university research programs within the immediate future. Curiously, the NSF (1989a, 3) states "A research plan for the federal establishment does not exist and there is no mechanism in the Congress for dealing with such a plan, should one appear" Such cavalier euphemisms abound in Washington, where positions and plans of great influence are deliberately understated. Unfortunately, this statement like all euphemisms can be misleading. The statement is true only, if one expects to find one comprehensive research plan—of course, there are many, many research plans for the federal government. As we have just discussed, strategic planning occurs continually in the executive and legislative branches of the federal government and in all of its agencies. Once again, the research administrator must know where to look for agency plans and know who in the agency can influence those plans.

The National Science Foundation's *Long-Range Plans*; the National Institutes of Health's *NIH Health Research Strategy for the 1980's*, the current *NIH Research Plan*, and the *Health Research Activities of the Department* and the NIH specific strategic plans for intramural and extramural research; the Veterans Administrations Medical Research Service's *Long-Range Plans*; and the other research agencies strategic plans usually look at the technological revolutions now in progress and identify opportunities for breakthroughs in their respective fields. Current agency plans have serious implications for university strategic plans as agency research plans will affect funding in specific fields immediately and for the long-term.

The *Five-Year Outlooks*, the agency long-range plans, the NSF *Science Indicators*, and the *Condition of Education* are vital to university strategists as they draw for their institution a number of overarching policy implications from national assessments of trends. These and other documents help them to see long-term national development in specific disciplinary areas. Executive agency reports should be included in every scan of the enterprise as agency programs grow from the recommendations of advisory groups to the agency.

The environmental scan to determine the needs and resources of sponsoring agencies should include copies of the organizational charts of agencies such as the NIH, Department of Energy, Department of Defense, and the NSF.

Comparison of the organization plan included in the enabling act of the Congress (England 1982, 363) and comparison with the National Science Foundation Organizational Chart for 1986 illustrates the growing complexity of the NSF organization. For the research strategist a current chart provides a great deal of information for locating specific interest areas. A comparison of the 1986 NSF Organizational Chart with the 1989 NSF Organizational Chart reveals the addition of the Office of Science and Technology Centers Development, a new directorate, and several new programs. These additions point to NSF's current areas of intensive development and herald coming appropriations in these areas.

Although it is a prosaic planning activity, the research administrator should order the guidelines and the annual reports from each of the program offices and have them in the University Office of Research Services Library as these documents are vital to principal investigator planning. The P.I.'s most frequent requests from the Offices of Research Services are for specific guidelines and program reports. Also, a copy of the agency's organization directory helps with planning as it allows the research planner to obtain and send information directly to the agency's grant tracking system, to personalize their communications to program officers, and to select a particular contract specialist.

The Washington Establishment's Influence on Planning

The Washington establishment (those Washington insiders who are not in the Congress nor presidential term appointees) is tremendously influential in planning university research. The congressional staff, the bureaucrats in the executive offices and mission agencies, the staffs of associations at #1 Dupont Circle, and the numerous professional association officers in the national capital form the core of the Washington establishment for university research.

Since 1976, the American Association for the Advancement of Science (AAAS) has held colloquia on research and development policy issues and the have studied with regularity the impacts of government budgets on national agenda. Shapley (1979) and Teich's (1981) reports to the AAAS Committee on Science, Engineering, and Public Policy provide some idea of the information exchange and the influence that is exerted on government strategy by the Washington establishment. The formal and informal exchanges of information among members of this group and the complementary planning efforts of the establishment make Washington the locus for much of the federal strategic planning. Roschwalb in Chapter 8 provides greater insights into this area of influence.

NATIONAL SCIENCE FOUNDATION
ORGANIZATION AS OF JUNE 30, 1954

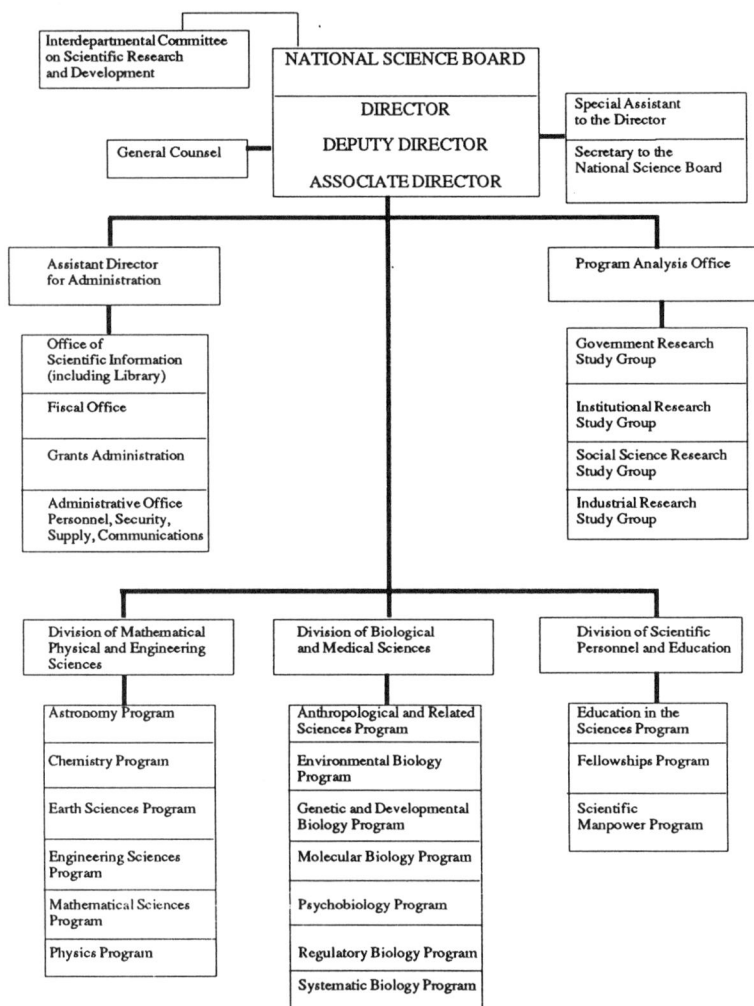

Interdepartmental Committee
on Scientific Research
and Development

NATIONAL SCIENCE BOARD

DIRECTOR

Special Assistant
to the Director

General Counsel

DEPUTY DIRECTOR

Secretary to the
National Science Board

ASSOCIATE DIRECTOR

Assistant Director
for Administration

Program Analysis Office

Office of
Scientific Information
(including Library)

Government Research
Study Group

Fiscal Office

Institutional Research
Study Group

Grants Administration

Social Science Research
Study Group

Administrative Office
Personnel, Security,
Supply, Communications

Industrial Research
Study Group

Division of Mathematical
Physical and Engineering
Sciences

Division of Biological
and Medical Sciences

Division of Scientific
Personnel and Education

Astronomy Program

Anthropological and Related
Sciences Program

Education in the
Sciences Program

Chemistry Program

Environmental Biology
Program

Fellowships Program

Earth Sciences Program

Genetic and Developmental
Biology Program

Scientific
Manpower Program

Engineering Sciences
Program

Molecular Biology Program

Mathematical Sciences
Program

Psychobiology Program

Physics Program

Regulatory Biology Program

Systematic Biology Program

National Science Foundation as of 1986

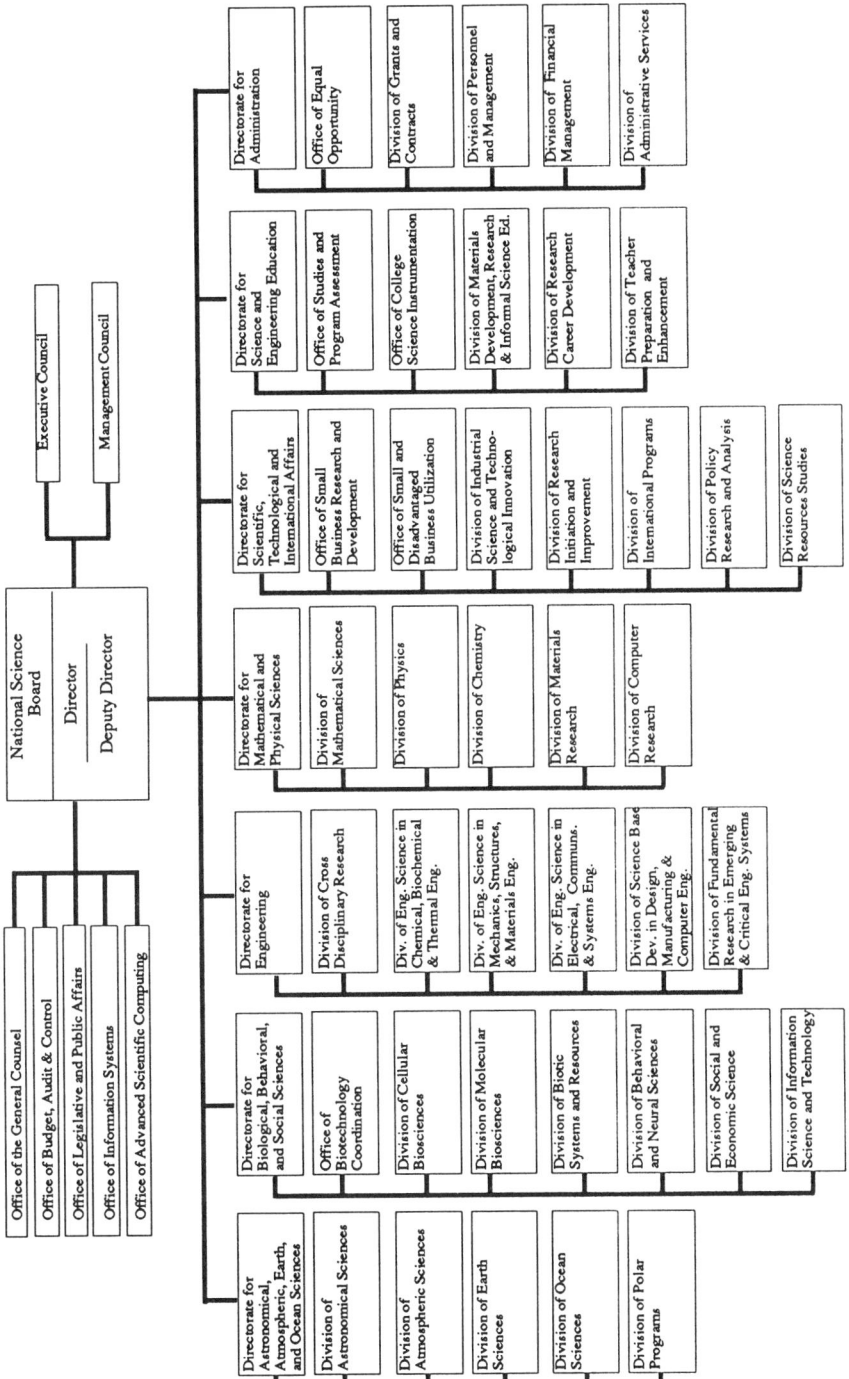

Executive Council

Management Council

National Science Board

Director

Deputy Director

Office of the General Counsel

Office of Budget, Audit & Control

Office of Legislative and Public Affairs

Office of Information Systems

Office of Advanced Scientific Computing

Directorate for Astronomical, Atmospheric, Earth, and Ocean Sciences
- Division of Astronomical Sciences
- Division of Atmospheric Sciences
- Division of Earth Sciences
- Division of Ocean Sciences
- Division of Polar Programs

Directorate for Biological, Behavioral, and Social Sciences
- Office of Biotechnology Coordination
- Division of Cellular Biosciences
- Division of Molecular Biosciences
- Division of Biotic Systems and Resources
- Division of Behavioral and Neural Sciences
- Division of Social and Economic Science
- Division of Information Science and Technology

Directorate for Engineering
- Division of Cross Disciplinary Research
- Div. of Eng. Science in Chemical, Biochemical & Thermal Eng.
- Div. of Eng. Science in Mechanics, Structures, & Materials Eng.
- Div. of Eng. Science in Electrical, Communs. & Systems Eng.
- Division of Science Base Dev. in Design, Manufacturing & Computer Eng.
- Division of Fundamental Research in Emerging & Critical Eng. Systems

Directorate for Mathematical and Physical Sciences
- Division of Mathematical Sciences
- Division of Physics
- Division of Chemistry
- Division of Materials Research
- Division of Computer Research

Directorate for Scientific, Technological and International Affairs
- Office of Small Business Research and Development
- Office of Small and Disadvantaged Business Utilization
- Division of Industrial Science and Technological Innovation
- Division of Research Initiation and Improvement
- Division of International Programs
- Division of Policy Research and Analysis
- Division of Science Resources Studies

Directorate for Science and Engineering Education
- Office of Studies and Program Assessment
- Office of College Science Instrumentation
- Division of Materials Development, Research & Informal Science Ed.
- Division of Research Career Development
- Division of Teacher Preparation and Enhancement

Directorate for Administration
- Office of Equal Opportunity
- Division of Grants and Contracts
- Division of Personnel and Management
- Division of Financial Management
- Division of Administrative Services

Federal Laboratories

In viewing the Federal Impact Area, the strategic planner should recall that the federal government performs research under two management systems—in-house federal laboratories such as the Environmental Protection Agency's Environmental Monitoring and Support Laboratories and Federally Funded Research and Development Centers (FFRDCs). The in-house federal laboratories account for about 70 percent of the federal activity and the FFRDC's do about 30 percent. The development of joint plans with these laboratories greatly enhances the university's research opportunities.

The federal government laboratories have enjoyed a rapid growth in funding over the last three decades by increasing their funding 450 percent in constant dollars. Precise partnerships with government laboratories and FFRDC's such as the Argonne National Laboratory can be most beneficial to universities. Argonne is operated by the University of Chicago for the Department of Energy. In forty years, it has developed into a multidisciplinary research center with primary focus on engineering research, particularly for nuclear power and other advanced energy technologies; basic science, particularly chemistry, physics and material science and biomedical and environmental science and technology.

In 1986, Argonne's director, Alan Schriesheim laid out the laboratories major initiatives in his plan for *The Next 40 Years*. Schriesheim based his strategic planning on specific assumptions of future national needs. He discussed in some detail Argonnes (1) leading in the development of the Integral Fast Reactor, (2) leading in the design and development of the six billion electron volt synchrontron x-ray source; (3) initiatives in advanced computing, fundamental chemistry of energy processes, and basic and applied surface sciences; (4) proposing initiatives in experimental waste treatment and advanced environmental control technology; (5) pioneering research programs to improve competitiveness in cooperation with the steel industry, off-road equipment firms and a plant biotechnology consortium; and (6) work on technology for arms control and treaty verification, and national security applications of its reactor expertise and accelerator technology.

Research collaboration between Argonne scientists and visiting professors from Argonne affiliates lead to many successful research projects to be conducted on the university campus. Knowing the initiatives of Argonne or any federal government lab is the first step in assessing the impact of the FFRDC's on a university's research. The second step is beginning joint planning with the FFRDC on a specific initiative.

THE STATE GOVERNMENT: A CRITICAL IMPACT AREA

Because the states charter and regulate institutions of higher education, both public and private, state executive agencies and legislatures are critical elements in the state impact area with which research administrators must work.

State-University Liaison for Strategic Planning

The planning liaison between university representatives and state planners is extremely important at this time as the state governments are promoting an environment for technological growth that will support the commercialization of university research by industry, revitalizing existing industry, and introducing new industry.

The political liaison for state-government–university planning is explained more fully by Darling and Hensley in Chapter Six. William Webb in Chapter Ten provides a comprehensive explanation of the importance of state strategic planning for the coordination of higher education institutions and outlines the twenty-two formulas employed in that planning.

State government representatives come into strategic planning sessions with the expectation that their funds will be used to promote economic development within the state. In Chapter Nine, Roger Tellefsen, a pioneer in the development of state science and technology councils, explains in detail the strategic planning process for the state councils and the expectations legislators have for the state-government–university partnership.

This section will deal only with the strategic planning performed by two relatively new offices in state governments—the Divisions of Research Programs (DRP) in the State Higher Education Coordinating Boards and the governors' State Science and Technology Offices (SS&TO). These two offices are emphasized as critical impact areas because they have been given the routine strategic planning functions for research in the states. The Research Administration offices in the universities are primarily responsible for maintaining liaisons with the DRPs and SS&TOs. The state research liaison with universities is frequently performed by a director of research in the state's higher education coordinating board and by the governor's director of the state science and technology office, or both.

The State Science and Technology Offices (SS&TO)

The State Science and Technology councils are new but exceedingly important units in state research planning. Their general activities have been widely reported in recent publications and national meetings including: *State Technology Programs in the United States* published by the Minnesota Governor's Office of Science and Technology in 1986, the

transcriptions of the SRA national meetings of 1985, 1986, and 1987, in-
dividual state brochures, and the publications of the National Governors'
Association (1983, 1985a, 1985b, 1986, 1987). This author has extracted
information related to strategic planning from these sources and from the
*NGA/SRA Survey to Determine the Structure and Functions of State
Science and Technology Offices* and summarizes it here.

The State Science and Technology offices are organizations within the
state impact area that universities must contact for joint planning. In 1987,
the National Governors' Association and the Society of Research Administrators undertook a study of the structure and function of state science
and technology offices. The investigators, Hensley, Clarke, and Peterson
(1987) found that 31 states reported currently maintaining S&T offices.
They found that most of the reporting states conducted planning through
staff that is assigned the responsibility for maintaining liaisons with the
state's universities, the governor's office, legislature, federal agencies, industrial associations, and small business innovation research programs.
Some state S&T offices also maintain liaisons with international associations, research parks, and professional associations.

The NGA and the SRA study found that input into and knowledge of state
S&T strategic plans were essential functions for the university research administrator to perform. The study found that university faculty, industrial
scientists, and legislative leaders were key to state strategic planning. For
example, presidents of the major universities in Oklahoma served on the
Oklahoma Science and Technology Advisory Committee (OSTAC) and
played a major role in drafting a very comprehensive *Five-Year Plan 1986-
1991* for the state of Oklahoma. This plan illustrates the driving role that
economic development currently has in state long-range planning. An
analysis of the Oklahoma plans shows how the university presidents were
able to link the state plans for economic development with the research
needs of the universities. The plan states "The ultimate purpose of the five-
year plan developed by the OSTAC is to expand and diversify Oklahoma's
economic base by cultivating one of its relatively unnoticed but highly
promising segments—science and technology-based research and industry. The goals, objectives and actions recommended herein are
designed to create a climate in which the science and technology segment
of Oklahoma's economy can flourish." The Oklahoma plan called for the
use of state and federal funds to increase the success of Oklahoma's researchers in federal grant competitions; established a competitive peer
reviewed funding program in health research; and initiated an Eminent
Scholars and a Research Equipment program that offered matching grants
in targeted areas for newly endowed chairs and research equipment. Supplements to the five-year plan were the specific plans for *Oklahoma*

Programs for Science and Technology that planned for specific amounts of funds to be appropriated by the legislature. The legislature provided a plan for attracting and retaining high calibre researchers to the higher education institutions by planning for the development of basic and applied research in certain centers. Specific programs were planned for the creation of: (1) a Regular Research Program, (2) a New Investigator Program, (3) a Small Project Program, and (4) a Faculty Recruitment Program. These comprehensive reports were followed by the quarterly *Update*, which kept the state planners current with programmatic progress and new legislative goals.

H. Graham Jones (1986), one the countries first directors of a SS&TO, explained for the SRA membership the importance of strategic planning to the state of New York's program for technology development. His office used a number of university faculty and industrial scientists to plan the following five part strategy: (1) support and encourage closer collaboration between the State's major universities and the industrial community, both in cooperative research and development, and in business development activities; (2) ensure that education and training programs meet the emerging needs of technology-based industries; (3) improve access to capital; (4) give special attention to the needs of technology-based industries in all of the State's economic policies and development programs; (5) increase awareness among both business decision makers and the general public of New York's assets.

Jones stressed that strategic planning was necessary for individual states to counter the Japanese and German national focus on directly transferring the results of basic research to commercial application. He noted that for more than four decades the U. S. investments in research and development far exceeded that of other nations. However, these other nations were concentrating their efforts on transferring our basic research into commercial applications. As a result, the industrial primacy of the United States came under increasing challenge and the industrial bases of states such as New York were severely eroded. He indicated that university-industry cooperative arrangements have not constituted a major share of university research budgets and have not been central considerations in university planning. He suggested that New York's strategy to develop Centers for Advanced Technology (CATs) would be a direct response to this need for increased university-industry collaboration to stimulate economic growth within the state. He supplied a very comprehensive set of criteria established by the New York State Science and Technology Foundation for the planning and evaluation of each center in the Advanced Technology Strategy.

The southern states formed the Southern Technology Council because as Governor Baliles (1987: 1) noted, "None of us has the resources or expertise to pursue all the opportunities that science and technology offer. Through cooperation and collaboration, however, each state can strengthen its efforts to research, develop, and transfer new technologies faster than it could working alone." Academicians are frequently the key planners in state science and technology efforts. Ronald E. Carrier, president of James Madison University was asked to take a leave of absence to develop Virginia's Center for Innovation Technology and to plan the work of the Southern Technology Council. The fact that a university president was asked to leave his post for a year to co-chair the development of an organization such as the Southern Technology Council shows the value and the level of commitment that governors are willing to give to the planning activities of their science and technology councils.

The *Regional Forum*, the Southern Technology Council Newsletter, The *Authority Report*, a quarterly newsletter for the Arkansas Science and Technology Authority, and the New Jersey Commission on Science and Technology's *Quarterly Report* provide summaries of these organizations' planning actions, budgets, progress reports on specific programs, reports on collaborative research with industry, and plans for technology transfer. These reports are vital to academic research strategists.

The Divisions of Research Programs (DRP) in Higher Education Coordinating Boards

Roger Elliot, director of the Texas Higher Education Coordinating Board, Division of Research Programs distributes to universities, state agencies, and industrial concerns by electronic mail each Friday an informal newsletter that advances research planning for Texas. Elliot established the newsletter to: announce research and technology transfer meetings within the state, apprise the universities and cooperating industries of planning activities of organizations such as the Technology Industry Legislative Taskforce (TILT), request help in planning sessions with the State Auditor's Office to discuss auditing requirements for state grants and other matters, and inform university planners of scheduled meetings in Austin with NSF and coordinating board personnel to discuss planning and evaluating science and engineering programs. The electronic newsletter also provides information about research opportunities, the status of state research programs, and changes of personnel in the state research establishment.

The Illinois Resource Network (IRN) (1980), the prototype for state research information networks, allows the research administrator to input and obtain information from the state research agencies. The IRN is an innovative statewide electronic directory that can supply names, campus addresses, current research activities, and educational backgrounds of Illinois faculty members. Through a key word or phrase, the research administrator can obtain the identity of specialized consultants in a myriad of disciplines from agriculture to zoology.

Rodman and associates (1987) developed the Texas Innovation Information Network System (TIINS), a research-information system designed to assist the state of Texas in its efforts to improve its technological research efforts. This computerized system, now operated by the Texas Engineering and Experimental Station (TEES) contains information on current scientific research, technology businesses, and professional and business services in Texas. The network reveals technology transfer efforts, new business starts, and research planning by providing access to thousands of experts in all fields of science and technology, information on ongoing research at Texas universities, the technology capabilities and needs of Texas industry, all types of professional business services related to research commercialization, and information on new and emerging occupations in Texas. TIINS helps the university research administrator plan for the transfer of new technologies to the private sector, for more efficient utilization of technological resources within the state, and for speeding up the commercialization of new products and processes. Best of all, by using a computer search, it lets any user know where the strong research capabilities are in the state. It contains detailed information on more than 4,000 researchers in university, government, and other nonprofit institutions. Multiscreen profiles describe areas of research expertise, important publications, current research projects, patents and licenses, and the professional and the technical training capabilities of Texas scientists and engineers. TIINS offers unlimited possibilities for the research planner to define the specific types of information they need to obtain. As an example, most professionals speaking Chinese with expertise in a specific technical area can be located immediately through a key word search.

Bob G. Davis, founder of the Texas Technology Transfer Association—T^3A and editor of *Technotes* publishes lists of corporations in Texas specifically created to commercialize technology invented at Texas educational institutions. There are many excellent reasons for research planners to have access to such a list. Primarily it gives the planner familiarity with university researchers who have been fortunate in developing technologies into new companies as well as giving a brief description of the products of these new companies. Davis (1989), in talking of the advantages of networking, suggested that research planners should strongly consider as first contacts T^3A corporations when they seek to license inventions that are compatible with their product lines. He stated: "I would also suggest that each of us consider looking to other T^3A members first whenever we have special needs that can be filled by our talented fellow members. Most of us are aware that we have associate members who are patent attorneys, venture capitalists, certified public accountants etc. It seems to me that true, and profitable, networking occurs when we use the contacts we've made for mutually rewarding business alliances. The opportunity that membership in T³A affords for such fruitful networking also lends real meaning to the word Association."

INDUSTRY: A NEW IMPACT AREA

Although universities and industrial organizations operate under two very different missions, there are many mutual needs that can be satisfied when cooperative research relationships are developed through joint strategic planning. Today, there is a growing awareness among leaders of the research enterprise that government-industry-university partnerships can develop the research that is beyond the capabilities and scope of any of the three individual research performing sectors. Strategic planning is seen as a way that the three sectors can advance together to produce synergistic results through programs of cooperative research.

Traditionally, industry and universities have been seen as separate performers of research. Isaiah Bowman, (1945) president of Johns Hopkins University expressed the separate performer relationship when he stated that philosophy which dominated the thinking of the research enterprise for years and is still very strongly held by academicians. Toulmin, (1988) and Rothschild (1972) described the suspicion of industrial motives and the disregard that academicians have held for applied problems. Since the Nixon advocacy of research applied to national needs and the Carter initiatives for economic revitalization, the attitude toward joint research has turned 180 degrees in government circles.

One of the university research administrator's most important responsibilities in strategic planning is providing information about corporate interests in university research to their researchers and sending brochures about university research capabilities to targeted industries.

The National Commission on Research (1980) produced a report that holds that improved university-industry cooperative research can produce significant benefits to the nation. They recognized that difficulties arise because of the different character of the institutions and the responsibilities of the participants. The commission reviewed the state of research and innovation in the United States and identified a variety of needs and philosophies that are believed to have direct application for assessing the impact of strategic planning for university research on the industrial sector. The following assumptions should be considered when the university is making joint plans for cooperative research with an industry.

1. The final products of industry-university planning should be agreements that result in better products and services useful to the public and that enhance the mission of both organizations

2. Universities are better prepared to do basic research and should take the lead in planning the exploration of fundamental concepts needed by an industrial sector.

3. Planning within affiliate programs for specific inventions for a particular industry should strengthen the innovation process in an industrial sector and should lead to an enhancement of the universities instructional program as well as contributing to product improvement in the industry.

4. Joint planning should result in equitable financial rewards to an industry and to a university for development of an explicit objective.

5. With careful policy formulation the hazards to university academic freedom are manageable.

6. Strategic planning allows universities to exploit opportunities for cooperative research with industry and to avoid subversion of traditional university purposes.

7. State and federal governments should be involved in government-industry-university partnerships as facilitators of strategic planning rather than as an active manager or performer in specific projects.

8. Strategic planning requires the early identification of the types of research to be performed and an appropriate parceling of funds to support the basic as well as the applied research necessary for the long-term development of an industry.

9. Strategic planning must include provisions for informing the public of the nature and rationale of specific industry-university cooperative programs and for highlighting the social benefits that accrue from such partnerships.

10. Strategic planning provides a new technology for alleviating much of the misunderstanding and mistrust that exists among members of industry, university students and faculty, and the general public.

The National Commission on Research (1980,ii) provided an excellent set of recommendations for the performance of industry-university research, which are incorporated into the following suggestions for consideration in university strategic planning with industry.

1. Plans should be designed around important scientific areas of mutual interest, individually tailored to the characteristics of each participant. The protocol should emphasize initially investigator-to-in-

vestigator planning and continued interaction once the research is begun.

2. Strategic plans should have clearly stated objectives that preserve each partner's purposes and policies, recognizing that the two sectors have differing modes of operating that must be respected in joint efforts.

3. Strategic planning should encourage the individual researchers from both universities and industry to determine the specific choice of research topics.

4. Strategic planning should consider very carefully how financial rewards will be distributed among the participants based on their assumption of the risks of bringing highly uncertain research to the market place.

5. Every strategic plan should include opportunities for demonstrating ethical and performance requirements that further mutual respect for performing good science and technology.

6. Planning should be for the long-term recognizing that research results are rarely achieved in short periods of time.

7. University strategist should review with their industrial partners the needs of a particular industry and explore the possibility of combining their resources with a number of companies and universities in working distances of one another.

8. University researchers should plan to promote applications of their research and should plan for an equitable share of profits resulting from commercialization of their work that was not part of a work-for-hire.

9. University planners should have programs that advocate to legislators tax incentives for the development of cooperative research projects.

10. University strategists should study successful industry-university partnerships and should incorporate into their plans provisions that have proven effective elsewhere.

In addition to planning for contracts for the delivery of specific university research to industrial corporations, university researchers should work with their advancement officers in designing plans to develop corporate matching gift programs to support particular centers of research excellence in the university. University advancement officers seem to be able to stay abreast of planning for matching gifts for research by reading CASE's monthly magazine, *Currents*, and attending professional meetings. *Matching Gift Notes*, a quarterly newsletter from CASE informs the research administrator of trends and issues affecting matching gift programs, provides current information about changes in corporate matching gift programs and furnishes updates on national development activities.

Industry Checkoff Programs are major contributors to university research. The Electric Power Research Institute (EPRI) sponsored by the nation's electric utility industry began supporting research and development in universities in 1973 with the purpose of advancing capabilities in electric power generation, reliability, economy, and environmental concerns. The Soybean, Corn, and Cattlemen's Associations tax themselves to support research on advancing their products.

The impact of research on beef cattle has particular interest for the author because Texas Tech University has the Burnett Center for Beef Cattle Research and Instruction. During the later part of the 1980s, the Cattlemen's Beef Board has reported that state and national collections for the Beef Promotion and Research Program have exceeded $73 million annually. It is important that strategists for beef research invite the assistance of members of the beef board to join them in strategic planning as half of the total funds are directed to state beef councils. Also, national programs are committing a record amount to fund beef research programs.

THE NONPROFIT SECTOR: THE SOCIAL BENEFACTORS

The research university is stabilized by the funding that comes from foundations, philanthropists, voluntary associations and corporate giving. In making the environmental scan to determine sources of funding for university research, the professional meeting and publications of the organizations within the nonprofit sector should be carefully considered. Also, the research administrator may find the annual reports of the individual foundations to be most helpful with campus planning activities. The research administrator will want to link their campus planning with the advancement (development) office in their university.

Obtaining funds from the nonprofit organizations to support university research is much more personalized than applying to government offices. The network of development officers is most useful in placing ideas before key decision makers in a foundation or voluntary association.

The influence paths within the Nonprofit Impact Area revolve around three organizations the Council for Advancement and Support of Education, The Foundation Center, and The National Society for Fund Raising Executives.

The Council for Advancement and Support of Education (CASE) is a professional organization that exists to advance the understanding and support of education. Most research universities have an advancement office that specializes in the art of asking foundations for funds to support higher education. The university advancement staff will have plans for developing major gifts, raising money through gift clubs, sustaining a successful capital campaign, finding new sources of revenue, and obtaining matching funds for research. Each of these advancement mechanisms for soliciting funds are excellent sources for research support that require considerable joint planning. Within the advancement office a professional development officer should be building an alumni program to support research, communicating the achievements of the institutions arts and sciences through their publications, marketing select institutional instructional programs and publicizing its areas of research excellence, and most importantly making personal visits to foundation headquarters.

CASE's *Planning in the Alumni Office: the Decade Ahead* is very interesting reading for research administrators and its videotapes such as *Reachout and Raise More Funds* are particularly helpful in training deans and department heads to work with the advancement office in planning for nonprofit support for research.

CASE has conducted workshops and conferences to assist the senior advancement officials develop their institutions. CASE's Annual Assembly is an excellent forum for senior advancement professionals and interested faculty and university administrators to exchange information about current activities and to enter into cooperative planning with sponsors or other institutions. Similarly, the CASE district conferences enable all members to meet with colleagues in their region of the country and to share plans, techniques, and problems with others having common concerns. CASE senior profession programs provide senior advancement officers with opportunities to discuss pressing issues facing education and research, institutional strategies for developing research, and for developing their management abilities and asking expertise.

The Foundation Center's publications and services have provided for over three decades, university planners with the primary tools of strategic planning. The members of the research enterprise can consult a broad range of factual material on private philanthropy contained in the Foundation Center database files, directories, guides, and monographs. University strategists find current information on all private, community, and corporate foundations in one or more of the center's recording of their meetings or in their publications.

Thomas R. Buckman, president, in 1989 made a sustained effort to update all files and directories. The "financial profile" for the previous year provides at-a-glance the corporate business status of organizations that might give money to support research. Also, the sections on "Purpose and Activities" and "Programs" are helpful in getting a line on the current giving interests of foundations so university planners can match their research funding needs with foundation funding programs. The history of how much the particular foundation gave and the size of its awards is essential information in the search for funds to support a neophyte investigator with great potential. *The Foundation Grants Index* provides factual information about what areas the foundations are currently placing their money, not what the foundations state they are willing to support. The difference is sometimes amazing. Strategist must be aware of what is actually happening not what was planned five or ten years ago. This easy to read index provides an excellent analytical introduction and a series of statistical tables that outline significant trends affecting the research support environment. No other source gives academicians planning to use nonprofit funds to support their research such a clear and total picture of foundation grantmaking.

The center's COMSEARCH provides printouts of actual foundation grants for research occurring in twenty-three broad areas of activity. Its broad topics related to professional societies and science and technology programs have been particularly useful to the author as they include nonprofit grant making to education and research institutions, scientific societies, museums, libraries and disciplinary associations primarily for capital support, program development and research. COMSEARCH helps the planner to find out which types of organizations receive funding, which foundations give in particular locations, and which foundations are currently giving in targeted subject areas.

Your author has found the following publications to be standard references for strategic planning when approaching the non-profit sector:

> *The Foundation Directory* (1989) is the best single source of current information on the nation's largest grantmakers. The new 12th Edition contains comprehensive information on over 6,600 corporate, independent, and community foundations holding $107 billion in assets and awarding more than $6 billion in grants annually. Five indexes help the planner to identify foundations that fund in subject or geographic areas and to pinpoint key foundation officials. Types of support are shown according to 185 subject fields and 33 types of support categories. *National Data Book on Foundations*, lists basic information on every active grantmaking foundation in the country, *Source Book Profiles*, provides a comprehensive review of the country's 1,000 largest foundations.

National Directory of Corporate Giving, supplies planners with key data on the foundations and direct giving programs of more than 1,500 leading corporations. In 1988, corporations donated well over $4 billion to nonprofit organization and community development projects. This directory describes program policies for 1,200 corporate foundations and nearly 500 direct giving programs. It covers both cash awards and in-kind gifts such as staff time, products, and real estate. The complementing and special features such as the state of corporate charity today, and the extensive bibliography for further research are very useful guides for the university planner.

National Guide to Foundation Funding in Higher Education features over 3,000 foundations with a proven interest in higher education. The National Guide concentrates its information on foundations that have made a commitment to the long-term support of colleges and universities. It is of considerable value to research development and academic planners. The internal consistency and reliability of source data from the Foundation Center assures the research community of accuracy of information for their planning purposes.

Two examples of investigator and foundation officer joint planning help to show the great influence the nonprofit sector has on the development of university research. In the nonprofit sector, the officers in private and company foundations, the voluntary associations, and individual philanthropists provide guidance in the development of university plans that are in accord with their long-term interests and current funding priorities. The Texas Tech Development Office maintained a personal liaison with the private foundations and advanced the research plans of the university by talking directly with foundation representatives about specific proposals that they had included earlier on their monthly "brag sheet." As an example, the Caesar Kleberg Foundation for Wildlife Conservation was a very active partner in planning and sponsoring the study for waterfowl on playa lakes. The strategic planning for the waterfowl research was conducted by Horn Professor Eric Bowlen who with the directors of the Kleberg Foundation mapped out an extensive plan for the study of waterfowl on the Great Plains.

McCartney (1989) informed us of the value of long-term planning with the voluntary associations. The special relationship that a number of departments of ophthalmology have with Research to Prevent Blindness, Inc. illustrates the worth of a continuing relationship between organizations with the same goal—preventing blindness—yet, serving different functions in the research enterprise. The ophthalmology departments are the performers of research, whereas Research to Prevent Blindness, Inc. is the sponsor for over fifty different medical units. This sponsor is the world's leading voluntary organization in support of eye research. It has given the Texas Tech Health Sciences Center, Department of Ophthalmology and Visual Sciences an annual grant of about $50,000 for departmental research. These unrestricted monies are most valuable in supporting an aggressive research program in preventing blindness.

The flow of information among the principals in the nonprofit sector is enormous. Knowing how to access that information and where to find a particular plan is an interesting management information problem for research administrators who must work very closely with university advancement officers in organizing nonprofit sector information.

THE DISCIPLINES—THE ARBITERS OF KNOWLEDGE

The Government-University-Industry Research Roundtable

The Government-University-Industry Research Roundtable, sponsored by the National Academy of Sciences, the National Academy of Engineering, and the Institute of Medicine was created to foster strong American science through effective working relationships among government, universities, and industry. The National Academies represent the nation's most distinguished scientists, engineers, and medical researchers. Any activity sponsored by the roundtable will have their members in active leadership positions. The agenda of the science disciplines will dominate any planning they sponsor. Research administrators making an environmental scan for strategic planning for university research should consider their reports as they have great impact on research, especially basic research.

In this section the author has summarized their conference report entitled, "What Research Strategies Best Serve the National Interest in a Period of Budgetary Stress?" This report came from a roundtable conference held in Washington February 26 and 27, 1986. Four-hundred science leaders attended the conference. They represented a cross section of federal and state research officials, university presidents, research administrators, industrial heads, professional society representatives, and working academicians from the scientific and engineering disciplines.

The conference was called because many scientists in the mid-eighties were very concerned that the projected national deficits, which were exceeding $200 billion, were so enormous that the federal government strategy as expressed by Gramm-Rudman-Hollings goals for deficit reduction would have a serious negative impact on existing and future federal funding of research. The conference major emphases were on federal support for basic research at federal laboratories, universities, and other sites. They looked at the possible impact that severe, successive Gramm-Rudman-Hollings budget cuts of 15 percent per year would have on the mission of specific research performers and sponsors, on a broad range of administration and management problems, and on the retention of science and engineering research personnel.

Although there was no set of directions advocated by the conferees, the following issues were highlighted in the Government-University-Industry Research Roundtable Report (1986, 3-8).

1. There is a risk that the important contributions of basic research to national goals may be seriously curtailed by a long period of constraint in federal funding. Basic research produces the new knowledge (organized by the disciplines) and fresh talent needed to enhance the nation's economic and military strength in relation to other countries.

2. The nature of research makes it particularly vulnerable to instability in support. In particular, a field of research (a discipline or disciplines) can suffer long-term damage if the best students and young talent are not attracted and retained.
Active research teams once disbanded, cannot easily reassemble. And loss of access to the most advanced equipment is often the difference between world-class work and second-rate work.

3. The federal budget constraints compound a preexisting problem. U. S. research is presently beset by serious shortfalls in science and engineering personnel and by deterioration of scientific facilities. The participants pointed out that universities and the science disciplines also are affected negatively by declining level of financial aid to students, more restrictive tax laws on charitable giving, and reduced access to tax-free bonds for construction.

4. Other sources of significant support for basic research can not compensate for decreases in federal funding. These planner from across disciplines posed the question of whether managers of large federal development efforts should substantially increase their support of basic research in disciplines pertinent to their missions.

5. In preparing for some very difficult trade offs, it will be necessary to reexamine key features of the U. S. research enterprise. Basic research in the universities was assessed with the idea that research management should be streamlined, that the number and roles of research universities should be reduced, and that international cost-sharing for expensive research facilities should be explored.

A special working group discussed strategies for allocation of resources between (1) Larger Scale Interdisciplinary Projects and Programs, (2) Disciplinary Research, and (3) Smaller Scale Research Initiatives. Roland Schmitt, senior vice-president of the General Electric Company for Corporate Research and chairman of the National Science Board, concluded that Gramm-Rudman-Hollings will be implemented by the Reagan administration and the Congress will have to address a very serious deficit. He felt that universities should consider the potential impact of Gramm-Rudman-Hollings solution as the deficit is not an aberration, but a major force that is going to be with us for a long time.

The university strategic planner must include the reports of the National Research Council (NRC) in the environmental scan for they frequently point the direction that a particular discipline is heading. The NRC's project, *Mathematical Sciences in the Year 2000* (MS 2000) is a report that points out the importance of the NRC to disciplinary planning. In January of 1990, the chair of the MS 2000, William E. Kirwan, president, University of Maryland presented a preview of the report to the National Association of Mathematicians at their annual meeting. This preview served to alert mathematicians of the major parts of MS 2000 and the question and answer period between the audience and members of the MS 2000 committee provided the planners of the NRC strategy with considerable input from the rank and file of the national associations of mathematicians. At such meetings the mathematical community had an opportunity to help in shaping the project's final report, which is due for publication in the fall of 1990 (FOCUS 1989, 20).

The International Sector

American research universities have become very involved in global strategic planning. Inexorably, as the sun rises, the globalization of research occurs and the need for global strategic planning increases. Research institutes exist in almost every country. Many of the scientists in foreign countries have been trained in American research universities by American researchers. The masters and their students remain in touch. They plan joint projects. They plan by using integrated services digital networks. They plan with one another through telephone, telex, facsimile, computers, electronic mail, messaging, and conventional paper transmissions. The research community is an important part of the global village. Their efforts must be linked for the welfare of this planet. Globally, they must plan strategically.

Most research universities have an office of international affairs that provides information on scholarships and fellowships available in different countries. They maintain school listings of the institutional characteristics, tuition fees, unique features, size, and specialties of cooperating institutions. They use international faculty profile systems that allow researchers to make new contacts according to their needs for a particular area of expertise, facility, and site in a certain country.

The United Nations and the Organization for Economic Cooperation and Development gather and publish a great deal of information about research internationally. We have seen the importance that international firms have placed on planning strategically with American research universities in a preceding section on the Industrial Sector. In Chapter Six, a detailed description of strategic planning between universities and a foreign country is provided. The topic of global strategic planning is of such importance that a Society of Research Administrators International Research Symposium has been conducted. Information from that symposium is to be presented in a future SRA monograph.

THE PUBLIC—THE ULTIMATE SPONSOR

The public is an impact area often neglected by universities. Research administrators must gently, but constantly, remind academicians that the taxpayer in the final sponsor of government research and that the consumer is the eventual sponsor of industrially funded research; consequently, the public must be considered in any strategic plan. How to help the public appreciate the value of the research university and the specific advances of individual researchers is a prime responsibility of the research administrator.

Speeches by prominent civic leaders stressing the value of university R&D to the nation and the significance of strategic planning are very potent communication mechanisms as they create among regional leaders an awareness of the major problems facing university research. E.G. Jefferson (1983), chairman of E. I. du Pont de Nemours and Company, outlined for New England business leaders, at a meeting of Commercial Club of Boston, a pro-industrial strategy that recognized M.I.T.'s pioneering "Technology Plan of 1920," which encouraged industry utilization of knowledge developed at the school. He stated:

> Such industry-university cooperation in the Boston area produced impressive research and manufacturing interaction, contributing to the prosperity of this region and the nation.
>
> We should nurture such industry/university cooperation. As we do this society as a whole will be the winner.

Chairman Jefferson being a good strategist explained his plan to the public by first identifying the need for a specific strategic plan. He observed:

> I take comfort that in the past year there has been growing recognition that an economy as large and complex as ours cannot abandon its manufacturing base. The "post-industrial" idea has given way to an understanding that manufacturing, service, and high tech sectors are linked; that we must enhance the competitiveness of all three if our economy is to function well. . . . But if we have made progress in correcting the post-industrial and central planning notions, we have not yet taken decisive action to address problems which imperil our world competitiveness. To adjust to new realities, I believe such action should come in the form of a pro-industrial strategy—not a bureaucratic industrial policy, but an ongoing process

designed to enhance the competitiveness of all U. S. industries in a changing world marketplace. Tonight, let me suggest elements of such a strategy in both the private and public sectors.

General plans for the university and other research sectors put forth by distinguished citizens such as Jefferson should be carefully considered by the academy as the faculty needs to know what the public figures expect of the university. They lead public opinion. The research administrator also needs to pay attention to what the public polls have to say about the general public's perception of research and the university.

Updating the Public's Image of the Institution

In every university there is a constant discussion of what the institution is and what it should be in the future. Institutions must change to keep up with social expectations or they wither. Institutions of higher education become what they and the public think they are. The conceptual models of institutions presented in documents (bulletins, catalogs, brochures, faculty handbooks, directories, etc.) are a cardinal factor in creating a general impression of the institution. This image is critical to the recruiting of faculty and students as it strongly influences their choice of institutions. Moreover, it is the institutional model that guides the activities of faculty and students after they become a member of the institution. The public image establishes a general expectation for everyone in the institution. Therefore, modeling the institution is of prime importance and keeping the public informed about the changes should be considered in every strategic plan. One must bring the public along with the planned changes.

Since the 1940s, institutions of higher education have been involved in lengthy and emotionally charged debates about their changing purpose. Research administrators must communicate the changes in the institution to the public. The public is accustomed to supporting multipurpose state universities with a range of program offerings that provide the opportunity for a liberal education for all students and for professional training at the undergraduate and graduate levels. In addition, the public recognizes the value of universities participating in community service and the public expects scholarly research leading to effective dissemination of knowledge. The public is not accustomed to the research university with its emphasis on elegant education, sophisticated science, and advanced technology. It is the responsibility of the research administrator to keep the public informed about changes in purpose and about the research activities. The research administrator should maintain a steady flow of information about research to the university office of news and publications and these offices should have a strategy for putting that information before the public. Chapter Six provides some very specific examples of how the public is brought into the strategic planning of the university.

The public image of a university will ultimately work its way into the thinking of state and national representatives who do the specific planning for the advancement of research. Therefore, the strategic planning that occurs in each of the previously discussed sections will be strongly influenced by public opinion. Consequently, research administrators must constantly present to the public a positive image of the research university. They must create an awareness in public of the wonderful and socially beneficial contributions of this unique institution.

WORKS CITED

Baliles, Gerald L. March 1987. Governor Baliles to Chair Council, Regional Forum 1:1. (Southern Technology Council Newsletter.)

Bennett, William J. 1986. Education Secretary Calls for Fundamental Changes in Colleges. *The Chronicle of Higher Education*. 33 (7):1. (October 15, 1986)

Bloom, Allan. 1987. *The Closing of the American Mind*. New York: Simon & Schuster Inc.

Bowman, Isaiah. 1945. Report of the Committee on Science and the Public Welfare. In *Science—The Endless Frontier*, ed. V. Bush, 70-122. Washington, D. C.: National Science Foundation.

Bush, Vannevar. 1980 [1945]. *Science—The Endless Frontier*. Washington, D. C.: National Science Foundation.

Carnegie Foundation for the Advancement of Teaching, The. 1987 *A Classification of Instituions of Higher Education*. Princeton, N.J. Princeton University Press.

Carnegie Mellon University. 1988. *Goals and Strategic Plans, A Report Prepared for Middle States Association of Colleges and Schools*. Pittsburgh: Author, February 1988.

Council for Chemical Research. 1984. New Ways To Get Industry Dollars to Academe. Chemical Week, 4 July 1984 Reprint.

Davis, Bob G. 1989. *Technotes, The Newsletter of the Texas Technology Transfer Association*. Houston, TX. P. O. Box 20334, Vol. 1, no. 2, Summer.

England, Merton J. 1982. *A Patron for Pure Science: The National Science Foundation's Formative Years, 1945-57*. Washington, D. C.: National Science Foundation, NSF 82-24.

Falk, Charles E. 1982. *1990 R&D Funding Projections*. Washington, D. C.: National Science Foundation, NSF 82-315.

FOCUS. (Publication of National Association of Mathematicians) 1989, 20.

Foundation Center, The. 1989. The Foundation Directory. New York: Author.

Government-University-Industry Research Roundtable. 1986. *What Research Strategies Best Serve the National Interest in a Period of Budgetary Stress?* Washington, D. C.: Author Conference, 26-27 February 1986.

Hanson, Harold P. 1985. Federal Strategies on Research. *The New Research Environment— Responding with Plans and Strategies*. St. Louis, MO. 19th Annual Meeting of Society of Research Administrators, 29 September-2 October 1985.

Hensley, Oliver. 1987. Texas Tech—Opening Doors To Tomorrow. *Lubbock Avalanche-Journal*, Sunday Morning 22 February 1987.

————, Peterson, N. and Clarke, M. September 19, 1987. The Structure and Functions of State Science and Technology Offices. *SRA 21 Annual Meeting*. New Orleans: Fairmont Hotel.

————, Peterson, N., Waugaman, P., and Wills, J. September 16, 1986. The Significance of State Science Councils to the Development of Research. *The Climate for Research in North America*, 20th Annual Meeting of the SRA. Montreal, Quebec, Canada: Hotel Meridien.

Jefferson, E. G. 1983. Remarks by E. G. Jefferson, Chairman of E. I. du Pont de Nemours and Company before the Commercial Club of Boston, Boston, Massachusetts, 13 December 1983.

Jones, H. Graham. 1986. The New York State Science and Technology Foundation. *SRA Research Symposium, The Place of the State Science & Technology Office in the Research Enterprise*. Montreal, Canada: SRA 20th Annual Meeting, 14-17 September 1986.

Killoren, Robert A. Jr. 1979. *Planning for research. Journal of the Society of Research Administrators*. XI, 1:13-20.

Lance, Bert. 1977. OMB Memorandum to the Heads of Executive Departments and Agencies on Funding of Basic Research. Washington, D. C.: Office of Management and Budget, 15 August 1977.

McCartney, David L. 1989 "HSC Receives Eye Research Grant." Lubbock: Avalanche-Journal, Thursday, June 22, 2989, A-3.

National Academy of Sciences. Committee on Science and Public Policy. 1964. *Federal Support of Basic Research in Institutions of Higher Learning*. Washington, D. C.: National Academy of Sciences, 31.

National Cancer Program. 1973. *The Strategic Plan January 1973 Edition*. Washington, D. C.: Author.

National Center for Education Statistics. 1976. *The Condition of Education*. Washington, D. C.: U. S. Government Printing Office, March.

National Commission on Research, 1980. *Industry and the Universities: Developing Cooperative Research Relationships in the National Interest*. United States of America: Author, August.

National Governors' Association. 1983. *Technology and Growth*. Washington D. C.: Author.

————. 1985a. *Programs for Innovative Technology Research in State Strategies for Economic Development*. Washington, D. C.: Author.

————. 1985b. *State Programs to Encourage the Commercialization of Innovative Technology*. Washington, D. C.: Author.

————. 1986. *Revitalizing State Economies*. Washington, D. C.: Author.

————. 1987. *The Role of Science and Technology in Economic Competitiveness*. Washington, D. C.: Author, October.

National Science Board. 1978. *Basic Research in the Mission Agencies: Agency Perspectives on the Conduct and Support of Basic Research*. Washington, D. C.: U. S. Government Printing Office.

National Science Foundation, 1989. *The State of Academic Science and Engineering*. Washington, D. C.: Author, Division of Policy Research and Analysis, August.

National Science Foundation. 1959. *Scientific Research and Development in Colleges and Universities Expenditures and Manpower—1953-54*. Washington, D. C.: Author, NSF-59-10.

New York State Science and Technology Foundation. 1986. *The New York State Centers for Advanced Technology*. Albany, NY: New York State Science and Technology Foundation, May.

Nixon, Richard M. "State of the Union Speech and Health Message." Washington, D. C. 1971.

Oklahoma Science and Technology Advisory Committee. 1986. *Five-Year Plan 1986-1991*. Oklahoma City: Oklahoma Department of Commerce, December.

Rauscher, Frank J., Jr. 1973. *The Strategic Plan*. January 1973 Edition. National Cancer Program. 1973.

Rodman, John A. 1987. "TIINS, The Missing Link for Innovation and Economic Development," in the Proceedings of the 1987 Fall Joint Computer Conference, October 1987, Dallas, Texas.

Rothschild, Lord. 1972. Forty-five Varieties of Research (and Development). *Nature* 239:373.

Schriesheim, Alan. 1986. The next forty years. *Research Highlights*, Argonne National Laboratory Annual Report. Argonne, IL: Argonne National Laboratory.

Science Policy Task Force, 1990. *Science Policy Task Force Report, Draft Chapter Number 1:* Reports to the Congress on Science and Science Policy, Staff Report to the Committee on Science, Space and Technology, House of Representatives. One Hundred First Congress, Second Session. Washington, D. C.: U. S. Government Printing Office, January.

Shapley, Willis H. 1979. *Research & Development AAAS Report IV—Federal Budget: FY 1980 Industry International*. Washington, D. C.: American Association for the Advancement of Science.

Teich, Albert H. 1981. *R&D and the New National Agenda. Federal R&D Agency Perspectives, R&D in the FY 1982 Budget: Impacts*. Colloquium Proceeding June 1981. Washington, D. C.: American Association for the Advancement of Science, November. 25-26.

Thornton, Ray. 1976. Special Report of the Hearings before the Subcommittee on Domestic and International Scientific Planning and Analysis. In *Government Patent Policy* op. cit. p-1.

Toulmin, Stephen. 1988 A Historical Reappraisal. In *The Classification of Research*, ed. O. Hensley. Lubbock, Tx: Texas Tech University Press., 21-29.

U. S. Congress. House. Subcommittee on Domestic and International Scientific Planning and Analysis of the Committee on Science and Technology. 1976. *Government Patent Policy* (The Ownership of Inventions Resulting From Federally Funded Research and Development). Hearings before the Subcommittee on 23 September-1 October 1976. Washington, D. C.: U. S. Government Printing Office.

U. S. Congress. House. Subcommittee on Science, Research and Technology of the Committee on Science and Technology. 1980. *Analyses of President Carter's Initiatives in Industrial Innovation and Economic Revitalization*. Washington, D. C.: U. S. Government Printing Office, December.

U. S. Office of Management and Budget. (1973) Part I. Principles for Determining Costs Applicable to Research and Development Under Grants and Contracts with Educational Institutions. *Federal Register*, Vol. 38, no. 181, Wednesday, 19 September 1973, 26292.

CHAPTER TWO

PHILOSOPHICAL FOUNDATIONS FOR STRATEGIC PLANNING FOR UNIVERSITY RESEARCH

Oliver D. Hensley and Pamela A. Cooper

In the past half-century, American higher education has been trans-formed by a number of powerful social forces into a highly organized and functionally diversified enterprise composed of community colleges, teaching institutions, and research universities. About 200 of the present 3,300 higher-education institutions are now classified as research univer-sities. These elite institutions have evolved from teaching or technical in-stitutions into unique organizations offering distinctive education and sophisticated research activities. Several of the research universities have in their strategic plans transformation statements such as Carnegie Mellon's (1988, 2) "Over the years, Carnegie Mellon University has suc-cessfully made the shift from a regional technical college to a national university known for its excellence and innovation in education and re-search."

Research universities have developed separate administrative structures and extramural research programs that rely on modern strategic planning. Methods of instruction and types of research performed in research univer-sities have vastly expanded and improved from what they were prior to World War II and their philosophical foundations have greatly changed. And, although research universities continue to claim instruction as one of their three major functions (research, instruction, and service), they are now dominated by the research function rather than the traditional instruc-tional efforts of most higher-education institutions. Teaching has been relegated to an important, but secondary role for faculty who now spend the majority of their time on some sort of research-related activity. Research dominance is acknowledged by many universities in their discussion of the budget process. They make such statements as "Carnegie Mellon is a private university, funded principally by research, tuition, private giving, and endowment income—in that order of predominance." Carnegie Mel-lon (1988,140).

This chapter will consider the traditional and emergent forces that in-fluenced the gradual transition from teaching to research in many institu-tions of higher education and introduced a new set of planning modalities designed to meet the increasing complexity in the development and administration of university research.

The evolution of the research university and its planning techniques can be divided into several transition periods, which were motivated by powerful social forces that created new research partnerships. These partnerships incrementally transformed a number of technical and teaching institutions into research universities.

Setting the direction of American university research is in a large way the result of political and scientific partners planning jointly on a large scale which areas of research the government wants to support (See Chapter Seven). Once the federal government makes the decision to enter a field, Congress appropriates money and designates an executive agency to administer the government's funds according to the intent of Congress; the president and Congress approve agency research programs; and then the government agency solicits proposals from university scientists for fundamental knowledge and technological solutions.

This pattern of sponsor and performer planning government-directed research is observable in the research developed to meet the national needs for advanced weapons technology, improved health care, space exploration, and new energy sources. The federal-government–university partnership requires the university to give immediate attention to critical national needs leaving instruction and service functions with lesser priorities.

The accretion of government-sponsored research projects slowly transforms grantee institutions by changing the source of revenues, which in the composite changes the major purpose of the institution. Soon after the arrival of a sufficient mass of sponsored projects the climate of the university changes to support sponsored projects. It is in this stage of the evolution of a university that the philosophical foundations for strategic planning for university research are set.

We believe that the philosophical foundations for a research university are much different from those of other postsecondary education institutions, and that sponsored research is the major influence in creating this difference. We hold that all research universities have at one time been teaching institutions and that the transition from teaching institution to research university was facilitated by particular social forces that created a need for new classes of research that the university adopted. The social forces were of such a magnitude that university changes in structure and philosophy were eclipsed; consequently, these changes remain relatively unknown. These major social forces can be subsumed under the following transition periods: (1) the teaching era, 1636–1940; (2) the war years, 1940–1945; (3) the government foundation period, 1945–1957; (4) the Sputnik period, 1957–1965; (5) the industry-university partnership period,

1965-to-present; (6) the state economic-development period 1975-to-present; (7) the advanced research and high technology era 1980-to-present. The reaction to these forces will be discussed in subsequent chapters.

MODELS OF THE HIGHER EDUCATION ENTERPRISE

Although the lion's share of the research performed in the higher-education enterprise is performed at research universities, the scan of the university sector must include all types of postsecondary education institutions as these institutions are potential partners or competitors for specific research activities. The identification of types of institutions in the higher-education enterprise is a first step in determining the location of competitors and partners and their influence paths within the research community.

It is important for research strategists to understand that the university is the home of research and to know the functional differences in the various types of higher-education institutions. The research administrator must have the knowledge for informing the sponsors and the general public of the vast differences in postsecondary institutions. Automobiles, trucks, and busses are all vehicles, but they have very different purposes and they perform different functions. In a similar manner, academicans are employed by three functionally different types of higher education institutions: community colleges, teaching institutions, and research universities. Although researchers perform their work at many sites, their home is the research university. It is the place where they receive their professional training and where they return to conduct research.

A Model of the Functional Divisions
in the Higher Eduction Enterprise

There are over 3,000 colleges and universities in the United States. At this time, 200 of these institutions perform over 95% of the academic research in science and engineering. These institutions are the research universities of the United States.

Research Universities are valued institutions in our civilization. They can be distinguished from other types of higher-education institutions with different missions by their emphasis on research activities. Hensley (1988, 47) has shown that a set of rectangles can help us represent the fundamental relationships among functions within higher education institutions and see the vast difference in activity allocations among types of postsecondary institutions.

Figure 2.1 contrasts three major types of institutions within the higher education enterprise. In Figure 2.1 bottom, research is the dominant func-

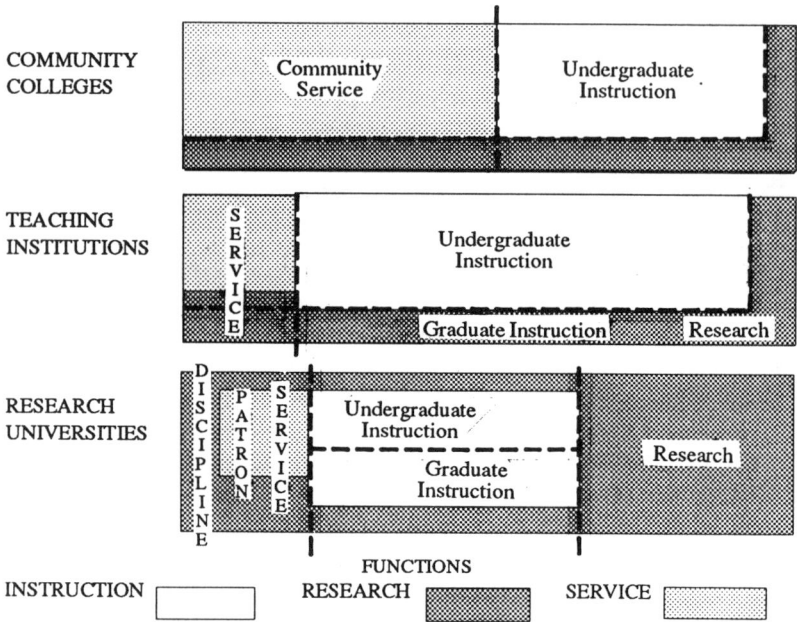

Figure 2.1. A Model of the Functional Divisions in the Higher Education Enterprise.

tion. In contrast, 2.1 middle shows the dominance of instruction activities in "Teaching Institutions" and in 2.1 top, it is apparent thât "Community Colleges" devote most of their efforts to community service and undergraduate instruction.

Each of these institutions play valuable roles in our technological society, but it is the research university that provides the environment for developing new ideas and the education of the next generation of researchers. Strategic planners must understand that the research university is the custodian of existing knowledge and the researcher produces new knowledge for the good of all society. Within our civilization, the research university has built the unique institutional climate to foster creative activities, the infrastructure to support special researcher needs, and the partnerships essential to fund elegant education and sophisticated science. The research university is the font of knowledge for our technological society.

As the higher-education enterprise has become more complex, one of the tasks of the research strategists has been to make within selected functional areas of work progressively finer distinctions to explain the benefits of those activities to a greater number of sponsors and to a public increasingly resistant to tax increases to fund higher education. Figure 2.1 shows how institutions in the higher-education enterprise can be grouped according to the functional activities they perform and how higher-education activities can be identified and placed within three general functional categories. It is important to convey in a strategic plan to the public and to the institution's partners the unique mission of the research university in our modern technological society.

We will analyze the Carnegie Foundation's and other schemes for classifying universities that allow the research strategists to make finer distinction among institutions. At this time, it is necessary only to make the point that strategists must help the sponsors and the public to functionally distinguish among types of postsecondary institutions.

National Science Foundation Ranking of Colleges and Universities According to Research Expenditures

In this section, several classification and ranking schemes are studied for their utility in helping the strategic planning process. The National Science Foundation (NSF) *Ranking of Colleges and Universities According to Research Expenditures* provides universities with a set of fiscal statistics that show the prowess of institutions of higher education in capturing funds for research. The Congress, in looking at strategies for developing the nation's research, uses the NSF *Five-Year Outlook on Science and Technology* and the Division of Science Resources Studies *R&D Expenditure at Universities and Colleges by Source of Funds* to rank annually the research universities. Johns Hopkins University, M.I.T., University of Wisconsin, Stanford, and the University of Minnesota usually are included among the top twenty institutions. The University of Arkansas usually is ranked in the sixth cohort and Texas Tech University usually is ranked in the seventh cohort.

The NSF ranking identifies for Congress the American research universities, and indicates, rather precisely, the amount of federal funds each institution is receiving and in which areas. It also indicates which of the nation's 3,300 colleges and universities have the capability to produce the sophisticated science and technology Congress is seeking to encourage through federal support. The NSF data are used frequently by university strategists to assist them in assessing university plans in relation to research expenditures by sectors and agencies. It is a current indicator of the standing of the institution within academe.

The Carnegie Classification Scheme

The Carnegie Foundation's (1987) classification of institutions of higher education is most useful in institutional planning and evaluation activities.

Its classification system is based on the levels of degree offered (ranging from prebaccalaureate to the doctorate), on the comprehensiveness of the institution's mission and on enrollment. The Carnegie classification, which follows, is useful in identifying the types and status of higher education institutions.

1. *Research universities I*—These institutions offer a full range of baccalaureate programs, are committed to graduate education through the doctorate degree and give high priority to research. They receive annually at least $33.5 million in federal support for research and development and award at least fifty Ph.D. degrees each year.

2. *Research universities II*—These institutions offer a full range of baccalaureate programs, are committed to graduate education through the doctorate degree, and give high priority to research. They receive annually between $12.5 million and $33.5 million in federal support for research and development and award at least fifty Ph.D. degrees each year.

3. *Doctorate-granting universities I*—In addition to offering a full range of baccalaureate programs, the mission of these institutions includes a commitment to graduate education through the doctorate degree. They award at least forty Ph.D. degrees annually in five or more academic disciplines.

4. *Doctorate-granting universities II*—In addition to offering a full range of baccalaureate programs, the mission of these institutions includes a commitment to graduate education through the doctorate degree. They award annually twenty or more Ph.D. degrees in at least one discipline or ten or more Ph.D. degrees in three or more disciplines.

5. *Comprehensive universities and colleges I*—These institutions offer baccalaureate programs and, with few exceptions, graduate education through the master's degree.

6. *Comprehensive colleges and universities II*— These institutions award more than half of their baccalaureate degrees in two or more occupational or professional disciplines, such as engineering or business administration, and many also offer graduate education through the master's degree.

7. *Liberal arts colleges I*—These highly selective institutions are primarily undergraduate colleges that award more than half of their baccalaureate degrees in arts and science fields.

8. *Liberal arts colleges II*—These institutions are primarily undergraduate colleges that are less selective and award more than half their degrees in liberal arts fields.

9. *Two-year colleges and institutes*—These institutions offer certificate or degree programs through the Associate of Arts level and, with few exceptions, offer no baccalaureate degrees.

10. *Professional schools and other specialized institutions*—These institutions offer degrees ranging from the bachelor's to the doctorate. At least fifty per cent of the degrees awarded by these institutions are in a single specialized field.

The Carnegie Foundation's classification serves the research strategist by providing a set of national student-production standards that are correlated with other data to which the planner can refer. They provide the external benchmarks that can guide regents and administrators in realistic goal setting for their institution.

The State of Texas Seven-Tier Model for Classifying Higher-Education Institutions

It is also important for strategic planners to know how legislators view the higher-education institutions within their state. For example, in the State of Texas the Seven-Tier Model is central to all strategic planning. Sage (1987) stressed the importance given to the classification system of higher education by the Texas Select Committee on Higher Education, which, as Arnold (1986) noted, had the responsibility of recommending to the governor and the legislature how Texas higher education would reach the twenty-first century and beyond in the best academic condition with the least possible damage due to fiscal stringency. The Select Committee discussed how the state would redeploy resources to enhance the research programmatic needs of the state. Fundamental to their recommendations for redeployment of resources was the following Seven-Tier Model reported by Sage (1987):

1. *National research universities*—Shall be a comprehensive, graduate research university offering an array of undergraduate, master's, doctoral and special professional degrees. Emphasis will be on excellence in teaching and research. Research endeavors benefiting the academic strength of the institution and the economic strength of the State of Texas shall be conducted with emphasis on maintaining a nationally and internationally recognized research institution. Funding for research shall be from private sources, competitively acquired sources, and appropriated public funding. [Texas A&M University (reference to land grant and sea grant), University of Texas at Austin]

2. *Emerging national research universities*—Shall be a comprehensive graduate research university offering an array of undergraduate, master's, doctoral, and special professional degrees. Emphasis will be on excellence in teaching and research. Research endeavors benefitting the academic strength of the institution and the economic strength of the State of Texas shall be conducted with emphasis on maintaining momentum as an emerging national research university. Funding for research shall be from private sources, competitively acquired sources, and appropriated public funding. [North Texas State University, Texas Tech University, University of Texas at Dallas (upper-level serving Dallas-Fort Worth metroplex), University of Houston/University Park]

3. *Comprehensive universities*—Shall be a comprehensive university offering an array of baccalaureate and master's degree programs. Doctoral programs meeting unique needs of the area served by the institution which are not unnecessarily duplicative are authorized. [Six institutions were listed.]

4. *Teaching institutions*—Shall be an institution primarily serving a specific region and offering undergraduate and graduate programs. Baccalaureate and master's degrees shall be granted. The emphasis of the institution shall be on excellence in teaching. Faculty research, using the facilities provided for and consistent with the primary function of the institution, is encouraged. Funding for research shall be from private sources, competitively acquired sources and appropriated public funding. [Twenty-one institutions were listed.]

5. *Other universities*—[The mission of several Texas institutions were discussed specifically in this section.]

6. Texas public community-junior colleges—Texas public community-junior colleges shall be two-year institutions primarily serving their local taxing districts and service areas in Texas and offering vocational, technical, and academic courses resulting in certification or associate degrees. Continuing education, remedial-compensatory education consistent with open-admission policies, and programs of counseling and guidance shall be provided.

7. *Texas State Technical Institute*—Texas State Technical Institute shall serve the State of Texas by offering occupationally oriented programs in highly specialized technical and vocational areas resulting in certification or associate degrees but which do not duplicate programs commonly offered by public community-junior colleges.

KNOWING WHAT ACTIVITIES ARE UNIVERSITY RESEARCH

The classification of research is of vital importance to the development of research in the United States. Congress uses terms and classification systems to react to national science and technology needs with broad political policies and appropriations, which are broken down in the mission agencies into thousands of projects. Federal plans and policies, as Watson explains in Chapter 7, are designed to promote research by appropriating funds according to agencies, classes, and expenditure categories (i.e., $64.8 billion for the conduct of research and developement (R&D) and $2.0 billion for R&D facilities in fiscal year (FY) 1988). In the public mind there is a need to find new solutions to national problems—the need for a strong modern defense force results in a particular national defense policy from Congress, which specifies how much money will be spent on certain classes of research.

The Bowman Model for Classifying Research

In the original modeling of the American research enterprise, Bowman (1945, 70-122) set the nation to seeking research in three sectors: universities, industry, and government. He believed these sectors conducted three broad types of research: (1) pure research, (2) background research, and (3) applied research and development. In his report, he described what university research was in the 1940s and established for many years the roles of the various sectors in the research enterprise. Although outmoded, that model is retained by the public and national research policy makers and appropriations are made according to it. Despite many discussions of inadequacy of the Bowman model for modern research planning, universities generally collect their R&D statistics according to the amount of expenditures associated with NSF form 411 (11-82) definitions and classification of research and development, which are only slightly different from Bowman's.

The Input/Process/Output Model for Classifying Research

Hensley and Jauch (1984, 1988) suggest that Congress and universities should adopt the model for classifying university research shown in Figure 2.2.

The model shown in Figure 2.2 is more appropriate for university planning because it shows the additional responsibilities for the conduct of research that go beyond the discovery and stewardship of knowledge, and places the university into direct partnerships with particular industries and the state for R&D efforts. Such a model is more realistic because it calls for the collection of data related to specific measures of output—research articles, technical reports, patents, copyrights, prototypes, new-product lines, productivity improvements, product enhancements, and technology innovations. The public and Congress can measure these things and could tie dollar amounts to them. Most important for our purpose, it allows the university research administrator to plan cooperatively with many sponsors for specific research developments over the long term.

Classes Of Activities	Basic Research	Applied Research	Development	Production Research	Technology Innovation
A. Input	Disciplinary Imperatives	Social Utility	Organization Priorities	Market Mandates	Social/ Disciplinary Needs
B. Process	Exploring Natural/ Human Phenomena	Rendering an idea into Practice	Stepping Up a Model Solution	Product or Productivity Improvement	Introducing New Technology into a Discipline
C. Output	Knowledge Articles Algorithms	Inventions Patents/Trade Secrets/ Copyright	Prototypes Pilot Plants	Improved Products Goods/ Services or Reduced Costs	Adoption of an Innovation

Figure 2.2. A New Model for Classifying University Research Activities.

Basic Research

Within this new model for classifying university research activities, the first university research activity is *basic research*. Basic research is new explanatory problem solving. An activity can be classified as basic research if it meets the following tests: if its purpose is to generate new theoretical knowledge; if the process includes thinking in a disciplined manner about why some natural or human phenomena occurs; and if the final product is a journal article, technical report, or other manuscript that explains why something occurs.

The primary motivation of the basic researcher is to increase knowledge for the sake of understanding. This type of activity has traditionally been performed by academicians within loosely organized bodies called disciplines. Although academicians and society place great value on the products of these efforts, basic researchers give their knowledge without reservation to all who will accept it. Because knowledge seems to be free, the products of basic research often times appear to be worthless to the uninformed.

The traditional inputs for basic research are disciplinary imperatives and the personal interests of the individual faculty member. The process is thinking and verifying that thought in a disciplined manner. The work is not completed until the results of the inquiry have been transmitted, reviewed by disciplinary means, and accepted into the professional repertoire of problem-solving concepts. A paper delivered at a professional meeting, journal articles, abstracts of research, and professional exchanges on professional electronic networks are all products of basic research.

It sounds trite to say basic research is generated by the researcher's desire to make a contribution to an academic discipline, and that such knowledge will usually end up as a public good in a professional journal and will probably be incorporated in advanced courses of the researchers' discipline. But the fact remains that the majority of basic research in the United States is conducted by academicians who attempt to have their work accepted first by their professional colleagues and then disseminated to the public. Consequently, any realistic definition of university research must consider the very special relationships among academicians, their disciplines, and the structure of knowledge within the discipline. With these relationships in mind, the strategic planner must remember that (1) the core disciplines are the groups charged with organizing our studies of natural phenomena and the observations of social problems into easily transmitted forms of knowledge and (2) the university has been for centuries the institution charged with the mission of creating, organizing, and disseminating that knowledge. The outputs of basic research hold particular significance to the research planner because research products are the ammunition in their arsenal for defending appropriations for university research. The sponsors (Congress, taxpayers, foundation trustees, state legislators, and industrialists) must see the results of their earlier support if they are to continue their sponsorship. The strategic planner for the institution must also keep in mind that the researcher's primary commitment is to the discipline, and not necessarily to the employing institution. This concept of commitment must be taken into consideration throughout the research planning process.

The outputs produced by basic research must also be kept in mind when funding is being sought. As an example, there are several obstacles that have prevented any close collaborations between the university and industry in the funding and conduct of basic research. Problem areas include: differences in research objectives (the creation of knowledge versus saleable product orientation); the timing of the publication of research results; and ownership and patent rights.

The preference for the conduct of basic research within universities has been reiterated numerous times throughout the years. In 1985, the National Research Council noted that:

> As a general rule, the closer a university comes to the activity of product development, the less likely it is that the purposes of the university will be served. . . . University faculties and students serve their publics best when they produce information that is broadly generalizable (National Research Council, 1985, p. 107).

The faculty's general preference for basic research versus industry's predisposition for applied research has led to the skepticism of each organization toward the other. As noted by Baer (1978, 85), "the professor's condescending attitude toward the commercial exploitation of knowledge and the businessman's disdain for ivory tower research are familiar stereotypes that need to be overcome." A nationwide survey commissioned by the Carnegie Foundation for the Advancement of Teaching asked faculty for their opinions regarding the performance of privately sponsored research. Of the 5,450 faculty who responded, 25% agreed strongly, or agreed with reservations, that performing sponsored research for a private company is not a proper university activity (Mooney, 1989).

Bartlett Giamatti, former president of Yale University, noted that although the activities of industries and universities are complementary, "the academic imperative is to seek knowledge objectively and to share it openly and freely, while the industrial imperative is to garner a profit, which frequently creates the incentive to treat knowledge as private property" (Peterson, 1983, 76).

Daniel Zaffarano, who retired in 1988 as Iowa State University's vice president for research and dean of the graduate college noted that:

> If graduate students can't publish their findings, then we couldn't use their services. And then we may as well become an industrial laboratory instead of a university. We simply would no longer be fulfilling the functions of education (Gibson, 1988, 15).

The faculty's desire to publish research results as soon as possible and make the knowledge freely available to everyone comes into direct conflict with industries' preference to postpone publication and impose conditions of confidentiality on the research so they can benefit from information that the competitors have not accessed (Baer, 1978; National Research Council, 1985).

In contrast, from the industrial perspective there is a need to maintain some protection of the confidentiality of the research results and to obtain proprietary rights to any discoveries that they have funded. Baer (1978, 85) noted that:

> Telling an industrial research manager that his firm cannot have proprietary rights to research it sponsors at a university is as difficult as telling a professor that he can only publish his results anonymously. Neither approach is likely to generate much enthusiasm for joint research projects.

In addition, the conduct of basic research is typically of little interest to industry. David (1982, 8), then president of Exxon Research and Engineering Company, noted that:

> . . . with its connection to basic science, most university research is not geared to invention and innovation. That is why colleges and universities have never earned large sums from patents and licensing. Their ideas usually require too much development work and entail too much risk to be commercially attractive.

Applied Research

The second class of work in the new model for classifying university research activities is *applied research*. Applied research is defined as original practical problem-solving activities that are directed primarily toward a specific utilitarian purpose. It is a combination of thinking and manipulation of resources that develops ideas into some new useful device or process. Basic researchers generally are concerned with why a phenomena occurs, whereas an applied researcher is concerned with how things work and how they can work better. Accordingly, an applied researcher is not required to advance a theoretical explanation of why his invention works nor to worry about acceptance of his concept into a disciplinary structure. Oftentimes, it is to the applied researcher's advantage to make no public disclosure of his discovery. Applied researchers have no obligation to share their knowledge, in fact, they may want to keep the recipe, the microcircuitry, or the bonding process secret. The applied researcher wants to create an invention or a process for solving a practical problem. For research to be applied, the researcher must have in mind the acquisition of a patent, copyright, or trade secret as his final product.

Applied research has its input from social utility. The inventor creates an original problem-solving device that meets the needs of the individual, a social organization, or a government. With increasing frequency, university professors are involved in solving problems that have direct utility for a vocational field or for a commercial establishment; and sometimes their ideas for problem solving lead to an application for a patent. In this case, the university, the sponsor, and the academicians who hold the patent have the legal right to exclude others from making, using, and selling whatever is covered by the claims of the patent anywhere within the United States for 17 years from the date of issue of the patent.

Universities and their faculty are pursuing patents at an increasing rate. According to a survey by the Association of University Technology Managers, the number of patents issued to universities nearly doubled from 619 in 1986 to 1,145 in 1989. Patent revenues are also increasing, and universities and faculty reportedly received an estimated $60 million in royalties in 1989 (Grassmuck, 1990).

Although the purpose of patents and patent law is to encourage the disclosure of new, useful inventions and to contribute to the advancement of practical knowledge, knowledge that is destined for a patent has limited dissemination, and the users of the embodiment of the idea must pay financial tribute to the originator of the knowledge. University researchers who conduct applied research can, if they wish, apply for patent protection and collect the royalties or they can publish the knowledge and give the world their ideas. At this point in our discussion one should see the importance of motivation to a classification scheme for university research. When an academician elects to keep a discovery secret, there is immediately a conflict of interest between his individual rights and the mission of the university. When an inventor elects to keep a discovery secret, he is exercising his right to protect a potential commercial advantage.

When looking at the processes of the various types of research, the research planner should always consider the time frame and remember that once an invention is publicly disclosed the time in which the inventor may apply for a patent is rigidly limited by statute. Premature public disclosure (a journal article or a paper delivered at a conference) may preclude patent protection.

Since the passing of the Bayh-Dole provisions (Public Law 96-517) timing has become more important to classifying research as basic or applied. Treaties, small-business research partnerships, and agency program officers may decide the category of a university research activity. For example, a faculty member may be investigating with government and or business support, a subject of great import to disciplinary knowledge, but it may also involve an invention that has great commercial potential for the small business. In this case, the investigator may be prohibited from publishing the results for several months from the university's election to apply for a patent. Is this research basic or applied? Categorization would probably depend upon the election of the sponsor to apply for a patent and the principal investigator's decision to publish the results.

This type of applied research allows university researchers to be rewarded financially as well as to be recognized at promotion and tenure reviews. Since the late seventies, university researchers have been encouraged to patent their inventions. The results of university researchers rushing into patenting arrangements are creating radical revisions in campus policy that now allow investigators a fair return on their intellectual investment.

Development

The Industrial Research Institute (1978) defines *development* as:

> The translation of research findings or other knowledge into a plan or design of new, modified, or improved products/processes/services whether intended for sale or use. It includes the conceptual formulation, design, and testing of product/process/service alternatives; the construction of prototypes; and the operation of initial, scaled-down systems or pilot plants. It does not include routine or periodic alterations to existing products, production lines, manufacturing processes, services and other operations even though these alternatives may represent improvements.

Development serves as the interface between theory and the real world, and the decision to engage in most development work is a corporate decision, not an individual one. This is a great change in the mode and scale of investigation on the university campus, and requires a level of planning that is more complex than that associated with basic and applied research. With basic research and applied research during the bench-science era, a single academician usually could make unilaterally the decision to conduct a particular piece of work and could (usually with only institutional resources and perhaps some modest sponsor resources committed to him) solve his individually chosen problem. This is not the case with development research. Development has not only a different set of products, but also a much different set of inputs and a different decision-making process. The purposes are not usually established by the individual scientist or engineer, but by government agencies, boards of trustees, trade associations, departments or colleges, and other organizations. It is usually a collaborative undertaking requiring large, annual investments that produce multiple outcomes for a particular field of production. Pilot plants and development centers operated by universities have complex organizations and networks that support their purposes. Though they serve the instruction and basic research needs of the parent university, they are usually financially independent of the general education appropriation.

With most development, no new theories are discovered, and the product is judged to have been merely changed in size, proportion, degree, or composition. Rather than creating what is considered a change in kind, the novelty in development is deemed to be obvious and therefore not patentable. Also, no manufacturer will publish development results because public knowledge removes their production advantage and gives a price advantage to the competition.

We do not count the pilot plants, prototypes, and centers of excellence created and maintained by universities to measure scientific output. We should. They can be identified and counted in the same manner as we count the publications and sometimes the patents of the institution. Also, we should learn to value their products as they enhance the reputation of the institution and advance the public good.

Production Research

Production research, the fourth class in the model, is a rapidly expanding class of university investigation that is oriented toward product-service enhancement or manufacturing process improvement for a particular company or trade association. The purpose of production research is to increase a company's or trade association's profitability by creating a new product line that may be produced under existing trade secrets or patent licenses, by increasing the number of products sold through product improvement, and by improving the production process. Production research frequently takes place in the factory with university researchers assisting the firm in automating an assembly line, in creating robots that will replace manual labor, and in finding a more efficient catalyst for a chemical process. It also takes place in the university laboratory where different products are enhanced for a company or where a service activity is significantly improved.

The motivation for this class of research is a market mandate that has potential for producing a profit in a commercial organization. Usually an entreprenuerial university researcher or a company has a research idea that promises to capture a new market or an increased share of a market through production increases. The problem solving is developed with the intent of profiting from the findings (improved products or production increases), which should be taken directly from the laboratory to commercialization by a particular company or trade association. Businesses will use university researchers because they do not have the resources of the university for that particular type of research or they find it expedient to do so. The company buys the time of the researcher and pays for the research costs. In return for the company's sponsorship of the investigator's research, the firm completely or partially owns the output of the university researcher.

Recently, the proprietary considerations have greatly changed. The motivations are still market mandates and attendant profits, but the universities and their researchers are demanding a share of the company's profits when their research is directly commercialized.

University production research was originally conducted through the hiring of university professors as occasional consultants, and these consulting arrangements were seldom formally identified by the university. In the last decade, the incidence of faculty conducting this type of activity and the scope of the work has increased to the point that companies are hiring entire teams of university researchers and in some cases forming long-term partnerships with special university institutes for the commercial exploitation of an entire branch of disciplinary research that has the potential to enhance their product lines. In the sixties and seventies, this new type of joint venture and class of research would not have been considered respectable on campus and would not have been attempted. In many institutions, these activities would have been classified as service not research.

If classified as research, productivity improvement is seldom given equal consideration with basic research. Frequently, the output of production research must be placed under the service functions or justified under other research activities and accomplishments when the faculty member is reporting achievement on standard college forms. This ad hoc treatment of production research places the academician conducting such research at a disadvantage in promotion and salary reviews as they must always justify their work, a very difficult task for those doing non-conventional work.

In their evaluations of their peers, traditional scholars place a high value on basic research published in "A" journals and look with some disdain on production research. Yet, if academe is to support the economic development thrusts of the state and the nation, academicians must come up with new ideas for industrial improvement, design new molds, jigs, and tools that are outputs of production research, and they must be given credit by the university and professional organizations for this increasingly valuable effort.

Technology Innovation

Technology innovation, the final class of generic research in the new model for classifying university research, is defined broadly as the first-time use of new practices and new devices in a particular field. Technology innovation in universities usually occurs in one of the following forms (1) the invention of new technology; (2) the adaptation of existing disciplinary technology; and (3) the transfer of technology from one discipline into another knowledge field or sector. It is the process of showing for the first time in a particular field how a new or existing device or methodology can solve a technical problem of the particular field. Technology innovation is the novel thinking associated with extending man's capabilities in practicing an art or science.

A clear understanding of the previous definitions for the other classes of university research becomes very important at this point in building the model for classifying university research. Adaptation and transfer were carefully selected words for describing the introduction of new technology. If society had to rely only on novel tools and completely new techniques for every new problem identified in a discipline, our society would not develop very quickly. Fortunately, academicians are not limited to using technology that is invented by their fellows for the specific discipline. They can, and in fact are encouraged to, look outside their discipline for technology that could be useful to their practice.

Technology innovation creates considerable controversy when it is included as a legitimate university research function. Many academicians feel that it is not of the same worth as basic or applied research. Some feel that it is not really research. Despite efforts to impugn its research legitimacy, it should be seriously considered now by the higher-education community as many of the research-oriented institutions are establishing more and more specialized innovation centers of one form or another. Small-business development centers, agriculture extension centers, and industrial technical-assistance centers have the expressed purpose of transferring technology to an expanding number of biotechnology, high-technology, and materials-science industries within a certain region.

TRADITIONAL PHILOSOPHICAL ASSUMPTIONS
AND THEIR INFLUENCE ON CURRENT RESEARCH PLANNING

The traditional philosophical foundations of research universities must be understood if research administrators expect to design a successful strategic plan for modern university research. Sponsor influences, social needs, disciplinary imperatives, and changing organizational priorities have caused profound changes in the traditions, beliefs, motivations, commitments, and attitudes of the university faculty. Throughout this book, the effects of academic philosophy on the conduct of university research are discussed. In this chapter, we summarize a number of powerful academic concepts that hold sway over university activities. Although they are not always expressly stated, traditional assumptions are implicit in any plan. Academicians hold the following assumptions about themselves and their institutions.

Faculty are professionals and will act like professionals—Most faculty hold terminal professional degrees and licenses—the licentiate, which allows them to practice a specific profession and the doctorate, which allows them to teach at any university that invites them. If their degree is in medicine, they could open their individual practice and become a resident in certain hospitals. It their degree is in law, they could practice law individually or join a firm provided they were admitted to a state bar association. Engineering, accounting, chemistry, architecture, music, and other faculty could practice their profession outside the university. They have the skill to practice a profession. Many have been practitioners at one time in their career. Professionals police themselves and perform their craft independent of supervision. Faculty, although they choose to teach in the university, retain the independence of action associated with professionals. They adapt to university schedules, policies, and professional codes; yet, they are expected to act independently without supervision. They know their trade and the people in it. They are expected to exercise independent judgment on the selection of knowledge for dissemination and to choose their areas of practice and teaching specialties. The faculty is constantly pulled by the need to act independently as a professional and to respond to the directions set by the mission of the university.

Compensation will dictate where the faculty will work—Faculty are motivated by many factors related to compensation. Income is a major consideration for they, like the rest of society, must earn a living from their work. The satisfactions of teaching, the fulfillment of colleague interaction, and joys of research are important compensations. Many academicians are attracted to a university because it offers financial compensation for their particular talents and intellectual labor and it provides an environment that will promote their work.

Universities are the great depositories of man's knowledge—The faculty creates, organizes, and disseminates that knowledge. This long-standing assumption has been touched on in Chapter 1 and has been discussed in an earlier section of this chapter.

Academicians are dedicated to advancing knowledge within disciplines—Knowledge is organized into disciplines and academicians are trained in certain modes of inquiry within that discipline. They have always considered themselves to be the guardians of the tenets of their discipline and the leaders in the promotion of scholarship among colleagues within their respective disciplines. Chapter 1 has shown the vital role the disciplines play in organizing and disseminating knowledge.

Instructional affairs are determined in departments or programs—The fundamental organizational unit within the university is the department. The members of a department understand that they individually prosper according to the reputation of the department. Standards are set and enforced at this level of administration. Collegiality among faculty is demanded. The traditional departmental philosophies and planning efforts are discussed in Chapter 6.

Academic freedom is to be preserved at all costs—Academicians have always insisted that they should be treated differently from the rest of the world. Their work is uniquely important—the future of the world depends on it. To perform it objectively they must keep the influences of the world at arms length, sometimes retreat to the ivory tower. After all, their credibility rests on their ability to determine the truth. They are the final arbiters of knowledge. They must be untainted in rendering decisions on the acceptance of new theories and in determining the new areas of exploration. Imbedded in the assumption of academic freedom is the concept that sponsors of research may influence the investigator's objectivity. Therefore, anytime a new generic sponsor—federal government or industry—attempts to form a research partnership with the university, there is an immediate reaction to resist the partnership until adequate safeguards are installed in the institution to prevent the new sponsors from exercising pressure on the principal investigator's objectivity.

Rational humanism governs academic thinking—Generally, academicians subscribe to a rational way of thinking. Whatever philosophy currently is being debated is rooted in the Greek heritage of rational thought and the supremacy of man. This basic way of thinking colors academic opinion and influences the decision of the institution to conduct certain types of activities. For example, in the sixties the campus rallies against defense research, the protests against ROTC on campus, and recently the animal rights movement are manifestations of a rational humanism that dominates academe.

Academic traditions are to be preserved—All institutions have traditions to give them the stability to navigate in the social tempest. Only the church enshrines tradition better. For change to occur, there must be a consensus among the faculty. In departments, instruction and governance issues often are debated endlessly with little action. To introduce significant innovation, new administrative units must be formed away from the control of the instruction-oriented majority. Then, these new administrative units must either prove their efficacy to the institution very quickly, or face the likelihood that they will be phased out. Chapter 3 follows specific changes in tradition through several transition periods and calls attention to their effects on strategic planning.

The primacy of the principal investigator—The researcher is the primary figure in the research university. The principal investigator (PI) is the most important person in the university for they are the source of new ideas and they do the research. Their work is the development of new knowledge, new tools, testing of innovative devices under various conditions, improving existing industry, and transferring technology into new fields. Researchers are entrepreneurs and sometimes they behave like the prima donnas of the institution. They are compelled by the ultimate responsibility for success or failure of their plans to demand absolute control over their activities and the institutional resources necessary to support research.

Moreover, they want to do their research and they want their projects to be served by the rest of the university. This is as it should be, for research is an unpredictable activity requiring immediate reaction to capitalize on the newest insights. All of the responsibility rests on the researcher as the person looking and stepping into the unknown. They must have absolute control over their work and supporting services. The institution must trust their professional judgment in all activities. Teaching activities do not have the urgency for meeting the unknown that is demanded by research; consequently, instructional-based administrative systems often do not work for the researcher. Researchers must have their own planning and administrative systems that are governed by researchers, not bureaucrats or teaching faculty. The section on Organized Research Units (ORUs) places attention on the evolution of new administrative units to preserve faculty governance over their work.

Functional duties of the university must be balanced—Research, instruction, and service are the major functions of the university. They must be balanced to keep the institution on an even keel. Traditionally, faculty have balanced individually their teaching, research, and service activities for these functions are complementary activities that are difficult to separate. Despite the inextricability of functions in scholarship, modern researchers must account for what they have done and plan for future work. Accountability for their time and effort is recorded in functional areas on faculty activity reports that help decision makers in planning and administering research.

Traditionally, basic research has been the dominant class of research in the university—Basic research has the purpose of creating new knowledge. In the section on the Classes of Research, the problems of universities performing many new kinds of research were addressed. Although institutions in the teaching era were organized to support the instructional function, a climate and simple administrative mechanisms for research were developed through three forms of intramural research—independent research, departmental research, and organized research. Each of these types advanced basic research. The motivation for intramural research was to aid the faculty in creating and organizing knowledge in their respective disciplines for teaching purposes. Colleges and departments were the administrative units responsible for planning and supporting intramural research to advance their discipline and to enhance departmental reputations with the intent of attracting the best students.

There is a partnership thesis that governs the development of university research—There is a general feeling that every tub should stand on its own bottom in the academy. Academicians feel that individuals or agencies that want research performed should pay for the full costs of solicited research and should help to keep the research university in a state of readiness. Because government, industry, and nonprofit sectors have recognized the efficacy of having universities perform research and advanced education for them, it is only fitting that they should form partnerships with the university to provide long-term support for these activities. The evolution of the research enterprise has created by project incrementalism an increasing complexity in the research process that now requires a number of partners to make long-term commitments to units for successful university research development.

There is an increasing complexity for planning and conducting university research—One of the major factors influencing the adoption of strategic planning for university research has been the increasing complexity involved in the planning and performance of research. To assist in explaining this incremental process, which is almost unnoticeable within a single year, but is profound within the century, the authors have developed a Complexity Index for Research (CIR) to quantify a phenomena that has only been discussed anecdotally. If we are to study the increasing complexity of planning and performing university research, the specific variables that explain this phenomena must be identified and related to empirical data. The CIR is a first step in that direction. The algorithm is explained in the next section.

In Chapter Three, the effects of the great waves of change on the research university can be easily seen when CIR's are applied and compared for different periods of the history of higher education.

Compensation and the faculty—The work of the faculty is teaching, research, and service. They are expected to advance knowledge, disseminate knowledge, and render service to their students, institution, disciplines, and sponsors. For centuries, instruction dominated the life of faculty members because the revenue stream was produced by student related activities. Lately, research and service have become major revenue sources and the faculty have begun to work for research sponsors and to serve as paid consultants to clients outside the university.

Faculty are hired by universities because they are reservoirs of knowledge. They are expected to transmit knowledge to students, to keep that knowledge current and relevant, and to create new knowledge. The value of faculty rests on their brilliance for it is their intellect that attracts students; it is their entrepreneurial endeavors that creates new intellectual property; and it is their professional expertise that obtains invitations to provide sage advice to practitioners.

A COMPLEXITY INDEX FOR RESEARCH

We believe that strategic planning is being performed by research universities because it is the technology that allows the university to manage change in an increasingly complex research environment and to remain competitive. The complexity of research increases for two major reasons.

Increasing complexity in the scope of the work—Research becomes awesomely more complex because of massive advancements in knowledge and technology in an increasing number of disciplines. Although the thought of the investigator is the seminal work of an investigation, investigators increasingly must rely on dedicated, cooperatively-built systems and shared, elegant, research-facilities to gather information to verify and support an individual's conjecture. Although this cooperation makes modern research possible, it also makes it more complex, but not easier— time is spent differently.

Increasing complexity in the administrative burden placed on the institution—Research conducted in the university environment has an expanding number of compliance procedures that increasingly encroach on the time and effort of the investigator. The investigator must comply with government regulations, university policies, and disciplinary standards. It is usually the investigator that must do the thought and paperwork associated with each compliance procedure.

The basis for university research is the creative thought of faculty and students. The more time researchers can spend on thinking and gathering information about their problem, the more productive they will be. The more time spent on dealing with the administrative activities, the less time that is available to be spent on the actual conduct of research.

The faculty have been subjected to a growing complexity of activity associated with the conduct of their research. As noted previously, this complexity is partially due to technological advances within their areas of research. As an example, the scope of the work necessary to prove or disprove the concept of fusion is much greater than that necessary to prove the existence of electricity.

But the complexity related to the conduct of research goes much further than the scope of work necessary to remain on the cutting edge of a discipline. Numerous factors related to the administrative aspects of the research have also entered into the picture. The university researchers of the early 1900s were able to pursue research in a chosen area with little influence, impact, or demands on their research activities by the employing institution of higher education or any external funding or regulating agency. In addition, the level of coordination that is required by today's development, production, and technology innovation research far exceeds the demands on the solitary bench scientist of a century ago.

It must be kept in perspective, however, that these early researchers also had little institutional or financial support for the conduct of their research. Today's researcher is in a far better position in this regard. Research universities now formally emphasize research as one of the most important goals in their institutional mission statements, and government and industry provide billions of dollars annually for research and development conducted by university faculty and staff. As might be expected, this increased level of support has been accompanied by increased demands for accountability. All of these factors have led to an increased complexity of the conduct of research.

We have developed an algorithm that takes into consideration both the technological advances in research methodology and the increased administrative responsibilities in an attempt to quantify the growth in the level of complexity associated with the conduct of research that has only been reported anecdotally in the past. Although universities have responded by supplying research support personnel to assist the faculty overall, the fact remains that the administrative burden increases the complexity of doing research. The CIR was designed to assist planners and policy analysts in demonstrating to the university's constituencies the increased administrative burdens that have been placed on universities and researchers in the last-half of the twentieth century.

Use of the CIR should illustrate the progressive complexity of planning and performing university research. The following symbols are used to represent the variables involved in the construction of the index numbers:

F = factors contributing to the complexity of the conduct of research

W = weighting values

t = subscript for the current (given) period

o = subscript for the base (reference) period.

As an example, the aggregate value of the complexity of a current research project, valued at current weights, is:

$$CIR = \Sigma\ W_t F_t$$

However, the CIR for any given research project has little meaning until it is compared with a standard or another project. The CIR ratio is defined as the ratio of one research project's aggregate complexity value over another research project's aggregate complexity value. This comparison of the complexity of the two research projects is accomplished through the following algorithm:

$$CIR\ ratio = \frac{\Sigma W_t F_t}{\Sigma W_o F_o}$$

The authors are particularly concerned with the measurement of the overall changes in the general complexity of conducting research over time. However, the index also can be used in a comparison of the complexity of two research projects being conducted at the same point in time.

The authors, using four decades of research and research administration experience and many focussed conversations with investigators and administrators during the seven transition periods, speculate that the following factors are responsible for contributing to the growing complexity of the conduct of research:

1. Sponsor and external regulatory agencies' administrative reviews (F_S).
2. Internal (institutional) administrative reviews (F_I).
3. Compliance procedures required by the institution and the cognizant agencies that must be followed in the process of planning, conducting, and reporting research (human subjects, affirmative action, animal welfare, environmental impact, etc.) (F_C).
4. Disciplines involved in the conduct of the research (F_D).
5. Persons involved in the actual conduct of the research (PIs, coPIs, research associates, and assistants) (F_P).
6. Research support personnel involved in assisting in various aspects of the research (clerical, technicians, etc.) (F_A).
7. Reviewing principles within the disciplines and other organizations that determine the significance and the acceptability of the research and its final products (i.e., peer reviews of proposals, journal editors, committees determining research priorities in sponsoring agencies, committees within the disciplinary associations that set the standards for the discipline) (F_R).
8. The scope of the work investigated-impacted during the course of the research (F_W). The scope of the work will include the modes of inquiry selected, the selection of the research design, the difficulty in gathering the data, and the complexity of analyzing and reporting the data.
9. Time factors (F_T). Meeting deadlines increase the difficulty of doing research. The absence of adequate time for contemplating the activities or forced scheduling can be a factor in increasing the complexity of the research. (For example, an immediate deadline for proposals and completion of project work according to a Program Evaluation Review Techniques (PERT) Chart creates a pressure that is not usually part of independent research. Such time factors, if unusual, should be considered as an increase in the complexity of conducting research.) Abnormal time factors may also result in the

researcher overlooking potential discoveries in the attempt to meet specified deadlines.
10. Omicron factors are the as of yet unidentified factors that impact research but are not included among the preceding factors (F_O).

Each of these factors are further comprised of subindexes that are necessary to quantify the full impact of each factor's contribution to the complexity of research. A factor is not simply the summation of the number of compliance procedures encountered during the course of a research project. Compliance procedures are impacted also by items such as the length, detail, and frequency of reports dictated in order to properly fulfill the requirements of the compliance procedures in a certain period.

Each of these factors do not have an equivalent impact on contributing to the complexity of the research. A thorough analysis of the impact of each of these factors on the complexity of research needs to be conducted before the weighting of each of these factors can be established. Once weighting values are established they must be reassessed periodically to retain correspondence to the standard. In addition, new factors may enter at a later point in time that further impact the complexity of doing research. Despite the problems of establishing the standards for the indices, the CIR offers a way of quantifying the growing administrative burden and disciplinary and social expectations that are being placed on the investigator. Without such a measuring concept, it is difficult to determine the complexity of a growing administrative burden.

The standard denominator of the CIR ratio is presumed to be independent research conducted during the teaching era (1636–1940). We offer, for purposes of explanation and speculation, the following empirically unestablished complexity indices for the transition periods associated with the evolution of the research university: (1) the teaching era, 1636–1940 (1-5); (2) the war years, 1940–1945 (5-10); (3) the government foundation period, 1945–1957 (7-15); (4) the Sputnik period, 1957–1965 (10-30); (5) the industry–university partnership period, 1965–present (12-40); (6) the state economic-development period, 1975–present (15-50); (7) advanced research and high technology era, 1980 to present (15-60).

Using these speculative numbers, a CIR ratio can be calculated that indicates that a research project sponsored by the federal government today may be three to sixty times more complex to conduct than the independent research in the teaching era.

$$\text{CIR Ratio} = \frac{\text{The CIR for a Project in the Advanced Research Era}}{\text{The CIR for a Project in the Teaching Era}} = \frac{(15\text{–}60)}{(1\text{–}5)} = (3\text{–}60)$$

Note in the Internal Administrative Reviews (F_I) for Texas Tech University (TTU) in 1990 there were rigorous budget checks in addition to 18 review elements (as outlined by the TTU "Internal Routing Sheet for Sponsored Projects") that had to be addressed before the Office of Research Services would process a grant application. The internal routing sheet requires the investigator to provide a descriptive title of less than 110 spaces, a list of cooperating investigators and their unit affiliation, and percentage of investigator time devoted to the project. If applicable, the investigator must show an administrative review from the Human Subject Review Board, the Animal Care and Use Committee, the Biohazards Review Committee, a license from the Office of Environmental Health and Safety, and so forth. Each of the aforementioned offices and other compliance offices require that the investigator provide written reports to them prior to their granting an approval from their committee or office. In most cases, the investigator personally touches base with all applicable review offices before providing an explanation of the project to his department head, dean, and central administrative officers. These reviews are time consuming and require completion of bureaucratic forms that call for redundant information.

In the teaching era there was no Office of Research Services and no Internal Routing Sheet. Research at that time on the TTU campus was mostly independent which yielded a one as the CIR in 1940. Because the teaching era has ended, the F_I for that period remains constant; consequently, the research complexity of that period was selected as the base from which other times are compared. The factors in the standard denominator will not change as most of the research was independent research with few if any administrative burdens. F_I will vary from 1 to 5 depending upon the institution and the type of research conducted prior to 1940. On the other hand, the numerator is constantly increasing as the university, sponsoring agencies, and regulatory agencies add more and more reviews of the investigators' research and as the scope of the research becomes more complex.

The CIR promises to be a powerful way of countering the bureaucrats insistence for incrementally imposing additional reviews and reports on the PI. The bureaucrat's argument is the same for each new compliance procedure, "It only requires a few minutes of the PI's time." Such statements are patently wrong, compliance requires hours and even days of the investigators time, not minutes. More importantly, there is not merely a single compliance procedure, but multiple compliance procedures with increasing numbers of elements in each procedure.

In some cases, the principal investigator may even elect not to conduct a particular piece of research rather than fight with the bureaucratic encroachments upon his or her time. Filling out giant applications that appear to the PI to be "novel length" may not seem worth the effort, particularly, if the possibility of receiving the funding is perceived as minimal. The increasing size of the guidelines that must be followed if a proposal is to be reviewed does in some instances deter an investigator from pursuing certain areas of research. This increased complexity has considerably eroded the research time of the investigator. The CIR can show the progress of that erosion. The accretion of administrative burdens slows the pursuit and attainment of knowledge in the United States. Moreover, we speculate that these bureaucratic accretions are contributing factors in the United State's declining competitiveness in international affairs.

APPLYING THE COMPLEXITY INDEX TO TRADITIONAL LEVELS OF ACADEMIC RESEARCH

In earlier sections of this chapter, we discussed the classification of university research and the measurement of the complexity of research. Within basic research there are three common levels of research support that help academicians account for their sources of support: independent research, departmental research, and organized research. This section provides an example of how the CIR can be used to measure the complexity associated with planning and conducting different levels of research and how that complexity impacts the strategic planning processes for research.

Independent Research

Independent research is research that is planned by a single individual or a small group of investigators who ask for no assistance from others and require no bureaucratic approvals. Generally, the CIR is usually less than five for such studies. The investigator has no commitment to gain other than his own (1), few if any impact areas to consider for partnerships or approvals (1), a limited scope of work (1), and personally established time frames (1). The Sponsor Factor designated as $F_S = 1$ included only the PI. The Internal Review Factor designated as $F_I = N/A$ was not applicable in the early transition periods.

Today, there may be several institutional reviews for the Compliance Factor (e.g., Human Subjects, Animal Welfare) associated with independent research. The Compliance Factor, F_C, was not applicable for investigators in the teaching era for Congress and state legislators had not regulated the conduct of research at that time. The Disciplines Factor, F_D, was equal to one as there was little multidisciplinary research conducted prior to 1940. The Principal Investigator Factor, $F_P = 1$ as the work was usually confined to a single investigator. This explanatory process could be continued with each of the remaining factors being declared as not applicable or being quantified as one. It would seem that the sum of these factors did not exceed five making the Complexity Index for Research to have a value from 1 to 5 during the teaching era.

Seaborg (1972, 6), Nobel laureate and co-discoverer of elements 94–102, in recounting the discovery of element 94, Plutonium, provides an excellent account of the lack of complexity that he and his colleagues had planning their independent research at the Old Varsity Coffee Shop and at the College of Chemistry seminars at the University of California–Berkeley. He also discusses the ease of working with senior professors and using E. O. Lawrence's cyclotrons in fundamental work in the late thirties and early forties.

Departmental Research

Departmental research in the teaching era consisted of a faculty member informally sharing ideas with the department chairman for the development of conference papers, articles, and books. If the chairman agreed, he might arrange for a lightened teaching load for the faculty member, assign laboratory space, graduate assistants and student help to the professor, and purchase small-priced equipment from the departmental account. Departmental research planning generally was limited to the faculty member and the chairperson. Departmental research for researchers is a very manageable undertaking that allows them to spend most of their time on organizing ideas and information within disciplinary models—little time is spent on development and administrative tasks. The CIR factors for departmental research are usually larger than independent research as the Sponsor Factor increases to (2) and the Institutional Review Factor also increases to (2). The other factors were generally the same as the quantification used in the independent research calculation. The instruction and research functions in departmental research are so closely tied that it is frequently classified as an instructional activity. The Office of Management and Budget (OMB) (1973) rules that "Departmental Research means research activities that are not separately budgeted and accounted for." Such research, which includes all research activities not encompassed under the term organized research, is regarded for purposes of OMB Circular A-21 as a part of the instructional activities of the institution. That is certainly a functional misclassification of an activity.

Seaborg (1972, 44), in describing his working at one of the premier research institutions in the world, the University of California—Berkeley, provided many interesting insights into university research in the teaching era. His comments are particularly revealing of departmental operating conditions.

In the fall of 1940, we were still thinking and working primarily in the traditional academic manner. There was no government support for our research. Fortunately, California believed in higher education and in the importance of graduate study and research in the university.

Our faculty salaries were paid by the university. We had some basic facilities, small funds for equipment, and when we were lucky, modest grants from generous private donors and foundations.

Organized Research

Organized research is defined by OMB (1973) as "all research activities of an institution that are separately budgeted and accounted for." Planning for this level of research project usually was confined to the institution as the supporting resources originated from endowments or a specific sponsor. The CIR for organized research in the teaching era was less than five.

Generally, the planning periods for all three levels of research were for as long as the investigator needed, there were no proposal deadlines and no sponsor termination dates; a single investigator at a bench was typical; one or two simple commitments were needed; a single output was expected; and there was only one impact area.

ACCEPTING SPONSORED RESEARCH

Bowman (1945) recalled that in 1939 there were only 150 universities in the Association of American Universities that had organized research programs. All universities at this time considered instruction their paramount function, for their revenues were derived largely from students or student patrons and their reputations were made by the quality of their graduates. The total research expenditures in 1939 was $26 million for all American universities. Most of these expenditures were associated with engineering and natural science basic research that derived much of its revenue from the university general fund or organized research funds.

The strategy of the teaching institution is to plan for the needs of students. In teaching institutions, the entire institutional administrative system is geared to supporting teaching. In the teaching era, the few subventionary projects that were awarded to investigators were administered within the instructional system by the principal investigator. Hensley (1986) found that only 13 institutions had enough externally sponsored research to justify a grants and contracts office prior to 1940. By 1980, 206 institutions had such offices.

The dominance of the teaching function led to the policy of the research buy out—the principal investigator planned on the sponsor buying the investigator's time away from his primary instructional duties, which averaged about twelve classroom hours per week (Bowman, 1945). If one uses the customary rule of two hours for preparation and one hour for follow-up for every class hour, it appears that the typical professor spent forty-eight hours a week on teaching activities.

Prior to World War II, basic or pure research was the only respectable research in the university. In discussing the traditional attitudes of their contemporaries, Kidd (1965), Rothchild (1972), and Toulmin (1988) noted that there is a long history of academicians recognizing only pure research, which is a class of research limited to providing explanations of questions in their disciplines. Historically, applied research had been performed by craftsmen making it not respectable in British and American academic circles. Academic attitudes toward applied research and development shifted slightly during the second quarter of the twentieth century as foundations such as the Carnegie and Rockefeller supported science research, and the federal grant program to the states sponsored in a small way both basic and applied research in agriculture.

World War II changed dramatically the attitude of academicians toward government-sponsored applied research. Government-sponsored research brought the government as a full partner into planning directly with faculty for the conduct of targeted research. Bowman (1945), in describing the roles of the performers and sponsors in the research enterprise, noted the proper work for universities was to perform pure research and conduct scientific training. Individual university scientists and engineers were recognized by the federal government as the driving force in developing the military technology that gave the Allies the mightiest weapons the world had ever seen. Early in the conflict, President Roosevelt realized that the nation's armed forces desperately needed a trained force of scientific and technological manpower to use in the development of its weapons systems. President Roosevelt did not see the universities as great military research institutes—he viewed them as a manpower pool from which the military could draw personnel to staff temporarily major projects planned and organized by the military.

The federal government made few efforts to develop the university. Federally supported research centers were developed that were administered by universities. The government needed only to acquire temporarily under their contracting mechanisms individual brain power that fit into the military strategy. Conversely, there was no university research strategy for meeting national needs, only the desire to do its bit by mobilizing its facilities and releasing faculty to the military for the duration. During World War II, the military provided the necessary infrastructure and direct support to its borrowed scientists for them to perform defense-related research. The military had no plan to keep the university professor in the government employ after the project or the war was over. Faculty were to return to teaching and basic research in their former colleges.

Two approaches to government research were developed at this time. The Federally Funded Research and Development Centers (FFR&DC), which were physically removed from the main campus, were sometimes administered by universities for a particular mission agency. And, the government used *project research*. Project research allowed the government to purchase specific research from the scientist who stayed at his university bench, but performed specific work as outlined in a government contract for an agency.

During the war period, a loose federal-government-university partnership grew from an unconnected series of specific agreements for scientific work between the principal investigator and a particular branch of the armed services. The planning process was relatively simple for most project research. A government agency made a request for a proposal and the university responded through a faculty conceived proposal that became a contract. The CIR in planning military-sponsored research was higher than departmental research but remained relatively low. The campus administrative approvals were often limited to signatures of the PI and an institutional officer, only two institutional reviews ($F_I = 2$), plus agreement of a program officer ($F_S = 1$) in the military. The output was applied research and development of weapons systems. The government contracted with universities for technological solutions in the same way they contracted with private industry for guns and airplanes. Applied research was respectable for the duration as the faculty wanted to do their part for the war effort.

Seaborg (1972) contrasted the ease of departmental research at Berkeley before the war and the increased complexity of planning that accompanied his broad program of sponsored research at the University of Chicago Metallurgical Laboratory of the Manhattan Project in 1942 where the "mission of the Met Lab was to develop (1) a method for the production of plutonium in quantity and (2) a method for its chemical separation on a large scale." Solution of these applied research problems required the planning and construction of a small city to service the large plutonium production reactors and chemical separation plants at Hanford, Washington.

These philosophical foundations and conventional administrative structures will be referenced frequently as they significantly influence the reaction of institutions to increasing social expectations for universities. To not recognize these philosophical forces in strategic planning is to court disaster.

WORKS CITED

Arnold, Victor. (1986, February 13) Testimony to the Texas Select Committee on Higher Education. Texas Tech University. 1986.

Baer, W. S. 1978. The changing relationships: Universities and other R&D performers. In *The state of academic science: Background papers*, eds. B. L. R. Smith & J. J. Karlesky, 61-103. New York: Change Magazine Press.

Bowman, Isaiah. 1945. Report of the Committee on Science and the Public Welfare. In *Science—The Endless Frontier*. ed. V. Bush, 70-122. Washington, D.C.: National Science Fouondation

Carnegie Foundation for the Advancement of Teaching. 1987. *A Classification of Institutions of Higher Education*. Lawrenceville, N.J. Princeton University Press.

Carnegie Mellon University. 1988. *Goals and Strategic Plans, A Report Prepared for Middle States Association of Colleges and Schools*. Pittsburgh: Author. February 1988.

David, E. E. 1982. The university-academic connection in research: Corporate purposes and social responsibilities. *Journal of the Society of Research Administrators*, 14:5-12.

Gibson, D. 1988. Same song, second verse. *Visions*, 1(2):12-17.

Grassmuck, K. 1990. Universities' efforts to protect their patents aggressively result in complex legal skirmishes and, often, lucrative results. *The Chronicle of Higher Education*, 25 July 1990, A21, A23.

Hensley, O. D., and Jauch, L. (1984, September 23). A new model for classifying university research. At *SRA/NSF Symposium on University Research*. San Diego, CA. Hotel del Coronado.

———. 1986. The importance of research support personnel to university research. In *The Identification, Classification and Analysis of University Research Support Personnel, SRA Monograph #2*, ed. O. D. Hensley, 15-46. Lubbock, Texas: Texas Techu University Press, 1986.

———. and Jauch, L. 1988. A new model for classifying university research. In *The Classification of Research, SRA Monograph #3*, ed. O. D. Hensley, 43-113. Lubbock, TX.: Texas Tech University Press.

Industrial Research Institute. 1978. *Definitions of Research and Development*. New York: Author, October 1978.

Kidd, Charles V. 1965. Basic Research—Description Versus Definition. In *Science and Society*, ed. N. Kaplan, 147-149. Chicago: Rand McNally & Co.

Mooney, C. J. 1989. Carnegie faculty survey: Professors are upbeat about profession but uneasy about students, standards. *The Chronicle of Higher Education*, 8 November 1989, A1, A18-A21.

National Research Council. 1985. *Engineering education and practice in the United States: Engineering graduate education and research*. Washington, D.C.: National Academy Press.

Peterson, I. 1983. Academic questions: Campus and company partnerships. *Science News*, 123, 76-77.

Rothschild, Lord. 1972. Forty-five varieties of research. *Nature* 233-373.

Sage, Frances K. (1987, January 21). *Summary of the Report of the Select Committee on Higher Education*. Austin, TX: Texas Faculty Association. Draft.

Seaborg, Glenn T. 1972. *Nuclear Milestones: A collection of speeches by Glenn T. Seaborg*, San Francisco, CA: W. H. Freeman and Co.

Toulmin, Stephen. 1988. A historical reappraisal. In *The Classification of Research SRA Monograph #3*. O. D. Hensley, ed. Lubbock, Texas: Texas Tech University Press.

United States Office of Management and Budget. 1973. Part I. principles of determining costs applicable to research and development under grants and contracts with educational institutions. *Federal Register*, vol. 38, No. 181, Wednesday, September 13, 1973. 26292.

CHAPTER THREE

THE HISTORICAL FOUNDATIONS FOR STRATEGIC PLANNING FOR UNIVERSITY RESEARCH

Oliver D. Hensley and Pamela A. Cooper

EVOLUTION OF THE RESEARCH UNIVERSITY AND THE DEVELOPMENT OF STRATEGIC PLANNING FOR UNIVERSITY RESEARCH

Killoren's Impact Model suggests that current university research requires a great amount of joint planning among teams of researchers, support personnel, students, and sponsors. This has not always been so—in fact, during most of the academic past the individual researcher has planned and conducted research in relative isolation.

As we have seen in the previous chapter, conventional thought about research planning is derived from a history dominated by solitary bench scientists and ivory-tower academicians. For a thousand years, the faculty member has been the most important producer of basic research and disseminator of professional knowledge. During this millennium, the faculty was supported primarily by student fees and collegiate teaching endowments. The traditional priorities of the faculty were first to teach and then to advance professional knowledge. In this teaching model, scholarly production was always ancillary to instruction because historically research was not the major revenue producer for the faculty. In the last four decades, immense government, industry, and state funding of university research has reversed completely the traditional faculty priorities in many departments of the research university. Today, the research university is dominated by the research function and by long-term partnerships with major research sponsors. Planning is a major activity for every investigator and university administrator.

Unfortunately, existing studies of higher education have not focused on the development of new partnerships, changing personal agenda of the faculty, the addition of separate research administrative structures, and the slowly modified mission of select institutions; consequently, conventional thought does not match reality. The lack of a national study of these modern changes prevents an updating of our knowledge of planning in universities, thus constraining our thoughts and actions on planning to personal experience and very limited institutional data.

THE TEACHING ERA (1636-1940)

Much of our thought about higher education goes back to the teaching era of American higher education, which started in 1636 with the planning and founding of Harvard College by the Massachusetts Bay Company. It was the intent of that puritan colony to establish in the New World an institution that would preserve the faith when its ministers lie moldering in the dust. The traditions of the early American colleges were imported from Oxford and Cambridge. In the teaching era, the sources of college revenue were from student tuition and fees and from state or church grants. Rudy and Brubacher (1976) explained in detail the evolution of our church- and state-supported teaching colleges.

The Great Waves of Change

Universities, like beaches, endure; yet, they too are altered significantly by great waves of change. During the transition periods, five great waves of change transformed 200 American universities from teaching institutions into research universities. We identify the following great waves of change: (1) federal land grants, (2) federal project support for research, (3) advent of organized research units (ORUs), (4) long-term, large-scale industrial support for university research, and (5) formation of research common grounds. These transforming forces will be discussed more thoroughly in the following sections.

Federal Land Grants: The First Great Wave of Sponsored Research and Its Impact on University Research Planning

The first wave of change came from the federal government in the form of federal land grants to the states. This created a federal-state government-university partnership that used new methods of planning and financing to achieve the intent of Congress.

In 1862, Congressman Morrill of Vermont introduced farsighted legislation that created the land-grant colleges and established a national network of applied research institutions, which would work closely with the U.S. Department of Agriculture. It also generated the first great wave of long-term federal support for "at least one college in each state where the leading object shall be, without excluding other scientific and classical studies and including military tactics, to teach such branches of learning as are related to agriculture and the mechanic arts in such a manner as the legislatures of the states may prescribe." Note that the state legislatures had to plan and prescribe the major areas of study. "Mechanic arts" was a nineteenth-century term describing the various branches of engineering. Setting aside of land revenues and mandating the teaching of agricultural and mechanical subjects assured that the industrial classes would have colleges to advance the technology of the day. This support of government-directed learning established the pattern for federal-government-university partnerships in the U.S. Installing the agriculture and mechanical (A&M) colleges required considerable planning and long-term commitments by state and local governments, which furthered a diversity of institutional missions according to state and local needs. Some states planned to use the revenues from federal land sales to add to preexisting state university endowments, others elected to divide the money among a number of competing colleges, and other states created new institutions.

In 1887, Congress passed the Hatch Act, a measure requiring each land grant college to organize an agricultural and engineering experiment station to "acquire and diffuse useful and practical information on these subjects." In 1890, Morrill secured federal appropriations for a grant of $25,000 per year to be devoted to research at each of the stations. This appropriation stimulated state legislatures to plan for research that would meet the agricultural and mechanical needs of their state. The combined monies from federal formula funding and state appropriations to A&M institutions have grown for almost a century. Today, this strong partnership formed from a century of joint planning continues to sponsor the most advanced and sophisticated system of agricultural and mechanical research centers in the world.

This series of federal legislation was of great significance to the development of higher education and our nation because it established state colleges and directed their research and instruction efforts toward advancing the agricultural and mechanical arts. The long-time dominance of U.S. agriculture in the international marketplace and the quality of American life are potent testimonials to the wisdom of long-term planning and directed research in a particular industry.

In the teaching era, most corporate support to universities came in the form of scholarships, annual donations to the chief executive officer's (CEO) alma mater, and endowments to the departments or colleges for the purpose of enhancing the teaching function of the university.

Although some scholars (National Science Board, 1982a) noted that the emergence of the research university in the late nineteenth century coincided with the development of the modern industrial corporation, there was no industry-university partnership for research development associated with that coincidental development. Despite the lack of a formal partnership, academicians established the philosophical foundations for industrial support for university research. Davis and Kevles (1974) called attention to the end of the nineteenth century as the time when researchers started arguing that pure research deserved support from industry because it ultimately yielded practical benefits that were used by industry.

From 1916 to 1930, the National Academy of Science planned to eliminate some of the problems of uncertain and inconsistent private funding of academic research through campaigns developed by the National Research Council (NRC). The NRC, which was established in 1916 and made a permanent agency in 1918 by an executive order from President Woodrow Wilson, was intended to be a cooperative agency that would bring together academic, governmental, and industrial research efforts (Davis, 1974). The NRC started a campaign in 1916 to raise funds from private sources for the support of basic scientific research in the universities. Industries, many of which were starting to develop their own research laboratories at this time, became the primary targets of this campaign (Davis, 1974; NSB, 1982a).

By 1925, the NRC's campaign effort had resulted in only a limited amount of support from industry. George Ellery Hale initiated a public campaign in 1925 in an effort to increase industrial support. The National Research Endowment was created, and a goal of $20 million was established. It was the intent that funds from this endowment would be distributed by the National Academy of Science to universities as research grants (Davis, 1974). The goal was cut back to $10 million, and those who had already made pledges were allowed to cut their commitments in half. By the time the goal was finally reached in 1930, the 1929 stock market crash and the depression that followed made it almost impossible for the NRC to collect the pledges. The few companies that had been interested in the concept no longer had any resources available to fund the program. The program was abandoned in 1932 (Davis, 1974; NSB, 1982a)

But even before the onset of the depression, the fund had been unsuccessful for a variety of reasons. Many industries, such as the automobile and railway industries, did not believe that they could benefit from an investment in pure science. Even those industries that had pledged funds were not convinced that they would receive any benefit. At one point, President Hoover noted that the National Electric Light Association did not "care a damn for pure science" (Davis, 1974, 214). He suggested that their pledge was prompted more by an impending examination by the Federal Trade Commission than by a commitment to research.

Probably one of the most significant factors that prevented widespread industrial support of the fund was a clause that specifically prevented any limitations on the complete academic freedom of the faculty conducting the research, including the freedom to publish the findings of the research (Davis, 1974). There was a general reluctance on the part of corporations to contribute to the fund because the publication of research findings by the faculty could assist competitors who had not financially supported the research (NSB, 1982a).

Federal Project Support: the Second Great Wave of Sponsored Research

Willner and Hendricks (1972) reported that Congress had supported academic project research for over a half century. In 1830, the Franklin Institute was given a contract to conduct a study of boilers explosions. In 1842, Samuel F. Morse was given a $30,000 grant by Congress to explore the feasibility for public use of the electromagnetic telegraph system. And in 1849, Charles G. Page was given a $20,000 grant to develop electromagnetic motive power. The former was successful and the latter was not. The passage of the Morrill Act of 1862, the Hatch Act of 1887, and the Bankhead-Jones Act of 1935 provided assistance to agricultural academic research. In 1937, Congress established the National Cancer Institute with authority to make grants to university researchers.

The second wave of sponsored research swept over many American universities when the federal government introduced project research directly into the university during World War II. This dramatic change allowed the federal government to purchase research of a specific type. During World War II, the Manhattan Project and other war-related projects produced in university laboratories some of the most deadly military weapons that have ever been known. Instruction was not a direct consideration in these early projects, and no institutional funds supported the research projects, although the greater facilities of the university provided indirect support for the government project.

The heart of federal project support is the faculty-initiated research proposal—a technical document that is prepared by a researcher for the purpose of finding a sponsor to support a specific investigation. The preparation of a simple government proposal during World War II greatly increased the Complexity Index for Research (CIR) because written proposals are considerably more difficult to prepare than the verbal requests or short memos needed for independent or departmental research. The length and format of this fundamental planning document will be discussed in detail in Chapter 5.

During World War II, proposals were simple, but they required the principal investigator (PI) to write or discuss verbally with a government officer the work that the government wanted for the war effort. Once the concept was reviewed and approved by someone in the military, the research was purchased. A minimum of paper work was required of the PI. Today, written proposals are required and assessed for technical competency by individual or study-group peer reviews. The feedback from these evaluations is an important aspect of revising specific proposals and of preparing long-range plans. If the technical proposal is approved, the contracting section of the sponsoring agency then negotiates an appropriate grant or contract with the institution through a research administrator and the investigator.

Targeted contract research broke many teaching traditions and imposed planning requirements and product and fiscal accountability on faculty researchers that had never existed before. Also, project funding created a number of "soft money" research support positions that had to be considered carefully in any research plan. With project funding, the project directors (faculty members) made a direct obligation to the government for the achievement of proposal objectives, whereas the institution was held accountable for the terms and conditions of the contract. This required close cooperative planning between the PI, the central university administrators, and the federal program officer. Although accountability has been resisted continually by academicians, government regulations were placed firmly by federal projects on all members of the faculty, not just federally-funded project directors. This greatly increased the complexity of planning for any type of university research.

After the introduction of the federal project, university investigators and administrators had to plan to balance three or more types of research—independent, department, federal project—along with the traditional functions of university service and teaching. With federal project funding, the university received the funds and provided the necessary laboratory facilities and faculty for the delivery of project research services. By the early seventies, it was apparent that research was the dominant function of many first class universities and that their reputations were made by their federal project research capabilities, not by their teaching abilities.

The significant feature associated with the second great wave of sponsored research is the reversal of the federal government's policy of providing general institutional or formula funding serving a broad mission to funding small grants and contracts for specific research accomplishing a very narrow project objective in a short period of time (two or three years). With this mode of funding—the government-university partnership—the particular ideas of a faculty member are central to the development process, but the federal government selectively funds university research according to national policy and nationally controlled competitions. Many thousands of these single-investigator projects are conducted annually by American academicians and funded by the federal government under acts of the Congress.

In the last quarter century, universities have developed separate administrative structures, policies, long-term plans, and extensive research facilities to conduct project research. The number of proposals and projects became so large (as many as 6,000 proposals annually in a single university) that offices of grants and contracts were created to provide the central coordination and liaison between investigator and government agency. Sponsored research offices, formed primarily to handle project research, have grown from thirteen in 1940 to 206 in 1985. They showed that the major growth in establishing these offices occurred in the period from 1950 to 1980.

Continuing from World War II to the present, the wave of government project funding has been swelled by each successive federal initiative to meet emerging national needs. This has caused the number of planning activities to increase with each new federal research program or national compliance issue.

In the early forties, the U.S. Office of Scientific Research and Development planned programs and coordinated research projects to further all aspects of the war effort. The National Institutes of Health (NIH) were established in 1944 to direct and encourage medical research. The institutes have relied upon the project method extensively to advance their mission for four decades. In 1950, the National Science Foundation (NSF) was created. It, too, has used a system of competitive projects to achieve its mission. In the fifties, mission agencies such as the Office of Naval Research, the Atomic Energy Commission (AEC), and the National Aeronautics and Space Administration (NASA) were established to meet national needs. They also depended upon university project research for much of their basic research. In the sixties, the Great Society philosophy of the federal government created hundreds of government programs that solicited thousands of university projects for the Law Enforcement Assistance Administration, National Endowment for the Humanities (NEH), and the Department of Health, Education and Welfare. The oil embargo of the seventies caused the federal government to appropriate huge sums of research dollars for energy research to the Department of Energy, which relied heavily upon university projects. Most of these federal agencies continue to enjoy large Congressional appropriations for support of mission research performed by universities.

The project-based research efforts required by World War II had a significant impact on the development of the industry-university research relationship. Research, development, and production efforts related to the war efforts led to an increased level of planning and cooperation among university, industry, and federal-government scientists and engineers (NSB, 1982a).

Vannevar Bush, president of the Carnegie Institution of Washington, led the formation of the National Defense Research Committee (NDRC) in

1940. Bush was a major proponent of the concept of the federal government funding university and industrial laboratories, rather than developing its own laboratories. "In some ways the NDRC fulfilled the functions of the hoped-for National Research Fund of the 1920s" (NSB, 1982b).

THE GOVERNMENT FOUNDATION PERIOD (1945-1957)

The government foundation period (1945-1957) was a time of serious reassessment for the academic community because the government formed several new agencies that included university researchers as major performers in their research and development strategy. The Office of Naval Research was formed in 1946 and began a vigorous extramural grant program during this period. The AEC was established in 1946 and formed a system of national laboratories from the university-operated laboratories that were left over from the Manhattan Project, and started a basic research program for grants to individual academicians.

The fundamental question that the government foundation period presented to universities was "Who would control government-sponsored research performed in the university?" When the government formed permanent foundations, it signalled universities that it planned to begin direct funding of academic research in targeted areas. If the government decided what research to fund, could the university researcher maintain the same degree of objectivity that society generally expected from academicians?

In the teaching era, the question of control did not arise because individual academicians in the university controlled all aspects of independent research or departmental research. During World War II, the university logically and loyally subordinated its goals and reordered its priorities to meet the needs of the military preserving democracy. In the post-war years, could the university allow the intrusion of government influence into a separate social institution, especially through the most sensitive of functions—research, the font of knowledge?

Glenn Seaborg (1972, 143), a University of California faculty member in the 1930s and chairman of the AEC in the 1960s, noted with grave concern the transforming impact of government monies on the university. He observed

> Those of us who had been privileged to explore this new realm of science during the war were gravely concerned about the prospects for the future. Research in the nuclear sciences would require equipment and financial support on an unprecedented scale, far beyond the capabilities of traditional sources in universities and private research institutions. Under the 1946 Act, the Commission had a leading role in creating new administrative machinery for federal support of research. The Commission also deserves credit for bringing into reality the new concept of the national laboratory. The research contract and the national laboratory (ORU) became the key instruments for a system of research on a national scale which has helped to

bring the nuclear sciences in this country to world preeminence. The impact of this system has extended far beyond the nuclear sciences to other fields of research and to American education in general. The commission program has established new standards that have come to be accepted as the norm in educational institutions.

It was, however, the planning of the NSF that focused the arguments of the federal government and the universities on how the partnership would be governed. On the one hand, the government had the responsibility of assuring that government-sponsored research would serve the purposes of the nation as defined by the Congress and the president. On the other hand, the faculty had the responsibility of preserving the integrity of the university. England (1982), in *A Patron for Pure Science*, informed us of the long debate over the structure and governance of the NSF and over the value of sponsored research that raged in the halls of Congress, academe, and in scholarly journals from 1945-1957.

The discussion over government-university control of research in the post-war period was moot because science had evolved to the point that the simply organized, single-investigator research using only departmental resources was no longer capable of solving many of the problems of science and the nation. World War II only hastened the formation of a partnership and an administrative structure that was inevitable. By themselves, universities did not have the organization and resources to take the next steps to advance knowledge in certain disciplines. Only the federal government had the massive financial resources and the centralized power to concentrate the intellectual resources on the problems of applied weapons research. This research was essential to providing the empirical evidence needed by basic researchers for the expansion of their theories. A federal government-university partnership was necessary for both parties.

Arthur Compton, an experimental physicist who won the Nobel Prize for his brilliant theoretical concepts on X-ray scattering, documents this change in terms of his own career:

> As I think back to those early experiments, one matter strikes me forcibly. It is the contrast between my first airplane experiments, which were done entirely with my own hands and with a minimum of contact with others working in the same field, and my last major engineering or scientific job, which was the atomic reactor, where thousands of people were engaged using the best available tools, and my part consisted largely in organizing the activities and thoughts of the scientists who were concerned with getting the job done. In the thirty-three years that intervened, my own scientific work, like that of the nation, went through all the stages from primitive pioneering, where one's own individual skill and resourcefulness, not only in ideas but also in handicraft was the basis of success, to what has now become a vast enterprise in which each individual contributes a small but expert part, but in which, nevertheless, the originator of the idea has still to take responsibility for it. (Seaborg, 1972, 81).

The control over the development of science had indeed shifted from the individual faculty member initiating work that was supported solely by his department to a "big science" so ably described by Price (1963). Price and others at this time saw predominantly the bigness of science and the potentially negative impact of government domination of science. This was understandable in the 1950s because the fate of science under the Nazi and other totalitarian regimes was still vivid in their minds. This bias caused them to miss the intrinsic advantages of the government-university partnership to universities that were changing their planning modalities and their management techniques for scientific investigations. Ikenberry (1972) was one of the first to point out that universities were moving beyond the traditional teaching functions and instructional administration to a system designed for the administration of research. Unfortunately, the needs of science and the university for restructuring during this period too often were ignored by academicians.

Federal support of big science kept American universities doing the major part of the world's basic research. The federal government could have elected to build its own laboratories and American universities probably would have remained primarily teaching institutions. Also, the universities could have refused the federal support. They did not because they benefited greatly from the partnership. They lost no capabilities, but they did have to adjust to the planning and managerial arrangements of a partnership.

Despite tolerance of individual government projects, which did not seem to affect too adversely the instructional program, the academic mind remained unchanged regarding the respectability of sponsored research. The majority of the faculty of the time maintained their rugged individualism and intellectual integrity by relying on traditional student support and by dedicating themselves to only one type of research. They took the stand in the formation of all government programs, foundations, and institutes that they would tolerate no government control and no institutional direction of their individual research. Project planning allowed them to have their way.

All planning and performance responsibilities for the project rested on the PI in this period. The planning and approval points within the university were limited to three points:(1) the proposed work was approved by a single agency program officer; (2) the scope of the work was performed mostly by a single investigator at the bench, and was explained in a narrative outlined by the investigator. The time frames were single years with automatic extensions for satisfactory work; and (3) fiscal planning consisted of a summary budget.

The work centered on a single project, which cost less than $18,000 on the average in fiscal year (FY) 1954 (NSF 1959). The NSF study provided some interesting benchmark figures that show there were of a small number of federal grants and contracts in this period, about forty-five projects for the average institution. Only six institutions had over 250 federally sponsored projects. Total expenditures for 173 institutions receiving the 7,803 federal research grants and contracts was $142 million. Universities and colleges had an additional $64 million in research income for separately budgeted research from other sources. Seventeen million dollars came from the institutions' own funds, $23 million was given by foundations, industry provided $19 million, and $4 million was from private gifts. Note that the top fifty institutions did 89% of the government work. At all institutions, control of the work and preparation and administration of the budget was definitely in the hands of the PI. At the end of the government foundation period, the federal government had introduced a new administrative unit—the project—into the university. The department, college, and university had little control over the planning and conduct of a sponsored project. The planning was between the PI and the agency program officer, who was usually a scientist. Within the university at least three administrative levels for planning and approval existed: departmental, college, and university.

Bush (1945), in *Science—The Endless Frontier*, initiated the concept of long-term planning for university research, drafted government policy that would continue the federal-government-university partnership for research development, and advocated a plan that made the foundation period possible.

President Truman (1945, 16) committed the executive branch to the partnership when he said: "No government adequately meets its responsibilities unless it generously and intelligently supports and encourages the work of science in university, industry, and in its own laboratories." Truman assuaged the fears of faculty for government control of research and developed his concept of the federal-government-university partnership by declaring that "Although science can be coordinated and encouraged, it cannot be dictated to or regimented. Science cannot progress unless founded on the free intelligence of the scientist." He followed up on his policy statements by appointing a president's Scientific Research Board, which planned for expanded facilities and increases in trained manpower, heavier emphasis on basic research, and recommendations for progressive increases of annual expenditures. These government plans, which resulted in the founding of the NSF and the development of strong extramural research programs at NIH and continued appropriations, spurred university presidents to plan for the administration of project monies that would be awarded to universities after agency approval of individual research proposals prepared by faculty.

The discussions (extended and intense) concerning the acceptance of military and other government contracts cemented the federal-government-university partnership, but did not change most academicians' ideas on the respectability of research that was not academically oriented. The actual flow of projects into the institution did create a fait accompli of their acceptability. An indicator of this acceptance is seen in the creation of an administrative apparatus that handled awards and contracts long before the faculty acknowledged the acceptance of government-sponsored research.

Hensley and Burns' (1985) study of the growth of grant and contract offices in American universities has shown that prior to 1940 only thirteen universities had established grants and contract offices. These early offices had very limited operations. In the forties, twenty universities founded such offices. By the end of the 1960s, after the federal government had made a commitment to long-term support of basic research by establishing the NSF, NIH, and basic research programs in the mission agencies, 156 universities had grant and contract offices. During the government foundation period the number of grant administration offices more than doubled. In 1985, 206 universities reported having grant and contract offices.

Wolfe (1972) and Strickland (1967) and his associates in the American Council of Education chronicled the rise of sponsored research in American universities and colleges and discussed the major issues during the early stages of the federal-government-university research partnership. Although the government established with the creation of the new health institutes and federal foundations, a national research policy for the development of research in universities, the universities made no plan to serve national needs. They did, however, create policy that would allow their faculty to compete individually for federally sponsored grants and contracts.

As the 1989 Survey (Chapter 4) shows, strategic planning for university research was not performed during the government foundation period. The presidents of the colleges and universities felt that they needed to be true to the objectives of a teaching institution while accepting sponsored research that would fit into their instructional programs. A number of specific feelings in this regard are discussed in Chapter 5. We can see from the details of the major processes associated with the acceptance of a federal proposal that the complexity of planning necessary for federally sponsored research is considerably elevated above that required by "departmental research."

The establishment of federal-government foundations helped transform teaching and technical institutions into research universities and furthered the acceptance of strategic planning for university research by convincing academe that the federal government was going to support basic research in perpetuity. This meant the institutions would preserve their integrity; yet, they had a federal partner who would support research in the future. The PI anticipated other projects in the future. This long-term commitment by the federal government caused a dramatic transformation in academic thinking and in university organization. During this foundation period, private foundations (Ford, Rockefeller, Hughes) made many long-term commitments to developing university research. While the federal government led in establishing mechanisms for long-term support for university research, the other sectors of society also were establishing foundations that promised to advance university partnerships for research development during the foundation period.

THE SPUTNICK PERIOD (1957-1965)

The placing of Sputnik I into orbit on October 4, 1957, launched the American Congress into an expansion of federal support for university research and brought about strategic planning on a sizable scale between the federal government and universities. In the Sputnik period, the CIR increases dramatically as the F_s factor (the summation of planning and approval points within the sponsor organization—see Chapter 2) increases by more than an order of magnitude.

Although Sputnik tarnished the image of the United States as the world's technological leader and created national anxiety, its constant beeping from space had a beneficial effect on American research by creating a public desire to leapfrog the Russians in space explorations. It advanced the cause of government sponsored basic and applied research in the university because mathematicians and a wide range of scientists and engineers saw unequalled opportunities in space exploration.

The desire to be the first nation to land a man on the moon led Congress to draft P.L. 85-568, the National Aeronautics and Space Act of 1958, which President Eisenhower signed into law on July 29, 1958. NASA was established on October 1, 1958 with a generous budget. Both Anderson (1981) and Rosholt (1966) stressed the critical role of Thomas Glennan, the first head of NASA, in immediately establishing a long-range planning office and installing the military system for strategic planning and procurement in a civilian agency.

Cooperative planning between the agency's program officers and the staff of the university's ORUs became essential to the achievement of mutual goals in space exploration. NASA's long-range planning system was installed when Congress considered in February of 1960 the first NASA Ten-Year Plan. This plan had the following broad goals.

1. To develop larger launch vehicles to lift heavier payloads.
2. To develop manned flight vehicles, first orbital, then circumlunar.
3. To develop scientific satellites to measure radiation and other aspects of space.
4. To develop unmanned lunar probes to photograph the moon and measure the lunar space environment.
5. To develop planetary probes to measure and photograph Mars and Venus.
6. To develop weather satellites to enhance our knowledge of the Earth's weather patterns.
7. To continue a broad range of aeronautical research.

Because NASA is and was an operational agency as well as a research agency, not only did it design and build space vehicles and satellites, it launched, tracked, and operated them. In addition, it had a tremendous amount of scientific data to gather and interpret. University researchers were essential in every operation.

The list of NASA's goals shows the broad range of research and development programs that NASA originally supported and shows the complexity of program operations in the new space establishment. Each NASA goal was to be achieved by organizing the work in agency programs that had to be monitored constantly and assisted by academic researchers and for which proposals had to be prepared and contracts negotiated. To deal successfully with NASA, particular ORUs of the university had to decide if they wanted to form a partnership with a NASA program for the long term to achieve specified national goals as articulated in NASA's Ten-Year Plan. If that decision was affirmative, the director of an ORU and his staff became immersed in NASA's long-range planning. Planning activities ranged from serving on national advisory boards to peer reviewing research proposals.

A cost-plus-fixed-fee (CPFF) contract was the government's usual contracting mechanism for R&D work prior to 1947. The CPFF contract required a short proposal outlining the work to be performed and a summary budget. In 1947, Congress passed the Armed Services Procurement Act (ASPA) to permit Department of Defense (DOD) agencies flexibility in conducting their procurements by the method of negotiation as well as by the traditional method of advertising for competitive bids. In 1949, the General Services Administration adopted most of the Armed Services Procurement Regulations (ASPR) for use by civilian agencies. In 1958, Congress provided that NASA procurement would be governed by ASPR. Ninety percent of NASA procurement dollars were spent by using the negotiation method. This is not surprising when one remembers that

NASA's operations were constantly on the frontiers of man's knowledge and that, in many cases, the agency program officer had to talk to a university researcher before conceptualizing the request for a proposal. The point is that the staffs of ORUs were involved on the front end of planning programs, writing proposals, and developing prototypes for a number of agencies. Academic planning was no longer a short chat with the department head, it had evolved into a high managerial art.

Rosholt (1966) described the major steps in the procurement process. To determine the increase in complexity for planning and performing research there are five major steps in which the PI might be involved.

1. Preparation of a procurement request (PR)—a description of the R&D work to be performed (program officer and PI talk).
2. Preparation of procurement plan (government procurement specialists and PI talk).
3. Soliciting proposal— a NASA invitation for bid (IFB) contains guidelines and essential project information, or
4. NASA issues a request for proposal (RFP) by announcing the project in the commerce's *Business Daily* allowing the university to request the RFP. A proposal conference may be held for interested parties.
5. A proposal is prepared.

The NASA effort was such a massive undertaking that it eclipsed the complexity of all World War II projects including the Manhattan Project. Within NASA, new organizational and planning modes were essential because no one center could handle the previously mentioned programs. A much expanded headquarter's team was needed to coordinate the efforts of the several centers and to plan the enormous mobilization of American industry and university effort.

The NASA effort also eclipsed the expansion of industrial support of basic research in the universities during the Sputnik period. During 1957-1967, industrial support of basic research in the universities increased from $21 million to $31 million, or by 47%. During the same period, however, government support of basic research increased from $155 million to $1,124 million, or by 625% (NSF, 1970)

Total support of university research, basic and applied, followed a similar pattern of change in levels of support from 1957 to 1967, industrial support of basic and applied research increased from $32 million to $45 million, or by 44%. Growth in government support of basic and applied research in the universities greatly exceeded the growth in industrial support. From 1957 to 1967, government support of university research, basic and applied, increased from \$217 million to \$1,346 million, or by 520% (NSF, 1970).

The industrial share of university research support dropped from 6% in 1960, to below 3% in 1965. However, this drop in percentage of support was due more to an increase in support by the federal government than a decrease in the actual dollars contributed by industry. In fact, from 1960 to 1965, the amount of industrial support remained relatively constant at just under \$60 million (in 1972 constant dollars) (NSB, 1982b).

The rapid growth in federally funded research during the 1960s resulted in universities becoming less reliant on the private sector for its research support (Baer, 1978). In addition, by the late 1960s strong anti-industry protests and attitudes had developed, particularly within the most prestigious universities (Baer, 1978). We can see from the patterns of funding that federal-government space initiatives increased more than fivefold the universities' research expenditures in a decade. Such radical changes in funding worked dramatic changes in university research administration and in university planning.

The expanded scope of scientific work, the F_W factor in the CIR algorithm, increased dramatically because the nature of space exploration by man's probes was entirely new. The complexity of NASA's management and planning was mirrored in the university research organizations.

The work of C. Stark Draper, of the MIT Instrumentation Laboratory, illustrates the increasing complexity of university research. Draper had two sets of problems. First, he had to bring together an academic team of mathematicians, scientists, and engineers who could develop a space navigation system that would guide and track a spacecraft leaving Earth and heading for rapidly moving stellar objects. The inscrutable problems of celestial mechanics called for many teams of basic and applied researchers supported by sizable groups of technicians. The scope of work at the Instrumentation Laboratory was of such a complex nature that it required a long-term commitment of the university in allocation of facilities, professional staff, and supporting services. Secondly, this type of research required research planners and managers to match the work of the laboratory to NASA goals. New ideas for new problems were not enough to get long-term NASA contracts to develop a key component for space flight—strategic planning and modern management were prerequisites. This was not bench science, but sophisticated science requiring huge amounts of joint-planning time and an incredible amount of coordination among a large number of partners.

The terms and conditions associated with space research partnerships were so complicated that universities immediately placed their planning and operating activities under the authority of ORUs because it was so difficult to develop and conduct three-sector applied and production research within the administrative units of the traditional instructional organization. The philosophy and practice of people in the instructional units were not oriented to the rapid pace demanded by applied research and development, and they proved to be a greater hindrance than help. Consequently, large contracts using tripartite planning and operations were housed in some type of organized research unit outside the control of instruction-oriented individuals and systems.

Organized Research Centers:
The Third Great Wave of Institutional Change

The establishment of ORUs in universities brought about a third great wave of internal change in universities. The ORUs dramatically changed the CIR because an ORU usually has multiple sponsors; consequently, the F_s factor, the summation of planning and approval points for sponsors increased by multiples of sponsors. Also, the F_I factor more than doubled because a whole new university research administrative structure was included in the planning reviews.

With the formation of university research centers, the planning and financing of research was no longer based on a single sponsor or on single sector support. Instead, these units had to initiate joint planning with many sponsors to garner support from multicompany and multiagency sponsors. These joint plans focused resources on particular research areas such as jet propulsion, radiation, coal research, or materials technology. These focal areas, once identified, were given specific names to describe their purpose, such as the Southern Illinois University Coal Center and Materials Technology Center and the Texas Tech University Textile Research Center and International Center for Arid and Semi-Arid Lands Study.

The center or institute continues the university's historical mission of originating and organizing thought about particular problems, but it moves problem-solving techniques to a much higher level of sophistication that allows the institution to solve increasingly complex social and technical problems. It also transfers the mechanisms for planning and investigating from the individual scientist to a group of researchers and their associates. This fundamental change improved the efficiency of the university in problem solving, because the collective mind now approached very complex problems that the single, bench scientist could not easily resolve.

The diverse characteristics and the commonalities of institutes and centers can be seen in the following descriptions of three of the well established organized research units listed in the *Research Centers Directory* (1980). Note the staff size and composition of these senior ORU's as well as their sources of support.

321 University of Massachusetts Cranberry Experiment Station,
East Wareham, Massachusetts. Chester E. Cross, head.
Founded: 1909.

Integral unit of Agricultural Experiment Station at University of Massachusetts. Supported by parent institution, U.S. government and industry. Staff: 5 research professionals, 1 supporting professional, 5 technicians, 2 others.

Principal field of research: Problems of cranberry producers in Massachusetts, including studies on control of insects, fungi, weeds and nematodes, cranberry breeding, fertilizers, drainage and mechanization of operations.

Research results published in technical journals and Experiment Station bulletins.

2063 California Institute of Technology, Jet Propulsion
Laboratory, Pasadena, California. William H. Pickering, director.
Founded: 1936.

Government contract research facility operated for National Aeronautical and Space Administration by California Institute of Technology. Supported by U.S. government. Staff: 1304 scientists and engineers, 674 administrators, 2100 technicians and others.

Principal fields of research: Physics, propulsion, electronics, communications, guidance and control, materials, structures and fluid dynamics. Conducts lunar and interplanetary exploration with unmanned spacecraft and a broad basic research program designed to further capabilities of the laboratory.

Research results published in technical reports, technical memoranda and quarterly summary reports. Publication: *Space Program Summary* (bimonthly). Holds seminar series annually in cooperation with University of California Council on Space Sciences for University personnel and graduate students. Maintains a library of 20,000 volumes dealing with space exploration and related sciences.

1911 New York University, Courant Institute of Mathematical
Sciences, New York, New York 10003. James J. Stoker, director.
Founded: 1946.

Integral unit of New York University. Supported by U.S. government, industry, foundations, and professional associations. Staff: 125 research professionals, 125 supporting professionals, 40 technicians, 60 others. Volume of research: 1961—$2,905,000; 1962—$2,950,000; 1963—$3,000,000.

Principal field of research: Pure and applied mathematics, including studies on computing methods, electromagnetic theory, magneto-fluid dynamics, quantum field theory, statistical mechanics, elasticity, fluid dynamics, statistics and mathematical physics. Maintains the university computing center.

Research results published in scientific journals and special reports. Publication: *Communications on Pure and Applied Mathematics* (quarterly). Maintains a library of 20,000 volumes on mathematics.

The establishment of university ORUs transferred a portion of practical problem solving from the industrial sector to the university sector. This too was a significant social problem-solving transformation that required a higher level of research administration and planning. With the formation and successful operation of a legitimate center or institute, a university gains a reputation for having the critical mass of researchers and the essential infrastructure to address broad-spectrum problems for a specific industry and to solve generic industrial problems. This reputation attracts research funds to the center from both government and industry.

ORUs are new administrative structures necessary to the survival of new types of university research. The center concept and the cooperative planning needed to operate an ORU are essential to university administration, because conventional instructional-administrative structures are not adequate to carry both instruction and applied research. The demands of applied research and development are such that they cannot thrive in an environment oriented to the slow pace and traditional procedures of an instructional program. Thus, new centers emerged and their plans became vital to a widening spectrum of university research that now includes multidisciplinary research, pilot plant development, regulation research, advanced process research, product-oriented research and development (R&D), classified defense research, and assorted technological developments.

Since 1940, when most universities were instruction dominated, over 4,800 university research centers have been established in American universities, which represents a sevenfold increase in less than half a century. Figure 3.1 illustrates the rapid growth of ORUs after World War II. Centers usually are not part of the traditional instructional structure of a university; therefore, separate administrative structures and new planning systems were established in universities to serve ORUs. Most persons employed by centers have a research function. The proliferation of centers has advanced the transformation of many higher education institutions from teaching institutions to research institutions. Today, research center activity rivals the activity of the academic department.

Number
of
Centers

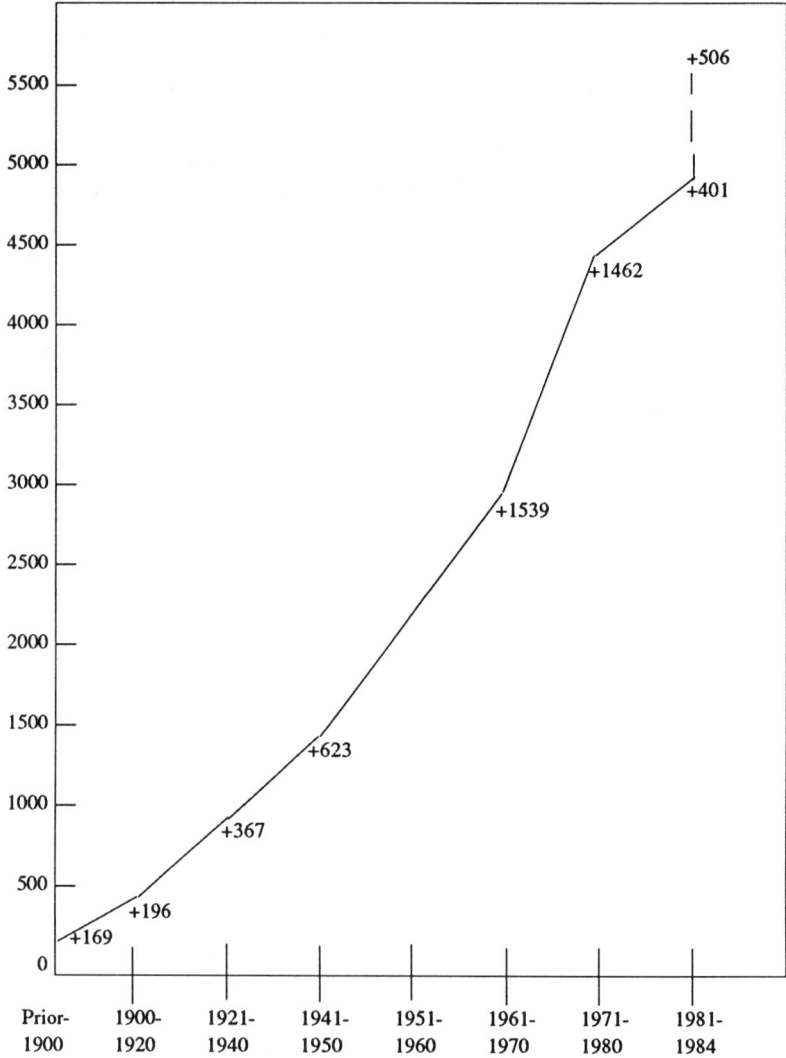

*508 centers were given with no date, making the actual number of existing centers in 1984 total 5,547.

The data for this chart was gathered from the *Research Centers Directory* 1984-85 and Supplements I and II.

Figure 3.1. Charted growth of organized research centers prior 1900-1984 (Hensley, 1986).

Prior to World War II, 600 research centers had been established in universities. These included all the major agricultural experiment stations, observatories, institutes, and laboratories. These early academic centers were predominantly basic research and instruction oriented and usually had a small professional staff. They were funded by modest endowments and small grants, generally, they had no strong ties with industry.

The cooperative centers, laboratories, and institutes that were established after the war were quite different. Many of the cooperative centers were based on the philosophy that there must be joint planning and long-term support for university research and development by both government and industry. This support was to be directed toward ORUs to find answers to scientific, technological, and commercial problems in a particular field. Funds were not given for general appropriations to an institution, nor as a grant to an individual project; instead the funds were given to the center. Organized research units are new, powerful, university mechanisms that are supported by national government policy and individual business commitments to advance focused university research in a particular field.

A few examples in the development phases of the cyclotron show the increasing complexity of research planning that accompanied a tremendous growth in radiation laboratories founded by Ernest O. Lawrence and his associates. In 1930, at the University of California-Berkeley, E. O. Lawrence and N. E. Edlefsen planned and built a small cyclotron to explore the nucleus of the atom. Four years later, Lawrence and Stanley Livingston were the architects of a 27-inch cyclotron. Although rather crude in appearance and housed in small, dingy quarters, this machine was used by many chemists, physicists, biologists, physicians, engineers, and agricultural scientists to achieve breakthroughs in their fields of knowledge.

By 1939, a team of eight senior scientists and a number of graduate students planned and built a 60-inch cyclotron that had a broader spectrum of utility and was central to the expansion of knowledge in many fields. The fields of nuclear medicine and nuclear chemistry became possible with the advent of this cyclotron. Because so many scientists and engineers wanted to use this accelerator, Lawrence was forced to develop a strategic plan that called for bigger and bigger cyclotrons and more and more sponsors. Lawrence's transformation from bench scientist to an ORU director is explained by Seaborg (1972, 87) who noted, "Dr. Lawrence, bold, adventurous and unfettered by the tradition that an academic scientist used only the tools he could make himself, brought engineering and technology into the basic science laboratory."

The vital nature of the cyclotron to the development of atomic weapons led to the creation of the 184-inch cyclotron in 1946. This sophisticated machine was conceived by Lawrence and associates and was housed in large, new quarters paid for by the federal government. The pinnacle of Lawrence's research planning and technological achievement came with the completion of the Bevatron, a giant particle accelerator that began operation in 1954. This huge accelerator was housed in a larger-than-a-stadium building. The complexity of the planning and management activities in this ORU are difficult to imagine. The accelerators planned by Lawrence and associates led to the University of California scientists filling in most of the periodic chart of the elements beyond uranium from element 93 through element 103.

Today, the hundreds of scientists and engineers in the Lawrence complex of buildings overlooking San Francisco Bay continue the goal of understanding the atom and its components. For a half-century, scientists from many countries came to this ORU to plan the next steps in exploring the previously unimaginably small units of matter and energy and in applying this knowledge to practical matters.

Although most ORUs do not reach the huge size of the Lawrence Radiation Laboratories, an ORU usually calls on the services of several disciplines within a university. The structure of a center or institute frequently includes several complementary laboratories and offices associated with applied fields of science. A center is composed of a number (10-1,000) of research associates who frequently have their own grant or contract research related to the purpose of the center. Each associate heads one or more laboratories and employs a sizable research support staff.

The complexity of the university administrative structure is shown in Hensley (1986, 201). His general titles for typical ORUs provide some indication of the diversity of research organizations within a research university and the complexity of planning for research development and performance in such a complex environment.

Networks	Coalitions
Consortiums	Foundations
Research Parks	Institutes
Centers	Stations
Departments	Areas
Systems	Bureaus
Programs	Studies
Offices	Groups
Teams	Laboratories
Projects	

A typical cooperative research center has a large number of sponsoring affiliates (for example, industrial companies that provide long-term support for the privilege of having an early look at what is occurring in the university laboratories and for the advantage of having the center's top scientists periodically to come into their organization for joint planning and technical consultation).

International industrial competition has done much to advance university research centers. McLaren and Wachtman (1984) recognized that "Japan has set national goals to assume world leadership in ceramic materials and has carefully structured its policies to have the best of cooperation between universities, government, and industry in order to attempt to win the scientific, technical, and commercial race in ceramic materials." They warned that "If we are to maintain the science lead in electronic ceramics and to expand U.S. participation in supplying this growing market, we must make every effort to maintain our scientific research efforts in these areas with commitments to such central activities as the NSF cooperative research centers."

Because the U.S. does not have a government entity similar to Japan's MITI (Ministry of International Trade and Industry) to coordinate industry-government-university cartels, American national research policy relies upon the NSF to encourage the industry-government-university endeavor through NSF's program for industry-university cooperative research centers.

Schwarzkopf (1981) explained that NSF programs promote basic and applied research in various scientific disciplines and generic technologies that may lead to new products, processes, and services for the participating companies. Generally, the research agenda is established by the participants and is not subject to NSF control. Joint support by NSF and industry in launching a center allows the university to develop a broad-based research program that can respond to the scientific needs of industry and test the ongoing interest and commitment of the industrial sponsors.

After a planning and organizing period of about one year and funded up to a level of approximately $100,000, the annual budget of a typical center (including some government and private funds) is normally $300,000 to $500,000. At first it is co-funded by industry and NSF, but the center is expected to become self-sufficient within five years. As the center research program matures, industry acceptance and support grow, while NSF support is phased out.

Before NSF provides any money for university-industry arrangements, the university must convince NSF that it has the critical mass of scientists, support personnel, and equipment to help a particular industry. Also, there must be a strong, long-term, institutional commitment to the research center and a pledge of continuing financial support from specific firms and manufacturing associations to the center, not to an individual or institution.

Eveland and Hetzner (1982) provide an excellent summary of the development of the major NSF-sponsored cooperative research centers.

In the Foreword of the *1965 Research Centers Directory*, Alan T. Waterman (1965), former NSF director, made the following comment on the significance of the center movement:

> The large increase in the number of these research centers is evident from the contents of this edition which lists from 3,200 centers as compared with the 1,200 of the previous edition. This increase may be said to reflect the similar increase in the nation's research and development effort over the same period. The movement is interesting and significant in that it represents a realization of the advantage of a degree of autonomy on the part of research groups with specific objectives. This autonomy is also useful in identification of the unit for purposes of recruiting and fund-raising.

THE INDUSTRY-UNIVERSITY PARTNERSHIP PERIOD: 1968 TO DATE

The industrial partnerships furthered the transition of teaching institutions into research universities by creating large amounts of long-term revenue for university research. In this period, the leaders of the nation began to see the need for formal planning among the major performers and sponsors of research. The vast amounts of money and the complexity of the research associated with the industrial partnerships forced a number of new administrative structures for research administration and new planning modes for research development.

In this period, the traditional ambivalence that the universities and industry held for each other began to change. By the late 1960s, Turner (1967, 96-97) forecasted that:

> With the rate of increase in federal research funds slackening and the increase in industrial funds for basic research (particularly) rising, a decade from now faculty researchers may well come to look to industry and industry-related activities for research support as a major alternative to government.

These predictions held true because during the 1970s, inflation resulted in a relative decline in federally-sponsored research, and universities were once again forced to seek new sources of funding for research. At the same time, industry's revitalized interest in sponsoring research was motivated by growing concerns in the areas of productivity and innovation (Beasley, 1982).

In 1976, the past president of the Industrial Research Institute was prompted to note that:

> As a start there must be strong support by government and industry for a major commitment to undirected basic research at the universities . . . . Only if we can be assured of a strong, viable university structure in its own right do we then have the basis for the integration of some added university efforts into broad national missions. (Baer 1978, 88)

The dollar amount of industrial support increased significantly during the 1970s, and in 1980 universities received approximately $235 million dollars from industry for basic research (more than $120 million in 1972 constant dollars). By 1981,the industrial share of sponsored research had risen to almost 4% of their total research dollars. (NSB, 1982a).

Although universities had been doing business separately with industry and the federal government and as we have just seen some industrial support was developing for basic research, the Research Applied to National Needs (RANN) program initiated in 1970s brought the federal government on a broad scale into the planning for the three-sector partnership that would have academicians performing applied and production research. Thus the federal government helped bring about a radical change in academic philosophy that greatly altered the research universities' practice.

Following World War II, as the federal government formed basic research programs and established government foundations to support academic research, single corporate support of basic research diminished for a time. It has been suggested that this reduction of support was due in part to the fact that industry management was overly optimistic about the impact of, and the potential financial returns that basic research would have on industrial operations. When the returns on their investment did not materialize as quickly as had been anticipated, the eagerness to support basic research diminished (NSB, 1982a).

In the early sixties, there was some concern among the leaders of United States that the nation's companies were at a competitive disadvantage in existing and future markets. A few United States' manufacturers said that foreign competitors were playing by a different set of rules than U.S. companies and that the nation needed to recognize the threat that dominance of foreign manufacturing of products would have for our quality of life.

Their warnings were supported by indicators of export market shares. Export market share indicators and plant closing suggested that there was a beginning erosion of U.S. competitiveness in world markets.

These early warning were not alarming for almost two decades. After World War II, American business had dominated the domestic and international markets for manufactured goods. Most Americans in the early 1960s saw the beginning decline in exports as a temporary aberration in trade that would be soon corrected. They fully expected a favorable balance of exports to continue. However, by the mid-sixties, many U.S. companies were experiencing considerable difficulties in competing with Japan and West Germany in the steel, ship building, and textile industries. In the fifties, these industries had been targeted by Japan and West Germany in their strategic planning for economic development. Both countries then set favorable national policies that allowed their companies to capture these international markets in the next decade.

In the late sixties, U.S. manufacturers of consumer goods and automobiles began to lose their share of international markets for most consumer goods. Concern over our industrial competitiveness arose in the Midwest and on the East Coast where the steel related industries were badly damaged by plant closings. By the early seventies, Japan and certain of the more advanced countries had captured a large share of the American market for consumer goods and automobiles. Since the seventies, U.S. business has experienced a steady decline in exporting automotive equipment, furniture, textiles, rubber products, copper manufactures, dyes, leather goods, metal working machinery, steel, and domestic electrical equipment. This decline in manufacturing exports coupled with the U.S. oil import dependency created a mounting trade deficit.

Despite the fact that the United States has been blessed with the most favorable of natural resources, it was apparent by the mid-seventies that U.S. manufacturers were in serious trouble for the following reasons.

Lag in Domestic Investment in American Industry

The Joint Economic Committee in 1980 warned that U.S. industrial capital expansion had for two decades trailed that of our major foreign competitors. Capital resources available per worker in United States grew at about 2.2% per year through the sixties and seventies. On the Pacific Rim, capital available per worker grew at more than 10% per year. This indicator reinforced the anecdotal information associated with individual company failures, product-line discontinuance, and export indicators. They explained that Americans save only 10% of their GNP, compared to 15% in West Germany and 20% in Japan. Such shortfalls in capital formation contributed significantly to obsolete factories and inhibited the introduction of technological innovation in American companies. Moreover, much of American expansion capital went into service companies, rather than into manufacturing industries.

Lagging Productivity In American Industry

American productivity growth for manufactured products followed all our major foreign competitors, except Great Britain. In the seventies, our manufacturing productivity increased by an average of 2.2% per year. In Japan and Germany, the average rate was better than 5% per year. A large contributor to the U.S. small growth rate was the management-labor antagonism that was a carry over from past eras. Large foreign productivity increases allowed wages and profits rates to rise above those in the U.S.

This led to surplus capital in the foreign countries which was available for venture capital.

Foreign Trade Barriers

While the U.S. was developing social policy to advance the goals of President Johnson's Great Society, the leaders of foreign countries were developing tariffs to U.S. exports and non-tariff barriers to their own products in the U.S. The lack of an aggressive U.S. policy to encourage the development of domestic manufacturing and to counter protectionist policies in foreign countries proved to be serious impediments for purchase of U.S. products in the international markets. Despite two decades of multilateral trade negotiations there has been little reduction of tariffs and few cases of the elimination of non-tariff barriers. Restrictive foreign government policies on purchase of some type of American high technology and agriculture products have prevented U.S. company penetration into the foreign countries. These tariffs on Americans products were oftentimes as high as 25% of the selling price.

Technology Development

The U.S. production of airframes, power generating machinery, computers, paper, photographic equipment, and scientific measuring and controlling instruments constitutes a majority of the U.S. manufactured exports. Although the U.S. had dominated these markets for some years, other countries have steadily increased their R&D expenditures in these areas in an attempt to "double jump" the U.S. companies and thus place a more advanced technological product on the market before the U.S. does. Although the U.S. still leads in total R&D expenditures, this indicator is misleading because the Pacific Rim and West European nations purchase or appropriate our R&D and beat us to market with our advanced technology built into their products.

Government Industrial Policy

Earlier we mentioned that Bush's *Science—The Endless Frontier* established the federal government's long-term plans for scientific development. Isaiah Bowman in his paradigm for university science development carefully separated industry and university roles. He suggested no economic development strategy based on the commercial exploitation of university research. In fact, he would have been horrified by the thought. His laissez faire attitude toward the development of the different sectors in the research enterprise was typical of the thought of the times. With the notable exception of government subsidized agricultural research to the state land grant colleges, the laissez faire doctrine and the antimercantilism philosophy dominated the government's industrial policy. There was little thought given to fostering cooperation between government, industry, and universities until American industry began to lose its competitiveness in the marketplace. This nondirective approach of the U.S. should be compared with the Japanese approach that had MITI target a number of industries for economic development and then supported university research to achieve those objectives. The U.S. House of Representatives, Subcommittee on Trade (1980), in seeking a strategy for economic development for the U.S. government, reviewed how Japanese industrial policy from 1954-80 helped the development of the Japanese semiconductor, computer, and telecommunications industries.

University Fear of the Military-Industrial Complex

One of largest barriers to the industry-university partnership was the academicians' resistance to working with industrial partners. They recognized that industrial partnerships would change drastically the university. During the Vietnam War era, American industry was viewed by many of the liberal and fine arts faculty as being too big and too influential. They did not want a military or an industrial presence on campus. Traditionally there is an intellectual snobbishness on campus that has many academicians frowning at the crassness of the money grubber in industry. Many academicians felt the academy would be corrupted by accepting industrial dollars.

There is also a competitiveness among departments within the university that retarded the acceptance of industrial partnerships. The nonscientific departments recognized that industrial dollars would go exclusively to science and engineering departments. Thus, strengthening them and further eroding the power of nonscientific disciplines. This philosophy also colored the attitude of scientists and engineers whose expertise was not needed by industry.

Industry's Need for the Partnership

Successful competition in free international markets depends upon the delivery of goods and services that are wanted by consumers. The consumers of the last quarter of the twentieth century demanded quality manufactured products and personal services at affordable prices. The prime measure of the quality of the product and service was technological advancement of the product. For example, consumer electronics such as radios, televisions, and phonographs have been developed to the point that the customer has an immense number of choices for entertainment, on the receiving product (radio, television) selection of entertainment is individualized and is directly controlled for client preference, the products are powerful, and they become less and less expensive. To keep a product technologically ahead of the competition requires the commercialization of research. Company laboratories cannot produce all of the ideas for advancing technology. Universities are the place where ideas are spawned and nurtured. Consequently, industries had to head for the universities in order to acquire ideas that are not generated in-house.

At the end of the seventies, many U.S. and foreign companies were realizing that the industry-university partnerships were potent mechanisms to increase innovation and to improve manufacturing productivity. They saw universities providing the basic research for industry to use to develop new products and improve production processes.

Companies, in their strategic planning, scan the universities to determine which ones have the knowledge that they need and who is doing research that they can commercially exploit. For this reason, in the seventies and eighties industrialists began coming to the research universities in droves seeking windows on emergent technology. When they found a principal investigator or laboratory that was doing work in one of their target areas they established some sort of liaison and if the university research was judged to have specific applicability to their company's objectives, they encouraged the investigator and university to enter into a cooperative agreement or a joint venture.

On the reverse side of this industrial need is the need of universities to have their research thrusts supported both for the short- and long-term. The industry-university partnership is a symbiotic relationship. It has worked for decades in informal ways and through consultancies. During the industry-university partnership period, we witnessed 1) the formalization of ways of performing cooperative research, 2) the shift from industry consultancy relationships with PIs to industrial support to the PI through a project grant, 3) the support of research centers through center affiliation fees, 4) an enormous increase in the number of partnerships, and 5) a sharing of financial rewards with the PI and university. These changes brought about further transformation in the research universities.

Most universities neglected the development of research supported by industry prior to the seventies. However, in the late sixties, it became apparent to many of our education, business, and political leaders that American manufacturing was losing its competitive edge in the international marketplace and that industry-university partnerships for research development were seen as the solution to returning United States products to dominant positions in their markets. From 1970 until 1980, the faculty and other university constituencies had to debate the major issues related to industry-university partnerships before they could accept this innovative partnership. Many of the research control and institutional integrity issues that had been associated with the adoption of the federal-government-university partnership were reassessed and new issues peculiar to industry were examined in the light of assisting another sector in need of university research. Also, during this period special administrative structures, policy, procedures, and support personnel were developed to respond to the needs of the industrial sector. These debates and adoption of newly organized research units for industry created additional changes in the research universities.

Long-Term, Large-Scale Industrial Support: The Fourth Great Wave of Change

Long-term large-scale industrial support of university research was a powerful transforming force that profoundly modified the purposes of many units in the university and significantly altered the directions of investigators and expanded their thoughts about what research could be. In the preceding section, we saw the need for American industry to work with universities to improve their competitiveness in international markets. In this section, we will look at these partnerships and their effect on the university.

Industrial Liaison Offices

By the seventies, many research universities had established industrial liaison offices for the purpose of developing university research with industry funds. Massachusetts Institute of Technology's (MIT) Industrial Liaison Program founded in 1948 provides a model to help us understand the functions of industrial liaison offices and the changes that long-term large-scale industrial support brought to the research university. James D. Bruce, (1980) director, and Kay Tamaribuchi, assistant director of the Industrial Liaison Program (ILP) at MIT have discussed the operations of their liaison program at several SRA meetings. From their addresses, the authors have gained the following understanding of MIT's program.

The ILP has the objective of providing efficient and timely access to the research and staff resources of the institute because the benefit of its members fits very neatly under the original mission of MIT, which was chartered by the Commonwealth of Massachusetts in 1861 for the purpose of the advancement, development, and practical application of science in connection with arts, agriculture, manufactures, and commerce.

As all research administrators know, MIT, one of the great research universities, is a rather diffuse institution with five schools, twenty-three academic departments, and over forty ORUs to administer. It has an annual research budget of almost $300 million. Tamaribuchi (1980) is fond of saying that "The most valuable resource at MIT, of course, is its faculty and staff." The director of the ILP often commented that MIT's research programs and staff represent tremendous potential resources for industry and commerce. And he noted that it was difficult, or even impossible, to have systematic and efficient access to the wide spectrum of the institute's resources without some special link to MIT. Bruce and Tamaribuchi (1980) provided much of the following information on their office structure and activities.

The ILP staff of eleven full-time liaison officers link MIT and member firms through a number of services. The staff usually have advanced degrees from MIT, research experience at MIT, and several years of experience in industry. They are experts on MIT and their technical field. Each officer travels regularly to the principal locations of the firms he serves. While there, he learns of the companies interest and research development plans; he meets with company scientists and managers to describe the ways a member company can make use of ILP. On their home campus, they carefully determine the capabilities of MIT's faculty and staff. Most are distinguished academicians with international reputations for industrial problem solving.

The liaison officer recommends faculty experts for in-depth consultation of specific problems a company might have. In these circumstances, financial arrangements are made privately between the company and the faculty consultant. In 1979, over 2500 visits occurred between MIT faculty and staff and member company staff.

The MIT researchers travel widely and often extend their trips a day or two to visit member companies. Such visits may include a seminar on a topic of interest to the member company, informal discussions with key staff, and planning with company scientists and engineers for future work. Over 250 of these visits are to locations throughout the United States, Europe, and the Pacific Rim countries.

The MIT Institutional Liaison Program publishes annually a *Directory of Current Research* that includes a comprehensive summary of over 2,500 MIT current research projects. There is a bibliography listing related theses, papers and reports for each project. The ILP compiles and distributes manuscripts and preprints, laboratory periodical reports,, working papers, internal memos, patent awards and applications, and so forth.

Members are informed of about a dozen symposia per year of special interest to industry representatives. These two-day meetings attract about 100 scientists, engineers, and chief executive officers intent on reviewing the latest developments with other experts in the field in an informal setting. The 1980 symposia focussed attention on the following topics: advances in modern control theory; computer graphics; management of research, development, and technology-based innovations; solar energy utilization—possibilities and probabilities; biotechnology: status and prospects; future demands for energy; materials research; office of the future; how microprocessors are changing product design; toxicology research; polymers research; and IC engine operation fundamentals. Many of these symposia were held around the country in order that staff of member companies would find it more convenient to attend.

Research seminars are sponsored by the ILP to focus attention on specialized research efforts. Seminars are designed for about thirty people who can draw a sharper focus than the larger symposia. These half-day programs are held on site or in the vicinity of member companies, which maximizes the benefit to member companies. A large number of seminars are offered in this country and nineteen were held in Japan in 1980.

Industrial Interest in Supporting University Research

The fourth great wave was a powerful transforming force that profoundly modified the purposes of many units in the university and significantly altered the directions of investigators and their thoughts about what research was. This wave of change rushed into the university from many quarters changing the positions of traditional disciplines and creating new ones.

Recall that the MIT ILP sponsored symposia in 1980 to review the latest research and industrial developments with the experts in a dozen fields that MIT had developed strong research programs. One of symposia focused on biotechnology—a new field of academic study that was attracting long-term industrial support in several universities. The use of biotechnology has been with us for ages. Agriculture, one of man's oldest practices, is a traditional form of biotechnology.

Fermentation too has been studied for thousands of years. In recent years wine has not only been consumed, but studied on the campus. Enology has developed into prominent study on several campuses. At Texas Tech University two or three chemists interested in the fermentation processes and several of the plant and social scientists worked for a decade in creating and developing the distinctive West Texas wines of Llano Estacato Winery and Teysha Cellars, which now produce international award winning wine annually. These superior wineries and scientifically managed vineyards of West Texas have created a multimillion dollar industry for the region and respectable areas of university study.

When Crick and Watson unlocked the genetic code of living organisms by explaining DNA, they created the field of molecular biology, which rapidly developed genetic engineering—the laboratory-based technology of directly manipulating the genetic material of microorganisms, plants, and animals to create new organisms. This technology has the potential to revolutionize medicine, agriculture, waste processing, and the clean up of oil spills. Murray (1983, ii) in discussing the issues of corporate sponsored research in biotechnology noted

The revolution in technique is also radically changing the way research is done. Traditionally, universities in America have concentrated on something called "pure" research, leaving "applied" research to corporate laboratories. But the line between research and marketplace is blurred in genetic engineering, where a "pure" research technique can just as readily be used to manipulate a commercially important organism.

Furthermore, developments in the new field have come at a rapid pace. As a result, many companies were caught off guard, and they turned to universities to do research, both to discover what the new field was about and to begin to develop new products. Since universities at the same time were subjected to increasing costs, uncertain enrollments, and decreased Federal funding, many of them welcomed the industrial initiatives.

United States industry began investing heavily in molecular biology in the mid-seventies, when they realized that huge profits could be made from genetic engineering. Harvard Medical School received $6 million from DuPont for genetics research and Washington University received $4 million from Mallinckrodt, Inc. for investigation of antibodies (Begley, 1981). A year later, Washington University put together a partnership with Monsanto Chemical Co. that provided a prototype for future collaborative efforts between industry and higher education. This $23.5 million agreement focussed university research on proteins and peptides, but did not specify the topic of individual projects. The structure of the governing body of the Monsanto-Washington University partnership shows the joint development of direction for industry-university research. Their eight-person committee is split evenly between industry and university. The partnership encourages Monsanto scientists and engineers to work in the Washington University Medical School laboratories to facilitate the transfer of technology to Monsanto and in turn the Washington University faculty were invited to use the company's nearby isolation and tissue culture laboratories, in addition to using company biological materials.

The Monsanto-Washington University partnership allowed faculty members to publish the results of any research done under the Monsanto funding. The company has the right of prior review for patentable technology and requires a short delay of publication or other disclosures to allow for patent filing. Patents generated from the research will be held by Washington University with Monsanto having an exclusive license to any patents that it chooses to market expeditiously. Washington University retains the right to license the patents to other corporations if Monsanto chooses to not license them. To allay the fears that its university investigators would get rich on their research done in university labs, Washington University insisted that the royalties go to the University rather than to individual investigators. This lack of sharing with the principal investigators created considerable controversy among investigators and caused speculation that the policy would hurt that unit's recruiting efforts in the future. Washington University's position in the early eighties on nonsharing of royalties with investigators is an example of the conservative policy that is rapidly disappearing on most university campuses.

Yale University after considerable debate over forming industry-university partnerships and an investigation by a presidential commission, established in 1982, a director of cooperative research to explore research opportunities with industry. Immediately after university acceptance of the new partnership concept, Yale found an honest confluence of interest with the Celanese Corporation, which supplied $1.1 million for a three-year period to support basic research on enzymes in the Yale biology department and medical school. Long-term agreements with other companies quickly followed. For example, Bristol-Meyers a leader in anticancer pharmaceuticals provided $3 million for five years to support research on the development of anticancer drugs in Yale's Department of Pharmacology. In addition, Britol-Meyers agreed to screen drugs developed by ten Yale researchers for anticancer potential, a very costly procedure that probably would not be done by the university. In return, Bristol-Meyers had an option of first refusal to pursue at their expense patents filed in the university's name. In return Bristol-Meyers is entitled to an exclusive license to produce the university discovered drugs for a limited period. Moreover, this agreement provided the company with the right of first refusal on any discoveries outside of the field of anti-cancer drugs made by faculty members participating in the program.

Murray (1983) reviewed how Hoechst, the giant German chemical company, announced its partnerships with Massachusetts General Hospital, a teaching and research affiliate of Harvard Medical School and how that partnership created a national controversy. In 1981, Hoechst committed to spend at least $70 million dollars in the next decade if the hospital would establish a department of molecular biology. The department of fifty senior faculty was to be built around Howard M. Goodman, a distinguished researcher in recombinant DNA work. Hoechst was to be the departments sole support. Hoechst was to receive first rights to any patentable discoveries made by the department, while reserving to individual researchers partial interests in patents, the right to collaborate with colleagues and the right to publish their findings. The Hoechst-Mass General partnership caused considerable concern in Congress. Congressman Albert Gore of Tennessee, a member of the Investigations and Oversight Subcommittee of the House Science and Technology Committee was anxious about the intent of the Hoechst proposal and called for an investigation of the terms of the agreement. The General Accounting Office found that although there was some potential conflicts of interest with federal regulations governing government support, which totaled $30 million annually, the contract as written did not violate any law. It was Congressman Gore's contention that the "exclusive rights provision" of Hoechst-Mass. General agreement and the inability to segregate Hoechst and Federal money allowed the foreign company to exploit research that had been paid for by American taxpayers. Congressman Gore threatened to use the "march-in rights" provided in PL 96-517 to take control over any research that Congress might view as having been paid for by the taxpayer but benefiting a foreign company.

Edwin C. Whitehead, who made a $400 million fortune in developing laboratory instruments, was so convinced that biotechnology was man's great breakthrough on curing genetic disease that he gave MIT $7.5 million in 1981 for start-up costs and another $20 million to house the Whitehead Institute. Moreover, he supplied $5 million annually for operating expenses, and promised a $100 million endowment at or before his death. Interestingly, MIT was not the first choice of Whitehead, Duke University, where Whitehead was a trustee, and another major research university had declined the honor of housing the Whitehead Institute.

Much of the stumbling in the university quarters was caused by Whitehead's insistence on setting the composition of Institute's board, which was to be dominated by Whitehead's children and associates. This was later changed to give the MIT faculty more control. Also, Whitehead insisted that the Institute might serve as a model for other wealthy persons and corporations in establishing common grounds where researchers would be given joint appointments in university departments and hold positions in the Institute. Twenty new positions from the Whitehead Institute in a department of forty would give the department a further emphasis in molecular biology, which the traditional biologists resisted. Moreover, many MIT faculty were concerned that the Whitehead Institute would be the first in a series of "satellite institutions" around MIT, what we refer to as "common grounds". They were worried that such institutes with jointly appointed faculty would have undue influence on the university.

The greatest innovation in the industry-university partnership and in the establishment of common grounds came from the West Coast. Eugenics provides the most inventive variant of the industry-university partnership arrangements. Eugenics Corporation is formed around Harvey Blanch of the University of California who was interested in focusing on bioreactor design and scale-up to aid the transfer of biotechnology from the laboratory to the marketplace. Six corporations financed Eugenics—Bendix, Elf

Technologies, General Foods, Koppers, Mead, and McLaren Power and Paper. They invested $7.5 million to capitalize Eugenics. They own 35% of the stock. The Center for Biotechnology Research owns 30% of the stock and 35% is owned by the founder of Eugenics. Eugenics does not directly fund biotechnology research. Funding comes from the Center for Biotechnology, a nonprofit corporation initially funded by the same six companies. The center, which is the common ground, is governed by an independent board of trustees who represent industry, the universities, and Eugenics. The center then supports research at Stanford, the University of California, and MIT. The center receives from the cooperating universities royalty-bearing licenses to any patents developed in the sponsored research. Eugenics then arranges to do the develop work or makes the patent available to the sponsoring companies. This arrangement ensures the integrity of the university, protects the investment of the companies, and assures that the principal investigators can legally commercially exploit their intellectual property without being placed at the sufferance of traditional governing bodies.

Eugenics is a new model for cooperative research, which can help solve the future research needs of universities by providing the long-term support from industry. It does require a great deal of strategic planning among the principals. Note that the CIR increases dramatically as investigators are now involved in checks at the following points of progress: scope of the work; duration of the agreement and continuation; payments and schedules; prior publication review; post publication dissemination to sponsor advisory committees; patents; licenses and best efforts; royalties; termination; confidentiality of information; use of PI's name with product; keeping a work-log; reporting competing research; indemnities, liabilities and insurance; warranties by corporations; settling disputes; and reporting on progress and final reports.

The previous examples of long-term large-scale industrial support for biotechnology reveals the enthusiasm of industry to support university research that promised a high commercial payoff. Earlier, we listed the MIT ILP symposia, which included biotechnology as one of a dozen development areas for MIT. Space and time allowed us to look at only one area, but similar types of partnerships were being formed to exploit the other eleven areas. The sudden rush of large amounts of industrial monies for extended periods and the distinctive terms of the industrial agreements profoundly altered the way universities did research and the way they thought about the mission of the university.

The purpose of strategic planning with industry is to give both partners maximum freedom of action in the joint development of research, while sharing fully their intentions for their respective execution of research.

Joint planning for specific projects is the most popular type of cooperation, which is very flexible in as much as it leaves the partners operating as independently as possible while sharing a common goal. The industry-university partnership is spreading rapidly in the major research universities for the long-term large-scale financing from industry meets the needs of the university.

Economic Benefits of Industry-University Joint Research

The usual benefits from industry-university joint research are quite simple: 1) the opportunity for the faculty to have long-term large-scale funding for a problem of their interest with an opportunity to gain financially from development of their intellectual property; 2) the development of new and improved products for industry outside of their internal initiatives and increases in productivity. The benefits are derived from several sources. One is the pooling of technical talent and financial resources that would not be possible by any one of the participants. A second source of benefit from strategic planning is the conservation of resources. Also, joint projects avoid unnecessary duplication of research facilities and pilot plants.

Expanding membership abroad has prompted the development of intensive short courses that are of special interest to member companies in Europe and Japan.

Long-term industrial support accelerated the transformation of research universities from teaching and technical colleges into research dominated institutions. The industry-university partnership grows out of industry's need to commercialize university research. This partnership is developing rather rapidly in the last decades of the twentieth century.

THE STATE ECONOMIC-DEVELOPMENT PERIOD
(1955 TO PRESENT)

Although it is true that the states have been using their universities to promote economic development through general education and departmental research for more than a century, the establishment of state-initiated common grounds; state offices such as the state offices of science and technology, technology transfer programs; and divisions of research programs in state higher-education coordinating boards is quite recent and significant. The impact of these state research initiatives on university research cannot be overestimated for they are changing radically the research activities of universities. The entrance of states with programs to influence the commercialization of university research was a major innovation in the research establishment. It created another revenue stream into the universities and created the need for universities to plan jointly with state economic development offices for the long-term development of new industries, new technologies, and advanced research programs. That revenue stream is presently a mere trickle—we believe that revenues from state initiatives will become a raging torrent in the twenty-first century.

In Chapter One, the functions of the state science and technology offices and the divisions of research programs in coordinating offices were discussed in some detail. This section of the historical foundations for university research focuses attention on emergence of the university-centered state economic development efforts and the reawakening of state government leaders to the potential impact of university research on the economic development of their states. We will consider the following transforming influences: research parks, technical assistance centers, state advanced research and advanced technology programs, state higher-education general appropriations, state line-items to support centers of excellence, state science and technology offices, divisions of research programs in coordinating boards, and regional development associations.

The Fifth Wave of Change:
The Development of Common Grounds

A common ground is a site that is not located on the main campus. It may or may not be owned by the university. Frequently, the common ground is owned by the state or local government. Sometimes they are owned by private businesses. In any case, they are sites where researchers from the various sectors come together to work on cooperative endeavors.

Although the research triangle was founded in the 1950s to promote the development of collaborative industry-university research, the concept of the research common grounds did not become popular until the 1970s (The North Carolina Science and Technology Research Center, 1983). Forming common grounds for university-industry cooperative development of research marked a dramatic change in the university mission, its planning and its operations. The research park not only took the faculty members out of the departmental classroom and away from traditional sponsors, it also took them off the campus to a common ground and placed the researcher or university in a partnership mode of planning and operation with a particular industrial firm.

Movement to a common ground required much more than physical movement—it required radical changes in campus philosophy, planning, and policy. Long-term, joint planning was necessary to commit university resources to the development of specific industrial objectives with the idea that the nation or state would be economically served through the attraction of business dollars to develop high technology products in a particular region.

These new partnerships brought into existence new industries and greatly expanded the number of scientists and technicians working in local industries. The increased payrolls greatly improved the economy of the region. Your authors believe that the success of the Research Triangle was duly noted by the governors of the southern states, especially Governor Jimmy Carter. Recall from Chapter 1, President Carter's Industrial Innovation Initiatives and his Economic Program for the Eighties had the industry-university partnership theme running through both programs. The Research Triangle was a model for his national strategy.

Since 1950, more than 100 research parks have been established to actively promote industry-university collaboration (Lee, 1982). Most universities see no alternative to planning the development of common grounds if they want to be internationally competitive with the major research universities around the world. Presently, the United States and other developed nations are experiencing a fundamental change from industrial-based economies to technological economies that are dependent on the rapid commercialization of research. It is a change that is as profoundly altering as the transformation from an agricultural economy to an industrial economy. Authors such as John Naisbitt use "megatrend" to describe the change, whereas conventional economists call it "structural change." Regardless of our selection of terms to describe the economic upheaval, it is real and universities are caught in it because they are the institutions that are expected to have a plan that meets the knowledge and research needs of local industries striving to compete in international markets.

The increased sophistication of a technological society demands greater cooperative planning between universities and industry. For example, in the semiconductor field, the development of many new products requires the exact positioning of artificially synthesized, layered structures or superlattices of materials grown from molecular beam epitaxy, a technique in which crystals are assembled layer-by-layer in an ultrahigh vacuum by beams of atoms. This technology requires strategic planning to direct the long-term work of a large contingent of university and industrial scientists supervising huge research support staffs on a common ground. It also requires mutual planning for basic and applied research, product development, and marketing operations. Technologies other than the semiconductor industry have different, but equally comprehensive, plans for developing new products and highly trained technicians to support their researchers.

The fifth wave of university research support was brought about by industry and universities cooperatively planning for industry to switch from established manufactured products to new products and new services; to convert a work force that was predominantly blue-collar grade-school graduates to a lab-coated professional staff of graduate-trained scientists and engineers; to move from bench science to sophisticated science; and to change from heavy, rigid manufacturing to automated, flexible technologies. To accommodate these social and technological changes, the structure of research universities has changed from conducting work in a departmental laboratory that is predominantly used for instruction to conducting work in partnership laboratories that encourage advanced students to work on industrially identified problems, and from the single investigator-oriented research project to center-focused research that has applied as well as basic research intent. Although basic research will be conducted on these common grounds, a great deal of planning time will be given to research for new products and for improvement of production capabilities. The planning for such profound changes was very complicated and raised considerably the CIR because the F_S factor, planning and approval points within sponsoring agencies (industrial companies), multiply dramatically with production research.

On the common ground, academe and industry are merged. In a research park it is difficult to distinguish whether one is standing on the campus or on company turf, as industrial high-tech facilities are nestled in handsome landscapes that complement the beauty of adjoining campuses. The common ground promotes a blurring of roles among researchers because the academician spends much of his time in an affiliate's lab, whereas his industrial counterpart has an adjunct appointment at the university to teach. Scheduling for this type of research requires continuous joint planning. The phenomenal growth of research corridors, research parks, and beltway research areas is creating a greater physical and organizational change in universities than did the post-WWII student enrollment surge. Selecting and planning the site is mind boggling because of the involvement of boards of city development, state science technology councils and state legislatures. On the common grounds there is an astonishing amount of joint planning between the industrial and university sectors. Today, university planning is not just for the university laboratory; it must consider every facility on the common ground.

Most of North Carolina's Research Triangle park's 45,000 total employees work on a joint venture directed by faculty, but paid for by industry. Senior administrators such as Hart (1985) have estimated that 70% of the employees in Research Triangle Park affiliate institutions are directly or indirectly working on some joint project. He also recognized that an enterprise such as Research Triangle Park could not exist without joint planning and without the presence of a large number of research support personnel.

The research support personnel are as important to the technological economy as factory workers and managers were to the industrial economy. However, in an advanced research and high technology environment, researchers must plan for the continual updating of knowledge for research support personnel (RSP). Although the instructional side of the university must implement the training component of the research strategic plan, the researcher must select and organize the knowledge content. This too raises the CIR; however, failure to include training for the RSP in the strategic plan will have the PI doing work that should be done by a technician.

In addition to training the RSP for advanced research and high technology jobs, the current wave of common grounds promises a new and expanded training role for research universities. It is in the research university that training for entry-level professional positions into high technology industries occurs. Research universities are the only institutions that have faculty who understand the advanced technology. Educators must have on a common ground real-environment instructional facilities that ensure the technical training essential for an easy transition to tomorrow's world of practical work. Most conventional academic facilities are totally inadequate for these new technological training demands. Such facilities exist only on common grounds and are owned by industry. To use industrial facilities requires the instructional side of the university to plan closely with industry for the use of these common ground facilities.

Today, business and industry seek to hire the graduates of research universities affiliated with research parks, and industry encourages its industrial researchers to collaborate with universities in the development of instructional programs and personnel exchanges that meet industrial objectives. The instructional relationship between the industrial sector and higher education is no longer separate and sequential; in this new era it has become increasingly interactive and lifelong, requiring a strategic plan to develop a common ground for instruction as well as for research. Many advanced technologies will require customized training programs planned and developed between industry and research universities on common grounds. This may become the normal way of developing university curricula. Research universities have much to learn—and to offer in return—from the practical experiences of corporate training programs conducted on a common ground.

This increase in industrial education needs has created a sizable cadre of continuing education support personnel who assist the faculty and the university's industrial partners in planning for the technical training needs for industry. The staffs of continuing education units frequently operate apart from the traditional graduate and undergraduate instructional programs. They operate more like ORUs than like conventional instructional programs. For this reason they must articulate their plans with research administrators and enter into the strategic plan for university research.

North Carolina's Research Triangle: A Prototype

The research triangle has become a prototype for state economic development efforts using university research. The influence of Governor Luther Hodges of North Carolina and the success of the research triangle to the development of state initiatives is a major milestone in the history of university research. Hodges, representatives from the university community, and business leaders in North Carolina began to seriously consider the "Research Triangle" project in 1955. It was hoped "that the development of research facilities attracted by, and located near the state's three neighboring major universities—would, in turn, attract manufacturing plants to produce goods and services conceptualized through this research activity" (Franco, 1985, 82).

Governor Hodges appointed education, business, and government officials to a Research Triangle Development Council to oversee the development of the project. A working committee of academic leaders was also established to review the three universities (the University of North Carolina at Chapel Hill, North Carolina State University in Raleigh, and Duke University in Durham) to identify their various research activities and potential (Franco, 1985).

In 1957, University of North Carolina-Chapel Hill sociologist George Simpson, who had been given a leave of absence from his faculty duties, presented the committee with a three-part outline that established the first clear concept for the development of the research triangle project. That outline proposed: "1) a vigorous promotional campaign to attract industry and government research facilities; 2) the purchase of contiguous land parcels on which to establish a research concentration, or park, and 3) the establishment of a research institute" (Franco, 1985, 84).

The next step was to sell the concept to industry. Governor Hodges, Simpson, other committee representatives, and faculty began highly visible campaign efforts to sell the concept of the research triangle to the nation's industries. An example of these efforts included a thirty-member delegation led by Governor Hodges to New York City to attempt to develop industry and news media interest about North Carolina.

At the same time, the concept of the proposed research institute was being developed. One of the key considerations in its development was the concern that the "integrity of the universities' traditional research autonomy" be retained (Franco, 1985, 84-85). Although the faculty were sensitive to the potential conflicts of interest resulting from ties to business, they viewed the research institute as a vehicle that would protect them against inappropriate pressures from the private sector. The park-based contract research facility would remain primarily accountable to the three universities.

The institute was able to attract research work from both the private and public sector, and was operating in the black within three years. By 1984, forty-six research operations and fifty-seven support groups (lawyers, doctors, a hotel, restaurants, engineering firms, etc.) were housed in the park.

Other research parks have been established through mechanisms that do not involve the initiative, or even the cooperation of the state government. For example, the first research park established by a university was the Stanford Industrial Park, founded in 1953. The approximately $1 million development costs for the initial 450 acres of the Standford Industrial Park were all borne by Stanford University (Lee, 1982). In contrast, other research parks have been commercial ventures, such as the Waltham Centers and several other parks in the Boston area. These research parks were established by the real estate development firm of Cabot, Cabot and Forbes Company, and interact with M.I.T., Harvard, and several other institutions of higher education located in the area (Lee, 1982).

Technical Assistance Centers

States have become actively involved in providing direct incentives, and even mandates, to their universities to help in the development of the state's industry and the economy. The incentive to establish three-sector partnerships of state government, industry, and university often comes from the state in the form of a grant to a university to establish technical assistance centers to serve the needs of local industry.

The Pennsylvania Technical Assistance Program (PENNTAP) was established in 1965 to provide a technical information network to assist private and public sectors throughout the state to obtain and apply appropriate scientific and technical information. PENNTAPP has used a variety of media activity to respond to service requests and conduct program awareness operations (Beasley et al., 1982).

In 1978, the Ohio Technology Transfer Organization (OTTO) was proposed to assist small businesses in the application of new technologies to improve their market position. A statewide network of eleven community and technical colleges was established to work with Ohio State University in their efforts to provide information, training, and technical assistance to small businesses (Beasley et al., 1982).

The University of Tennessee's Center for Industrial Services (CIS) central office and field offices have provided technology transfer training, marketing, engineering, and field applications to advance industry located in Tennessee (Beasley, et al., 1982).

In all research universities, the schools of industrial engineering and business management for over a half-century have been dedicated to the solving of production improvement problems. Dudek and Smith (1986) worked with integrated circuit manufacturers in the United States to realize large gains in productivity by developing for the computer industry extremely high production techniques. Their new techniques went beyond existing CAD/CAM (computer aided design and computer aided manufacturer) programing, eliminated costly manufacturing production by creating extremely low work-in-process schedules, and custom designed extensive robotics and flexible automation systems that resulted in enhanced products and improved productivity in integrated circuit manufacturing for Texas companies.

Macy (1988), director of the Texas Center for Productivity and Quality of Work Life, contracted to deliver the following work activities in a Houston plant: 1) train job analysts, 2) observe and interview job incumbents, 3) develop task lists and administer task inventory, 4) complete and score position analysis questionnaire, 5) task clustering, 6) develop selection-assessment program, 7) develop performance assessment program, and 8) other activities as determined by the owner. When university researchers are engaged in the aforementioned activities, they are performing "production research," which is frequently not identified within the university and which is traditionally not recognized as "good research" for promotion and tenure.

Every company in the United States can have a research capability as good as Bell Laboratories if they can find university centers of excellence and then link particular centers to the company's research and training problems. Linkage is an important factor in today's university-industry partnerships. The Texas Innovation Information Network (TIINS) located at Texas A&M University provides such a linkage by maintaining an information data base containing current research and development, engineering, technology, management, and education information describing the capabilities and needs of Texas scientists, engineers, entrepreneurs, advanced technology companies, professional services (accountants, attorneys, bankers, venture capitalists) and continuing and professional education programs. These brokerage organizations help in the development of common grounds because their long-term existence depends upon their effectiveness to improve the flow of innovations from the university laboratory to the marketplace.

In all the aforementioned programs, the state has provided at least a portion of the funding the educational institutions needed to provide services to industry. Other sources of funding for these programs include federal and private grants and contracts, institutionally provided services and funds, conference fees and other miscellaneous income (Beasley, et al., 1982). For a more complete discussion of state efforts in strategic planning for technological innovation, see Tellefsen's discussion of the Ben Franklin Partnerships in Chapter 9.

State Advanced Research and Advanced Technology Programs

Governor Mark White in an effort to reform the higher education system of Texas and to promote the use of universities in the economic development of Texas formed the Select Committee on Higher Education in the mid-eighties.

The select committee's recommendations brought about clear definitions on the differing roles of higher-education institutions and recommended differential funding. In this strategy, top-tiered research universities will receive a higher rate of funding for all functions when compared to the lower-tier institutions. To actively promote more university research, which would revitalize the state economy, the committee recommended to the legislature the funding of four new research development programs that were to direct more than $60 million biennially into Texas research universities. The state legislature targeted research by using such new terms and definitions as the following:

"Research Enhancement" Program—provides university support for basic research and creative activity in all disciplines.

Advanced Research Fund—provides support for basic research in selected disciplines.

Advanced Technology Fund—provides support to selected disciplines for technological research in area with potential for improving the economy of Texas.

Research Assessment Program—provides for the Coordinating Board to arrange for merit reviews of "Special Line-Item" research programs.

Advanced technology programs support faculty projects in eligible research areas such as agriculture, biotechnology, aquaculture, and manufacturing science. In these programs, a pool of money is established and advanced research or advanced technology proposals are solicited through a statewide competition with peer review panels recommending successful proposals. These special appropriations (in accordance with the definitions in the bills) direct support for university research to politically targeted areas in the form of grant awards.

Hennessey (1987) provided a specific example of the value of university production research. In the mid-eighties, she delivered several enhanced computer programs for a California company. Her research produced very specialized modules in standard ANSI 74 COBOL to be operated in the UNIX and MSDOS (Microfocus COBOL) environments. Her production-research contract to convert several proprietary programs supplied by the company and its affiliates required that during the term of company sponsorship, university employees supplying the services could not serve as a consultant to any person, firm, or corporation who manufactured any product whose function was the same as that of any product manufactured by the sponsor. The work products of the services, any writings, discoveries, inventions, and innovations resulting for the services, were promptly communicated to and were considered the property of the sponsor. This project partnership between the university and company provided for sharing the receipts from the sale of licenses to use the software developed under the agreement. The original general techniques for relatively inexpensive conversions of software were pioneered by Hennessy. Now, through contracts with individual companies, the specific intellectual outcomes of her work became shared property among the principal investigator, the university, and the company according to the very precise terms of a particular contract.

Hennessey has multiple production-research contracts amounting to several hundred thousand dollars annually, which support several graduate students and purchase the most advanced equipment and software. In addition to production research, her work on computer inspection of microchips was funded by the Texas Advanced Technology Program in 1987 and 1989. The combination of production research and Texas Advanced Technology Program funding create in Texas a university-based common ground that lends assistance to the advanced technology industries of the state. The strategic planning for such common grounds requires the gathering of several groups of industrialists, campus associates, and personnel from the coordinating boards division of research programs.

Despite some strong opposition to her operations, Hennessey remains a strong proponent of university researchers conducting production research and advanced technology. She makes a convincing case that production research and advanced technology have great potential for assisting the investigator in locating an area of basic research. She believes that as investigators work on industrial research problems their learning curves accelerate dramatically for a particular area of study; oftentimes, to the point that the university researcher sees basic research problems that would not have been seen if a university researcher had not performed the industrial work.

She also understands the downside for academicians performing production research when departments, colleges, and institutions do not have the mechanisms for recognizing the outcomes of this activity. She has called to university administrators' attention the difficulty in getting college merit-advisory committees and departmental committees to consider production research as "research" and not a "service" activity in promotion and tenure reviews.

Higher Education General Appropriations: a Significant Element In Developing the Research University

The term "sponsored research" has special significance for state strategic academic planning and policy analysis because "sponsored research multipliers" are used in state formulas to provide the research universities with significant funds to pay for research administration and research development. For example, the Texas Higher Education Coordinating Board appropriation recommendations included a formula of 7.5% times the amount of "sponsored research" for general administration and .02 times faculty salaries + .20 times "sponsored research" for organized research funding. These are significant sums that provide the research university with some assurance that its major sponsor, the state, supports the research functions of state institutions. State Deputy Commissioner of Higher Education Webb provides a thorough explanation of foundations for state funding of the research university in Chapter 10.

It is easy to overlook the tremendous influence of the higher-education general appropriation on the development of the research university because the general appropriation is considered to be directed toward support of instructional activities. Unfortunately, accounting principles and definitions misplace research under the instructional function making it difficult to see state support for research. Despite its nonrecognition, the state higher-education appropriation is of immense importance to the development of university research and to state economic development because it provides the infrastructure for all researchers as well as a sizable fund for departmental research, which is usually considered by accountants as an instructional function. Using current accounting models and classification schemes it is difficult to show a direct relationship between state higher-education appropriations and state economic development efforts. However, such a relationship exists but is obscured by traditional accounting models. This topic was discussed at length in the 1990 SRA symposia on Financing Science and Technology.

State Line-Item Appropriations in the University Budget

Most states have special line-item research appropriations (up to several million dollars annually) to an individual university to perform research in areas vital to the state interests such as water conservation, brush and noxious weed control, efficient beef production, and robotics. This topic is discussed at length in Chapter 6.

State-Capital Located Science and Technology Offices (SS&TO)

The state-capital located science and technology offices and the division of research programs (DRP) coordinating boards and their contributions to the development of the research university are discussed in Chapter 1.

Regional Development Associations

Hensley (1981), a university research-development officer, noted that during the late 1970s he worked for several years with southern Illinois business leaders to develop government-industry-labor-education partnerships as a strategy for development in southern Illinois. At that time, Illinois business and political leaders were concerned that their companies were at a competitive disadvantage in existing and future markets. Southern Illinois Incorporated (SII), a regional development association, was concerned about foreign competitors such as Japan and West Germany. SII leaders, John McCarty and Joe Bennett realized that southern Illinois businesses must develop new products, technologies, and markets that not only matched the new competition, but advanced to the next generation of technological development. They realized that to remain on the competitive edge, southern Illinois businesses must remain one step ahead of their competition.

These southern Illinois leaders recognized that local companies were no longer just competing among themselves. They were now faced with competition from huge joint-venture companies formed by national governments, business consortiums, and national labor. Although many ideas were presented as to how the development of this technological advancement should occur, there was general agreement that new partnerships had to be developed to meet the rapidly changing conditions being imposed by the competition. To form these partnerships, representatives from each of the major sectors within the region were brought together to talk about specific issues, particular problems, and practical solutions.

A workshop for "Exploring Government/Industry/Labor/Education Partnerships: A Strategy for Development" was held in October, 1981 to get people together to talk about long-term partnerships that ultimately could solve existing and emerging problems. The major goals of the conference, as noted by Hensley (1981, 148), were:

1. To bring the leaders of four major sectors of our society together to focus on development of technology, new products, and larger markets;

2. To increase the number and influence of four sector partnerships by extending an invitation to key area leaders to identify critical problems facing their communities and to have them form for their areas development teams who could design a workable development strategy for particular segments of the community;

3. To create in all levels of the participating organizations and communities an awareness of the value and obligations of the four sector partnerships to area development; and

4. To create a climate dedicated to the development of Southern Illinois.

The objectives of this conference were intentionally broad, but specific outcomes were expected from the development teams. "The Conference Advisory Committee stressed that this Conference was not to be a 'talk and listen to generalities' but a time to plan solutions for problems that impeded development in certain fields" (Hensley, 1981, 148).

The conference structure included five broad dimensions that impacted various aspects of southern Illinois economy: 1) energy development, 2) agricultural development, 3) community development, 4) international development, and 5) industrial and capital development. The coordinators for each of these dimensions selected three or four major-strata leaders, who in turn selected development team leaders. These development team leaders and their teams were selected from leading practitioners in their fields, and guided the major conversations during the conference.

The speakers at the ten plenary sessions addressed broad issues relevant to their sector and presented their overall views on future development. In addition forty-three small group meetings were held in which the dimension leaders had prepared "precept papers" designed to focus discussions on current problems within the respective five broad dimensions. The development groups took the next steps in designing development strategies that could be achieved with the resources of the partners.

Current problems encountered by the region were identified, future problems and opportunities were forecasted, and specific recommendations for developing partnerships, new products, technology, markets, and training programs were made in the team sessions. Although each team had a different agenda, they all had the common task of developing partnerships that would enhance the development of their field. Development strategies for attaining team goals were established. These strategic plans would serve to guide the new partnerships toward specific agreements.

As an example, the critical issue of easing the adversarial relationship that existed in the labor-management partnership was addressed. Both sides acknowledged that their survival was dependent upon long-term agreements that were economically viable. "New protocols were formed between these two sectors with government and education playing a large role in assisting the development strategies for a particular industry" (Hensley, 1981, 150).

Other issues addressed during the course of the conference included: the changing allocation of resources by federal and state agencies; new provisions for corporate tax credits for local development; and the framing of legislation to meet new requirements or to remove regulations that were counter-productive to local development. In addition, international consultants provided information on how to develop joint ventures and foreign leaders described how Japan, Great Britain, West Germany and Canada had been able to use a four sector partnership to project certain segments of their economies into dominance of world markets.

The conference provided a true strategy for development. More than 500 leaders from the four sectors engaged in frank and open discussions of emergent issues, and cooperatively designed specific strategies for the development of their organizations. The open forum allowed for the presentation of ideas and an opportunity to work with new people on problem areas. The conference provided the basis for the next steps of joining the appropriate partners and of implementing the specific recommendations that had been devised by the development teams. State support for two new centers emerged from this strategic planning conference and increased funding was pledged to several others.

The State-University Pilot Plants

The states have assisted industry and universities in establishing pilot plants, constructing prototypes, forming dies from which thousands of a new device can be rapidly and cheaply reproduced, and refining or testing an invention for wide-scale use. The states have found that universities can add to man's repertoire of problem-solving activities by operating pilot plants. These pilot plants and prototypes serve as the interface between theory and the real world.

Organizational Priorities

The decision to engage in most development work is a corporate decision, not an individual one. This is a great change in the mode and scale of investigation on the university campus. With basic research and applied research during the bench-science era, a single academician usually could make unilaterally the decision to conduct a particular piece of work and could (usually with only institutional resources and perhaps some modest sponsor resources committed to him) successfully solve his individually chosen problem. Not so, with development. Development not only has a different set of products, it has a much different set of inputs and a different decision-making climate. The purposes usually are not established by the individual scientist or engineer, but by government agencies, boards of trustees, trade associations, departments and/or colleges, and other organizations. It is usually a collaborative undertaking requiring large, annual investments that produce multiple outcomes for a particular field of production. States frequently establish a line-item in the general higher-education budget for the support of a particular pilot plant that will advance a major industry in the state. These pilot plants are frequently located in industrial buildings some distance from the campus. Location on common grounds have several advantages: sizable quantities of raw and finished material requires large storage areas that are difficult to obtain on campus, laboratory space and office space are easier to acquire and less expensive than space on campus, and indirect cost rates may be substantially lower.

Parker (1984) noted that at the Texas Tech University Textile Research Center (TRC) (a pilot plant for spinning, weaving, and testing of fibers and fabrics) was established when, in 1969, the Texas legislature and the University decided to establish in West Texas the nation's finest textile research facility. To accomplish this, the State of Texas decided to provide many millions of dollars over the decades to build in stages this internationally known facility. The prime objective of this research partnership was the improvement of the cotton, wool, and mohair industries of Texas. In setting its priorities, Texas Tech University placed the construction of TRC and the hiring of faculty and staff for the establishment of an engineering textile instructional program to complement the research program above other areas of academic interest. These were carefully considered group decisions that were to commit the state, the institution, the Natural Fibers and Food Protein Commission of Texas, and several trade associations to long term support for a pilot plant to test and develop a variety of fibers and fabrics.

Today, the trade associations are pleased with the TRC, which has enhanced the marketing of Texas natural fibers through long-term research. The TRC laboratories test annually more than 60,000 samples of cotton and their researchers report to producers and manufacturers how to obtain optimum utilization and maximum profit for a particular bale of cotton, wool, or mohair. TRC has developed an extensive data base describing the characteristics of fibers and with the assistance of their computer programs can select the exact bales for the production of quality yarns and fabrics. This creation of a model solution for the use of raw fibers has upgraded the use of Texas natural fibers providing to Texas cotton, wool, and mohair growers, many millions of additional dollars, attracting textile plants to West Texas, and improving vastly textile quality.

Input into the TRC's operating funds is mostly from fee generation for development projects and special line-item appropriations. Their staff of fifty-two professional and support personnel provides an impressive annual report summarizing the hundreds of projects conducted for the sponsoring partners. The TRC director and principal investigators maintain close personal contacts with several advisory boards composed of legislators, producer association leaders, and individual manufacturers. With TRC's considerable input into the decision making of key organizations, the fiber producers and the legislators perceive the TRC as a very modest investment for the return it produces. Manufacturers throughout the nation are most grateful to pay for its unique services. It is no wonder that the TRC retains the legislature's commitment to a special line-item appropriation and receives continuing support from the Natural Fibers and Food Protein Commission. Its international reputation for textile research excellence enhances the image of its parent institution.

Most pilot plants operated by universities have similar types of organizations and networks that support their purpose. These development centers serve the instruction and basic research needs of the parent university, but are usually financially independent of the state general education appropriation. They are partially dependent upon a special line-item appropriation. Strategic planning is essential for the pilot plant because they must have the backing of a number of industrial principals, state legislators, and campus administrators.

Prototypes may involve the assembly of many inventions to make a system function according to some theoretical construct. The problem solving ability for this type of activity is more organizational than investigative in the disciplinary sense. The purpose is to discover if a complex system can work under different conditions by testing the limits of the unit and its individual components under real conditions. The development and testing of prototypes is an expensive activity for industry because they must shutdown production lines to test innovations or to adjust existing machinery. A pilot facility allows development and testing to occur without sacrificing production schedules.

In this age of advanced technology, the university development processes become very important to national industry. The semiconductor industry is a case in point. Computer chips, the sine qua non of modern computers, require "cleanrooms" (particle-free environments) that are astronomically expensive to construct and even more expensive to operate. Once these high-tech facilities start a production run, it does not shut down until the production schedule is completed. It is not uncommon to have three-fourths of a production run scrapped. Quality control of the process and changing of manufacturing machinery settings are manipulated from the outside by trained scientists and engineers. It is too costly for production equipment manufacturers to test their equipment during production runs; consequently, they need a cleanroom at a pilot plant where they can test and do research on their own equipment.

Marcy (1984) conceived the development of the SMART Lab, a university-operated cleanroom where manufacturers could test their equipment and where there was a critical mass of university scientists, engineers, and research support personnel to help the manufacturers' engineers with applied and production research. The SMART Lab concept calls for the university to construct a cleanroom. Computer-equipment manufacturers then pay an annual fee to be an affiliate of the SMART Lab, which entitles them to early briefings on all nonproprietary research and special consultation services. Computer equipment manufacturers may use, for a full-cost fee, the SMART Lab to test their equipment under a variety of controlled situations. The remainder of the time, the SMART Lab is used for basic and applied research and for instruction.

The Advanced-Research Era (1980 to Present)

One hundred American universities have been transformed in about a half-century from teaching institutions into research universities. A second one hundred universities are struggling to emerge as research universities. Most research universities entered the advanced-research era around the 1970s depending on their stage of evolution. Today, research universities are dominated by an advanced-research environment. Their constituencies demand that they offer an elegant education, sophisticated science, and advanced technology that is entirely different from the education and research in the teaching institutions. The rare environment of the research university creates a unique individual that is much sought after in our technological society. Graduates from research universities think and act differently from the rest of mankind.

In the teaching era, universities were dominated by teaching. The students entered their freshman year expecting to be taught the subject matter of their chosen discipline and to graduate with a baccalaureate, which would admit them to practice routine science or engineering. In the advanced-research era students enter research universities expecting to be taught a mode of inquiry that will allow them to conduct advanced research in the world's high-tech industries or go on to professional school and graduate school.

In the teaching institution, faculty come primarily to teach students. In the research university, faculty come primarily to perform research. In the teaching institutions, students are taught by teachers to be practitioners. In the research university, the student are taught through example and by formal instruction to be researchers. Many students will leave the research university after having acquired a baccalaureate to serve as a scientist or engineer in a research support position in an R&D operation of a high technology industry. Others will go on to graduate school with the expectation that they will graduate as a doctor of philosophy and enter some part of the research enterprise as a principal investigator conducting advanced research.

Research jobs are plentiful now in the high tech areas. Most companies investing in the bright research minds for business want to commercialize their inventions. The legal, accounting, and business divisions of industry are requiring that their personnel be trained in research universities because they have the best background to perform in the highly competitive international marketplace. It is almost a requirement for the research division heads and the senior executive officers of high tech companies to have earned both a Ph.D in a scientific or engineering discipline from a research university and a professional degree in such areas as law, accounting, finance, or marketing.

The world's population is being stratified by education. At the top are elite groups of researchers who have been elegantly educated in advanced technology and sophisticated science who enter the research enterprise at high-salary levels and who receive a large share of the profits obtained from the commercialization of their intellectual property. At an upper-middle level is a group of practitioners who enter positions calling for routine practice. They enter the world of work at good salaries but do not share in the wealth generated by the commercialization of intellectual property. At the lower-middle level is a group of technically educated people who perform repetitive tasks. They enter the work force at modest hourly rates or on piecework payment. They manufacture objects and have minute shares in the wealth of the company. And, there is a large group of people who have little or no education for a technological society. They live on the subventions of the nation.

In the research era, there are numerous expectations that are placed on the research university. The federal government has the expectation that the research university will assist in the defense of the nation, in the promotion of the health of its citizens and in the training of its leaders. The federal-government-university partnership is well developed. Although the expectations of the federal government expand with each internal and international crisis, the partners have reached a good understanding of the other's roles. The state-government-university partnership has the expectation that the research university will assist with the economic development of industry in the state and the education of its citizens. Generally, the long-standing relationship of this partnership carries the partners through good and bad economic cycles. The expectations of industry for the development of new products and enhanced productivity from university partnerships are burgeoning. This partnership is not well established. Industry and universities must work diligently to develop common grounds and to encourage joint efforts. The disciplinary partnerships traditionally have fared very well in the university environment. Researchers are expected to create, organize, and disseminate knowledge within disciplinary structures. The creation of knowledge is occurring at a geometric rate. The challenge of the next decade is how to structure knowledge within each discipline so researchers and practitioners can find knowledge that is organized by function for problem solving. Knowledge organization and efficient dissemination are the next generic problems that must be seriously studied by the university and its many disciplinary partners. Strategic planning is the mechanism for future research development among the partners. We hope the following chapters will provide appropriate insights into the present status of strategic planning for university research, its technology and its problems of adoption.

WORKS CITED

Anderson, Frank W. 1981. *Orders Of Magnitude, A History of NACA and NASA, 1915-1980.* Washington, D.C.: National Aeronautics and Space Administration.

Baer, W. S. 1978. The changing relationships: Universities and other R&D performers. In *The State Of Academic Science: Background Papers.* eds. B.L.R. Smith and J.J. Karlesky, 61-103. New York: Change Magazine Press.

Beasley, Kenneth, et.al. 1982. *The Administration of Sponsored Programs.* San Francisco: Jossey Bass.

Begley, Sharon. 1981. A $127 million gift horse. *Newsweek.* October 12, 1981. 87.

Bowman, Isaiah. 1945. "Report of the Committee on Science and the Public Welfare." In *Science—The Endless Frontier.* V. Bush. 70-122. Washington, D.C.: National Science Foundation.

Brubacher, J.S. and Rudy, W. 1976. *Higher Education in Transition: A History of American Colleges and Universities, 1636-1976.* (3rd ed.) New York: Harper & Row.

Bruce, J.D. 1980. The MIT Liaison Program. In *Industry/University Cooperative Programs.* Proceedings of a workshop held in conjunction with the 20th annual meeting of the Council of Graduate Schools in the United States Dec. 2, 1980. ed. Thomas R. Williams. 22. Washington, D.C.: Council of Graduate Schools and the National Science Foundation.

Bush, Vannevar. 1980 [1945]. *Science—The Endless Frontier.* Washington, D.C.: National Science Foundation.

Compton, Arthur. 1972. Quoted in *Nuclear Milestones: A collection of speeches by Glenn T. Seaborg.* San Francisco, CA: W. H. Freeman and Co. 81

Davis, L. E. and Kevles, D. J. 1974. The National Research Fund: a case study in the industrial support of academic science. *Minerva, 12,* 207-220.

Dudek, Richard and Smith, Milton. 1986. *Productivity in High Tech Manufacturing*. A research project funded by the Texas Advanced Technology Research Program at Texas Tech University

England, Merton J. 1982. *A Patron for Pure Science: The National Science Foundation's Formative Years, 1945-57*. Washington, D.C. National Science Foundation, NSF 82-24.

Eveland, J.D. and Hetzner, William. 1982. *Development of University* Industry Cooperative Research Centers: Historical Profiles (NSF 82-47), Washington D.C.: National Science Foundation.

Franko, Michael R. 1985. *Key Success Factors for University Affiliated Research Parks: A Comparative Analysis*. Unpublished doctoral dissertation, University of Rochester, Rochester, NY.

Hart, Donald. 1985. *The Development of Research Parks and Other Commongrounds*. Symposium held at the 19th Annual Society of Research Administrators Meeting, St. Louis, MO: September 29, 1985.

Hennessey, Kathleen. 1987. *Automated Visual Inspection Using Syntactic Representation of Images*. A research project funded by the Texas Advanced Techology Research Program at Texas Tech University.

Hensley, Oliver D. 1981. *The Proceedings of A Working Conference for Exploring Government/Industry/Labor/Education Partnerships: A Strategy for Development*. Carbondale, IL.: Southern Illinois University, October 26-27, 1981.

————. and Burns, Debra. 1985. *Growth of organized research units*. Paper presented at the National Council of University Research Administrators Region V and Society of Research Administrators, Southern Section joint spring meeting, Galveston, TX, April 19, 1985.

————. 1986. Organized research unit personnel. In *University Research Support Personnel, SRA Monograph #2*. ed. O.D. Hensley. 189-226 Lubbock, Texas: Texas Tech University Press.

Ikenberry, Stanley O., and Friedman, Renee C. 1972. *Beyond Academic Departments*. San Francisco: Jossey Bass.

Lee, Charles Alan. 1982. *University Related Research Parks: A Michigan Case Study with Selected Comparisons*. Unpublished doctoral dissertation, University of Michigan, Ann Arbor.

Macy, Berry. 1988. *Job Analysis: Timelines, Budget Estimates and Product Production*. Contract with the Clorox Company, Huston Division and the Texas Center for Productvity and Quality of Work Life Lubbock, TX. Texas Tech University.

Marcy, William M. (1984, August). *The SMART LAB Planning Conference of 1984*, Lubbock, TX.: College of Engineering, Texas Tech University.

McLaren, Malcolm and Wachtman, John B. 1984. Converting ceramic science into technology. In *Converting U.S. Scientific Leadership into Technological Leadership. Proceedings of the 1984 Conference on Industrial Science and Technological Innovation*. eds. D.O. Gray and N. Koester, 152-168. Raleigh, N.C.: North Carolina State University, May 14-16, 1984.

Murray, Dennis J. and O'Connor, Patrick J. 1983. *A Guide to Corporate Sponsored University Research in Biotechnology Issues, Contracts, Models, and Personnel*. Washington, D.C.: McGraw-Hill Publications.

National Research Council. 1985. *Engineering Education And Practice In The United States: Engineering Graduate Education And Research*. Washington, D.C.: National Academy Press.

National Academy of Sciences, Committee on Science and Public Policy. 1964. *Federal Support of Basic Research in Institutions of Higher Learning*. Washington, D.C.: National Academy of Sciences. 31.

National Science Board. 1982a. *University-Industry Research Relationships: Selected Studies*. (National Science Foundation Publication No. NSB 82-2) Washington, D.C.: U.S. Government Printing Office.

National Science Board. 1982b. *University-Industry Research Relationships: Myths, realities, and potentials*. (National Science Foundation Publication No. NSB 82-1) Washington, D.C.: U.S. Government Printing Office.

National Science Foundation. 1959. *Scientific Research and Development in Colleges and Universities Expenditures and Manpower—1953-54*. Washington, D.C.: Author. NSF-59-10

National Science Foundation, 1970. *National Patterns of R&D Resources. 1953-1971*. (National Science Foundation Publication No. NSF 70-26) Washington, D.C.: U.S. Government Printing Office. In *The Home of Science: The Role of the University*. ed. D. Wolfe, New York: McGraw-Hill.

The North Carolina Science and Technology Research Center. 1983. *Research Triangle Park, North Carolina Directory*. Research Triangle Park, NC: North Carolina Department of Commerce. January 1983.

Parker, James. 1984. *A Strategic Plan for the International Center for Textile Research and Development*. Lubbock, TX.: Texas Tech University.

Price, Derek John de Solla. 1963. *Little Science, Big Science*. New York: Columbia University Press.

Research Center Directory. 1980. Detroit, MI: Gale Research Company.

Rosholt, Robert L. 1966. *An Administrative History of NASA, 1958-1963*. Washington, D.C.:National Aeronautics and Space Administration.

Schwarzkopf, Alex. 1981. An introduction to what the National Science Foundation has accomplished. In *The Proceedings of A Working Conference for Exploring*

Government/Industry/Labor/Education Partnerships: A Strategy for Development. O. Hensley, ed. 69-73. Carbondale, Illinois: Southern Illinois University. October 26-27, 1981.

Seaborg, Glenn T. 1972. *Nuclear Milestone: A collection of speeches by Glenn T. Seaborg*. San Francisco, CA: W. H. Freeman and Co.

Strickland, S. ed. 1967. *Sponsored Research in American Universities & Colleges*. Washington, D.C.: American Council on Education.

Tamaribuchi, Kay. 1980. MIT's industrial liaison program. In *Sustaining Vitality: A Challenge for the 1980's. The Proceedings of the 14th Annual Meeting of SRA at Chicago*. ed. O.D. Hensley, 174-177. Santa Monica, Cal.: Society of Research Administrators, October 5-8, 1980.

Truman, Harry S. (1945, September 6). Quoted in National Academy of Sciences, Committee on Science and Public Policy. *Federal Support of Basic Research in Institutions of Higher Learning*. Washington, D.C.: National Academy of Sciences. 1964. 16.

Turner, W. Homer. 1967. Private sponsorship, public gains. In *Sponsored Research in American Univesities and Colleges*. ed. S. Strickland, 91-118. Washington, D.C.: American Council on Education.

U.S. Congress, Joint Economic Committee. (1980, December). *Research and Innovation: Developing a Dynamic Economy*. a Staff Study on Economic Change. Washington, D.C.: Author.

U.S. House of Representatives, Subcommittee on Trade of the Committee on Ways and Means. (1980, October 1). A Committee Print on *High Technology and Japanese*

Industrial Policy: A Strategy for U.S. Policymakers. 96th Congress, 2nd Session Washington, D.C.: U.S. Government Printing Office.

U. S. Office of Management and Budget. 1973. "Part I. Principles for Determining Costs Applicable to Research and Development Under Grants and Contracts with Educational Institutions." *Federal Register*, Vol. 38, No 181, Wednesday, September 19, 1973. 26292.

Waterman, Alan T. 1965. In *Research Centers Directory*. eds. A. M. Palmer and A. T. Kruzas, Foreword. Detroit: Gale Research Company, 1965.

Willner, William, and Hendricks, Perry B. *Grants Administration* Washington, DC: National Graduate University, 1972.

Wolfle, Dael. 1972. *The Home of Science: The Role of the University*. New York: McGraw-Hill.

CHAPTER FOUR

THE PRESENT STATUS OF STRATEGIC PLANNING FOR UNIVERSITY RESEARCH

Pamela A. Cooper and Oliver D. Hensley

As the data from the tables and analyses in this chapter indicate, strategic planning for research is an innovative technology for universities. In the early 1970s, the authors had not been able to identify which, if any, universities were using strategic planning techniques. Although strategic planning had been firmly established in the military and many government agencies by that time, universities generally had not accepted the concept nor adopted the technology.

Many research administrators believed that strategic planning was appropriate for universities and that it should be adopted for the development of university research. The problem with adopting strategic planning in the 1970s was the lack of information about the subject and the inordinate fear of academicians that such planning would direct or stifle their work.

Research administrators used other types of planning but ignored the advantages of this efficient tool. In the late 1960s and early 1970s, Schoppmeyer (1972) and Hensley (1968) (1970), as principal investigators, experimented with and wrote about a total systems approach for long-term cooperative regional planning to introduce innovations into education systems. Hensley (1979), in predicting new roles for the research administrator in the 1980s, suggested that university research administrators were the architects of the future and that cooperative planning with sponsors would become the dominant role of senior research administrators.

The Society of Research Administrators (SRA) decided in the early 1980s to study strategic planning because it held considerable promise for the membership and their institutions. The progression of this study is shown in Figure 4.1.

The first steps in speculating on the value of strategic planning for research came from specific membership interest. Thomas Collins, vice-president for research at the University of Missouri, and Hensley discussed the subject during formal presentations and at informal meetings of the Society of Research Administrators in the early 1980s. Both were convinced that strategic planning technology should be adopted by research universities because it was the logical next step in the progression toward better research development and grants administration. Both were experimenting with the technology on their respective campuses and shared

149

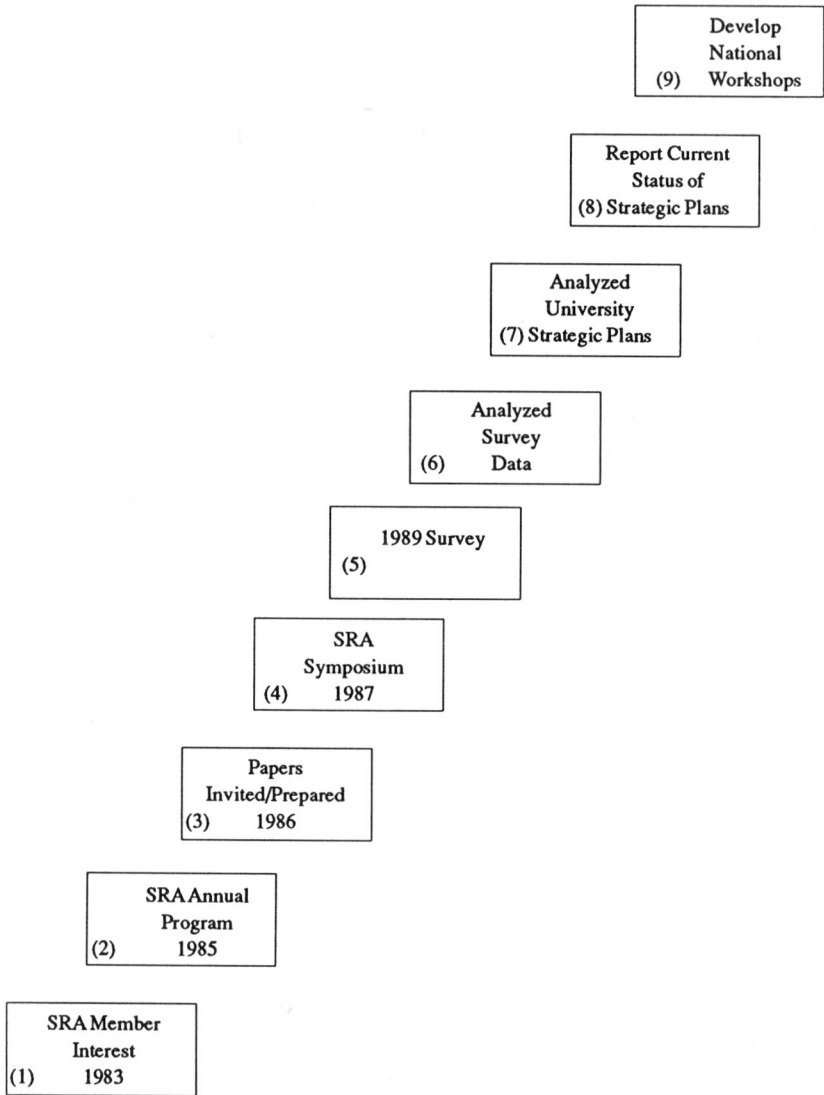

Figure 4.1 The Steps in Determining the Present Status of Strategic Planning for University Research

informally information on their techniques, progress, and failures. Darling (1979) and Hensley (1981) used strategic planning techniques for university research at Southern Illinois University-Carbonale and reported their results to their constituencies in published papers.

Collins took the second step in the formal study of the subject by persuading members of the midwestern section of SRA that the 1985 program in St. Louis should be entitled "The New Research Environment—Responding with Plans and Strategies." The 1985 program provided for a dozen experienced administrators who delivered anecdotal information about strategic planning in their agencies. These program sessions were well attended and membership interest in this new planning technology was high.

In 1986, the SRA Research Committee issued a national call for papers on the subject and invited several speakers to present papers at the 1987 SRA research symposium "Strategic Academic Research Planning" held as part of the SRA 21st annual meeting in New Orleans. These papers were refined and expanded in 1988 and are included in this volume.

In 1989 the authors conducted a national survey. This chapter presents the result of that survey.

The fourth SRA Monograph is the compilation of nearly a decade of SRA study of strategic planning. The next step in the study will be the presentation of the data and models at workshops for individuals interested in discussing, developing, and implementing the technology from their campus perspective.

INSTITUTIONS PRESENTLY ENGAGED IN STRATEGIC PLANNING FOR UNIVERSITY RESEARCH

The analysis presented here is based on a survey of university administrators that the authors conducted during the summer of 1989, in an attempt to determine basic information related to the institutional use of formal strategic research plans. The surveyed population was based on the 150 institutions that the National Science Foundation (NSF) reported as receiving the largest amounts of total research and development funds in the United States in 1980. Each of the institutions was mailed a postcard questionnaire inquiring about the presence of formal strategic research plans on their campus. Eighty-four (56%) of the institutions responded to the survey. Of the responding institutions, sixty-two were public and twenty-two were private institutions. Institutional administrators who indicated the existence of strategic research plans were asked to submit a copy of the plans. The full plans of seven of these institutions, and the table of contents, executive summaries, and goals and objectives of five institutions were reviewed and analyzed. The plans of an additional five institutions that had lower levels of research and development funding were also reviewed.

A relatively small number of the responding institutions indicated that they currently have, or are in the process of developing, a strategic research plan. Approximately 64% of the institutions indicated that they do not have a formal strategic plan for research (see Figure 4.2). Only 27% reported that they currently have such a plan, and an additional 8% indicated that they were in the process of developing a plan (see Table 4.2). Although in some cases the research plan is an independent document, in most instances it is one part of an overall institutional plan.

SRP Initiated?
(84 Institutions Responding)

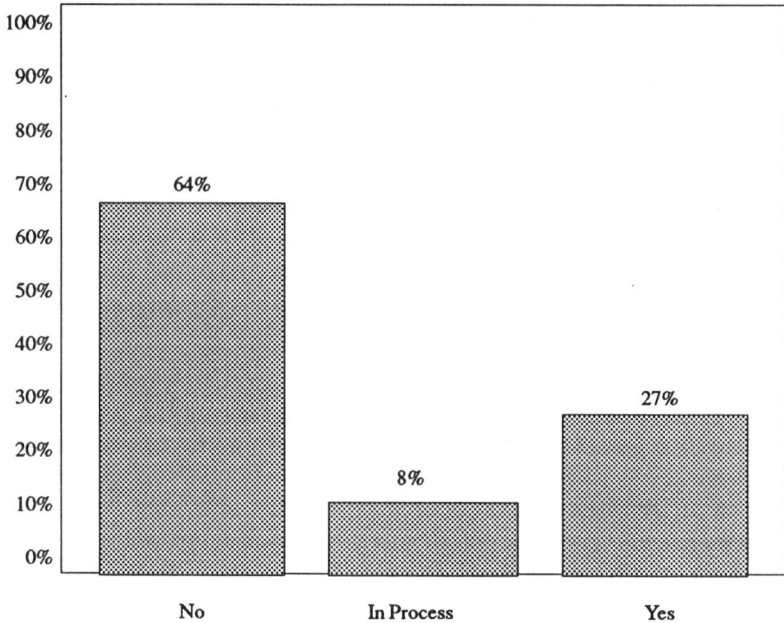

Figure 4.2 Does your institution have a strategic research plan?

The number of institutions that are becoming involved in strategic research planning is increasing at a rapid rate. Less than 4% of the responding institutions indicated that they were involved in strategic planning for research prior to 1980. This number has increased dramatically in the past ten years. Twelve percent of the responding institutions indicated that they had become involved in strategic research planning during 1980 through 1984. Another significant increase in the total number of institutions becoming involved in strategic research planning occurred during 1985 through 1989. An additional 20% of the responding institutions reported the development of such plans. Although only three (3.6%) of the responding institutions reported involvement in strategic planning for research

Rank	Institution	Rank	Institution
17	University of Southern California	64	University of Kentucky
20	Pennsylvania State University	65	Carnegie Mellon University
21	Texas A&M University	79	University of New Mexico
24	University of Arizona	91	Temple university
28	Purdue University	96	Georgetown University
33	Georgia Institute of Technology	101	Univ. of Texas Med Branch-Galveston
34	The University of Georgia	102	University of Oklahoma
35	Louisiana State University	114	University of Idaho
37	Oregon State University	119	University of Houston
46	Colorado State University	120	Tulane University
47	University of Hawaii at Manoa	121	U of Medicine and Dentistry of NJ
51	University of Iowa	129	Medical College of Wisconsin
52	The Rockefeller University	131	Dartmouth College
57	University of Missouri - Columbia	135	Lehigh University
61	Washington State University	143	South Dakota State University

Table 4.1 Institutions Among the Top 150 in Financed Research and Development Expenditures (1980 ranking) Reporting the Use of Strategic Planning to Advance Research

prior to 1980, the next ten years saw a tenfold increase in that number. By 1989, 30 (36%) institutions reported involvement in strategic research planning.

Approximately the same percentage of responding public and private institutions indicated that they currently have strategic research plans either in existence or under development (22 public institutions or 35% of the responding public institutions, and 8 private institutions or 36% of the responding private institutions), although private institutions got a head start on developing such plans. None of the public institutions indicated that they had developed a strategic research plan prior to 1980, whereas 37% of the responding private institutions that currently have strategic research plans had initiated them prior to 1980—including one that was initiated in the early 1900s! Rockefeller University's Executive Vice-President Rodney W. Nichols noted that their institution had originated its first plan during the period 1901-1910. A more modern format of the plan was instituted during the 1950s, and a systematic update was implemented during the 1970s.

The majority of the responding institutions have not implemented a strategic research plan. In fact, some institutions apparently do not feel there is a need for such plans. It is interesting to note that of the eleven responding institutions ranked among the top fifteen institutions in total re-

Number of Institutions with SRPs
(84 Institutions Responding)

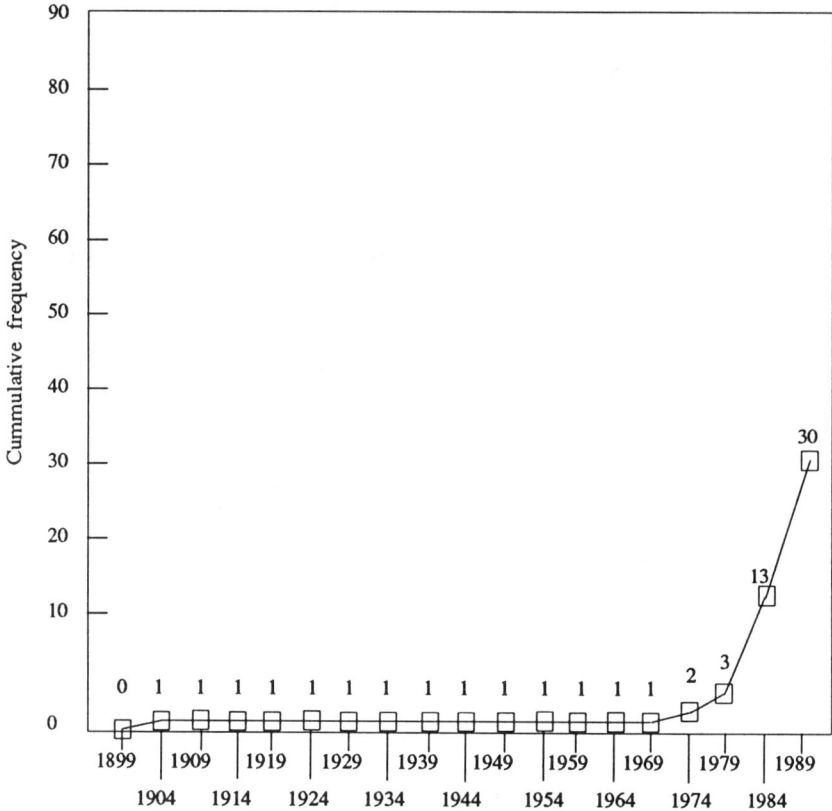

Figure 4.3 Cummlative Frequency of Responding Institutions with Strategic Research Plans—by year

search and development funding in 1980, not one had an institutional strategic plan for research. In fact, the vice chancellor of one of these leading research universities indicated a perceived lack of need for a strategic plan for research when he responded that "It (research) doesn't require a plan-just a strong research faculty."

Only 21% of the responding institutions ranked among the top twenty-five in research and development funding indicated that they have such plans. Institutions at somewhat lower rankings in total research and development funding (NSF, 1980) are apparently more convinced of the necessity for and benefit of such planning, perhaps because they view it as a mechanism through which they can raise their level of research and development funding. Approximately half of the responding institutions ranked twenty-six through seventy-five, and 101 through 125 have institutional research plans (see Table 4.2).

Does your instituion have a strategic research plan?

Rank by R&D Funds	Total # of Institutions Responding	# of Responding Institutions w/SRPs Developed/in Process	% of Responding Institutions w/SRPs Developed or in Process
1-25	19	4	21%
26-50	13	7	54%
51-75	13	6	46%
76-100	14	3	21%
101-125	13	6	46%
126-150	12	4	33%
Total	84	30	36%

Table 4.2 Institutional Initiation of Strategic Research Plans (by institutional rank — 1980 R&D Funding)

Physical Characteristics of Plans Received

A total of eighteen plans and/or the executive summary-table of contents of the plans from twelve different universities ranked among the top 150 institutions in research and development funding and six additional colleges and universities not ranked among the top 150 institutions were reviewed. The plans for the twelve ranked research universities accounted for 40% of the institutions ranked among the top 150 institutions that indicated they have instituted a strategic plan for research. The six additional colleges and universities not ranked among the top 150 institutions included: Farleigh Dickinson University, Gallaudet College, Lehigh University, Loyola University, Medical College of Hampton Roads, and the Oregon Graduate Center.

In most of the plans that were reviewed (94%), the strategic plan for research was only one component of an overall institutional strategic plan. The only exception was Pennsylvania State University. Penn State developed, and has subsequently updated, a plan that deals exclusively with the various research components of their institution.

The length of the plans varied considerably. The primary document of the plan ranged in length from fourteen to 186 pages, with an average length of approximately sixty-five pages. Of course this length was impacted by the style of type, page size, use of photographs, charts and graphs, and layout and design of the plan. Institutions such as Texas A&M, the University of Hawaii, the University of Oklahoma, and Lehigh University used separate documents for items such as executive summaries, mission statements, timetables, planning assumptions, and statistics.

There was a wide variation in the physical characteristics of the thirteen full plans that were reviewed. The primary document was strictly a written presentation in most cases (62%). Graphics, particularly for the presentation of statistical information, were used in the primary documents of 32% of the plans. In a few instances (15%), black-and-white photographs were used. Only one institution, the University of Oklahoma, used a four-color, glossy, photographic production process as a component of their document.

THE PLANNING AND REVIEW PROCESS

Reasons for Plan Initiation

The conduct of research has become the predominant means for universities to obtain national and international stature. At the same time, institutions of higher education have realized that the growing competition for a limited amount of funds, coupled with a tremendous expansion of knowledge in a growing number of disciplines, and the increasing demands made by government, industry, and the public, make it impossible for them to be all things to all people. If the institutions are to establish themselves as leaders in research, they must accept the fact that they have the potential to do so only in selected areas, and focus their efforts predominantly in those areas. They must have a critical mass of resource—human and physical—to produce knowledge in an area that can set them apart.

Institutions of higher education have begun to rise to this challenge. The setting of priorities, focusing of effort, and development of research within specific disciplines have become recurring themes in the institutions' strategic research plans. Institutional commitment to assisting in the economic development of the state in which the institution is located is also prevalent in many of the plans. In some instances, institutions such as the University of Oklahoma have initiated their strategic plans in response to specific directives from the state. Some of the strategies developed for the University of Oklahoma have been initially outlined by the state's previously developed state economic plan.

Critics and skeptics of formalized plans such as strategic research plans tend to point to the very real danger of these plans being developed, but never implemented. If institutions of higher education are to be successful in their research efforts, they do not have this luxury. Jean Wadlow, provost at the University of Oklahoma-Norman campus, noted regarding that institution's recently developed strategic plan:

> I am reminded of an incident that occurred early in our deliberations. I was handed a dusty, old plan someone had pulled from the bookshelf with the admonition, "This is what will happen for the Strategy for Excellence too." I assure you, the University of Oklahoma Strategy for Excellence is not and will not become a "Shelf Plan." Indeed, since the State Economic Plan calls for AAU membership in five years, we need to move faster and farther than other schools. This is no time to put the "plan" on the bookshelf! (University of Oklahoma, 1988, p. 3).

Participants in the Planning Process

Because planning for research was only one component of the majority of the institutional strategic plans reviewed, it was only a portion of the plan's development process. In many instances, an overall committee for long-range planning was comprised of top administrative personnel and faculty members. This committee often was assisted by numerous subcommittees in key areas of focus such as research, academic affairs, computing, development, facilities, finance and operations, libraries, and student services.

Oregon State University (1987) developed its plan through the efforts of a long-range planning commission, three subcommittees, twenty-three planning units, and six task forces. More than 100 faculty and staff participated in this process. In addition, a survey was distributed to faculty, staff, students, and external constituents in an effort to obtain these groups' prioritization of twenty proposed goals.

The University of Hawaii received ideas for the development of its plan from more than 200 faculty through a strategic planning colloquium and task group process.

Planning Principles or Assumptions

Initial steps in the planning process include an analysis of current conditions and consideration of future environmental factors that will impact, or have a high probability that they will impact, the institution's research efforts. This includes a consideration of the external factors over which the institution has limited, if any, control, as well as the internal factors that the institution may more readily modify. Following is a list of some of the environmental factors that were considered in the development of the strategic plans that were reviewed. Although this list is not all-inclusive, it will give strategists an idea of the environmental factors that should be considered during the development of a strategic research plan.

The External Environment

External factors that strategists for institutions of higher education have taken into consideration in the development of strategic plans include the following.

Demographic and Societal Trends—Some of the demographic and societal trends that are taken into consideration when developing a strategic plan for an institution include: the institution's geographic location and service area; changes in population characteristics including size, age, sex, and race; decreases in the number of traditional students and increases in the nontraditional student population; changes in household composition; and the increased entrance of women into the work force.

Economic Trends—Economic trends are another factor that can significantly impact the planning and decision-making process related to research. Strategists have considered, among other factors: the reallocation of resources; the decline of federal funds; voluntary and state-directed commitments to assisting with economic development within the state; increased employment in the services, retail, and wholesale trades rather than manufacturing; areas of employment specific to the location of the institution (e.g., oil production in Texas and agricultural-related businesses in Iowa); the impact of automation; increased collaborative research opportunities with industry; the increased demand for technology transfer; the impact an increased level of international trade will have on the local economy and institutional areas of research; and an increased participation in international research activities.

Trends in Federal and State Policy—Trends in federal- and state-government policies and areas and levels of research funding provided, are instrumental in setting the focus, direction, and level of research activities within an institution. Strategists are sensitive to the impact of decreasing levels of federal support; increases in the level of competition among more institutions for available federal and state funds; increases in oversight and control over research activities imposed by the states; the growing emphasis of state support on near-term economic development rather than long-term basic research; and the increased dependence upon higher education by the states to help shape their public policy.

Technological and Scientific Trends—Changes in science and technology continue to have a major impact on the conduct of research. The sophistication of equipment used in the conduct of research allows for increased levels in quantity, precision, and complexity, of research. Strategists take into consideration: the continued integration of computers, automation, and telecommunications into research activities; the increased demand for interdisciplinary research; as well as the increased sophistication and cost of research instrumentation.

The Internal Environment

In some cases, institutional strategists will be more able to alter or impact the internal environmental factors than the external factors. This is not always the case, however, particularly for public institutions. Factors such as institutional mission and enrollment policies are often set by the state, and institutional administrators must abide by these legislative intents. Although technically there exists the capability to impact an institution's internal environmental factors, the implementation of any change must be politically acceptable to the various populations within the institution. Such change is often not easy or immediately attainable. As was once noted by Woodrow Wilson, "the only thing harder than changing a university is moving a cemetery" (Davenport, 1990).

Some of the internal factors that institutional strategists have taken into consideration as they develop their strategic plans follow.

General Assumptions and Institutional Mission—Most of the plans include discussions of the designation and pursuit of an institutional mission. These mission statements vary based on the organizational structure of the institution from very individualized and distinct, to coordinated mission statements developed for multicampus institutions. In many cases, an intent to compete with the top research institutions in areas of specific research strengths is indicated. In addition, periodic internal and external reviews of programs are established to maintain and enhance the quality of the efforts to attain the institutional mission.

Research—There exists, for most institutions, the ultimate goal of the advance of excellent research and scholarly activity. To accomplish this goal, one of the key components that is included in the consideration of the institution's internal environment is an attempt to increase the research funding base. Factors that impact this effort include the intention to capitalize on existing research strengths in the pursuit of additional research funding and an increased level of competition for external research support. Other components of the internal factor of research that strategists consider include increased participation in international research, collaboration of research efforts with other institutions and industry, programmatic need and research productivity in the decision-making process related to budget and space allocation, the increased demand for technology transfer, and the potential effects research efforts can have in shaping public policy.

Faculty and Staff—As previously noted, one survey respondent noted the need for a strong research faculty to develop research within an institution. To obtain, develop, and retain a high quality faculty, strategists note that high priority must be given to the recruitment, selection, evaluation, compensation, and retention of the faculty. Other factors that can have direct or indirect impacts on the development of faculty at a research university include: tenure and promotion criteria, consideration of faculty workload, extramural funding of scholarly work augmented with internal funds, collegiality, faculty morale and satisfaction, career-development activities, and an increased level of research support staff.

Students—One of the primary roles of higher education is the education of the student, and many factors regarding the make-up of the student body typically are taken into consideration in the development of the strategic plan for an institution. Admissions policies, student enrollment patterns, and the availability of financial support for graduate students can have a significant impact on the direction and development of the plan. In general, attempts are made to increase the number of students, particularly minority, female, nontraditional, out-of-state, international, and graduate students.

Educational Programs—The focus and direction of the educational programs can be highly reflective of research efforts within an institution. Strategists often call for a systematic review of the curriculum, resulting in the discontinuation of marginal or ineffective programs and the consolidation of overlapping areas of study. There is a demand for increased interdisciplinary and interinstitutional activity, as well as an increased level of interaction with the community colleges.

Service—The strategic plans include references to the dissemination of knowledge to the state and the surrounding community, the accountability and obligation of the institution to the public, and the institutional function of creating solutions to problems.

Finance—Another factor that can have a major impact on the overall strategic planning for research, and that also directly impacts many of the other internal factors, is the financial aspect. To increase the funding base for research, strategists identify the need for more active relationships with public and private sectors to attract funding for research. But an assessment also must be made of the institutional priorities related to research; they must be balanced with the available resources, and when necessary, a reallocation of available resources must be made. The recovery and subsequent use of indirect costs also should be evaluated.

Resources, Equipment, and Facilities—The plans often include discussions related to the resources, equipment, and facilities available for the conduct of research. Consideration is given to the quality of the library, computer, and telecommunication resources that are available for the conduct of research. In addition, the physical condition and limitations of the infrastructure are evaluated, as is the cost effectiveness of renovation versus new construction. Consideration is also given to modernization, maintenance, the possibility of shared facilities equipment among disciplines, acquisition and expansion without build-up of excess capacity, leasing rather than purchase, and cost factors related to on-campus versus off-campus facilities.

Organizational Components—The plans often include consideration of organizational structures for the institution including single- versus multi-campus, as well as the development of research institutes and centers within the institution.

Review and Evaluation Process

Slightly less than half (44%) of the institutions that responded to the 1989 survey that currently have strategic research plans indicated that those plans are updated on an annual basis. Other institutions tend to review their plans on a less frequent, but specified basis. These reviews are completed at least once every five years. On the average, institutions that update their plans at specific time intervals do so every 1.9 years. However, not all institutions have such a formal review process. Whereas some institutions indicated that their plans are being updated continuously (9%), others either did not have a specified time period established for this review process or noted that their plans are updated on an "as needed" basis (17%).

In most cases, an official in the upper administration of the institution is ultimately responsible for the institution's strategic plan. That official is typically a vice-provost or vice-president for research (33%), some other vice-president (planning, academic affairs, etc.—22%), or a provost (22%).

The Characteristics
of the Strategic Planning Document

Executive Summaries

Almost all of the strategic plans reviewed began with some type of an executive summary, preamble or introduction. These sections tended to be relatively short, typically less than two pages. An exception was Texas A&M's executive summary, a separate document in excess of sixty pages that has been updated annually.

One of the primary components of the executive summary is to identify the purpose of the strategic plan. It typically indicates that the plan is to be used as a general guide for the future development of the institution, either in maintaining its existing direction or in pursuit of a new course of action. Oregon State University identifies its "Preparing for the Future" as "a guide for change and a call to action" (1987, 4). An institution's executive summary may reaffirm its existing commitments, or it may indicate a desire and intention toward change and growth as it moves from a teaching to a research institution.

The executive summary also may identify the plan as a presentation of a specific course of action necessary in order to achieve the institutional direction. This identification of a course of action often is related to a series of briefly defined, broad objectives that the institution plans to accomplish within a specified period of time. The executive summary for the Oregon Graduate Center's (1987) strategic plan identifies strategic positions that the institution plans to achieve in a five-year period within the following aspects of the institution's operation: academic excellence, board of trustees-faculty working relationship, faculty career enhancement, financial health, institutional management, physical facilities, federal support of research, industrial education and research, and local and national institutional recognition.

Mission Statement

Strategic plans tend to include in the institutional mission several generalized commitments to teaching, research, and service, and to address the desire to use the plan as a mechanism to guide the development and improvement of the institution's national and international reputations. Many of the institutions' plans, particularly those of the state and land-grant institutions, indicate an institutional commitment to meeting the educational, societal, and economic needs of the state in which they are located.

In addition to these generic statements of mission, there is often an attempt to develop missions that highlight the uniqueness of the particular institution. The University of Hawaii sees itself as a link between the East and the West and recognizes that "its special mission is to provide the leadership necessary to assure that Hawaii and its people are full participants in the Pacific arena" (1984, 5). Loyola University, a Jesuit Catholic University, exists to "preserve, extend, and transmit knowledge and to deepen understanding of the human person, the universe, and God. Loyola values freedom of inquiry, the pursuit of truth, and care for others, especially the young, the poor, and the sick" (1989, v). The University of Medicine and Dentistry of New Jersey is a major provider of health profession education in New Jersey, but also sees the mitigation of "the health problems of the state's most disadvantaged populations" as a part of its mission (1989, 3).

Motivating Factors and Statement of Value of Strategic Planning

Perhaps one of the most succinct discussions of a motivating factor for the development of a strategic plan is presented by a series of questions in

the preamble to the University of Oklahoma's *Strategy for Excellence.*
"Where are we now? . . . Where do we want to be and how, realistically,
might we get there?" (1988, 4). The plan goes on to note that "events of the
last decade at the University of Oklahoma brought home the message that
the only certainty for higher education during the last years of the twentieth
century is uncertainty" (1988, 4).

This level of uncertainty, precipitated by changes in external and internal
environmental factors, can be a major motivating factor in an institution's
decision to develop a strategic plan. The University of Oklahoma noted
that "no university can afford to drift into so uncertain a future. Planning is
essential. OU must set priorities, focus resources, and seize opportunities
as they arise" (1988, 4). Michigan State University noted that its strategic
plan is "an effort to address intentionally the changes that will be powerful
influences on the future of this University" (1989, i).

A desire to be able to restore, replace, or otherwise deal with drops in
funding from specific external sources is one of the areas of uncertainty
that is identified in many of the plans. Declines in resources can have the
compound effect of negatively impacting the level of faculty salaries and
the upkeep of facilities and equipment, both of which can lead to a departure of, and an inability to attract, desirable faculty and staff.

The concept of change can be a positive influence on the institution.
Colorado State University noted that "change is fundamental to the vitality
and creativity of any university" (1989), and the University of Oklahoma
pointed to the opportunities that will arise as "technological and societal
change inevitably stimulates initiatives in the nation's leading universities"
(1988, 4). In 1984, the University of Hawaii projected that "the next ten
years will be one of rapid and, perhaps, radical change. It is assumed that
the University and State will respond to that change in active and creative
ways" (1984, 7).

The progress and direction supplied through strategic planning can help
to alleviate the uncertainty associated with change, and positively impact
the institution. Strategic plans are identified as guides for change and a call
to action. Texas A&M University (1988, vi) noted that its earlier *Five Year
Plan 1985-1990* "plus the board of regent's endorsement of the 'Commitment to Texas,' facilitated tremendous progress in high-technology research and departmental programs. These strategies have also served as the
catalyst to develop greater interdisciplinary and intercollegiate research
programs." The drafters of the A&M plan explained in some detail how the
previous strategies brought about the upgrading and introduction of new
laboratory facilities, and the updating of the way students participate in
numerous educational and research activities.

Spotlighting the Uniqueness of the Institution

As more and more universities become involved in increasing their levels of externally funded research, these institutions are finding it necessary to point to their areas of uniqueness to attract faculty, students, and funding. It is no longer sufficient to note that the institution participates in research. The level and focus of the research are important, as are many other aspects of the institution's external and internal environments.

Carnegie Mellon pointed out that its size allows it to offer many of the educational advantages of a small liberal arts college, while its research emphasis "provides students with the stimulating atmosphere of a major research university. With the combination of these two attributes, coupled with excellent and innovative educational programs, Carnegie Mellon has carved out a successful niche in the higher education arena" (1988, 3). The University of Hawaii noted that as "the only public higher education institution within a 2,400 miles radius, the University has a unique responsibility to provide quality higher education and post-secondary vocational and technical training opportunities for all qualified residents of the State" (1984, 7). In addition to its service to the state, the University of Hawaii added that its "mission extends in its areas of strength into the Pacific and Asia and to the intellectual communities of the world" (1984, 7).

The strategic plans often identified the general strengths and weaknesses of the institution. Specific strengths and weaknesses were identified when the strategic plans included sections dealing with the individual colleges within an institution. Some of the general institutional strengths and weaknesses that were identified in the plans follow. It should be kept in mind that what is viewed as a strength for one institution may be seen as a weakness for another institution, or that two institutions may indicate strengths that appear to be at opposing ends of a continuum. This difference in attitude is not due to a lack of earnestness or comprehension by any one institution, but rather due to differences in philosophies and missions among institutions.

Institutional Strengths

Programs—clear and precise professional programs; broad scope.
Faculty—dedicated and committed.
Students—high quality, dedicated, and committed.
Reputation—graduates that have become visible leaders in their professions; growing strength and recognition of educational and research programs.
Philosophy—institution guided by a single philosophy.

Interdisciplinary Opportunities—available for the education of all disciplines.

Planning—used to define institutional mission and goals; enables response to innovation while maintaining a commitment to fundamentals and basics; built on current and selectively developed strengths.

Support—institutional; administrative; political support by the state's governor; high levels of financial support for research; essential nature of institution's services to the state's population; collaboration with external public and private organizations.

Organization—geographic advantages of multiple campus locations in densely populated areas.

External Environment—sole public institution of higher education; quality of life; natural environment; multicultural peoples and attitudes.

Institutional Weaknesses

Scope—narrowness that could result in a tendency toward vocationalism.

Funding—inadequate amount of external funding necessary to achieve desired levels of research; inadequate funding available for development of space and supporting services necessary to keep pace with growth in research.

Location—distance from east and west coast is seen as a disadvantage in attracting and retaining faculty, particularly in the artistic and high technology fields.

Campus Organization—need for contiguous space for departmental activities.

Interdisciplinary Activities—inability to increase the level of educational and research interdisciplinary interaction among departments.

Support—declining governmental support; political pressures at state, county, municipal, and community levels.

Competition—other educational institutions; other service providers.

Discussion of Criteria for
Determining Research Program Priorities

One of Colorado State University's goals was to "continue to build and to maintain quality teaching and research programs, recognizing that some programs should achieve national and international reputations for excellence" (1989, 1).

Institutions recognize that they cannot expect to achieve a level of research excellence within every discipline. They realize that the requisite resources are not available for this level of development, and the competition among institutions is too great for any one institution to presume that it can be the leader in every area of knowledge. To accommodate these factors and still maintain a level of excellence, institutions have focused their efforts into selected areas of study. As an example, Oklahoma State University noted that it

> has the potential to lead the nation in research in selected disciplinary and interdisciplinary areas. But to realize that potential, the University must not try to be all things to all disciplines; it must focus its resources carefully and monitor its programs, remaining ever ready to augment support for a program that faculty have developed into a likely national leader . . . and through resource allocations we must support the efforts of faculty whose research programs are demonstrably or potentially strong (1988, 6).

This inability to excel in all areas is evident at the departmental level as well as at the institutional level. Temple University acknowledged the inability of departments to excel in all areas when it noted that the departments that are selected for strengthening "will not be able to achieve national and international status in all sub-fields of their disciplines. Our goal is to achieve excellence in a reasonable number and variety of departments by developing selected sub-fields of those disciplines" (1986, 16).

Michigan State University indicated that its research program priorities will build upon current and selectively developed strengths, and later noted that in reassessing its priorities, it is necessary to "continue to direct careful attention to the identification, preservation, and extension of areas of institutional strengths" (1989, iv). The institution's planning, which includes an analysis of the relative purposes and roles of areas of research within the university in addition to relative positions within national peer groups, relies on unit-level self-assessment with a review by the institution's upper administration.

Texas A&M University developed a list of high-priority research areas that have "the potential to make significant contributions to natural resources management, the health and welfare of Texas citizens, and the expansion and diversification of the Texas economy" (1988, 56). Temple University set a goal of becoming a top research institution in the United States within ten years by "maintaining the strong research programs which presently exist, establishing University research centers in several areas where we have realistic expectations of excelling, and by strengthening existing departments" (1986, 16).

However, the ability of institutions to attain excellence in specific research areas is highly impacted by the willingness of external sources to fund research in those areas. Funding situations for particular research areas do have a tendency to fluctuate over time. Carnegie Mellon noted its disappointment that funding by external sources has become more goal directed when it stated that "it seems that funding agencies are particularly interested in short term results and deliverables. The danger exists that high-risk research and research with long-range goals will not be suffi-ciently funded. It has been very difficult to make government and industry aware of this situation" (1988, 35).

Despite the fact that the strategic plans often identify the institution's need to prioritize, focus, and develop research activities in specific areas, there is relatively little discussion on how these research priorities will be set. Other than some cursory comments about allowing faculty input in the process, emphasizing those research programs that are currently the strongest (typically those bringing in the most external funding), and developing those research programs that will in return promote the economy of the state, there is little detailed discussion within the planning documents that specifically delineates how those research priorities are es-tablished.

Identification of Goals and Objectives to be Pursued

The development of a strategic plan for research includes the estab-lishment of goals that, when met, will help to advance an institution's re-search efforts. The strategic plans that were reviewed typically included goals for a variety of areas, including research. Some of the goals set by the institutions that relate specifically to the institutions' research activities in-clude the following.

1. An enhancement of the quality and an increase in the quantity of scholarship and creative activity.
2. An increase in the level of research funding to be obtained from government, foun-dations, and industry within a specified time period.
3. The establishment of, or an increase in the level of funding for, internal research support mechanisms.
4. The development or expansion of incentives that will entice faculty to become more involved in the research activity.
5. The development of the administrative services support structure to assist faculty in the conduct of research.
6. The establishment of centers to market technology for industrial research, consult-ing and as a means of promoting an advanced technology image.
7. The establishment of research appointments such as post-doctoral fellowships, re-search professorships, endowed chairs, and research chairs.
8. The fostering of interdisciplinary and intercollegiate research.
9. An increase in the interaction of faculty with professional and scholarly com-munities outside the university.
10. An increase and improvement of the facilities, equipment, materials, library, and computing services used for research.
11. An emphasis on the recruitment of research faculty and graduate students.
12. An increase in the level of financial aid and in the number of fellowships, traineeships and research assistantships for graduate students.

Interdisciplinary Efforts

As research becomes more complex, the ability for any one person to be familiar with all aspects of a research problem diminishes. Institutions are finding it increasingly necessary to engage in interdisciplinary and intercollegiate research to address properly all components of the research problem. Unfortunately, institutions typically have found this interdisciplinary or intercollegiate interaction lacking or relatively insignificant in the past, and slow to develop. Oregon State University characterized the need for interdisciplinary research and lack of institutional change to meet this need when it noted that:

> Universities are agents of change, but the world invariably changes faster than universities. Discoveries, new technologies, and ideas create alternatives for meeting societal needs. They generate new bodies of knowledge. Many significant advances occur in interdisciplinary areas of inquiry that transcend traditional fields of study at universities (1987, 30).

There are constraints that have tended to inhibit the desired and needed interdisciplinary interactions. Faculty evaluation and reward systems are based on the traditional discipline-based organizational structure. Considerably more time and effort frequently is required when there is interaction between programs. Many times, the administrative structure and policies of the institution are not conducive to interdisciplinary cooperation.

At one point in its planning sessions, Temple University considered a massive restructuring of the present academic organization of fourteen independent degree-granting schools and colleges into three large colleges or divisions in an effort to achieve university-wide priorities and goals without the many "constraints and 'territorial barriers' inherent in virtually any system of schools and colleges" (1986, 21). It was decided to retain the current organization and attempt to achieve the desired flexibility "through cross-departmental, cross-collegial activities and commitment to the academic goals of the institution, as well as those of the individual school" (1986, 21).

Oregon State University suggested that "outstanding universities find ways to accelerate progress by encouraging interdisciplinary studies and research among students and faculties who have different interests and expertise" (1987, 30). Efforts are being made to foster the desired interaction through the development of new organizational structures, such as the establishment of multidisciplinary research centers, that will foster interdisciplinary research programs.

Additional actions proposed by institutions to increase the level of interdisciplinary activity include:

1. Consideration of the need to strengthen interdisciplinary activities in the evaluation and modification of the existing academic structure, and development of new organizational structures.
2. Stimulation and reward of interdisciplinary efforts through: the recognition of interdisciplinary efforts in promotion, tenure, and salary adjustments; and an emphasis on interdisciplinary scholarship in the hiring of departmental chairs, creation of endowed chairs, awarding of distinguished professorships, and selection of program development leadership.
3. Establishment of administrative policies that encourage interdisciplinary cooperation, including: clarification of personnel policies related to joint appointments, cross listing of cotaught courses, and provision of budget support for interdisciplinary graduate programs.
4. Establishment of new graduate programs in evolving interdisciplinary fields.
5. Development of ways to increase space utilization in a flexible way.
6. Provision of university support for external proposals that request long-term support for large-scale interdisciplinary research programs.
7. Establishment of seed grants to initiate interdisciplinary research activities.

Organized Research Units (ORUs)

One of the mechanisms that has been successful in stimulating and advancing interdisciplinary research efforts has been the development of new organizational structures within institutions of higher education. The traditional institutional organization structured strictly on the basis of academic disciplines has had a tendency to narrow the focus of research activity to one field of study. The development of ORUs has increased the cooperative efforts among the disciplines as they attempt jointly to solve a problem, rather than approaching the problem from a single disciplinary direction.

Temple University noted that:

> Meaningful research crosses the boundaries of traditional disciplines. Beyond this obvious point, at Temple not every existing discipline can become self-sufficient across the discipline lines in both equipment and faculty expertise. The reason is that the University cannot bear the operating costs needed to bring such a critical mass to each virtually autonomous department. For too long, however, we have operated as though we could afford such vertical baronies. That day is over. For these reasons, we are establishing University-wide Centers, which bring together persons and equipment from several disciplines, departments and schools. (1986, 18)

The use of ORUs by institutions of higher education is becoming more prevalent. Expenditures by the intercollege research programs at Penn State increased from less than $10 million in 1983-84 to approximately $16 million in 1987-88. By 1987-88, Penn State had eighty-three faculty with joint appointments between an intercollege research program and a tenuring unit, and an additional ninety-eight faculty associated with an intercollege research program on a temporary basis. These programs also provided financial support for 274 graduate students. A total of 996 individuals were supported wholly or partially on intercollege research program budgets during 1987-88.

Carnegie Mellon had more than forty recognized research centers and institutes established to conduct research in focused areas of expertise, ranging from high technology to education to basic industry to management to the arts. Some of the strengths that were noted for three of their largest centers and institutes included: the interdisciplinary nature of project activities; strong technical capabilities due to access to academic research through the faculty consultants; the broad base of support received as a result of the nature and immediacy of the problems investigated; and the ability to recruit top-quality personnel as a result of the reputation of the units and national scope of the work that is conducted.

At the same time, the current weaknesses of these units had been recognized, and strategies had been developed at Carnegie Mellon to alleviate these weaknesses. Additional efforts will be made to increase interaction and decrease the number of one-on-one type of research projects. These efforts will include increased interdisciplinary interaction, and increased levels of participation by industry beyond the contribution of funding to "address real world problems and solutions" (1988, 135). Another problem that Carnegie Mellon had experienced was the lack of discretionary funds when a center or institute was funded entirely by research grants and contract. It was suggested that "this weakens the flexibility of the Institute to react to problems and issues it feels are important to the United States" (1988, 135).

Seek Partnerships with Public and Private Sector

Universities are including in their strategic plans mechanisms through which their faculty can seek public and private partnerships through collaborations with industry and national laboratories. Interaction between industry and ORUs is particularly encouraged. This allows for an increased interaction of faculty with professional and scholarly communities outside the university, expands the faculty's working relationship with the private sector, and serves the state's industries and businesses. Mechanisms developed to foster these partnerships include the clarification of contract and consulting policies to encourage faculty participation with the private sector, and the encouragement of departments to appoint scientists from the private sector to courtesy faculty appointments.

Economic Development

Institutions of government and higher education realize the important role that research can play in the economic development of the state, and are developing stronger correlations between the universities' research arm and the business community. The states are making more direct demands on the universities to take on a higher level of responsibility for the state's economic development. As an example, the state of Oklahoma included in its recently adopted Five-Year Economic Development plan for Oklahoma a call to the University of Oklahoma to augment its research faculty and to increase federal research-related expenditures on external grants and contracts as one mechanism to assist in that state's economic development (1988, 6).

Institutions of higher education also are realizing their responsibility for the economic development of the region in which they are located. Penn State saw its institutional commitment to economic development as an "increasingly important, politically sensitive University mission" (1988, 27). Carnegie Mellon noted that its continued research efforts in the area of computing is not only to build upon its leadership role in this area, but also to "provide major impetus to the economic transformation of the region" (1988, 5). Texas A&M pointed out that the "rapid internationalization of the economy requires increased attention to the global environment for Texas agriculture, business, and industry" (1988, ix), and included as one of its priorities a continuation of research and service programs that will help to diversify the state's economy and allow it to become competitive in the international markets.

Land-grant institutions have long felt this responsibility for the state's economic development, and are placing additional emphasis in this area. Penn State noted in its strategic plan that:

> Technical assistance and economic development have long been missions of land grant universities. The recent decline in the competitiveness of U. S. industry, and its implications for our national security and standard of living, have resulted in heightened societal emphasis on these university missions. In this context, the Board of Trustees . . . directed the University to undertake an eight-point program initiative to increase and strengthen the contributions of the University to the economic development of the Commonwealth of Pennsylvania. Given these developments, there is a significant opportunity for the University to accelerate transfer of knowledge and technology and thereby to develop expanded dimensions of public service (1988, 26).

One mechanism through which institutions of higher education plan to assist in the economic development of their region is to provide technical and economic development assistance to the business community. Penn State noted the necessity of an organization with the specific purpose of state technical assistance and economic development as that institution strives "to fulfill the industrial extension aspects of its land grant mission in a highly visible, substantive fashion" (1988, 28). The strategic plan goes on to indicate that this type of transfer of knowledge from universities to the private sector "has served to educate the Pennsylvania business community in technologies which make them more competitive in the national and international marketplaces" (1988, 28). Penn State also proposed in its strategic plan that technical and economic development specialists be placed at locations throughout the state to educate key people in the private sector of the potential uses of new technologies which could make their companies more competitive (1988, 27).

Small-business development centers are being established to assist faculty and other entrepreneurs in the development or expansion of small-business ventures. These centers make use of faculty and students in the evaluation of business ventures, and focus on the mechanics of capital formation and setting up small businesses.

In addition to this provision of technical assistance to businesses, institutions of higher education also realize the importance of accelerated technology transfer as a key component in their capacity as a facilitator of economic development. Penn State suggested that "the enhancement of the Intellectual Property Office, with functions and resources commensurate with Penn State's status as a leading research university, is a key aspect of the . . . technology transfer strategy" (1988, 28). The following are listed as principal functions:

1. As technology is disclosed to faculty, find licensees willing to underwrite the cost of patent filing and R&D required to bring concepts to the commercialization stage.
2. Encourage faculty to disclose concepts with commercial potential.
3. Coordinate disclosure/patent management.
4. Develop industry-university research projects based on faculty inventor 'prior art.'
5. Participate in the negotiation of research contracts with industrial sponsors.

International Programs and Research

In contrast to their commitment to the economic development of their state and local communities, institutions of higher education are also expanding their scope of influence by becoming more involved in research with an international focus, and developing campuses and programs in other countries. Texas A&M noted that there is a need to increase the amount of attention institutions of higher education give to the global environment as a result of the impact that the rapid internationalization of the economy has had on local businesses and industries. This expanded scope of influence was reflected by Oregon State University when it suggested that it "reflects the trend of global interdependence in serving not only the people of Oregon but the people of the world" (1987, 22). The University of Hawaii sees a unique opportunity to serve as a bridge between the East and the West by playing a direct role in developing contacts within that region and in serving as a center for technical and cultural interchange.

But the institutions caution that these international activities need to be efficiently and effectively managed and appropriately focused. Temple University, which has campuses and programs in a dozen countries, noted that they have "established prominent programs in the international areas, but the left hand often does not know what the right hand is doing. We must manage this enterprise much more efficiently. With the proper planning and organization, we are capable of having a much greater impact" (1986, 20). Oregon State University also identified the need to focus its activities within its efforts to broaden the institution's international perspective. The University of Hawaii suggested that such a "focused effort will strengthen the University's position as one of the leading research institutions in the nation on Pacific/Asian matters and will enable the University to become the research, training, and cultural center of the Pacific basin" (1984, 17).

Attempts are being made to deal with the potential problems of inefficient and ineffective organization and lack of focus in international activities. The provost at Temple conducted a comprehensive study of the international and foreign activities, programs and personnel at that institution, and identified a need to have a central clearing-house function "to avoid unnecessary duplication among departments or Colleges, and to marshal resources to reach the critical mass needed to make a difference" (1986, 26).

Some of the activities that the institutions proposed for further development of international programs and research include:

1. Expand and coordinate collaborative research opportunities between the institution and institutions in other countries.
2. Support proposals that will increase faculty scholarly activities outside the United States.
3. Expand the development of cooperative research activities, and student and faculty exchange programs, particularly in African and Latin American countries.
4. Insist on reciprocity in the development of international programs to ensure that American students also have the benefit of studying abroad.
5. Increase enrollment at overseas campuses.

College Planning

In some instances, the strategic plans included in the 1989 Survey contain a section on strategic planning at the college level. Goals for each college are outlined, and commitments to particular philosophies, standards and directions are summarized. As noted by Temple University, these college plans are typically "developed in the spirit of and within the constraints set by the University plan" (1986, 21).

Specific research strengths and weaknesses are typically identified for the colleges, as are goals and objectives. Most seem to focus on clarity and precision in program definition, on faculty and student dedication to existing program thrusts, and on commitment to future program plans. The need for further development of graduate programs to attain the status of a major research university is identified. The standards for admission of students to graduate programs and the reputation generated by the significant roles played by graduates in attaining leadership positions in their professions are common themes in college plans.

The college plans also point out the advantages of the total context of college resources and emphasize the graduate specializations and unique research facilities under their authority. The administrative arrangements for housing units with very diverse goals under one roof or in several locations in the region, and for continuing to guide them by a philosophy that promotes the creation of strong joint graduate and cooperative research programs are recurring emphases in these plans. College plans stress the interdisciplinary nature of their programs and highlight specific opportunities for joint research.

The college plan is frequently used to state a college philosophy that contends that strategic planning offsets a drift toward narrowness and sponsor domination. It was apparent from the context of many of the college plans that the college leaders were using the strategic plan to create in their faculty and administration an awareness of the value of defining further the goals of the college and the objectives of the departments and ORUs. They seem to think that such refinements enable the college to respond to sponsor needs while maintaining a firm commitment to fundamental beliefs and basic principles.

A discussion of the strength or lack of university support for specific programs are frequently included in this section. Problems of declining undergraduate and graduate credit-hour generation, a lack of influx of new faculty, and excessively high percentages of tenured faculty are noted by some of the colleges. In contrast, other colleges, often within the same institution, are experiencing tremendous growth in undergraduate and graduate credit-hour generation, and are experiencing difficulty in attracting and retaining faculty.

Resource requirements, including the need for a reallocation of existing resources and for the commitment of additional resources is identified. Plans to bring in new programs, to phase-out obsolete programs, and to restructure and reorganize existing programs are also prominent components of the college plans.

Colleges of Arts and Sciences typically are viewed as the providers of a university-wide core curriculum. However, from a research perspective, there is often a tendency on the part of those areas outside of the hard sciences, engineering, and medicine to comment on the lack of external funding equal to that received by science and technology. In addition, liberal arts and fine arts schools often note the disorganization of the professions they serve and the failure of their professional practicing colleagues to recognize the need for new ideas that can be generated by academicians.

The hard sciences, engineering, and medicine acknowledge the significant amount of time and effort the faculty devote to acquiring research funds and to the conduct of research. The faculty teaching-research workload is of concern, and the shortage of well-equipped space and the insufficient support of the research infrastructure are often cited as weaknesses for these colleges.

Human Resources

Some institutional strategic plans included projections for the number of faculty, graduate, and undergraduate students, and support- and administrative-unit personnel. The growth of the faculty and staff over the past decade in relationship to the growth of the institution in enrollment and research is discussed in several of the strategic plans.

The growth in the number of research support personnel in comparison to the growth in the number of faculty is another factor considered in many plans. Carnegie Mellon University's (1988, 8) comparison of the growth in support personnel to faculty is a particularly good example of the past and projected changes in this ratio (see Figure 4.4). The accompanying narratives usually analyze the past and projected growth in nonfaculty positions in the professional research and technical-paraprofessional staff positions in response to growths in the volume of research.

Institutional planners realize that for a strategic plan to be successful, a significant commitment must be made to the faculty, students, and staff who are instrumental in achieving the goals outlined in the plan. It is suggested that creative research requires attention to the development of a scholarly and physically supportive campus environment which "blends stability and change and provides intellectual stimulation" (Temple University, 1986, 10). The University of Oklahoma's plan noted that to achieve excellence, policies and programs must "support professional development, preserve cultural diversity, and encourage and reward optimum performance" (1988, 18).

Supportive Campus Environment—Scholarly Support. Several of the plans stress the importance of the development of an intellectual climate that encourages both professional and social interaction among faculty, staff and students. The overall aging of the current faculty is often identified, and the large number of retirements in the near future is seen as an opportunity for the institutions for bring in new faculty—with either established reputations or exceptional promise— who will bring new ideas to the campus. At the same time, it is proposed that systems be developed to

Full-Time Staff and Tenured and Tenured-Stream Faculty
Fiscal Years 1979 to 1988*-1989 to 2000 Projected

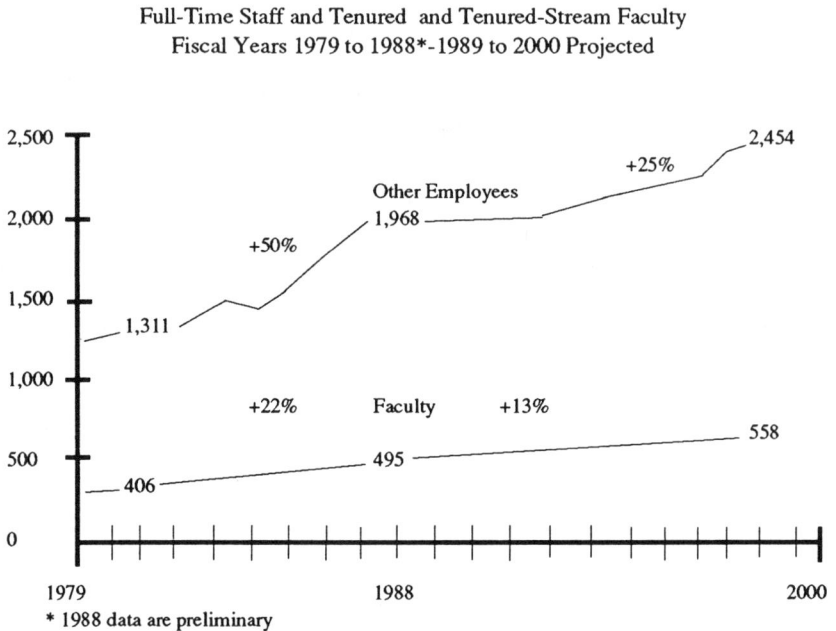

Figure 4.4. Actual and Projected Growth of Full-Time Staff and Faculty at Carnegie Mellon University (Carnegie Mellon University, 1988).

interview departing faculty to obtain their suggestions, criticisms, and recommendations, which can be considered in institutional decision making. The need to develop supportive institutional policies and programs and to remove obstacles to the conduct of research is also identified. Programs suggested for development include: the establishment of mentor-protege systems, role models, and support groups; state, national, and international faculty exchange and visiting scholars programs; and the provision of graduate assistants, post-doctoral scholars, and international scholars to work with faculty members. It is suggested the procedures for awarding tenure and promotion be reviewed, that award and recognition programs be developed or expanded, and that more endowed chairs and distinguished professorships be established. In addition, it is suggested that the strengths and interests of faculty and staff be taken into account in the apportionment of responsibilities within a unit.

Fiscal and Physical Support—The need to provide faculty with the appropriate fiscal and physical support for the conduct of research is identified in the plans. One of the most frequently cited fiscal factors is the need to provide competitive and equitable salaries and benefits to attract and retain quality faculty. Some of the benefits that are mentioned include:

retirement, faculty housing assistance programs, maternity leave policies, and evaluation of the access of child care. The need to increase the amount of graduate financial aid and assistantships is identified. The development of equitable workload assignments for faculty and staff also is discussed. It is suggested that new faculty be provided with start-up money to initiate their research, seed money be available to all faculty to initiate and develop new research, and that funding be provided for faculty to attend national and international conferences. To assist faculty in the conduct of their research, it is suggested that the proper physical support be provided. Some of the physical items of support that are presented in the plans include: a strengthened research infrastructure; up-to-date equipment; regularly maintained offices, classrooms, and laboratories; increased library holdings and services; clerical support; and an attractive and safe campus.

Encourage and Reward Optimum Performance—It often is suggested that institutional support of the faculty needs to go beyond the provision of academic, fiscal, and physical support. Methods of encouraging and rewarding optimum performance in the conduct of research often are suggested. Temple University noted that: "Scholarship and research should also be rewarded and encouraged through direct incentives to seek research grants, including a policy of grant overhead distribution and a more attractive study leave policy" (1986, 10). Other methods that are suggested include: develop faculty and staff incentive plans to recruit and retain high quality personnel; increase the awards for excellence in research and graduate education; institute policies for compensation and evaluation that recognize involvement in interdisciplinary programs for those persons who want to extend their interests beyond traditional disciplinary programs; and create awards to recognize staff excellence.

Professional Development—The need to encourage and provide opportunities for continued education and professional development for faculty and staff is identified at several institutions. Before a professional development program is developed, it is suggested that a needs assessment be conducted. This will enable the programs to take into account existing areas of desired and needed professional development, as well as identify areas of expertise among faculty and staff that can be incorporated into the development programs.

In addition to faculty seminar programs in subject-specific areas related to research, it also is suggested that faculty and staff development opportunities be provided regarding the use of campus resources, organizational participation and management skills.

Cultural Diversity—Some of the colleges located at a distance from the artistic and technological centers of the east and west coasts found it difficult to attract and retain faculty and research support personnel who wanted frequent face-to-face interaction with professional colleagues in proximate universities and industry, and who liked the ambience of urban areas. As a result of this need, several universities mention their cooperative agreements for the development of the cultural and educational institutions outside, but near the university. Other institutions chose to assume the social and cultural responsibility of making their own contributions to the cultural life of the area through the provision of art galleries, museums, theater productions, and musical programs. It also is suggested that the intellectual and cultural environment within an institution can be diversified through an expansion of the geographic area from which faculty, staff, and students are obtained. The recruitment of minorities and women, particularly in the sciences and engineering, often is cited as an area of diversification that is being pursued within the institutions.

Upgrade of Library-Information Resources

The need and importance of a quality library system within institutions of higher education to support properly the faculty in their research endeavors is recognized. Financial problems in the late 1970s and early 1980s often resulted in less than appropriate maintenance of the library collections. In order to better meet the needs of the research faculty, strategic plans often identify the need for the conversion of library card catalog systems to computerized systems; the development and expansion of circulation capabilities with other libraries; surveys of users on a regular and recurring basis; the expansion of and the recognition of the need for changes in priorities for acquisitions; the expansion of space for faculty and student use; the employment of additional personnel and the extension of hours of service; an increase in the level of funding—including funding through external funding sources and capital campaigns—for acquisitions, services, and facility expansion; and the transformation of the library into an advanced electronic information service.

Facilities and Equipment

The growth in the number of research faculty and staff, increased enrollment of graduate students, and the dramatic addition of sponsored research projects over the past decades have placed significant demands on university physical plants. Many institutions report that modest increases in requirements for classroom space over the past ten years were accommodated through reduction of slack-in-classroom scheduling and construction of new classrooms. Office and lab space has grown rapidly in some institutions in the past decade.

However, new construction of laboratory space is expensive. Consequently, fiscal constraints often require that institutions plan to build new research facilities when funds become available from capital development funds. Many institutions are meeting current demands for expansion of research facilities through leasing of new facilities built by boards of city development or private business, and through renovation of facilities given to the university by industries that have closed plants. In most instances, physical plant expansion plans are cautious and seem to be contained in a framework that minimizes university exposure to a build-up of excess research space capacity. Stanford University, on the other hand, had launched a very ambitious plan for developing the Stanford Industrial Park and its campus research facilities. The need for contiguous space for departmental activities currently located on- and off-campus was cited frequently, and the need for appropriate maintenance of existing facilities also was seen as important.

The need to purchase, replace, upgrade, operate, and maintain the institutions' current research equipment also is identified. The failure to maintain properly equipment in the past has resulted in equipment that is now beyond repair. Other items have become obsolete and the need to secure state-of-the-art equipment for research faculty is identified. New projects also may require laboratories and offices that are appropriately equipped for the specific research activities. However, Temple University noted that "these difficulties are exacerbated by the high cost of research and teaching equipment and the lack of external funding (Commonwealth and federal) to assist the University in meeting these needs" (1986, 41). The efficient conduct of research is becoming more reliant on the use of computer facilities and equipment. Plans for future computing needs within the institution, including the decision to move into supercomputing, are being considered. There is often a desire to upgrade mainframe computing to state-of-the-art research capabilities, at a considerable financial investment. The financial needs for moving into supercomputing are particularly substantial. The provision of personal computers is also a factor within the plans.

Financial Planning to Achieve Objectives

Most of the strategies involved within the strategic plans for research in some way impact the financial component of the institution. If the strategic plan is to become more than a wish list that ends up on a shelf, then a significant amount of attention to the financial planning necessary to attain the desired goals will be required. Funding requirements must be successfully and sufficiently matched with funding sources. The University of Hawaii had established as one of its objectives the intent to strengthen the relationship between planning and budgeting. Texas A&M acknowledged that: "the planning that produced those ultimate goals involved a level of sophistication that speaks well for the capable individuals who worked together to achieve the results. The only problem with the plans proposed is that all worthy and reasonable goals cannot be supported from levels of funding expected to be available" (1988, 97). The goals were subsequently prioritized within Texas A&M's plan in such a manner that the goals of highest priority were more likely to be funded.

The budgeting and financial review processes often incorporate financial projections and identify planning assumptions for future increases in institutional revenues. Funding priorities are then established based on those assumptions. In some instances, the goals of the strategic plan cannot be met through the anticipated increases in funding, and as a result, the reallocation of resources are incorporated into the plan. Although the operating budget is a very important component of this entire process, capital budgets are receiving an increased amount of attention as the level of capital spending for buildings and equipment rises. There is also a growing movement from annual to long-term budget projections.

The future opportunities for continued and expanded funding from external sources is often analyzed. The goal of pursuing increased funding from private foundations, the federal and state governments and other countries is often identified. It is likely that an institution will experience a growth in external funds as proportionately more of its faculty becomes involved in externally funded research.

WORKS CITED

Carnegie Mellon University. (1988, February). *Goals and Strategic Plans*. Pittsburgh, PA.: Author.

Colorado State University. (1989, April). *The Vision of Colorado State University: Its Goals and Objectives*. Fort Collins, CO: Author.

Darling, John R., et.al. (1979). *Technical Report on the Middle Management Education Program-Egypt*. (USAID-NEC-1700). Carbondale, IL.: Southern Illinois University.

Davenport, D. (1990). A stitch in time. *Visions*. 2(4), 12-17.

Farleigh Dickinson University. (1988, October 1). *Farleigh Dickinson University Strategic Plan: 1989-1994*. Rutherford, N.J.: Author.

Gallaudet College. (1985, August). *Strategic Plan: Mission and Goals*. Washington, D.C.: Author.

Hensley, Oliver D. (1968). "A Study of Factors Related to the Acceptance and Adoption of a Cooperative Supplementary Educational Service Center." unpublished dissertation, Southern Illinois Univerity-Carbondale, February, 1968.

———. (1970). Regional long-range planning for public school desegregation. *State Department of Education Planning Workshop for School Desegregation*. Jackson, Mississippi. February 20, 1970.

———. (1979). New roles for the research administrator in the 80's: the university research administrator—the architect of the university's future. *SRA Looks to the 80's, Proceedings of The 13th Annual Meeting of Society of Research Administrators*, September 16-19, 1979. San Francisco, California.

———. (1981). *A Working Conference for Exploring Government/Industry/Labor/ Education Partnerships: A Strategy for Development.*

Lehigh University. (1988, October 7). *Lehigh University Plan: Progress and Priorities.* Bethlehem, PA: Author.

Loyola University of Chicago. (1989, February 6). *A Proposed Plan for Lake Shore and Water Tower Campuses: Loyola University of Chicago in the 1990's.* Chicago: Author.

Medical College of Hampton Roads. (1988, September 13). *Strategic Planning Project.* Norfolk, VA: Author.

Michigan State University. (1989, January 23). *The Refocusing, Rebalancing, and Refining of Michigan State University.* East Lansing, MI: Author.

National Science Foundation. (1982). *Academic Science R&D Funds Fiscal Year 1980.* Washington, D.C.: National Science Foundation, NSF 82-300.

Oregon Graduate Center. (1987, December). *The 1988-1992 Strategic Plan for the Oregon Graduate Center.* Beaverton, OR: Author.

Oregon State University. (1987, September). *Preparing for the Future: Strategic Planning at Oregon State University.* Eugene. OR.: Author.

Pennsylvania State University. (1988, November). *Strategic Planning Revision and Resource Request.* (City & State)

Schoppmeyer, Martin W., and Hensley, O. (1972). *A Total Systems Approach to Regional Planning. Boston Mountain Cooperative Annual Meeting. Fayetteville, Arkansas, November 15-16, 1972.*

Temple University. (1986, May 13). *The Academic Plan for Temple University.* Philadelphia, PA: Author.

Texas A&M University. (1988, June). *Long-Range Plan: 1990 - 1993.* College Station, TX: Author.

Texas A&M University. (1988, September). *Executive Summary: Long Range Planning into the 1990s.* College Station, TX.: Author.

Texas A&M University. (1989, July). *Executive Summary Update: Long Range Planning into the 1990s.* College Station, TX.: Author.

University of Hawaii. (1982, April 16). *Mission of the University of Hawaii.* Manoa, HA.: Author.

University of Hawaii. (1984, July). *A Strategy for Academic Quality:1985-95.* Manoa, HA.: Author.

University of Medicine and Dentistry of New Jersey. (1989, June). *Strategic Directions: 1990 - 1995.* New Brunswick, N.J.: Author.

University of Missouri. (1986, October 26). *Toward Excellence: The Next Decade of The University of Missouri.* Columbia, MO.: Author.

University of Oklahoma. (1988, December 8.) *Strategy for Excellence.* Norman, OK: Author.

CHAPTER FIVE

THE TECHNOLOGY FOR STRATEGIC PLANNING FOR UNIVERSITY RESEARCH

Oliver D. Hensley and Martin W. Schoppmeyer

THE CONCEPTUAL FRAMEWORKS

Research strategists should recognize that universities use at least three different types of planning to develop research. It is important to distinguish the three major types of planning for university research because they are quite different in scope and time frames. Most research planning can be subsumed under one of the following types of planning.

TYPES OF PLANNING	TIME FRAME	SCOPE
OPERATIONAL PLANNING	Day-by-Day—1 day-1 year *individual, daily activities are outlined according to operating periods.*	The Unit Plans the *Means* for Achieving Sponsor Goals. Planning and budget formats are set by the sponsor.
TACTICAL PLANNING	Semester-5 years—Plans for ORU's *Academic Time Frames. (Semesters or Quarters. Legislative Appropriation Periods. Accreditation Board Visits.*	The Unit Plans the *Means* and *Objectives* for Achieving Sponsor Goals. Planning and budget formats are set by the sponsor
STRATEGIC PLANNING	1-50 years—Institutional planning *Periods set the time* frames. Institution five-year plans.	The Unit Plans the *Means, Objectives, Goals* and *Strategies* for achieving the *Mission* of the university and sponsors. Planning and budget formats are set by the university.

A brief discussion of various types of planning and the structure and functions of the operating and planning systems will provide descriptions of the products generated by the processes. The success of the planning process can be evaluated by measuring the completion of certain products and phases and valuing them.

Operational, tactical, and strategic planning are complementary activities that must be integrated for any one type to be effective. Strategic planning could not be conducted without building on the operational and tactical planning of the institution. Similarly, operational and tactical planning are more difficult and less effective without strategic planning.

THE TERMINOLOGY FOR PLANNING

When we use the word "planning," we mean a detailed description of the future work being proposed by a particular university unit. The unit is described clearly by a purpose statements that defines the unit, its work, and its products. Understanding the differences among purpose statemnents and their heirarchical arrangement is essential to for strategic planners. The following section discusses the importance of writing clear purpose statements.

Purpose Statements—General Guides in University Strategy

Strategic planning requires very precise purpose statements to guide the work of the university. Every word in the plan should have a specific meaning that relates to the work to be done and to specific research administrative levels. Also, each system's terms should be reserved for use with a particular characteristic of the system. Without precise definitions and the proper matching of terms with the appropriate level of administration, vague and inappropriate statements will govern the processes of unit planning with a resultant product of unknown character. When such a situation exists, people in the greater system have difficulty understanding what is expected of them. Consequently, they can not prepare an agenda for the future. Without an agenda their units will fall short of anticipated accomplishments. An accumulation of inadequately achieved goals, or nonrecognition of successful goal completion, causes frustration for the researcher, university administrators, and sponsors. Too many unrecognized accomplishments or unrealized goals will bring about the failure of the research program and an erosion of unit and university reputation.

Unit Plans project the future responsibilities for work to be performed by the unit, by subsuming under clearly defined purposes: (1) exact statements of the functions of the unit, (2) statements of outcomes to be produced, (3) statements of the resources needed and their costs, and (4) criterion statements.

The planner should consider the following in the development of any plan:

Do the words used in the goal statements clearly define the purposes of the unit? (What is the unit to do.)

Do unit plans specify the products to be achieved in a specified time frame?

Can the desired outputs be stated so they can be measured according to specified levels of production and support?

Can the goals be stated so they can have estimated costs assigned to them?

Can the goals be stated so the principals in the research development process will understand the unit plan's place in the institution?

Use of Standard Terms are Essential in Goal Formulation in Strategic Planning

Everyone who is involved in the production of the strategic plan should have an understanding of standard terminology and should use common time frames and common formats for reporting of data. It is important in the formulating of institutional goals that the leaders of the planning teams adhere to institutional standards so they will present without ambiguity what it is they intend to achieve in the various units of the university.

Ostensibly, insistence on using a technology for planning statements and on ordering a hierarchy of purpose statement seem a bit fatuous. However, after a couple of rounds of reconciliation arguments, the merit of uniform, precise meaning becomes apparent. This section will provide specific terms for purpose statements that correspond to the traditional administrative levels in academe and discuss positions and technical documents that are associated with a particular level of planning.

Every administrative unit within the education and research enterprises was created for a particular purpose. There is an enabling act or a board policy that authorized the establishment and operation of the unit for definite purposes. Many of these purpose statements are buried in the archives of the institution and are known presently only to the intimates of the unit. As we shall see in the following sections, it is the duty of the planner to uncover these governing statements, to assess their current relevancy and then, if necessary, to reformulate them. These ordered statements form a *goals hierarchy* that correspond to the administrative units shown in Figure 5.7, which shows the major planning divisions within and outside the university. It also illustrates the relationship between purpose statements in a goals hierarchy for university research. This model will help us order our thoughts when discussing unit planning.

The first consideration in drafting a purpose statement for a research unit is to determine where the unit fits into the university administratively. Notice in Figure 5.7 the first dimension of the planning model is divided into three administrative divisions: academic-unit purpose statements, organized-research-unit (ORU) purpose statements, and joint-venture purpose statements.

These administrative divisions are necessary as they usually have a different legal status and different revenue sources. Such differences create a need for new organizational structures and management techniques. Therefore, when university strategists are developing unit plans, they must first consider the purpose, legal status, and revenue sources of the research unit. Secondly, they must consider the units relationship to the university. That relationship needs periodic assessment because over time the work of the unit evolves, perhaps to the point that the activities of the unit change enough that the unit purpose statement no longer coincides with the objective of the parent unit. When that happens, it may be advisable to change the relationship by the unit assuming more autonomy from the parent unit. These changes should be reflected by changed purpose statements. The purpose statement should define the research unit and the work it is to do.

When developing the unit plan, the strategist must ask, "How is the research unit presently administered?" and "Should it be administered differently?" Colleges, departments, and departmental research projects are administered by the vice-presidents for academic affairs, deans, department heads, and faculty as instructional activities. Institutes, centers, research groups, laboratories, and sponsored projects are often administered separately from the academic affairs under a vice-president for research. And, coalitions, consortia, cooperative programs, and research parks operate on common grounds administered under some type of cooperative agreement that requires joint funding arrangements.

The planning teams must assure that the administrative elements in the unit plan reflect the purpose and the functions of their units.

The University's Adoption of Planning Terminology

Some of the greatest arguments associated with the development of unit plans originate when the discussants do not understand the differences in management terminology and the purposes and functions associated with a particular type of research unit. In Chapter 2, the functional differences among institutions in the higher education enterprise were discussed and the distinguishing mission of the research university was stressed. All of the units within the research university have unique functions and purposes that contribute to the mission of the university. Strategic planning requires a hierarchy of purpose statements that allows planners to make finer and finer distinctions in work units and to manage smaller and smaller units that progressively narrows the scope of the work being done.

One of the problems of understanding the development of hierarchical statements of purpose, process, and need stems from the numerous organizational environments in which specific terms associated with statements of purpose have universal currency but different meanings, values, and relationships among the different universities, disciplines, and sponsors.

Academic and Military Use of the Terms "Mission," "Objective," and "Goal"

The Department of Defense was the forerunner in the race for improving the management of projects through the use of purpose statements. This is because the Department of Defense was an early architect in operations research and systems management. As with program evaluation and review techniques (PERT), and planning, programming, and budgeting systems (PPBS), the educational concepts and terms for purpose and process statements were derived from early military models, which were diffused from one federal agency to another, then transferred from Washington through federal projects to the university research administration offices, which then imposed the federal regulations, systems, and terms on all university research planning.

The United States Office of Education (USOE), the federal government's cognizant agency for the fiscal affairs of most universities, was quick to adopt the Defense Department management techniques but changed some terms. It seems well to compare the military usage of purpose statements with their operational management definitions and to match them with the research terminology shown in the hierarchy of purpose statements for the research university.

Mission Statements

Military practice has developed a goal hierarchy that is useful in managing large complex organizations and for this reason it has been adopted by management theorists in several disciplines. In the military frame of reference, every organization has, first of all, a *mission*. This is the broadest charge in the hierarchy of purpose statements. For instance, it means the mission of an army is to protect the state and its citizens. For an automobile manufacturer, it is to market a dependable, saleable car at a profit. For American research universities, it is to provide liberal and/or professional education opportunities for qualified students, to maintain an environment that encourages and facilitates research and to serve a variety of constituencies needing research and education services.

A mission statement is broad. It generates little if any disagreement whether within or outside the organization, and like Napoleon's ideal constitution, it is at best short and vague. This latter feature renders it almost useless for specific planning. A mission statement is usually so general and means so many different things to different people that it can only give broad direction rather than pointed impetus to planning. It is one of the highest goals, but in accordance with Aristotle's analysis, it should be broken down.

For research administrators to know what their institutions are, they must analyze first the mission statements established for their institutions by their governing bodies. The mission statements of American universities vary greatly. They have different responsibilities to perform because they are in different regional areas, they were established at different times, and their initial purposes were quite different.

The importance of the mission statement is recognized by the University of Hawaii, which published in 1982 a handsome brochure explaining the "Mission of the University of Hawaii." Inside the brochure, the "Mission" is boldly printed and its prime purpose clearly stated as "The fundamental mission of the University of Hawaii encompasses its broad responsibilities as the sole public institution of higher education in the state." It initially discusses the ways that the University is committed to the development of the state's greatest asset, its people, and recognizes that the university's responsibilities extend to the nation and to all humanity. The brochure then points out that more than any other American university, the University of Hawaii has a significant responsibility to serve as a bridge between East and West and to cultivate close human contact between Hawaii's people and their neighbors in Asia and the Pacific. The brochure states succinctly the outlook and the goals of the institution in the 1980s. This handsome brochure is an extremely useful document in the planning efforts of the University of Hawaii for it provides a concise picture of the university and a clear statement of where it is headed generally.

Goal Statements

For strategic planning in research universities, a "goal" may be considered as a specific breakdown of a mission statement in that it suggests at least a partial explanation of how the mission is to be accomplished. A "department aim" provides direction for the departments in a college, An "objective" describes the most specific activities and acts as part of the mode of accomplishment of the higher purpose statement. It should be apparent that descending from the summit of the hierarchy, purpose statements become more explicit, extend over a shorter duration, encompass narrower populations, and increase in number at each lower level.

In the early 1960s, many academicians were concerned that government-sponsored projects would present a great peril to the existing purposes of the institution by taking them in an unnatural direction. In this regard, President C. C. Furnas (State University of New York at Buffalo) (1967, 33) warned "The more serious hazards result from a lack of clear definition of purposes within the institutions and the lack of a strong administrative system dedicated to the fulfillment of those purposes." In a research university, colleges must have clear research goals. As Aristotle pointed out, goals are in a sense, "means."

The selection of research methodology and instructional techniques makes little difference in terms of a university's mission as they are tactical decisions made in terms of the specific problems at the operational level.

The formulation of goals do make a difference to the mission of the university because the different colleges will have different purposes and produce different products. Therefore, deans need to talk about the goals of the college and how these goals support the university mission. Goal formulation has to do with the purposes of the college and the success of its means, in reaching a greater purpose. Goals are properly determined at a lower level of management than a mission statement, but they must be developed in terms of the universal availability of materials, space, funds, and personnel within the institution or specific materials, services, and products must be paid for directly by outside sponsors. Somewhere within the institution, resources and products are measured and tied to goals and dollars. Deans are held accountable for resource management and goal achievement within their colleges.

Similarly, principal investigators should talk about objectives and their work should be measured on the outputs related to project objectives.

Statements of Objectives

Departments, programs, and laboratories have implicit objective statements that guide their work. For example, the Higher Education Program at Texas Tech University uses the following Implicit Objectives to explain their purpose.

The Higher Education Program is a community of scholars committed to excellence in

- the preparation and support of administrative leaders for higher education,
- the preparation of instructional leaders,
- the generation and support of research, and
- the delivery of public service in the field of higher education.

Subsumed under each of the implicit objectives are a series of explicit objectives for the faculty, students and program. Also, each higher education course and each research project has a specific set of explicit objectives which can be easily observed, measured, and costs attached to each explicit objective achievement. The faculty and students are held accountable for the achievement of the explicit objectives. This is the lowest level of administration in the university. It is at this level that specific products are delivered at a certain time for an agreed upon cost.

Certainly, the objective of the program or project should be in harmony with the college goals and the mission of the institution. If the project purposes are not the same as the mission of the institution, the administrators of the university probably will not allocate university resources to the project eventhough the principal investigator may be strongly committed to the work. A detailed discussion of writing objectives appears later in this chapter.

MODELING THE STRATEGIC PLANNING PROCESS

Recalling that strategic planning is mostly developing common under-standings of the future purposes of a unit with its chief partners and major constituencies, it is important for research administrators to model the strategic planning process and to use the technology necessary for such planning. Since the middle sixties, we have used and experimented with a total systems approach in several types of cooperative long-term planning for research and instructional development. We are convinced that al-though planners spend a great amount of their time informally developing cooperative agreements in others' offices, the planner must have a model in mind and the planning technology to manage the endless paper work that follows a handshake to cement a verbal agreement for the achievement of mutual goals over the long-term. And, although many units should be en-couraged to use a variety of techniques to a advance their planning, there must be a common model that guides large groups of people in joint efforts, that assures the exchange of compatible information in usable formats, and that reminds the planner of impending deadlines. Moreover, for the tech-nology to work there must be an adequate support staff who will develop and maintain the information systems. These diverse and multiple efforts require a synchronization of effort according to an agreed upon model of the planning process.

Presenting a conceptually valid model for strategic planning for univer-sity research is difficult because the generic process is extremely complex and as we saw in Chapter 4, the specific techniques vary widely among in-stitutions. Despite these difficulties, modeling the strategic planning process has great utility for the planner because basic models provide the framework for organizing the work associated with strategic planning.

Modeling the strategic planning process to be used by an organization is a fundamental technology for planners. Because strategic planning is such a complicated and continuing process, a planning model such as that shown in Figure 5.0 allows all who are involved to share a common frame of refer-ence for their planning activities and permits the planners to check their progress toward the development of an agreed upon series of outcomes.

We believe that strategic planning for university research can be modeled as occurring in the six phases shown in Figure 5.0. We include two phases that are seldom discussed by writers on the strategic planning process, but they are indispensable for strategists who intend to rely on the plan to bring about major changes. The first, "positioning the architects," stems from the authors' belief that university planning is totally dependent upon administrators getting the best minds to do the planning—anyone less, results in a second or third-rate plan. The latter phase, adopting the university strategic plan, comes from the belief that second and third generations of strategic planning can not continue without the adoption of the first generation agenda and without the faculty and sponsors seeing the implementation of their plans. The other phases "scanning the environment," "analyzing strategic options," "designing unit plans," and "accepting the university agenda" are rather standard fare in planning. We believe that the model shown in Figure 5.1 provides a valid, graphic representation of the strategic planning processes for university research. The accompanying narrative provides specific information supporting the model.

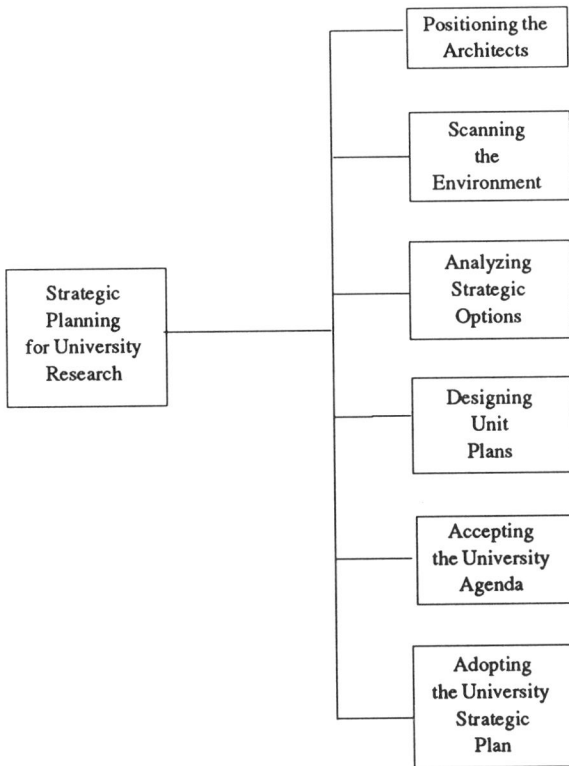

Figure 5.1 A Model of the Strategic Planning Process for University Research.

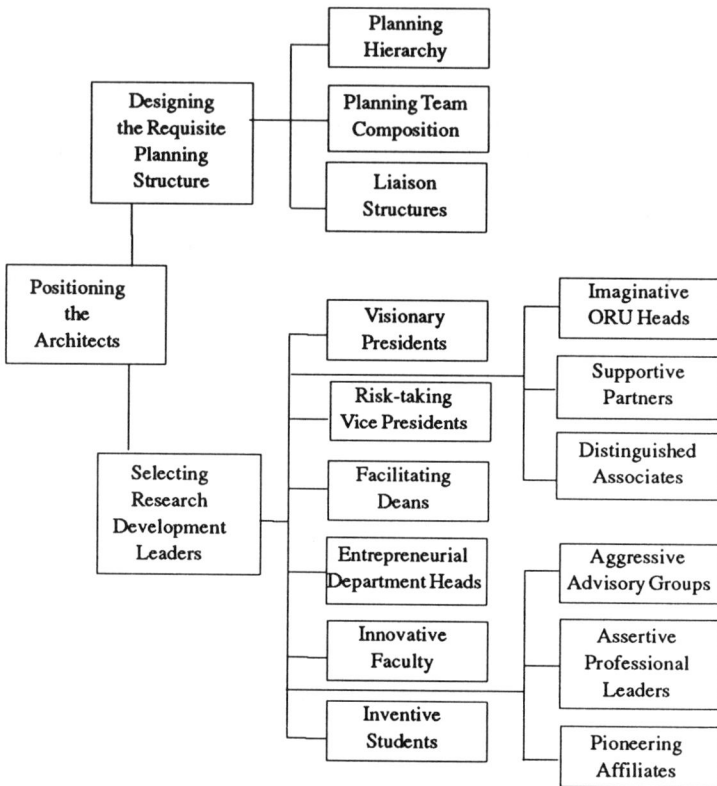

Figure 5.2. Positioning the Architects to Design the Future.

Positioning the Architects of the Future

The major theme of this monograph—research administrators are the architects of the future—is graphically illustrated in Figure 5.2.

To design the future, research administrators must first be given the necessary authority and direction for planning by the university president. Without this, they will never be taken seriously by sponsors or performers. Also, research administrators must conceive the requisite organizational planning structure for developing the strategic research plan. Next, they must select the best planners available, give them specific charges and delegate authority for planning. The design of a requisite structure for planning can follow the traditional administrative structures or functional divisions depending on the chief administrator's propensity for managing planning activities. Regardless of the efficacy of the organizational planning structure, the planning will be only as good as the selection of people to lead in the planning and the success of the planning will rest on the clearness and authority of the charges.

Designing the Requisite Planning Structures

The authors built this chapter on the belief that the principal investigator (PI) is the originator of ideas for strategic planning in the university, that the individual unit plans are the essential elements in the strategic plan, and that research administrators have the responsibility of facilitating the development of the PI's idea by designing the requisite planning structure.

Establishing the Planning Hierarchy—The design of an organizational structure for research strategic planning should include a planning hierarchy such as the following:

Administrative Level	Purpose Statement	Responsible Individual
For Academic Unit Plans		
University	Mission Statement	President
College	Goal Statement	Dean
Department	Department Aims	Department Head
Program or Group	Implicit Objectives	Program Coordinator
Project	Explicit Objectives	Principal Investigator
For Organized Research Unit Plans		
University	Mission Statement	President
Institute	Goal Statement	Director
Center	Aims	Director
Research Groups	Targets	Coordinator
Laboratories	Implicit Objectives	Director
Projects	Explicit Objectives	Principal Investigator
For Joint Venture Unit Plans		
Coalitions	Goal Statement	Executive Director
Cooperative Programs	Aim Statement	Coordinator
Common Grounds	Goal Statement	Executive Director

Figure 5.3. A Heirarchy of Purpose Statements for the Research University.

Such a planning hierarchy is necessary for institutional control over the planning process. Orderly planning occurs when the president has a general vision of what the university should be in the future and designs the requisite planning organization to achieve that vision.

A planning hierarchy establishes the formal planning structure that orders the planning activities of the university considering existing and future goals. A planning hierarchy usually follows the existing administrative structure and existing unit purpose statements on campus. However, a planning hierarchy can provide an option to the president for the appointment of people from outside the traditional administrative lines. The president can create an ad hoc structure that allows him to bypass unimaginative people who may be effective in maintaining a system once it has been developed, but who are not natural facilitators of the development process or who are not supportive initially of the chief executive's vision.

In a research university that has a well-established research climate, the existing administrative and goals hierarchy afford the president a natural planning hierarchy for strategic planning for research and it offers the best planning hierarchy because the established administrators are the researchers or former researchers. They will adopt generally what they have planned. In emerging research universities, the existing administrative staff may be so instruction oriented that they do not understand research development and do not want the institution headed in that direction. In this latter case, the president must build an ad hoc planning hierarchy composed of individuals with a research development orientation. In a university requiring dramatic changes in orientation, the president may have to hire consultants to buttress the core of researchers who should lead the planning within the university.

Properly administered this approach will lead to research development plans that usually will be adopted by the board of regents despite strong resistance from the naysayers. This latter approach will generate a considerable amount of internal resistance, but it will also produce a first generation strategic plan for research that can set the institution in the direction of becoming a research university. Expecting instruction-oriented administrators and faculty to design a strategic plan for research development leads to failure as the instruction-oriented individuals have neither the capacity to understand research nor the desire to plan and perform it.

The Planning Team Composition—Once the president has organized the university for strategic planning, the planning leaders must design the requisite teams. The composition of the planning teams should include representatives from the impact areas associated with the research unit. For example, representatives from the federal and state governments, industry, and nonprofit sectors should be included on the teams if they sponsor or consume research from the university's target areas. Also, representatives from the impacting disciplines and from impacting university units should be included. In Chapter 6, we will see how the vice-presidents, deans, and department chairs organized their advisory teams to accomplish their planning objectives. Also, we will look at the existing patterns of student-teacher organization and their role in planning research.

The Liaison Structures—The purpose of institutional liaison structures is to establish contact with the principals in the major impact areas. In strategic planning, the institution cannot limit its planning activities to input coming from outside sources—it must position its own representatives on the planning boards in the major impact areas and send its representatives to testify at hearings and to carry their plans to the outside world. Also, liaison officers learn first hand and at an early hour what opportunities are available in the sponsoring sectors and which competitors are initiating development efforts in their target areas. Liaison is provided by the president and his representatives serving on many sponsor advisory boards and on the boards of cooperating agencies. How institutions gather information and how they make their input into sponsor plans have been explained in Chapters 1 and 3.

Selecting Research Development Leaders

The unit plans are assembled under the following three administrative divisions that develop university research. Therefore, the division heads should be included in the planning hierarchy: academic units (AUs), organized research units (ORUs), and joint ventures (JVs).

One of the problems of selecting research development leaders is locating the planning units. There is a danger that some individual unit plans (IUPs) may be omitted from the strategic plan because there are several separate structures for the administration of research units. Within the university, unit plans may be designed under the conventional instructional administrative structure or they may originate with the assistance of a separate research administrative structure. In many institutions, both instructional and research administrative structures are employed to further internal planning while the executive offices of joint ventures develop plans by units outside the university. Individual research plans frequently originate in one of the following academic units and come under the authority of academic vice-presidents, deans, and department heads.

Academic Units	Administrative Titles
systems	chancellor
universities	president
colleges	dean
schools	dean
departments	chairpersons
laboratories	faculty members

Many universities place their ORUs under a vice-president for research or under a rsearch foundation president. There seems to be no best way of placing ORUs. However, a reasonable hierarchy for research units can be conceived in the following manner:

Consortiums	Teams
Systems	Areas
Foundations	Bureaus
Institutes	Programs
Centers	Studies
Stations	Offices
Departments	Laboratories
Projects, Projects, Projects, and more Projects	

In the aforementioned ORU hierarchy, "projects" are the basic organizational unit. Projects have a principal investigator who directs the work of graduate assistants and support personnel to achieve specified objectives. "Laboratories" are dedicated to a particular research thrust and are usually supervised by a group leader who is given a part-time administrative assignment that allows for the coordination of a small number of research fellows and research support personnel. "Centers" are led by full-time directors who develop an area of research excellence through the reputations of laboratories and their research associates. Generally, "institutes" have a full-time director and some part-time assistant directors who develop a wide spectrum of research activities as well as promote limited service and instructional projects.

Selecting Leaders for Joint Venture Planning Teams
Consortia
Research Parks
Common Grounds
Cooperative Agreement Facilities

Selecting research development leaders is a critical activity in strategic planning; yet, it is oftentimes neglected. For universities initiating strategic planning, it is often necessary to await the arrival or appointment of the right person to lead the planning of the unit. The appointment of a person without vision and imagination to a leadership role may take the unit in the wrong direction. This can be worse than no leadership at all.

Academic and business staff frequently occupy their positions because they conform to established ways and reflect the thinking of the majority. They form the university bureaucracy. They are not eager to lead in changes. Their rewards come from maintaining the status quo. They consistently perform the duties in established systems, but they have little time for planning and development activities. Strategic planning activities demand that the institution select a visionary president, risk-taking vice-presidents, imaginative organized research unit heads, facilitating deans, entrepreneural department chairs, innovative faculty, and inventive students. After development-oriented institutional officers are positioned in key planning roles, they must be able to select visionary and supportive planners from the sponsoring sectors and their cooperating units. Selecting research development leaders from the common grounds is not as difficult as it may first appear because their jobs require them to be very aggressive in planning and development. The model for this phase identifies the need for aggressive advisory groups, assertive professional leaders, and pioneering affiliates. The reasoning behind the model shown in Figure 5.2 is contained in Chapter 6.

Scanning the Environment

The environmental scan has the purpose of identifying the major impact areas and the principal performers and sponsors that may assist in the development of university research. Impact areas are an important consideration in every phase of strategic planning, but they are particularly prominent in scanning the environment and in adopting the university strategic plan. In scanning the environment the university must first identify the strategic impact areas. At this phase, the university is seeking information from the principal performers and sponsors of research before it sets its plans. Later, in the adoption phase, the university will be seeking the adoption of its plan by the principal performers and sponsors.

The scanning process is performed by each unit planning team focussing their attention on the research outputs to be produced by their unit in the future. The outputs are aimed at a consumer or client in a particular field. Within the consumer or client field, there is a target area where the unit's products must be placed. Each of these target areas will be impacted by the unit's strategic plan and in turn, the principals in and around the target area will influence the unit plans. There are an infinite number of research opportunities that could be pursued by a university—strategic planning has the purpose of targeting areas for developing selected opportunities because it is impossible for a single institution to react successfully to all opportunities. Also, there are many factors (government policy, economics, and industrial demands) that will influence the institution and its units. Only the trends of significant factors should be considered in strategic planning.

The university selection process begins with individual research units looking out on their impact areas. They must scan their fields of responsibility to determine their disciplinary imperatives, their client needs, their partners' priorities, market mandates, and disciplinary needs for technological innovation. The disciplinary imperatives, needs and mandates are the inputs for future research outputs. Which areas will the university investigate?

Target areas must be sighted in the strategic impact areas. The research scan is analogous to the submarine commander scanning the environment with a periscope. When the periscope focuses on a fleet or shoreline an impact area is located and information can be gathered about the many objects appearing in the scope. The impact area is huge. The target area is small—what appears at the crosshairs when the commander locks onto a target. Target areas are the specific areas in which the unit is already doing research or in which it plans to do research. For example, the target can be a small area in the structure of a discipline's knowledge, in a line of inventions, in an organization's sphere of success, in an industry's common request for assistance, and in the wide spectrum of professional technology.

Target areas are identified according to individual units assessing opportunities for future research outputs and the factors that will impact the units ability to produce the outputs. Usually, the target areas are determined by existing areas of operations or areas that are scheduled for exploitation. Second, the unit must identify their competitors and partners, the principals, in the target areas. Third, the unit must assess the strengths and weaknesses of the principals. Fourth, the unit planning teams should determine the research development assumptions of competitors and sponsors in their target areas. Fifth, the unit must consider the effects of significant factors such as national and state political winds, global and regional economic trends, the changing demographic characteristics of their clients, and the critical issues in their discipline. How easily the people doing the scanning find relevant information is determined by the power of the institutional and external information systems. This comprehensive scanning process can be modeled as shown in Figure 5.4.

Scanning the External Target Areas

Our model divides the environmental scan into looking outward toward the external target areas and looking inward at the internal target areas. In Chapter 1, the Killoren Impact Model showed the major quarters of influence in the environment and the subsequent sections of that chapter discussed methods of analyzing the assumptions of the principals in the research enterprise.

We believe that the first part of the environmental scan should determine the external principal's perceptions of the relevancy of the existing mission statement for the work that the university is currently doing and for what it proposes to do. Once a relevant mission statement is established by the legislature or board of trustees, the planners should direct their attention to reassessing the goals of the individual research units and their supporting

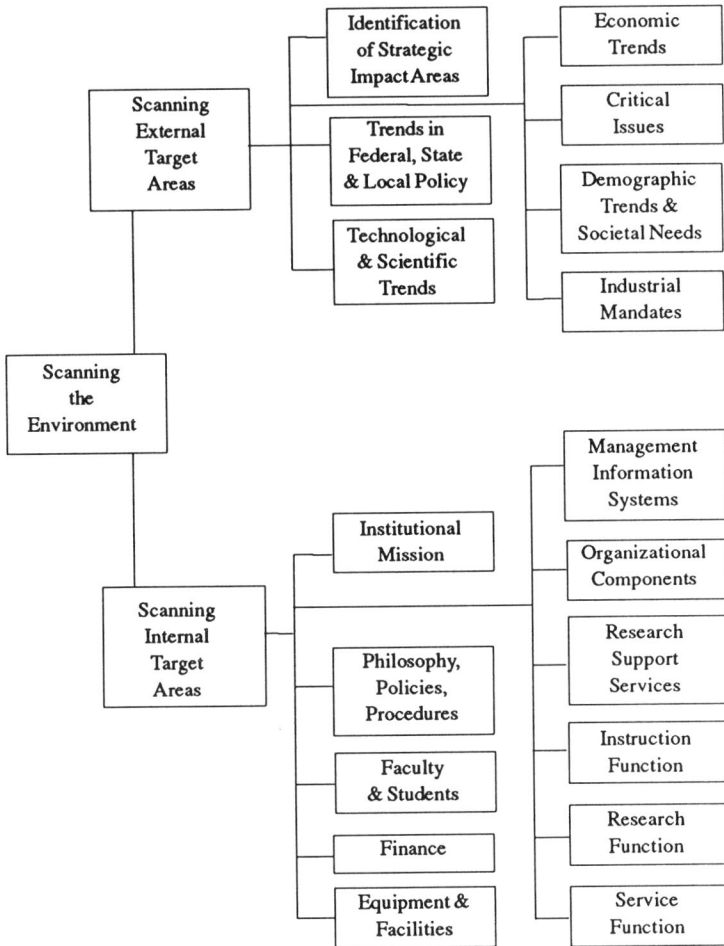

Figure 5.4 Identifying the Research Principals and Their Planning Assumptions.

services. At every level of planning, the unit planners should ask the following fundamental questions:

1. What are the patron and client research expectations for the unit?
2. Do patron and client expectations match the institutional mission statement?
3. What was the unit founders' intent?
4. Is that intent still relevant?
5. What are the research demands of the traditional and current external constituencies of the unit?

6. Does the faculty believe that they can accomplish the expanding expectations of the patrons and clients under the current goals of the unit and the current mission of the university?

If the unit purpose statement does not fit the times and circumstances, it must be changed.

Environmental scans should be made with the relevant university mission and the unit goals statements always in mind. We will consider two different mission statements drafted by the Texas legislature in 1987 to understand how the mission statement affects every planning activity of the institution.

1. National Research Universities.

Shall be a comprehensive, graduate research university offering an array of undergraduate, master's, doctoral and special professional degrees. Emphasis will be on excellence in teaching and research. Research endeavors benefiting the academic strengths of the institution and the economic strengths of the State of Texas shall be conducted with emphasis on maintaining a nationally and internationally recognized research institution. Funding for research shall be from private sources, competitively acquired sources, and appropriated public funding.

2. Teaching Institutions.

Shall be an institution primarily serving a specific region and offering undergraduate and graduate programs. Baccalaureate and master's degrees shall be granted. The emphasis of the institution shall be on excellence in teaching. Faculty research, using the facilities provided for and consistent with the primary function of the Institution, is encouraged. Funding for research shall be from private sources, competitively acquired sources and appropriated public funding.

Note the vast differences in legislative intent for the national research university and the teaching institutions. Excellence in research is expected of the former and not of the latter. This intent should guide the environmental scans of the individual units. In the research university unless there is an opportunity for excellence in research, the area should not be targeted for development. In the teaching-oriented institution, the primary function is instruction; therefore, the environmental scan of units in a teaching institution should target areas where excellence in teaching can be developed.

The mission of the institution will direct the environmental scans to those target areas that can advance the current mission of the institution and the goals of the unit.

Gathering Information About the Target Areas—Scanning the research environment according to target areas allows the planning teams to establish a planning framework by identifying performers and sponsors that may be partners or competitors. If the scan of both the external and internal environments are performed carefully, a number of opportunities and preemptions will be identified in the early planning sessions allowing the planners to direct their attention to opportunities and to eliminate the strong preemptions.

This part of the strategic planning process is the foundation for realistic goal setting in the design of the unit plan. An accurate presentation of the competition, a realistic assessment of the needs in the specific disciplines, and the actual inclusion of sponsor assumptions can reduce bickering and save time during later planning.

Trends in federal, state, and local policy for the support of research in general and in particular disciplines should have a decided impact on institutional planning. This is particularly true for those institutions that follow the megatrends of society in anticipation of legislative intent and research program establishment in the government. Brief statements should be prepared by individual research units and ordered by target areas. Statements related to technological and scientific trends, economic trends, critical issues, demographic trends and societal needs, and industrial mandates should be prepared by the planning teams and included under their reports on trends. Oftentimes megatrends are difficult to evaluate by the general university population; consequently, backup information should be clearly cited for those needing additional information. An extensive bibliography supporting economic indices, demographic features, the platforms of major political parties, community needs and the breakthroughs in specific technological areas is necessary at this stage.

Scanning Internal Target Areas

The internal environmental scan has the purpose of bringing information from the operating systems of the institution before the strategic planner of the university. The research leaders obtain their information from both formal and informal sources. Recall that Chapter 4 discussed the following internal factors: general assumptions and institutional mission; institutional research strengths; faculty and staff; students; educational programs; service; finance; resources, equipment, and facilities; and organizational components.

In this section the authors consider the systems that provide the information needed for strategic planning for university research.

A number of critical planning activities occur during the scan of the internal target areas of the institution. The academic leaders must ask of faculty, students, and staff the introspective questions of "What are we now? and What do we want to be next year, five years from now, and a half-century from now?" University leaders should have a feel for what the institution is presently as they deal daily with the routine activities of the university and their official duties place them in contact with the outside world. If they are astute, they have acquired a fair idea of internal and external trends. If they are imaginative, they have formed a vision of what the institution should be in the future based on assumptions derived from internal and external environmental analyses. They must communicate this vision by sharing operating information and advocating their assumptions.

Note that in Figure 5.4, the first task in scanning the environment requires the president and the board to determine if the historical mission of the institution correctly describes the institution. If the activities of the institution have changed over the years, is the current mission statement accurate and, more important, is it appropriate for guiding the institution into the future?

The president as the principal planner in the university has the responsibility for preparing the university environmental analysis and proposing a new mission and program initiatives. If the president has no vision of the future or can not share that vision and assumptions for future developments, strategic planning for research is severely handicapped.

If change is desired, or has indeed occurred, it is the responsibility of the president and his planning team to convince the board, faculty, and outside constituencies that a new mission statement should be adopted. This will require the president to present an analysis of the external and internal research factors leading the institution in a particular direction.

Evidence of the changing mission of the institution will come from the historical records of the institution. For example, the president must present the case that changes in faculty and student interests and changes in percentages of total revenue generation from the major functions of teaching, research, and service have led to a changed institution. This requires the president to discuss the changing balance among the institutional functions and to put forth certain assumptions regarding the future direction of the institution.

It is usually necessary for the president's advisors to show that over the last decades research dollars from grants and contracts have replaced a significant portion of the dominant instructional revenue source. After surveying faculty time-and-effort reports, comparing financial statements from the functional areas, assessing student and faculty interests, and analyzing equipment and facilities inventories, the board of regents should accept the evidence that the institution has changed. Next, they should adopt a mission statement that reflects current realities and the vision of the academic leaders of the institution.

Incorporating information from the management information systems into the scanning process is essential to strategic planning. With the exception of the institutional charter, legislative acts and institutional philosophy statements, the evidence of the past and current status of the institution will be supplied by research development and administration systems. The importance of the operating systems is neglected sometimes by writers on planning. We may err in the opposite direction for we found that planners at every level need from the operating systems vast quantities of data and numerous customized reports to develop their environmental analyses and planning assumptions. Strategic planning is greatly facilitated by having the heads of major university divisions present to research planners analyses of internal financial trends, changing personnel work assignments, and growth in research organizational structures and services. The following systems provide the baseline data, the existing goals, and the operating plans necessary for the environmental analyses that lead to developing a new mission statement and new unit goals or that lead to affirmation of the current mission.

One of the reasons strategic planning did not become popular on university campuses prior to the 1980s was that most universities did not have the computerized planning and operating systems that could gather efficiently and inexpensively the information required for integrated, long-term partnership planning. For example, baseline financial information is the key internal target area in any university plan. A chart of research accounts is the document that provides the planners with accurate information on the current distribution of funds on campus. The vice-president for financial affairs should make his or her planning assumptions about future internal institutional financial trends based on existing institutional conditions and external economic trends.

Also, the planner must determine what the institution does not have that is needed. This is usually accomplished by surveying the faculty and staff.

Hensley (1974) explained how the development of a chart of research accounts for sponsored research and a unitary computerized accounting system introduced computerized accounting to many universities and how these systems allowed university personnel to present timely fiscal information on thousands of accounts according to the following attributes: the university account number, principal investigator's (PI) or account manager's name and social security number, departmental designators, college designators, organized research unit designators, sponsoring agency, agency grant or contract numbers, initiation and termination dates, amount of the grant, and uniform expenditure object codes for all accounts.

If a unit wants to target the development of a metabolic biology program, it is necessary to know who in the university has grants in the area. Or, if central planners want to know the history of total support by a particular agency since 1960, they can request a customized report from the accounting office that presents trends according to sponsors.

A unitary computerized accounting system (UCAS) was necessary to bring some uniformity and order to grants accounting in the late sixties.

Prior to the introduction of UCAS, most sponsored university accounts were established under a general account number that permitted the investigator to spend monies according to the agency budget codes. This meant there were hundreds of different individual budget formats. Manual systems required individual attention to each account making it very difficult for the institution to determine how much was being spent on personnel salaries, fringe benefits, materials and supplies, and travel, etc. When manual reports were prepared, it required many accountant hours for preparation because the accounting office or the departmental secretary had to retrieve information from accounts individually for each desired report. The greatest problem with the manual system was the lack of confidence of fiscal managers in their data. The data was subject to so many internal variations and inconsistencies that projections for any system attribute were frequently off-target by as much as 20% for the next year. Five-year projections were wild guesses.

Today, detailed, accurate accounting information forms the financial base from which the vice-president for finance formulates the financial assumptions of the institution. The individual manual accounting systems of the sixties were very labor intensive and reporting was months, sometimes years behind current events. In the manually operated accounting systems, special reports for the target areas were impossible to obtain from the university accounting offices because they were prohibitively expensive. With computerized accounting systems, accounting offices can prepare internal financial trend reports for individual units for a few dollars. The new systems allow unit planners to track the number of outside grants and contracts according to research, service, and instruction functions for the last decades and to develop comprehensive trend reports on the development of research grants according to a variety of options.

Most importantly, the unitary computerized accounting system brought about a uniformity of thinking on all sponsored accounts by establishing a wide variety of expenditure object codes that enabled the PI to plan with some precision and to retrieve accurate operating information according to uniform expenditure object codes that were designed to meet their planning and management needs. While this was very handy for PI planning and management, it was essential for central administrators to do institutional planning and to administer large numbers of grants. The UCAS allowed the administrators to know immediately how much is being spent in any administrative unit according to any of the established expenditure object codes. Special operating and planning reports are easily prepared using UCAS. A unitary computerized accounting system reduced dramatically accounting overhead and provided current fiscal information instantly. Without the financial operating systems described, inexpensive internal scans of the financial environment would be impossible for the research university. Therefore, it behooves the planner to work closely with the custodians of these systems in developing special fiscal reports essential for accurate research planning.

Similarly, a program development system provides a broad array of current operating plans for the major units of the university. The vice-president for academic affairs must add his or her planning assumptions about future faculty and student interests grounded on existing faculty and student research and on the external scientific and technological trends for the academic constituencies.

The program development system included the following plans and files.

Department and College Operating and Development Plans—listed the colleges with their departments, administrators, staff size, and goals. Departmental operating plans listed faculty according to departments, position controls (number of faculty positions, graduate assistants, support personnel allocated to a department) and descriptions of the department programs.

Program Files listed the degree programs approved by the state coordinating board, and the institutional governing board and provided information relevant to their place in the instructional organization, student enrollment and graduate figures for the past five years, and abstracts for their five-year development plan.

Class Files listed courses in the current catalogs according to degree programs, purpose, instructor, level, section and room assignments by semester and year, and their five-year development plan.

Organized Research Unit (ORU) Files listed the approved ORUs, purpose of the unit, staff size, the ORU head, subordinate units within the ORU, list of ORU fellows, special facilities, titles of recent publications, list of affiliates, abstract of their five-year plan, demographic data, and fiscal data for the previous five years.

Sponsored Project Files listed all sponsored projects by principal investigator, project title, sponsor, project duration, amount of award, matching funds, and contained copies of the complete proposal and all correspondence related to the project, quarterly, annual and final activity reports, project results, and cross references to other relevant files such as the project accounts.

Faculty Activity Report File carried the time and effort reports of faculty according to their assignment to instruction, research, service, and administration for the previous operating years.

Theses and Dissertation Files carried information according to title, student name, chairperson, committee members, unit designators and locater information.

Continuing Education and Extension Course File contained information according to course, unit designators, site, CEU, and instructor.

Student Advisor Files included advisor name and number and names of students advised.

Faculty Development System organized information on the faculty according to the following files: faculty work loads for instruction, research, service, and administration; current research interests by key words; history of sponsored research awards by agencies and amounts; current research applications (decision elements, prospectus, and proposals) in the office of research and projects; research recognition; major research publications; facility responsibilities; and institutional and sponsor affiliations.

A *Facilities and Equipment Development System* contained a computerized system for a stores inventory, billing procedures, and a shared-use equipment inventory, and research facilities locater files.

A *Facilities File* listed the name and location of research laboratories and offices according to buildings. Costs for floor space were indicated. Building acquisition costs and subsequent improvements were listed. Use charges and depreciation rates were furnished. A wide range of information to satisfy the requirements of Sections F and J-9 of OMB Circular A-21 was set out in this file.

A *Stores File* included items in the stockrooms from computer paper and pencils through laboratory reagents, apparatus, hardware, small motors, and metal supplies.

A *Shops File* listed facilities that served development, construction, repair, and maintenance functions. It described their functions (glassblowing, machine work, computer repair etc.), gave their locations, and designated the unit head.

Specialized Service Facilities File provided descriptions of laboratories and centers with highly specialized analytical instrumentation (electron microscopes, mass spectrometers, lasers and x-ray equipment) vivariums, wind tunnels, reactors, and materials engineering research laboratories, pilot plants, and experimental farms.

Computer Facilities Files listed the campus computer facilities and described the hardware, software, and training and faculty support programs that emanated from the centers. It also listed the costs of services.

The Place of the Research Development Systems
in Long-Term University Planning

The outlines of the different systems were provided to show the types of information that are essential to the environmental scan in planning for university research. In the seventies, the authors found that research had reached such a complex level in most institutions that the development of many research proposals required up-front cooperative agreements and multidisciplinary approaches requiring a vastly modernized institutional information systems. Moreover, they found that their proposals were more attractive to sponsors when they joined efforts with other states. Finding out what others are doing requires that the institution have a research development system.

Strategic Analyses of Unit Options

In this phase of planning, the unit strategists should analyze where the unit and the university are and they should present a number of scenarios for research program development considering a number of options for each project in the research program.

In strategic planning for university research it is convenient to use a decision element to represent each project in the academic program or ORU. Each project is considered for its merit for advancing the unit purpose and the mission of the university under certain goals.

Strategic analyses of unit options are extremely important to research program development for it is this phase in strategic planning that the various project ideas are placed before the unit constituencies for judgment. The projects are the major building blocks of the research university. Which ones should be developed? There are thousands of good new ideas and many old ones that could be developed into a wide variety of research outputs. But resources are limited. Does the unit want to advance its basic research at this time or is it more interested in helping the local community revitalize a faltering manufacturer? Which of several sponsors should be approached for support and for how much? Where is the project best located for effectiveness?

Decision Element

The decision element conceived by Hensley and Schoppmeyer (1972) is a single page summary of a research project. It contains the following decision-making factors for standard consideration by the planners: project title, project period, project status, program development code, cooperating agencies, department person, purpose of the project, procedures (processes), benefits and achievements from adopting the project, consequences of not adopting the project, total resources required annually (input),and quantitative measures (output).

Every research unit to be considered in the research strategic plan submits scenarios for the development of the program to the unit planners. The

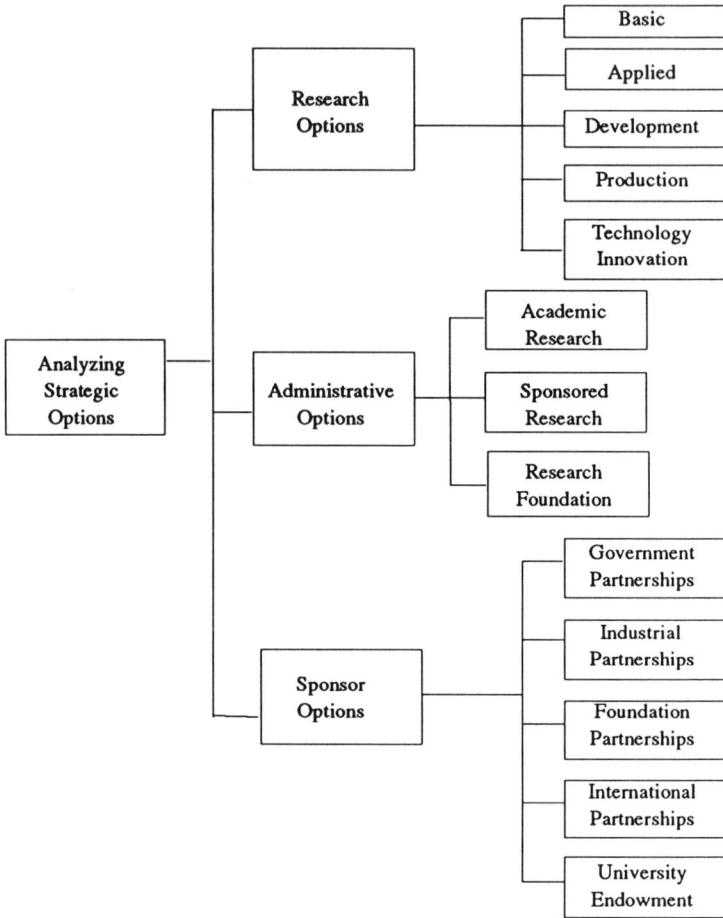

Figure 5.5 A Model for Analyzing Strategic Options.

following scenarios may be titled: present status scenario, reduction scenario, minimal expansion scenario, and maximum expansion scenario.

Each principal investigator has a number of options that should be considered when planning a project's development. For example, the decision element for each project calls attention to its research options—basic, applied, development, production and technology transfer. Under the quantitative measures factor the project director will estimate the number of basic research outcomes (articles, books, papers) to be produced from the project for each of the next five years. Estimates also will be made for outputs of applied research products (patents, copyrights and trade secrets), development products (pilot plants, prototypes, testing facilities), production research products (modified products, productivity increases) and technology innovation (interfield transfer of technology).

Outputs

Options are created by considering for every decision element the resource options needed to develop the program, the niche options associated with the program, and the program benefits, consequences and total priority value for each of the scenarios.

The present status scenario includes the decision-making factors for the existing projects in operation. The present status scenario summary sheet represents the real world of the program. The sophistication of present status scenario summary sheets varies from unit to unit. Most are nothing but fiscal data printouts of the projects in the program and associated output information items. Some units may use an options analysis matrix, which rates as good (5), fair (4), neutral (3), poor (2), and bad (1) the chances for each of the decision-making factors advancing the program under four possible scenarios.

Scenarios	Present Status	Reduction Goals	Minimal Goals	Maximum Goals
Decision-Making Factors				
ResourceOptions	5	5	5	4
Niche Options	2	1	3	5
Product Options	2	1	3	4
Consequence Options	3	3	3	5
Opportunity Options	3	1	4	5
Program Priority Options	4	4	4	5

Figure 5.6. Strategic Planning Options Analysis Matrix.

In the previous section, we discussed information obtained from internal and external scans. The trends in sponsor funding, critical issues, economics, and industrial mandates; and the university's financial bases, its support services, its faculty and student strengths; and the eternal balancing among functions are considered with each scenario. Also, the project is evaluated for its contribution to the research options. What is the project contributing to furthering the basic research outputs for the program or ORU. Each of the research class options is considered for its existing output. The unit scenarios permit the leaders of the university to consider many options for future action in regard to a particular class of research pursuit, ways of administering the research, and opportunities for partnership in the different research sectors. The visions of the university leaders will be telling factors as the planning teams prepare the scenarios shown in Figure 5.7. The planning teams should consider an options analysis for every program according to each scenario.

Research Scenarios

The unit options for developing research can be considered in five ways that are formed by the current classes of research. Each administrative unit on campus should consider their present goals and associated costs. They should contemplate the new goals and new budgets if they had to reduce their productivity, increase their productivity minimally, or increase productivity maximally. The basic research option is used to illustrate the types of questions that can be analyzed by considering a series of options in each scenario.

The Basic Research Option—Resource Factors—The resource factor addresses resources that are available for basic research. The greatest of these resources is the trained human mind. Research options should consider first the human capital that exists in the institution and then allocate adequate research time to the best research minds. Research time becomes the main resource factor in most research scenarios. Also, resource factors assess the facilities and equipment that can be devoted to basic research. And, it presents a series of possible sponsors for funding basic research. The following questions may be used to analyze the basic research options.

What amount of "faculty time" will be allocated to basic research and what are the costs associated with faculty time?

What is the present number of faculty in the unit and what are their basic research interests?

What number of faculty will be needed in the future according to reduction or increase options.

What are faculty plans for developing their basic research interests? Faculty decision elements, prospecti, and proposals must be considered in this option by the department and ORU planners. These research options and their costs are the foundation for all university planning.

What is the present mix of graduate students and post doctoral students and what are their basic research interests?

What research support personnel are needed for basic research?

What is the present number and purpose of existing basic research laboratories and other research facilities? What number is needed in the future and for what purposes?

What are the costs for each of the above options?

Niche Factors—What specialty areas of the discipline does the department or ORU intend to investigate and which ones are targeted for preemption? The critical question in this analysis is "In what knowledge area, does the unit want to be known as being the best?" The unit must consider which niche or niches it will occupy in its professional area. The niche factors include the following types of questions.

What are the possible disciplinary imperatives that should be targeted by the planning unit and what are the associated costs?

What are the research strengths of the unit?

Where in the international standings is the unit in regard to disciplinary specialty preemption and where does it want to be in the future?

What are the options for articulating the basic research products with the instructional functions in the university?

Where in the college and university can the recent research findings of the unit be incorporated into the curriculum to give particular academic programs the edge in quality of professional preparation.

Product Factors (Outputs)—This portion of scenario preparation deals with identifying the types and numbers of basic research products being produced in the individual research units of the university. Such planning requires the research unit to prepare an inventory of existing research and complementary function outputs and to consider what new products could be added to their production plan and how existing products could be enhanced. Factor analyses considers projections of product numbers and their payoffs for each product for year-one, year-three, and year-five of the plan using current faculty loads and distribution factors. It assesses what might happen to basic research productivity when work loads are varied to give faculty an additional 25%, 33%, and 50% release time for research. It addresses the following and related types of questions.

What percentage of total unit projects are basic research and what do they cost the unit?

Does this percentage give the unit the desired mix in the classes of research?

Are there emerging classes of research that the unit wants to consider supporting and what will the costs be?

What agencies are to be targeted for proposal submission to develop new projects?

What was the number of papers delivered, articles published, and theses and dissertation completed in the previous year in the department or in the ORU?

What is the quality of the papers, publications, and theses?

What are the possible departmental strategies for improving the quality of the products?

What are the scenarios for spreading the knowledge generated by the department beyond exiting methods of dissemination?

What are the plans of the department to place their members in nomination for awards from professional associations?

Consequence Factors—This section of the Research Scenario concentrates attention on people, facilities and events that may threaten basic research or complementary programs. Internal as well as external threats should be identified and options for nullifying the threats presented. In some cases, the threat is so powerful that it is better to delay or avoid planning in a particular area as planning for such programs could be unproductive and possibly fatal to larger plans. Questions such as the following should be asked.

What may happen if a reactionary group of faculty and alumni attempt to block every new program or change in administrative structure?

How can the faculty opponents of basic research be brought into the research faculty? (A great many of the teaching faculty may resist any effort to encourage research.)

How can the naysayers to basic research on the campus and in the larger community be neutralized?

What may happen when the flagship university of the state incorporates into their system a smaller, neighboring state institution that is in our research region?

What happens to our programs when the flagship institution converts the neighboring institution into an extension center for graduate and research programs that previously had been in our domain?

What are our options for continuing cooperative research and articulation agreements with the neighboring institution and for keeping that region's clients within our sphere of influence?

What may happen to our units basic research programs when a state select committee reviews universities and recommends new missions and revised service areas?

What are our options for influencing the select committee?

What may happen when the state budget board asks the coordinating council to review doctoral programs and ORUs in line-item appropriations with the intent of eliminating redundant graduate programs and low-priority ORUs?

What may happen to basic research projects and our teaching programs when animal rights groups begin to lobby against the use of animals in research and teaching?

What are our plans to prevent destruction of our laboratories and research by the activists in these groups?

What are the chances that our sponsors' basic research funding will be severely curtailed or redirected as Congress and state legislatures concentrate on applied research for economic development?

What are our options for fitting basic research into the economic development plans of the politicians?

Opportunity Factors—The research development administrator must always be aware of continuing and new funding opportunities and make the researchers on campus aware of those opportunities. Great universities are built by academic leaders seeing new possibilities and exploiting those opportunities.

What are the probabilities that the major sponsors will open new research programs to fund basic research? Having existing appropriations increased?

What are the options for bringing new partners into our plans for ORU development?

What are our chances for increasing the number of faculty who have outside funding for basic research?

What are the options for developing cooperative agreements with sponsors and other research institutions for joint development of research projects?

What are the opportunities for influencing legislators to increase the formula for organized research?

What are the options for having the state legislature permit the state institutions to retain for research purposes their recovered indirect costs?

What are the opportunities for developing state and national research facilities on our campus or on a neighboring common ground?

What are our options for developing a consortium to do the work a single institution could not individually perform?

Program Priority Factors—Program priority factors are the last words in the planning scenarios. It is at this stage of planning that planners must assesses the work to be done and to put forth the options that they like best. The advantage of strategic planning is seen by planners at this juncture, as the vast array of options is clearly subsumed in scenarios that look at a total systems approach to development. The best minds of the university and their partners peer into their crystal balls and do their best to order the future. If we have faith in expert opinion, the options analyses have presented the planners at every level with a variety of highly possible scenarios. Now, the planners must recommend a course of action by rating the projects they believe will best advance the purposes of university and the unit, in that order. The following assessment of previous questions are made in the prioritization analyses.

For purposes of illustration let us look at the main question in the resource factor— What amount of "faculty time" will be allocated to basic research. The planners must consider the trade-offs—where will the funds come from to support faculty basic research time. Faculty always want the institution to give them more released time for basic research. Students want the faculty to spend more time on instruction. The state wants the faculty to spend more time on the problems of production research that improves local industry. A commitment to basic research time subtracts from the instructional work that produces most of the university's revenue. An increase of 25% of time for basic research will result in the faculty member teaching one less undergraduate course with a correlated decrease in the departmental revenues from instruction. Also, the planning team should assess the outcomes of such action on the quality and competitiveness of the undergraduate instructional program.

Secondly, should an addition of 25% basic research time be given to all faculty? Or should only research faculty receive the 25% research time, leaving the nonresearchers with greater teaching loads? These are difficult analyses that have a long-term impact on the institution. They must be made first in terms of the present mission of the institution and secondly in terms of the long-term goals of the unit.

Administrative Options

The scenarios for choosing the administrative services of the university can be viewed by looking at the opportunities for the project when it is placed under the following three options: administration of research through the academic administration, administration for research through the sponsored research office, and administration of research through a university research foundation (not legally incorporated in the university).

A strategic planning options analysis matrix could be used in a strategic analysis of administrative services rendered to the university. Certainly, the administrative offices must be analyzed for their resources, the niche they will occupy in the total systems, the services they are to render, the consequences of their existence, and the trade offs for delivery of services. The strategic planning options must answer the following questions and provide estimates of associated costs.

Which of the offices optimize the development of research and what are the costs of those services?

What level of support service is wanted and needed by the principal investigators in order for them to perform research and where will the funds to support these service come from?

What are the supporting services needed by the other administrative units on campus?

What are the administrative services needed by the state agencies from a particular office and are these services useful or only bureaucratic encroachments?

What administrative services are needed by the sponsoring agencies and are the sponsors paying their fair share of costs?

What administrative services are needed by the central university administration to help the university comply with government regulations and ethical considerations.

Where are the best services delivered for the lowest cost?

Which of the administrative offices optimize the researcher's work according to classes of research and sponsor demands and which optimize the recovery of costs associated with the work?

Are different classes of research handled best in a particular administrative office?

The strategic analyses for administrative scenarios should focus on what is the long-term impact on research by evaluating the present services and assessing the potential services of administrative offices internal and external to the university. Again, keeping the total systems approach to research development in mind, the strategist must ask, "How will the university be advanced by the organization of specific administrative services and the quality of those services."

Sponsor Options

Again, the strategists at the unit level might create an options analysis matrix for the following sponsor options: university endowment options, government partnership options, industrial partnership options, foundation partnership options, and international partnership options.

In creating the specific sponsor options for the specific sponsor sectors, the strategists must consider the mix of sponsors needed to accomplish the goals set forth in each of the scenarios. Working out the particular options for research development depends on the recommendations associated with the research and administrative options. The university planner must develop strategic budgets for reduction goals, minimal goals, and maximum goal achievement associated with each scenario presented by the unit. This carries strategic budgeting to the lowest management level in the university and forces the department and ORU planners to develop their goals and output projections within the confines of realistic projected sources of income. It forces the researcher to create their development strategies based on a spending plan and it affords the researcher several possible plans of action that must be acted on after goal setting is achieved.

Continuation of trend lines for sponsor support created in the environmental scans are frequently developed by principal investigators and department heads for each project. Technologically advanced software programs provide "what if" routines for those planners interested in determining a wide range of changes in sponsor mix and levels of support. Lotus 1-2-3, SuperCalc, and other software packages allow planners to look at the impact of various sponsor commitments on project or department income projections, determine future financial positions, and analyze future and present values of investment and debt for the research units. At this stage of development the planning team members must consider articulation strategies as they must see how their scenarios will influence higher and lower planning decisions.

The strategic analysis should aggregate the best scenarios for each unit allowing the planners to recommend several courses of action at different levels. In the next phase of planning, consideration of the various scenarios should allow the unit to set realistic goals that should guide the unit and their partners for an extended period of time. The scenario allows all in the system to see all what has been recommended for a particular set of circumstances. At a later reasonable time, if a strategy is not working, alternative plans can be considered based on the rejected options.

Designing Unit Plans

Unit plan design is the most demanding phase of strategic planning. The principal investigators in the different administrative units of the university must examine what their current purpose is in relation to the goals of their many constituencies and the changing mission of the university and decide on what research work the unit will do in the future and how it will be organized and funded. Most importantly, in this phase, they must prepare and advocate the vision of what the unit can be.

The components for the planning document and concomitant technology for this phase are relatively simple; however, the reconciling processes at the various administrative levels are quite complex and the decision making is traumatic for the planning teams as they must make the unit's goals and work congruous with a series of other plans—a very time consuming and difficult activity.

Throughout this book, we have taken the position that the principal investigator is essential to any type of research development. This section demonstrates the truth of this thesis as we follow the aggregation of investigator ideas into progressively more complex plans prepared by higher level planning teams. Figure 5.7 shows the three major administrative structures and the units that plan the development and conduct of university research.

This section includes an in depth discussion of the following research administration structures: the academic research unit administrative structure, ORU administrative structure, and joint-venture unit administrative structure. This tripartite division is a good way of showing planning activities theoretically. However, in practice, the principal investigator and higher level administrators will be planning in all three structures simultaneously.

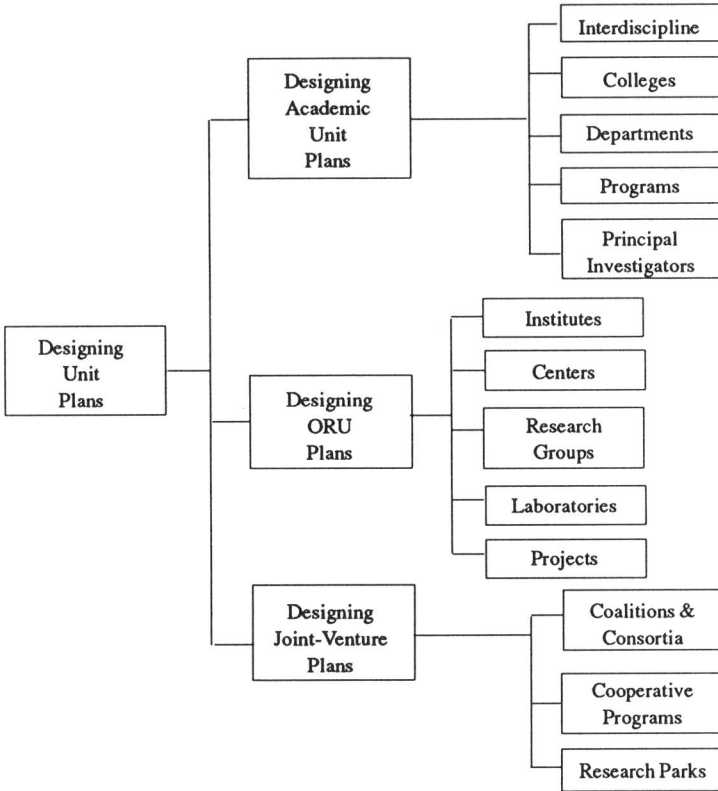

Figure 5.7 A Model for Designing Unit Plans.

Designing Academic Unit Plans

This section will deal with designing plans for the following five units: the PI, the program, the department, the college, and the interdisciplinary units.

The PI is the fundamental unit in each of the three administrative structures of the research university. Principal investigators must be engaged in unit strategic planning because it enhances their personal research development capabilities and their input is the foundation for all university unit planning. Although they are not paid for administrative responsibilities, the investigator operates as an administrator when they plan and conduct project research. They must plan for and administer thousands of dollars to pay for project salaries, equipment, travel, etc.; supervise research assistants and other support personnel; deal with sponsor and university bureaucracies; plan with their colleagues and sponsors for the development of a particular line of research; monitor their target areas; and maintain liaison with other professionals in their discipline. They have the creative and the practical know-how for developing and conducting a particular line of investigation. Without them there is no research, no research activities to administer, and no need for strategic planning for research. Chapter 6 further explains the role and value of the principal investigator.

Developing Principal Investigator Plans—Strategic planning for the faculty member involves important decisions on how much time the investigator wants to spend on research and on what problems. It is not uncommon for research faculty to devote 50-75% of their time to research and only 25% to teaching. The amount of time to be spent on research or teaching is an important planning decision as the decision will affect the career advancement of the faculty member. The faculty member who expects to devote more than 25% of his or her time to research, also expects to buy the additional time from the departmental teaching budget by obtaining sponsor funds to support particular projects. This means preparing planning documents advocating the adoption of certain projects.

The technology for planning at the principal investigator level requires the design of the following three documents, which correspond to three distinct rounds of planning at the departmental, collegiate and university levels of planning: the research decision element, the research prospectus, and the research proposal.

In the design phase of unit strategic planning, the planning team must ask for the preparation of the decision element, a one-page planning document. Its shortness should not belie its importance because it is the primary document for higher level planning. Recall that it was the major source of information in analyzing strategic options. It is the main document for wide dissemination of the unit plans.

In planning research, we must remember that principal investigators plan research work in terms of projects, which become the fundamental units for research administration. Projects grow out of the researcher's idea for investigative work. The decision element summarizes on one-page the proposed work.

A model decision element is shown in Figure 5.8. When planning their future work, faculty members must review their own and outside plans in light of the current mission statement and the relevant goals of the department and college. If the mission of the university and the goals of the department shift too far away from faculty members' interests, they may want to seek employment at another institution that plans to develop their areas of interest or they may want to change their research direction, or they

Texas Tech University
Office of Research Services

Project Title:_____ Project Start:_____
Filling Date:_____ Termination:_____

Proj. Status Devel/Operat/Term	Program Devel. Code	Cooperating Agencies	DEPT	Person	Cumulative Priority

Purpose Statements (objectives):

Process Statements to Achieve Adoption of Purpose:

Benefits and Achievements Expected from Adoption of Project:

Consequences of Not Adopting The Project:

Resources Required for year one: Souce of Resource Allocation

Total Amount:	Internal Sources					External Sources		
	Pers	Dept	Coll	CentAd	Other	#1	#2	#3
Professional Staff:								
Secretarial @ 40/wk:								
Research Ass't @ 20/wk:								
Student Work @ 15/wk:								
Equipment Purchase:								
Supplies:								
Space (Room number):								
Other:								
Other:								

Resources Required for year two: Source of Resource Allocation

Total Amount:	Internal Source					External Sources		
	Pers	Dept	Coll	CentAd	Other	#1	#2	#3
Professional Staff:								
Secretarial @ 40/wk:								
Research Ass't @ 20/wk:								
Student Work @ 15/wk:								
Equipment Purchase:								
Supplies:								
Space (Room number):								
Other:								
Other:								

Quantitative Measures:	Yr 1	Yr 2	Yr 3	Yr 4	Yr 5	Reviewer Comments:		
1.								
2.								
3.								

Figure 5.8. Decision Element.

may want to rely totally or partially on outside sponsors. The decision element (DE) has the purpose of putting the faculty member's ideas on one page in a manner that will allow an administrative review. Response to the DE should determine whether the idea falls within the mission of the institution and the current priorities of the sponsoring unit and whether the sponsoring unit has funds available during the planned project period. It provides the advantage of creating in planners an awareness of a potential work at an early stage of development. It helps the researcher by putting his ideas before the planning team and the unit decision makers who will determine whether the idea will be incorporated into the unit plan.

The preparation of a DE will avoid the wasted effort of preparing a full proposal that does not match the goals of the unit. It has the long-term benefit of introducing the principal investigator's ideas to key decision makers in the university units and among potential sponsors. It is the initial point of intellectual contact between research performer and sponsor. We must remember that departments and colleges are major sponsors of research. Their assignment of laboratories, support personnel, principal investigator time to a project, etc. makes the department or college a patron of the investigator. The DE is most helpful in creating an awareness and formal acceptance of the researcher's idea within his own unit. The DE will provide advocates of a project a one page document that allows them to present promising ideas to busy decision makers who may want to incorporate the project into their unit plans. It is a handy device for agency officials to circulate at staff meetings and within neighboring offices. It is capsuled information that is essential to any program officer preparing a development plan in a sponsoring agency.

The Proposal—The investigator or investigators prepare a proposal describing how they plan to study their selected research problem. A proposal may be as simple as a few verbal statements that obtain a commitment of resources to a project or it may be as complex as many printed volumes. In any case, a research proposal is a work plan. It projects how an idea will be developed in a particular setting using certain resources.

Developing Academic Research Programs—Academic research programs are subject to continuous planning, review, and evaluation. They are usually published in an official graduate school catalog or university bulletin. They are frequently associated with a degree program. They are arranged within an interdisciplinary program or organized under a college jurisdiction. The academic research programs are built by faculty and students conducting independent research along disciplinary lines. The research programs are built on outstanding faculty work that centers around a degree program. For example the Museum Science program at Texas Tech University has research programs in the fields of anthropology, biology, costume and textiles, education, geology, history, and the natural sciences. All of these depend on the Museum's extensive collections, the execution of accepted museum practices, and the need for communicating the results of research. In Chapter 6, the section on "The Primacy of the Principal Investigator" explains in some detail how Knox Jones planned and built the natural science research program in interdisciplinary programs of museum sciences.

Developing Departmental Plans—It is the wish of every department head to have unlimited resources to support research—that is a dream, not a plan. It is the duty of the research administrator to design plans, not to fantasize. This means that the department head must match the best ideas of faculty and students with their limited resources to achieve a specified output. Designing a departmental plan is not a trivial matter because personal careers and academic reputations will be affected greatly by investigator decisions to propose or not to propose departmental projects and by decisions of the departmental planning team to include or not include a particular individual or project. This last statement demands some clarification for the nonacademician.

There is an inseparable relationship between research ideas and people. An idea is a piece of intellectual property owned by its originator. Unfortunately, research ideas are sometimes stolen. It is the responsibility of the research administrator to keep the person and their ideas together until their ideas are developed to the satisfaction of their originator. Usually, researchers have significant ideas and can deliver what they propose. Sometimes, the work needed to develop the researcher's ideas is beyond the originator's capabilities or beyond the resources of their unit and university. The department head must decide, knowing the reputation of the researcher and the potency of the idea, how much of the unit's future resources should be allocated to a particular project. Determining which projects to include in the departmental plan is very difficult. All such determinations are largely subjective and have far-reaching consequences for the proposer. Therefore, they should be made responsibly and in the best interests of the person, unit, and university. Projects included in the departmental plan have a chance for departmental, collegiate, and university support, projects excluded will be denied these opportunities. Departmental planning is serious business that requires thoughtful analyses of the options and careful decision making.

The department head has the responsibility of gathering all of the DEs and arranging them into program development packets. Placing total dollar amounts on those programs, writing a description for the research program, assigning a program coordinator, assigning laboratory space and support personnel, and most importantly allocating faculty research and teaching time from the departmental budget to the program.

Many department heads use annual faculty planning and achievement reports to help them prepare the next years operating plan and the tactical plans for the department. Later, the operating and tactical plans are incorporated into the departments strategic plan.

The first step in designing a departmental plan is for the department head to request DEs from faculty and students, and requests for proposals (RFPs) from sponsors. The department head should obtain a DE for every research project that contemplates using departmental resources.

The new goals should grow out of the strategic analyses prepared by the unit. The architects of the unit strategic plan must formulate a goal for every scenario recommended by the planners and accepted by the unit. Departmental administrative officers prepare a packet of unit plans that incorporate program plans and any independent project proposals. The departmental plan is discussed thoroughly. The faculty is asked to make comments on the planning team's formulation of DEs for existing and new programs and for departmental research support plans. The section on "Designing the Departmental Strategic Plan for Research" in Chapter 6 provides an extended discussion of the technology and personal planning activities of departmental planners.

Designing College Strategic Plans—It is important to the adoption of the college strategic plan that all members of the college be involved in the goal setting phase for the development of its plan. The college strategic plans are mostly the aggregation of departmental plans and the independent research programs that are conducted under the direct supervision of the dean's staff. The greatest problem in designing college strategic plans is pulling together the disparate units to support interdisciplinary projects that cannot be done by a single department. The excellent planning that was done by Dean Sam Curl of the College of Agricultural Sciences at Texas Tech University stands as an example of good use of planning technology to advance an entire college while promoting several departmental initiatives. A fuller explanation of that planning is included in Chapter 6.

The authors recommend that planners at all levels send to all associates copies of their proposed unit plans. Part of the technology of strategic planning is establishing the lines of communication between the planners and the voting members of the corporate body. The planners should invite comments on the proposed unit plans and hold open meetings to solicit opinions on the proposed goals. The public meetings will bring out objections to the goals selected by the planning teams and evoke criticism of the means for achieving the proposed goals. Arguments over the direction the new plans will take the unit and the best way of getting there are time consuming, but unavoidable as these plans will very likely determine the units future and those in it. At the public meetings an objective tally of the opinions and comments on each unit plan should be presented to the audience and a reasonable period of debate on each goal and the direction it will take the unit should be encouraged. During these debates the quality of the strategic analyses will be telling. Well-prepared strategic analyses will put to rest most criticism. Several meetings may be needed to develop a body of supporters for the plans of the architects. It is seldom that a consensus will be achieved in the first round of planning, but without a core of stout advocates for a particular direction the unit plan will be very difficult to implement at a later time. Without organized opposition, a goal can be included in a plan with considerably less than majority support of the unit. However, significant support can be garnered at public meetings and problems anticipated by carefully considering the impacts of problems addressed in the written comments and voiced at open meetings.

At the public meetings, the skills of the planners and the support of the leaders of the administrative unit will be tested. Frequently, objections to certain goals can be overcome immediately by changing some objectionable words. In some instances, limiting phrases to protect against potential abuses or to eliminate existing, onerous policies and procedures must be added to the philosophy statements in the backup scenarios before support is given to a unit plan. Also, the modifying of a goal statement in a public meeting to bring about a consensus is often critical to acceptance of the unit plan by the corporate body at voting time. Sometimes compromise on the intent of the goal may be necessary to gain support, sometimes new information is needed by the corporate body before acceptance is given. The important thing for research administrator to remember about this phase of planning is to allow the process of criticism to take place. Frequently, criticism will emerge that will save the unit from a later disaster. It is wise to listen to your critics with an open mind. Despite the criticism, the architects of the unit plan must determine how much the changes in goal statements and the means for achievement will compromise their vision of the future. They must then set the elements of the unit plan to meet their vision of what can realistically be done in certain time frames. At this stage, they must have the courage of their convictions to set the plans according to the long-term benefit of the institution. This is very dangerous business. The antipathy of the opposition to a particular goal may (probably will) result in personal attacks on the advocates of the plan and create lingering animosities toward the advocates.

Appointment of planners to teams seldom creates a furor, conduct of environmental scans is an interesting learning activity for the campus, strategic analysis is a good natured extension of routine scholarly activity;

but unit plan development is a highly controversial activity that can make or break any institutional plan. It is at this phase that the higher level units incorporate subordinate units plans into their plans and recommend line-item appropriations for the future operating budgets. Can enough power be mustered to push a plan ahead? This long-range planning and budgeting is effective. Unit heads know that they must have their plans and budgets incorporated into larger plans. The scramble for program approvals and subsequent budget allocations locks competing forces in sustained intellectual combat. However, out of these critical conflagrations emerge plans that are substantially stronger and quite practical.

Similar techniques as those discussed above are used in the design of ORU plans.

The Format for the Unit Plan

In round one of the design process, the planners will reconcile the current plans with the new plans. In the preceding chapter thirty-eight elements were identified in at least one strategic plan. We have summarized the Cooper list into the following generic sections for a unit strategic plan.

The Architects of the Plan—The first part of the Unit Strategic Plan contains a message from the unit head presenting his or her vision of what the unit can become and their acknowledgement of services rendered by the planning team. It next lists the planning team members. The names of the members are listed alphabetically with their titles and organizational affiliation noted. As we discussed in a previous section, planning team members should be selected for their research development orientation and their influence in the field. Listing of leaders in the field give the strategic planning document credibility immediately.

Executive Summary— There is usually an executive summary that identifies the purpose of the strategic plan. It indicates that the plan is a guide to the future. It presents the leader's vision succinctly. It states that the unit will either keep the same direction or to make a change in course. It should identify a course of action based on the identification of a series of broad goals and the strategic positions that the unit plans to achieve in targeted areas within a series of five year plans. It will mention the general costs of the plan and the major benefits that are expected to accrue to the unit.

The Purpose of the Unit—The purpose of the unit is usually the third section that appears in the strategic unit plan. It contains: 1) a statement of purpose. This statement introduces the unit by telling what it is and what it expects to be for the next half-century. This statement provides the research development direction for the unit members and its associates and serves as a point of reference for discussing subsequent elements. 2) An expanded purpose statement that lists several long-range goals that are designed to lead the unit to a position of excellence within the next decade. The expanded purpose statement is concluded by listing ten to twenty near-term objectives that are action oriented and take deliberate steps toward achieving part of the unit's stated purpose within the next biennium.

The Philosophy and Guiding Principles of the Unit—The philosophy statement is a statement that says why the unit has been designated what it is. It outlines the responsibilities that it has accepted and explains why it wants to advance its research strengths. The philosophy statement reviews the unit's guiding principles, states what it is committed to, explains what it will foster, and distinguishes between different types of activities and prioritizes them if necessary. It defines research and the activities of the unit. It discusses the stewardship of knowledge and makes an affirmation of academic freedom and independent scholarship.

It provides a series of safeguard statements that protect the unit from encroachment upon any of its academic traditions. It generally acknowledges its long-standing patrons and invites dedicated scholars to join its faculty and students in their search for knowledge and their service to humanity. It sets in Jeffersonian language high standards for the unit.

The Unit's Point of Departure—This section places in front of the reader the following.

1. The dominant vision of the unit leaders. The leader's vision expresses the intent of reaching within the next half-century a position of preeminence in certain targeted areas. The vision tells very generally where the unit is going and about how long it will take to get there.
2. The assumptions of the unit leaders are expressed in a systematic manner. The assumptions begin by presenting the current facts of the field and calls attention to the opportunities. The assumptions outline the existing tactical plans of the unit and provide a series of short explanations of expected long-range developments with particular partners.
3. The unit's wide concerns for research development in its field. It lists from the relevant scans the patron and client expectations for delivery of future research outputs. It states the anticipated impact of these outputs on the socioeconomic infrastructure of the nation, state, and region. It discusses the major threats to the unit and the disciplinary field.
4. The critical issues of the constituencies of the unit are identified and their possible impact on the unit explained.
5. The targeted disciplinary problems to be addressed by the unit are identified and general solutions proposed.

The Unit's Destination—The unit plan contains statements of where the unit wants to go. This section addresses the following.

1. The challenge that the unit faces is couched in terms of why the field must develop certain areas of research. The challenge links the work of the unit with its target area problems and infers state and national benefits and consequences that will be derived from the proposed unit plans. The challenge statement reiterates the major points of the leader's vision and shares their understanding of the total process involved and the difficulty of the tasks ahead. It discusses in general terms the commitment that will be required by the major sectors and the principals in the research enterprise. It stresses the need for coordinated efforts that sustain the action initiated under the near-term goals. It provides a statement on how the unit leaders and affiliate leaders must make tough decisions that will ensure that the unit can reach a position of preeminence in the field.

2. The focus for the next decade concentrates attention on two or three promising areas that have been targeted for research development and explains how much of the unit's resources has been dedicated to direct exploration of each area. In addition, it tells approximately how much is expected to be budgeted by partners for cooperative ventures in an area. It lists the faculty and students working in each target area, explains what is being produced currently in each area by the unit, and projects what the unit expects to produce in the area.

3. The approaches for the unit reaching its destination are explained. The planners suggest ways that the unit can form research groups that will continue the work in the target areas. They recognize the quality of their partners and outline how the unit and affiliates will translate the disciplinary imperatives, social needs and organizational priorities into unit goals that must be met. It briefly states the old investigative approaches that will be used and explains in some detail the use of innovative approaches for particular types of investigation. In 1970 in order to plan and administer a three-state coalition, we elected to use a total systems approach to unit planning because it forces the unit to bring all relevant systems into the planning, and ties accountability for services to specific systems and their budgets. In the selection of any approach, the expectation of using a particular approach over another should be justified according to costs. This section mentions the current techniques that have proved to be ideal candidates for particular research breakthroughs as initial work has progressed beyond previous plans. The approach section stresses reaching the destinations of the unit and its affiliates by increasing

reliance on each other's strengths. It acknowledges that research development of the institution, state, and nation are dependent upon the strong government/industry/ university partnerships that develop new ways of sending the necessary feedback, corrective actions, and resources into the cooperating units to advance or keep them as world class competitors.

Designing Financial Budgets

Budgets are, of course, spending plans. Budgets are tied to a plan of action for a unit. The operating plan, tactical plan, and strategic plan each have a corresponding budget. Theoretically, the action plans form the structure for unit operations and for the setting of unit budgets. Practically, budgets often form the structure for the unit operations. Which is more important or which comes first is a chicken-or-the-egg argument. Both are important and one grows out of the other. They are complementary processes that should be considered together.

Designing Unit Operating Budgets—There are a number of technologies for budgeting that will be explained in the next section to assist the strategic budgeting process.

Research operating budgets are much more complex than instructional budgets. The instructional budget for the unit is usually derived from three or four major revenue sources—state appropriations, endowments, and student tuition and fees. Frequently, the instructional budget is based on formula funding tied to student credit hour production. See Chapter 10 for an excellent description of this budgeting process.

The research operating budget is derived from many revenue sources based on project or ORU budgets. There is the traditional allocation from the university general fund, monies from the organized research appropriation of the state, state line-item appropriations; direct costs for every project budget; and indirect-costs return to the unit, endowment income, funds from the advanced technology programs, affiliate fees, income from sales of goods and services of pilot plant operations, and income from sale and leasing of intellectual property.

A close inspection of the DE shows that each research unit director must consider revenue generation from several sources (university, federal, state, and private sponsors) and must consider their major objects of expenditure (salaries of personnel, fringe benefits, travel, equipment and supplies, and indirect costs). There are hundreds of expenditure object codes, which can afford the planner as much precision in budgeting and management as they desire. The authors believe that detailed budgeting for projects is very important in planning as it helps the principal investigator consider every person and anticipated physical resource needed. However, once the project goes into operation the changing demands of actual re-search operations are such that the investigator should be allowed complete freedom to transfer monies among expenditure object codes without ap-proval from the sponsor or university administration. The fastest way to ruin the strategic planning climate on campus is to have some accounting clerk or authoritarian administrator attempt during project operations to make the PI's spending conform to expenditure object codes prepared for a planning budget. If this caveat is remembered, the second generation of strategic planning and budgeting will be much more accurate and easier.

Reconciling Unit Plans

The designing of unit plans is difficult because the planners are required to reconcile the many ideal plans with the reality of the times. This development process demands several rounds of revisions and it requires the following types of reconciliation.

Unit Goal-Work Reconciliation—The planning team after careful con-sideration of unit scenarios and extant plans must affirm that the work and goals are congruous, or recommend changing the goals of the unit to fit the work, or recommend changing the work to meet the unit goals.

Past-Present-Future Goal Reconciliation—With the array of unit scenarios in hand, the planning team must make choices from among the various ideal options and design the unit goals to match current reality and/or strong trends.

Operating-Tactical-Strategic Plan Reconciliation—The planning team must review carefully the operating and tactical plans and budgets and determine the possibilities of shifting planning and budgeting formats and commitments to match the strategic plans of the unit.

Unit-to-Unit Goal Reconciliation—Again, the planning team must rewrite the unit goals to fit with the goals of units above and below them in the administrative structure.

Unit-Partner Goal Reconciliation—The planning team must rewrite the goal's statements or recommend a change in the work of the unit to match the goals of the major sponsor, affirm that the existing match is mutually beneficial and should be continued, or propose that the partner change their goals to match the unit's goals.

Incorporating New Proposals into the Strategic Plan

The designing activities not only involve reconciliation of goals and work among the existing research units, it involves the incorporation of new proposals and new partners into the strategic plan. The incorporation of new proposals begins with the unit requesting proposals to achieve their purposes. Once the proposals are received, the planning team must either incorporate the proposals into the unit plans or eliminate them. Incorporation is a critical activity of adjustment between unit goals and work. The incorporated proposals stand a chance of being supported by that unit's budget at a later time. Unincorporated proposals will probably not be considered further by planners in that administrative structure.

Designing unit plans is the proposing and consideration phase. It is a first cut that narrows the number of proposals that will be considered by the unit. The proposers and planners are like suitors. They are very anxious about the consideration of their proposals. The decision making is emotionally charged. The planning team is in both the position of being the proposer and being proposed to.

Accepting the University Agenda

Accepting the agenda of the university requires that planning teams affirm old goals or establish new ones for institutional associates , prioritize the plans under consideration, pledge their resources to specific plans, and advocate the acceptance of their plans to their partners.

The acceptance phase of strategic planning is often neglected by planners because they do not understand the difference between strategic planning and other types of planning. Most academicians have made unit plans that were in reaction to a higher authority's budget. These operational plans become the means of achieving sponsor goals according to a sponsor's budget Some have made tactical plans that determined the means and objectives for achieving the sponsor goals. These activities are planning efforts, but they are not strategic planning. Both operational and tactical planning are reactive planning that allows a single sponsor to set the direction and the rate of development of the unit.

Strategic planning is the process of establishing the future purposes of a unit considering common understanding for developing its agenda with its chief partners and major constituencies. It is proactive, not reactive. Strategic planning requires that the sponsor accept the plan of the unit according to the budget of the unit. This is much more difficult than tactical or operational planning. This key difference of acceptance of a unit agenda by partners must be understood and achieved or the plan remains a long-range unit plan with little chance for adoption. The process of planning reverses in the acceptance phase. The planners stop taking in information and reacting to it—they begin disseminating their plans and try to have others endorse those plans.

After months of designing the unit plan and delivering it to the unit head, academicians frequently assume that planning is finished. It is not. The unit plan is a raw product. A unit plan is a design that is the product of the "unit mind" after the environment has been carefully scanned, options analyzed, and goals set by the unit. An essential project is a product that has the support of the unit, but unit support does not make it a strategic plan. It may be an excellent long-range unit plan, but it does not yet have the endorsement of its agenda by its chief partners and major constituencies.

Strategic plans are not an assembled mass of unarticulated unit summary plans. Strategic unit plans are integrated into institutional budgets and plans. They are articulated with tactical and operational plans. Before the sponsors will approve the whole unit plan they must see prospectuses of the ideas they are expected to support and incorporate the individual ideas into the agency plan. Before affiliates can pay membership fees to support cooperative agreements and joint ventures, they must pledge long-term support and install specific revenue producing mechanisms in the association plans. At this phase of strategic planning appropriate decision ele-

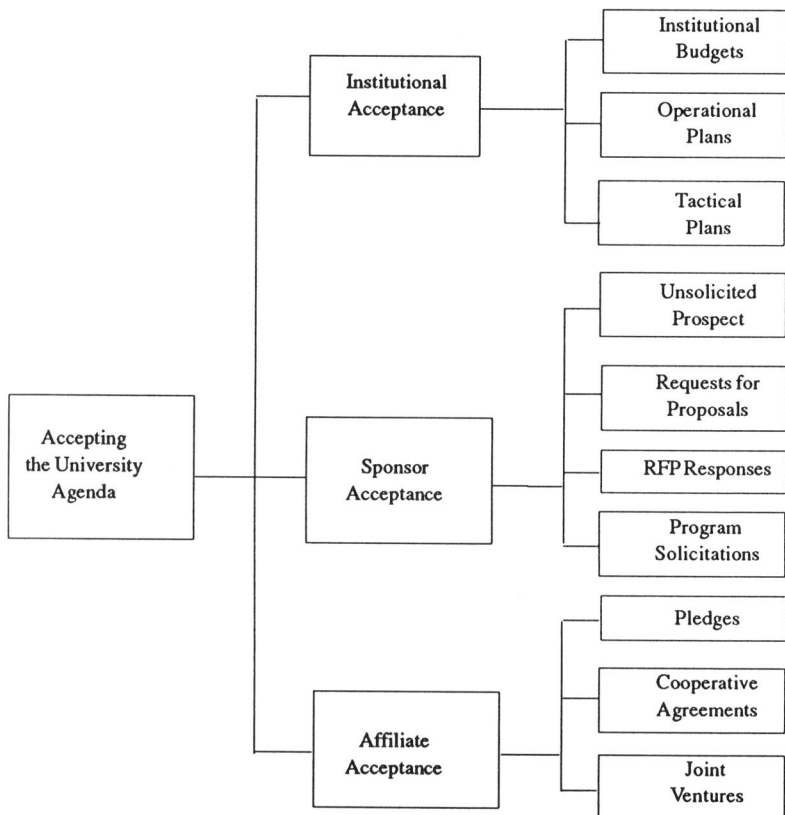

Figure 5.9. A Model for Gaining Acceptance of the University Agenda.

ments must be sent to the internal and external sources of resource allocation and to all of the administrative review offices. Figure 5.9 shows the
enormity of letting partners know what is being planned and seeing how
they are to fit into the plan.

This phase of strategic planning for university research requires the acceptance of the unit plan into the university plan, the commitment of the
sponsor to morally support the unit plan at a certain level of funding using a
particular set of priorities, and the approval of joint-venture affiliates to the
unit plan. Figure 5.9 shows three generic forms of acceptance—institutional, sponsor, and affiliate approval of the unit plan.

Institutional Acceptance

This phase of planning calls for the planner to obtain approval of a
schedule for plan implementation. Designing unit plans was mostly concerned with putting together a plan for a particular unit and articulating the
planned activities with the operating activities at one administrative level.
Accepting the university agenda goes beyond planning at the unit level and
routine administration—it requires the decision maker to articulate their
plans with other unit plans and approve generally the whole plan for the
university. We must remember that collegial power is characterized by
equal sharing of authority and resources within the university. Because
each planning team expects to have their unit plan accepted in the university agenda, the planning teams must now work on fitting their plans into
the university strategic plan and obtain from the other university planners a
commitment that their unit work is valued highly by their colleagues.

The acceptance of the unit agenda would be greatly enhanced if the
planner's colleagues would provide instant agreement that the unit plan
belongs in the university strategic plan, if sponsors would accept the planning propectuses exactly as presented from the unit, and if affiliates would
match precisely the development schedule offered by the unit. Unfortunately, colleagues, sponsors, and affiliates have different ideas and different planning and budgeting mechanisms from those of the soliciting
unit. This means that planners must make many adjustment to bring their
plans and budgets into sync with other plans and budgets. The accepting of
university agenda requires studying the acceptance process and examining
the mechanisms for achieving agreement upon the preferred work.

Accepting university agenda requires very precise analysis of the entire
plan by the three generic partners. It requires the partners to arrive at: 1) A
work agreement—mutual understanding of the work to be done and agreement upon the scope of the work; 2) resources allocation agreement—
mutual agreement on the level of resources to be committed for the planned

work; and 3) time of delivery agreement—mutual consent on the schedule for delivery of specific outputs.

The acceptance of the strategic plan requires various degrees of acceptance among different principals. A reader may completely accept or reject a plan. There are many degrees of acceptance between these two extremes. In accepting the university agenda, all units are interested in gaining acceptance for their plan. This is the phase where agreements must be reached concerning the tactical plans.

Strategic plans for university research require that all levels of the university administration review the unit plans above and below them in three rounds of review. The first round requires the acceptance of the plan by the reviewers. In some instance, the reviewer may believe there is no goal congruence between another's unit plan and their own unit plans. Consequently, they may reject a plan because it is in conflict with their own plans. In this case they assign the plan a low priority. If the plans of another unit correspond to their own thinking, they will probably accept it as being suitable for inclusion into the strategic plan and assign it a high priority score.

Round two of the internal planning process requires that the reviewer incorporate high priority plans into their planning if acceptable modifications can be made. Round three requires that the reviewer morally commit to supporting the plan at a certain level of funding for a certain performance level for a definite period of time.

Sponsor Acceptance of University Agenda

Earlier in this chapter we called attention to the function of the decision element in the design of unit plans. In this section, we note the importance of the prospectus in gaining acceptance for the agenda of university units.

Schoppmeyer and Hensley (1972) explained that the prospectus is a planning document used to secure from a sponsor an invitation to write a proposal for high priority work related to the mission of the agency. It has two planning functions. First, it attempts to convince the agency that the research question, training and/or service activities are of sufficient importance to the agency and of significance to a particular field of knowledge and/or client group. Secondly, it tries to convince the reader that the principal investigator and his research or service group are the best team to carry the research or service to a successful conclusion.

The prospectus contains in outline form the major elements of the final proposal. Therefore, the strategic planner finds it helpful to think through the entire operational features of the proposed project and to headline those features concerned with the need, significance, impact, and evaluation of the proposed project activities. The prospectus is a technical document that is to be read by experts in a particular field; therefore, the disciplinary imperatives, style, and language should be considered carefully at this planning stage of research development. Clear, concise prose is mandatory. A prospectus usually consists of three to five typed single-spaced pages composed of the following basic parts: the abstract, the purpose statement, the statement of the problem, procedures, evaluation, dissemination, budget, and institutional considerations (cooperative patent agreements related to disclosure, development, promotion, and licensing).

Abstract—The abstract usually does not exceed 150 words. The title is always descriptive of the work to be performed. "Cutesy" or "catchy" titles are never used. The first sentence states explicitly what the researcher proposes to do. Secondly, the problem to be alleviated by the planned actions is identified precisely. Next, the solution of the problem is explained briefly. Finally, the benefits of the project are enumerated and the unique qualifications of the PI and the special resources of the institution that are necessary to solve the problem at hand are recognized in a modest, but indelible, manner.

Purpose Statement—The purpose statement provides enough detailed information to clearly convey the intent of the project and yet it is general enough to serve as an effective overall guide in planning the project operations. Proposal objectives state in measurable terms exactly what is to be achieved during the project period. The objectives flow from the needs assessment; they are firmly anchored in the knowledge of the disciplinary field; and they are closely articulated with the goals of the parent institution.

The most commonly cited problem with objectives is their lack of specificity. This situation usually occurs when goals are submitted or general statements are written in the place of specific objectives. Note the summary example which follows.

Acceptable Objective:

The Institute for Research in Social Science intends to study voter decision-making in regard to Presidential, state, and local candidates in the 1968 Elections through 14 independent state-wide electoral analyses immediately after the election.

Goal:

The purpose of the Institute for Research in Social Science is to advance understanding of human behavior.

The goal of the Institute for Research in Social Science at the University of North Carolina is most appropriate to be included in the institution's strategic plan. It is too broad to be accepted by an external sponsor who wants to support a particular research thrust within the institute.

Those individuals who are writing in the area of the social sciences should remember the following principles and refer to Mager's (1975) slim, but excellent, volume. First, identify the outcomes by name; specify the outcome that will be accepted as evidence that the client has attained the desired behavior, received the designated service and/or produced a product. This may require a very precise definition of observable behavior, institutional policy and/or physical product. Second, describe the important condition under which the outcomes will be expected to occur; identify the selected population, describe explicitly the environment where the activities will be performed and specify when the activities will be performed. Third, define the parameters of acceptable performance or product by setting the criterion for the outcomes. If standardized tests or measurements are available and suitable, name the instrument; if you are using a newly designed instrument, name the instrument; and later in the prospectus give reliability and validity coefficients or cite prototypal results.

Statement of the Problem—The prospectus should identify precisely the problem as it relates to social needs, disciplinary imperatives, and institutional mission. The statement of the problem is usually evaluated on the following features.

1. The validity of the needs assessment—There must be an objective way of showing the need to find effective ways to increase productivity, improve products and reduce expenditures; to identify neglected clients, provide specialized services and expanded services at lower per-unit costs; and to train preprofessional and professionals to upgrade their skills, to transmit new knowledge, and to work under new conditions. Cite studies that identify the problem at the national and state levels. Needs assessments frequently begin with government reports.

2. The identification of disciplinary imperatives—The review of the literature should be structured to provide a conceptual framework converging upon the specific problems addressed. The literature review should be comprehensive, but not exhaustive. Cite national authorities who have previously identified the problem and recommend the proposed solutions. (*Note*: The prospectus is not usually the place for long quotations. Save the quotations for the proposal.) Citation trails to the proposer's present point of departure are recommended. If the project is interdisciplinary the proposer should remember that some of the reviewers will not be knowledgeable about the specifics of a discipline outside their fields; thus, a com-

prehensive bibliography across disciplinary lines should be supplied as an addendum. It is generally true that the prospectus will be strengthened by a systematic consideration of the theoretical foundations and the literature of the discipline upon which the project is based. Truly intuitional approaches will be downgraded if reviewers find that relevant findings of other investigators with which a proposer should be familiar have been neglected.

3. The recognition of institutional and individual commitment to developing solutions to the identified needs—It is in this section that the planner should provide evidence of individual commitment to the proposed project and a section on the institution's track record of success in similar types of activities. The historical record should show the institution's continuing commitment to the problem at hand. It should indicate how this project fits into the departmental priorities for development and, if possible, show the possibilities for continuation of the project after funding by the sponsoring agency is phased-out. Also, it should show the cooperative arrangements with other agencies when such operations are essential to the success of the project.

Procedures—When possible use classical methodology and research designs to convey to the reader the methods to be employed in investigating the problem, the activities to be used in delivering a service, the instructional strategies planned for training.

Information should by supplied on the following items: the specification of personnel and other resources that will be used for the project and how they will be used and organized; definitions of populations serving as subjects or clients; the research protocol; and statement of the plan for selection, gathering, and analysis of data.

If the protocol represents a significant departure from or improvement on existing practice, explain the advantages of the new procedures. If the writer is taking a new approach or one side of a controversial issue in preference to others, the existence of other protocols and the justification for the writer's selection of methodology should be discussed briefly. The proposer should state exactly the statistical techniques to be used rather than asserting that appropriate statistical techniques will be used. It is here that you must sketch a scenario of how you intend to achieve the outcomes. It is complete only when you have specified the settings, the role of the project staff, sequence of events, and calendar of planned activities. At this time you must constantly ask yourself, "Am I realistically providing a plan that can be implemented in terms of staff, space and funds allocated to the task?" If not, revise now. It is difficult to change directions once the agency program officer has invited you to submit a formal proposal. Also, the reviewers are knowledgeable about operating conditions within your field. Nothing else, other than poorly stated objectives, will disqualify a prospectus so quickly as an understaffed project, an unrealistic timetable, and inappropriate methods.

Evaluation—The evaluation statement should briefly explain the design of the evaluation protocol. The evaluation protocol should measure the impact of the project in the areas addressed in the objectives. (Without measurable objectives and the systematic collection and analysis of data associated with those objectives, it is difficult to convince an agency that their money will be spent appropriately.) It is the achievement of evaluation goals that ultimately establishes the reputation of the PI and the track record of the institution.

The evaluation protocol should assure the reader that beginning, continuous, and terminal measures will be taken. It should also convey to the reader that project personnel will systematically consider the processes involved as well as the end products. Information derived from evaluation activities should be used early on in the operations to determine the strong and weak points of the project and thus allow initiation of immediate corrective action. The agency must be assured that when baseline data is compared with terminal data it will permit project effectiveness to be determined and used as a guide for any future modification of project activities. The length of this section will depend upon the emphasis given to the evaluation component by the potential funding agency.

Dissemination—This section of the prospectus indicates the researcher's plan for publishing the results of the study. The classical path for placing results into the discipline is to supply the funding agency with a technical report (this is usually required annually by the sponsor), to present a paper on the findings at a regional or national meeting of a professional association, to submit abstracts and articles to professional journals, and finally to submit the published work to information clearinghouses. If special workshops, lectures, and seminars are to be arranged, this is mentioned here.

Budget—The prospectus requires a summary budget that includes the major expenditure items shown on the decision element. "Big ticket" expenditures may require a very brief justification for their inclusion in sponsor expenses. Fringe benefits and indirect costs are included in the prospectus budget.

Special Project Considerations—The research strategist uses the prospectus as a mechanism for determining the sponsors receptivity to special project considerations. If patenting and publication policies of a university are unusual, these and other special requirements should be mentioned in the prospectus so the sponsor and the university can determine if both parties can agree on a solution to the special considerations before the contract is signed. Special project considerations are often noted in regard to the assigning of rights for patents derived from sponsored research projects. Disclosure periods; ownership rights of investigators, university, and sponsor; patent pursuit; and development, promotion, and licensing consideration are mentioned here.

Affiliate Acceptance of the Agenda

The acceptance of the unit plan by industrial affiliates is no small matter for promoting its acceptance into the university strategic plan. There is a wide range of research development mechanisms that promote affiliate acceptance of unit plans. *Science* (1987, 987) reported that industry underwrites a sizable portion the research university's research budget. The same article noted that the Robotics Institute of Carnegie-Mellon has developed a range of partnership agreements to satisfy most industrial managers.

The following are illustrative.

Affiliate Grant Agreements—A company providing a multiyear grant of $250,000 to $1 million annually can stipulate the research goals of certain institute plans and receive the patent rights developed through its sponsorship.

Individual Industrial Affiliates—this program allows companies providing $10,000-$50,000 annually to receive specialized research newsletters and to support institute seed projects and to receive nonexclusive licenses for technologies derived from their sponsorship.

Group Industrial Affiliates—These provide a substantial affiliate fee can also sponsor research in their area of interest and can receive nonexclusive licenses for research they totally supported.

When industrial affiliates provide several million dollars annually to support an ORU, this becomes a strong incentive for the unit planners to be sure that they have affiliate acceptance of the unit plan. Such support also helps promote the inclusion of the unit objectives into the university strategic plan for research.

The acceptance process is so complex that only a hint of the major activities can be given by a model. Hopefully, after reading the anecdotal materials in Chapter 6, the reader will acquire a feeling for the vastness of activity that is subsumed under the general headings of the model.

Adopting the University Strategic Plan

In the previous sections, we saw the importance of partners assessing the other partner's purposes to determine the compatibility of their units to work together to develop mutual goals over the long-term, and accepting a new cooperatively designed agenda for their partners' research development that will in important ways match their own agenda. In this section, we will discuss the adopting of the partners' purposes into one's own strategic planning and then committing one's own resources to accomplishing specific goals in the mutual plan.

Chapter 4 allowed that strategic plans for university research ranged in length from 14 to 186 pages and included the following major divisions: executive summaries, mission statements, motivating factors and statement of value of strategic planning, spotlighting the uniqueness of the institution, discussion of criteria for determining research program priorities, identification of goals and objectives to be pursued, interdisciplinary efforts, organized research units, seeking partnerships with public and private sector organizations, international program-research development, college planning, developing human resources, upgrading of library and information resources, enhancement of facilities and equipment, and financial planning to achieve objectives.

In documents this large and comprehensive, adoption does not come immediately after publication of all objectives. It occurs gradually during the strategic planning process. In this regard, the planning process may be more valuable than the planning document itself. The strategic planning planning process, which may take two years or more to accomplish, brings a high degree of awareness of what was being proposed generally and in the early processes forges acceptance of the broad goals in many who are involved in the planning.

Figure 5.10 shows how the research principals use a series of adoption stages to gain commitments from the research performers and sponsors for new agenda. Chapter 6 will provide a case study of the adoption of a strategic plan for university research at an emerging research university. This section closes the discussion of the technology for planning by reviewing the six phases of strategic planning for university research and by noting the adoption of specific planning documents during the completion of the model phases.

Any strategic plan has much more of the old in it, than the new. In Chapter 3 we saw the incremental development of university research through a number of great waves of outside support and the gradual, internal restructuring of the university to meet the needs of society for more research. Much of strategic planning in the well-established research university is a reaffirmation of long-standing partnership purposes with the addition of some new terms in traditional agreements. In the emergent research university, much of the research infrastructure is also in place, but the purpose of the institution has to be reassessed and reformulated by the univer-

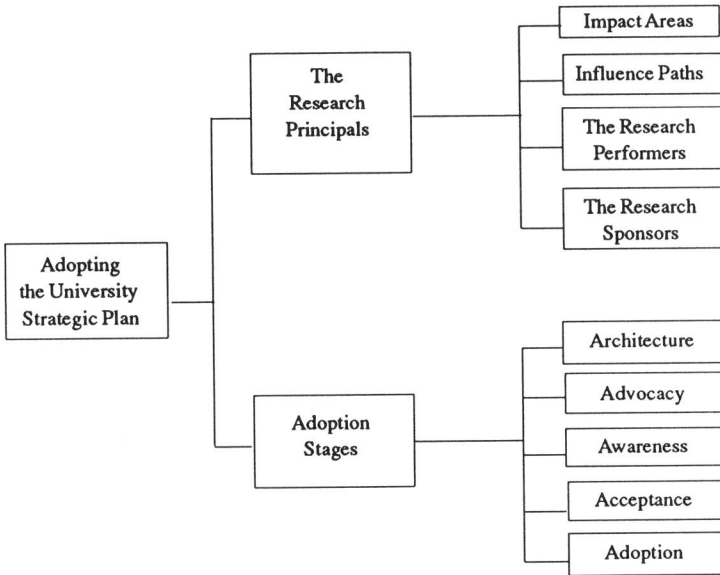

Figure 5.10 The Adoption of the Strategic Plan.

sity and its partners. Then they must accept or reject the proposed mission of being a research university and adopt a new agenda for its development. In the latter case, the adoption of a research mission and a research-oriented agenda occurs in following stages.

Architecture—Someone or some group of people must conceive the ideas for changing the institution and project that vision to the university's many constituencies and its partners.

Advocacy—Someone or some group must champion the plans that will transform the institution and carry it into the future.

Awareness—The principals in the research enterprise must be made aware of the proposed institutional changes and the new agenda for development of research.

Acceptance—The principals must incorporate the proposals for the future development of the university's research into their own plans.

Adoption—The principals must commit their resources to the advancement of specific plans that are incorporated in the strategic plan of the university or that are implied in the mission of the institution.

The adoption of the strategic plan was furthered when the unit leaders appointed the architects for research to critical planning positions. If the chief research officer of the respective units performed the following activities the architects of the university's future were positioned to project their vision for what the university could become.

PERIOD ONE
    Positioning the Architects

Inputs
    Identifying Research-Development Individuals
    Sharing the Leader's Visions

Process
    Designing the Requisite Planning Structure
    Selecting Reseach-Development Leaders

Outputs
    A Planning Hierarchy
    Appointment of Planning Team Members
    Cross Appointments Among Organizations
    Specific Charges to Planning Teams

This period is very important because it launches the institution into strategic planning. The appointment of personnel, the projections of leaders' vision, and the establishment of specific charges to planning teams creates an awareness of the direction that the institution is headed. The time frame for positioning the architects ranges from one to four months.

The time frame for conducting the environmental scan is quite lengthy if undertaken for the first time. This period may extend into several months. The environmental scan is a period that creates a high degree of awareness of what the units have been doing, of what patron and clients expect, of what current outputs are, and of what the trends and planning assumptions are. The awareness activities of this period are summarized below

PERIOD TWO
    Scanning the Environment

Inputs
    Program-Development-System Information
    General Information Releases
    Old Unit Plans
    Current Unit Outputs
    Research Opportunities
    Significant Factors
    Patron and Client Expectations

Process
    Locating the New Ideas for Niche Development
    Selecting External Target Areas
    Selecting Internal Target Areas

Outputs
>Ideas for Research
>Trend Papers
>Mission and Goal Assessment
>Information Integration
>Planning Assumptions
>White Papers

The third period for adopting the university strategic plan involves a great deal of awareness of the possible ideas for new research directions, a period of serious discussion of mission and goals, and consideration of alternative scenarios for research partnerships. Notice in the following outline of analyzing strategic options the importance that awareness of trends, mission assessment, and planning assumptions play in the acceptance of definite options in a scenario.

PERIOD THREE
>Analyzing Strategic Options

Inputs
>Ideas for Research
>Trend Papers
>Mission and Goal Assessment
>Information Integration
>Planning Assumptions
>White Papers

Process
>Formulating Decision Elements for Projects
>Analyzing Research Options
>Analyzing Administrative Options
>Analyzing Sponser Options

Outputs
>Scenarios for Classes of Research
>Scenarios for Research Administration
>Scenarios for Research Partnerships

The discussion of options probably should not extend beyond two or three months as information in the scenarios is tentative, highly speculative, and exploratory. Research breakthroughs, reversed economic and political trends, and the drastic modifications of operational plans cause units to weigh continuously a series of scenarios trying to find a proper fit between existing circumstances and scenarios. Also, in this period there is a rapid and diverse input of options into the scenarios. Scenarios are very tentative "what if considerations" that are intended to predict a unit's possible courses of action for a broad spectrum of changes in the internal and external environments. Scenarios are supposed to be speculative. Although they are done with care, they are not mutual plans. They are hunches on alternatives that should make the planners aware of their options. At this stage, scenarios and options require little discussion beyond the unit members and specific partners.

Despite the speculative nature of the documents developed during this period, people by nature begin to commit intellectually to certain scenarios. Emotionally, they lean toward certain development patterns and begin to advocate the inclusion of certain ideas in unit plans. At this time they may have committed to one small part of a strategic plan. The incorporation of this small part into a greater plan may help them ultimately accept the university strategic plans for they see an institutional commitment to their personal goals.

Period Four, designing unit plans brings about a great deal of emotional commitment to the strategic plans as the planner are highly aware of what is occurring inside and outside the institution, they know the emotional feeling of their peers and partners regarding certain options in selected scenarios. It is at this time that they must decide on unit plans. The investigators must decide to send their project decision elements forward to the organized research unit, the departmental unit, and the joint-venture organizations.

The ORUs, the academic units, the joint-venture organizations, and the sponsors must forward their plans to a higher authority and to their partners. This process has several iterations depending on the complexity of the organizations. For very large-scale and long-term research in a complex organization the design of a plan may take many months to develop. However, for strategic planning processes this period must be limited. The leaders must set deadlines for plans that correspond to the institutional schedule for development of the strategic plan. The following design processes and outputs can usually be achieved in six months or less for most plans.

PERIOD FOUR
    Designing Unit Plans

Inputs
    Proposed Agenda for the Units
    Operating and Tactical Plans
    Scenarios for Classes of Research
    Scenarios for Research Administration
    Scenarios for Research Partnerships
    Priortizing the Options

Design Process
    Formulating Unit Goals for the New Agenda

     Designing Academic Unit Plans from Select Scenarios
     Designing ORU Plans
     Designing Joint-Venture Plans
     Formulating Unit Decision Elements

Outputs
     A Unit Agenda for Research Development to Include:
     Unit Approved Decision Elements
     First Generation Interdisciplinary Plans
     First Generation Collegiate Plans
     First Generation Departmental Plans
     First Generation Program Plans
     First Generation ORU Plans
     First Generation, Joint-Venture Plans

In the adoption of the strategic plan, period five, accepting the university agenda for the future, is vital to the adoption of the whole plan as an intellectual endorsement for future activities must precede a persons' voluntary commitment of resources to a plan. In the preceding section, the value of the prospectus for projects in gaining acceptance from different partners was stressed. Also, the partners' acceptance of the units' first-generation plans becomes essential to long-term cooperative development. The following outline provides the major documents and activities associated with this period.

PERIOD FIVE
     Accepting the University Agenda for the Future

Inputs
     A Unit Agenda for Research Development
     Unit Approved Decision Elements
     First Generation Interdisciplinary Plans
     First Generation Collegiate Plans
     First Generation Departmental Plans
     First Generation Program Plans
     First Generation ORU Plans
     First Generation, Joint-Venture Plans

Acceptance Process
     Assessment of Partner's Purpose in Regard to Unit's Purpose
     Assessment of the Partner's New Agenda
     Prioritization of the Partner's First Generation Plans
     Submission of Prospectuses to Possible Partners

Outputs
     Institutional Acceptance, Revision, or Rejection of New or Reaffirmed Purpose State
       ments
     Partner's Acceptance or Revision of the Unit Agenda

Partner's Acceptance or Revision of First-Generation Unit Plans
Partner's Acceptance or Revision of the First-Generation Academic Unit Plans
Partner's Acceptance or Revision of the First-Generation ORU Plans
Partner's Acceptance or Revision of the First-Generation, Joint-Venture Plans

In the adoption stage of the strategic plan, the principals have already accepted the new agenda into their planning framework; they have reconciled unit plans with their partners; and they have endorsed the mission of the institution and the goals of their units. They strive in period six to achieve the adoption of the strategic plan.

Adoption of the strategic plan may require several years of stout advocacy and logical persuasion to achieve total implementation among partners. To achieve adoption of the strategic plan, legislative bodies and major sponsors must incorporate provisions of the university plan into their policies; they must commit their resources toward the achievement of specific plans; and they must endorse the long-term partnerships discussed in the strategic plan.

In this final period of adopting the strategic plan, the thousands of Proposals become in their unit organizations strategic documents. Proposals are plans for research development. They may involve several sponsors and the terms of the agreement may be established in five-year plans for the next quarter century. Some sponsors plan for perpetuity. In this sixth phase of strategic planning, project and ORU plans are forwarded to potential sponsors for their commitment of resources. In the research era, government agencies are demanding that university proposals fit into broad program plans and agency strategies; the non-profit organizations also have strategic plans that require university funds to match their long-term commitments; and industry sends proposals to universities and receives proposals to establish joint venture organizations and cooperative laboratories. These proposals cover multiple year operations, involve multiple sponsors and performers, and require multiple outcomes.

The following outline for inputs, processes and outputs illustrates the complexity of the adoption stage and points up its critical nature to the advancement of research development.

PERIOD SIX
Adopting the Strategic Plan

Inputs
Partner's Acceptance of the New Agenda
Partner's Acceptance of Reconciled Plans
Partner's Acceptance or Revision of Academic Unit Plans
Partner's Acceptance of the Reconciled ORU Plans
Partner's Acceptance of the Reconciled Joint-Venture Plans

Adoption Process
    Partners Mutually Adopt the New Agendas to Guide Future Operations
    Partners Commit Their Resources to Reconciled Plans

Outputs
    A New Agenda for Research Development
    Appropriations for Institutional and Unit Plans
    Grant Awards to Fund Projects
    Contract Awards to Fund Projects
    RFP Awards to Fund Projects
    Joint-Venture Program Appropriations

The proposal is the final part of the strategic planning technology that must be pursued if the ideas of an investigator and the plans of a unit are to be implemented. Partners must want to support proposals that clearly outline the development of future research. Without an aggressive commitment of planners to develop specific proposals, unit and institutional strategic plans will not be implemented. If proposals and plans are left on academic shelves, they will not be adopted by partners and faculty and research affiliates will not be eager to participate in future planning activities. Chapter 6 is devoted to showing the importance of the adoption of individual proposals to the advancement of the mission of the research university and to successfully adopting a strategic plan for research development. The adoption period is vital to planning because the success of the plan rests on the accomplishments of the plan. Well-drafted plans are academic exercises if there is no resolve to implement them. Achievement of plans establishes the reputation of the institution. Strategic planning success requires the adoption of the advice of President Harry S. Truman, who felt that individuals must adopt large goals and spend the rest of their lives accomplishing them. Strategic planning has occurred when groups of individuals commit to common goals and spend the rest of their careers accomplishing them.

WORKS CITED

Furnas, C. C. 1968. Coping with sponsored research: a special word to presidents. In *Sponsored Research in American Universities and Colleges.* ed. Stephen Strickland, 33-44. Washington, D.C.: American Council on Education.

Hensley, Oliver D. and Schoppmeyer, Martin. (1972, November 15-16). *A Total Systems Approach to Regional Planning.* Boston Mountain Cooperative Meeting, Fayetteville, AR. University of Arkansas.

———. 1974. Improving research fiscal management: a unitary computerized accounting system. *SRA Journal.* Vol. & pages.

Institute for Research in Social Science. 1971. A Ford Foundation project entitled, The thinking voter: national and state electorates in 1968. *Annual Report.* Chapel Hill, North Carolina: The University of North Carolina. 11.

Mager, Robert F. 1975. *Preparing Instructional Objectives*. Belmont, CA: Fearon Publishers.

Schoppmeyer, Martin W. and Hensley, O. (1972, May 11). Program planning and evaluation—a tool for project management. 2nd Annual Meeting of the Boston Mountain Cooperative. Fayetteville, AR. University of Arkansas, May 11, 1972.

Science. 1987. Corporations on campus. Vol. 237:353-355. July 24, 1987.

University of Hawaii. (1982, April 16). *Mission of the University of Hawaii*. Manoa, HA.: Author.

CHAPTER SIX

THE STRATEGIC-PLANNING PROCESS FOR UNIVERSITY RESEARCH

John R. Darling and Oliver D. Hensley

This chapter has some special thoughts for the vice-presidents for research who will have the final responsibility for preparing and implementing the strategic plan for university research. It is written from their perspective and we speak candidly to them about the advantages and difficulties of strategic planning. For over a decade, the authors have experimented with strategic planning as a technology to facilitate the work of researchers and to promote the development of new research in their institutions. We approach planning from our major orientation—the development of institutional climates where research can flourish. We believe the value of strategic planning resides in its affording people who are busy with routine activities an opportunity to step out of their daily thinking and to consider where they want to be at some time in the future. It provides all an opportunity to reassess their relationship with their unit and institution. Many administrators and faculty are so wrapped-up in their own narrow work and present activities that they can not see the broad picture nor the future.

When this occurs they will perform perfunctorily their activities without regard to institutional purposes and will continue only existing activities without introducing new developments.

Our culture is built on following the vision of far-thinking individuals. This phenomenon has been best expressed by "Where there is no vision, the people perish" (Proverbs 29:18). The essence of research is for a person to see a solution that others can not see. We believe that strategic planning is efficient and democratic. It is efficient because it places research development concepts in front of all people involved and invites other contributions under mutual terms. It is democratic because all ideas have an equal chance and it forces the leaders to place their agenda before their constituencies for immediate comment and later accountability.

We see the strategic plan for research as the focused collection of the long-term plans of the university and its partners for the development of research. We believe that these plans come from the university leaders and that strategic plans coincidental to the mission of the university should come from all units in the institution. We believe that the strategic planning process is particularly valuable for emergent research universities where all faculty are not doing research and are not convinced that their major function is research and graduate education. The strategic planning process reassesses the purposes of the units and helps the institution make the transition from a teaching orientation to a research orientation. The task for the vice-presidents for research is establishing the institutional climate that facilitates research planning and the conduct of research.

In keeping with this volume's unifying theme of studying research strategic planning through discussions of actual planning models, the authors have selected the change cube (Figure 6.3) and an academic orientation grid (Figure 6.2) to provide a common image for our analysis of the strategic-planning process for university research. Although our primary purpose is to provide useful insights into the generic strategic-planning process, most of our examples are drawn from personal views and experience, sample documents, and recent examples of the research planning process used at Texas Tech University (TTU) during the eighties—a time when we served respectively as vice-president for academic affairs and research (VPAA&R) and as associate vice-president for research-development (AVPR-Development). During our tenure, we were charged with developing and administering the institution's research.

The other chapters of this volume discuss impersonally and dispassionately the history, philosophy, and technology of strategic planning. This chapter will not be that way. Planning is a human process—some can do it well and others can not do it at all. We will talk about a particular institution and about particular personalities and we will do it from our point of view and from our personal experiences. We will attempt to analyze the character and professional qualities of people who made research planning work. We hope that the discussion of the character traits of exemplars in particular positions, the emphasis on the value of their research experiences, and the advocacy of placing individuals with a development orientation in key positions will provide some insights into the human aspects of planning that complement the technical studies and the academic models. Our introduction of specific personalities and positions into a study of strategic planning is necessary to show that people with a certain academic orientation do the thinking and the development work that is essential to research advancement. It is important for administrators to always consider the human aspects of planning for they weigh heavily in the equation for developing research.

As the success of implementing strategic planning depends on closeness of fit between the administrative orientations and philosophies of the planning members, the importance of appointing research development personnel to key planning teams is stressed. Organizational patterns and administrative orientations for building effective planning teams are analyzed. The value of teamwork and the importance of staying the course when certain plans are under attack are emphasized.

We operated on the assumption that there should be a high degree of congruence between an agreed upon plan and actual practice. Strategic planning has the purpose of showing the direction for future activities. It is a wonderful development tool that can facilitate the advancement of students, faculty, organized research units, and the institution. Strategic planning is an on-going process. To keep that process alive and well, administrators must preserve their credibility by implementing the development agenda once it is completed. Also, when planners know that they will be held accountable for implementation of planning goals, they have a tendency to keep their thoughts realistic and to promote these plans at every opportunity rather than leaving them on their bookshelf.

Finally, strategic planning should be done with a humaneness constantly governing one's actions. Planners should not become so enamored with the plans nor so caught-up in the process that planning becomes the end rather than a means. Plans are only the means that allow the research administrator to serve the institution and to help the researchers develop their ideas. Planning is a powerful administrative tool—it should be used in a wise and humane way.

THE PHILOSOPHY OF ORGANIZING BY ORIENTATION

The authors have held for some time that the best way to quickly advance and to sustain research in an institution is to establish strategic planning practices on campus. Although the strategic planning process is complicated and the plans difficult to formulate, bringing the university leaders into a systematic way of setting the direction of the university far outweighs the onerous features of planning. And, it allows all interested individuals to buy into what is being proposed or to organize resistance to it. Yes, strategic planning is a double-edge sword—Beware.

Prior to 1982, Texas Tech University had not been involved formally in strategic planning for research. In that year, Darling initiated strategic planning for the academic side of the university. Other divisions subsequently followed. The decision to draft a strategic plan for research meant that an administrative organization had to be constructed to develop the planning. Having been involved in research planning before, the authors were well aware of the time consuming nature of the work and the need to find the right people to lead the planning and attendant research development.

Institutions are in constant change. Its senior administrators by their personalities and actions will either attract people with vision who can anticipate and lead the major changes thus developing the institution in the areas targeted for change or they will run away the innovative faculty and students thus shrinking programs and allowing the institution to wither.

In organizing the planning teams, we worked from the following assumptions: 1) the institutional strategic planning for research should be coordinated from the office of vice-president for academic affairs and research, 2) the planning and research development process requires people who know how to develop new units and how to expand and improve the quality of graduate programs, not maintenance administrators, 3) when research-development-oriented faculty and staff are not available in the traditional administrative structure, the unit must reorganize to include such persons, and 4) the planning teams must work in concert to create a broad institutional agenda for research development.

Creating the requisite administrative mechanisms and giving university officers specific charges and adequate resources for the development of research are essential to the success of the strategic planning process and attendant development efforts. In 1981, President Lauro Cavazos recognized the need to reorganize the university for a development orientation. He shortly thereafter combined the two positions of vice-president for academic affairs and vice-president for research into one position—the vice-president of academic affairs and research, which was charged with improving university research and graduate education efforts rapidly. The uniting of these two areas under one administrator was aimed primarily at developing the research and graduate instructional programs at Texas Tech very rapidly. It also helped to bring a coordinated focus to those situations in which academic programs and instructional activities can be closely aligned with the various research activities of the faculty. This consolidation of academic administration enabled the university to bring a greater coordinated focus to graduate program planning and to externally funded research activities.

Modeling Administrative Activities on Knowledge and Stewardship Efforts

The planning and administrative activities associated with academic affairs and research are organized in many different ways in various universities. Darling (1982) organized his administrative functions according to a university administration grid shown in Figure 6.2.

This grid represents the authors' philosophy that in periods of rapid change, human capital must be organized according to specialized services that assist the institution move in the planned direction. The authors viewed academic and research administration as having two major dimensions—stewardship and knowledge. The knowledge dimension was seen as having research and instruction as its ends. The ends of university stewardship are advancement and maintenance.

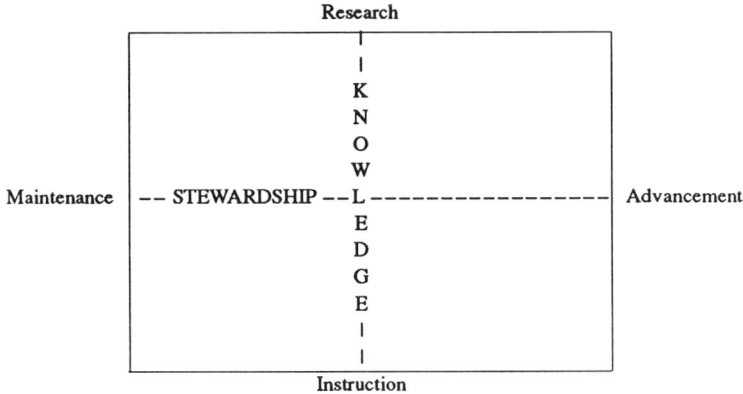

```
                           Research
          ┌─────────────────┬─────────────────────┐
          │                 │                     │
          │                 K                     │
          │                 N                     │
          │                 O                     │
          │                 W                     │
Maintenance│ ── STEWARDSHIP ──L ─────────────────│ Advancement
          │                 E                     │
          │                 D                     │
          │                 G                     │
          │                 E                     │
          │                 │                     │
          │                 │                     │
          └─────────────────┴─────────────────────┘
                          Instruction
```

Figure 6.1 The Major Functional Dimensions for Research Development.

This model follows similar ones suggested by Mehrabian (1971), Bolton (1984), and Darling (1986) who emphasized that behaviors of individuals can be grouped together in clusters giving them a particular social style.

The divisions formed by the major functional dimensions (knowledge and stewardship) create four quadrants that can be used to represent the four academic orientations of university administrators—custodial, development, undergraduate instruction, and graduate instruction orientations. Although all four orientations are necessary to university operations, the authors are convinced that development-oriented individuals are essential to successful strategic planning.

The Cluster of Development Characteristics

Development officers must be assigned at every level of university administration. Without the proper personnel assigned to research development and without adequate resources designated for that purpose, the routine administration will starve out the planning activities resulting in an aborted plan.

Most importantly, the senior administrators must find research-development officers who have a very distinct set of development characteristics. Above all else, research-development officers must be academic entrepreneurs and risk-takers who relish the challenge of the impossible dream. They must be able to walk with agency and corporate chiefs, yet not lose the common touch with principal investigators. They must be able to sift the wheat from the chaff. They must be innovators and leaders who

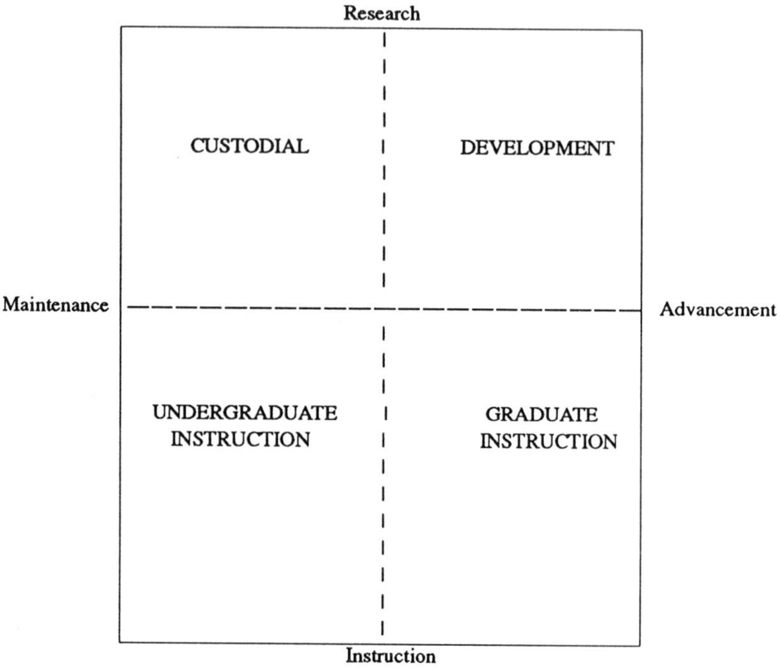

Research

CUSTODIAL	DEVELOPMENT
UNDERGRADUATE INSTRUCTION	GRADUATE INSTRUCTION

Maintenance ————————————————————————— Advancement

Instruction

Figure 6.2 A University Administration-Orientation Grid.

stretch the minds of their colleagues and who bring in the resources to make things happen. They must be able to organize groups to achieve goals that could not be achieved without them. They must be strong advocates of institutional plans. They must be bold in decision making and their activities must move at a reasonably rapid pace. They must know when to commit institutional resources in the planning process and how to develop first-generation plans far beyond what was initially proposed by the sponsor. Lastly, they must know where the sponsors are and how to put them into the university plan. In short, they must encourage the planning process and add value to the plan. Throughout this process, they have a primary leadership responsibility to correctly position the institution to effectively accomplish its research objectives.

As a consequence of this belief, Vice-President Darling decided to organize his staff by orientation thus capitalizing on their natural characteristics. The VPAA&R chose to use his academic council for his research planning team (RPT) and immediately recruited individuals with a research-development orientation to his council. Deans from the following colleges and schools formed the core of the academic council: College of

Architecture, College of Agricultural Sciences, College of Arts and Sciences, College of Business Administration, College of Education, College of Engineering, College of Home Economics, School of Law, and the Graduate School. They were expected to provide the leadership for strategic planning for research at the college level.

Although the academic deans would continue to look after the undergraduate programs, they were expected to rearrange their personal time and effort so they could develop new graduate instructional programs and research within their colleges and in conjunction with other colleges. Moreover, the deans were expected to reorganize their colleges around research-development oriented individuals who were expected to concentrate their efforts on research development and improvement in their professional and graduate programs.

The VPAA&R had the following directors of academic and research facilities reporting directly to him: director of Continuing Education, director of Libraries, director of the Texas Tech University Press, and directors of university organized research units.

The directors of the academic service units were expected to reorganize their units to provide optimal assistance to research and graduate education development.

The VPAA&R had four associate vice-presidents on his professional staff. To obtain the proper mix of people in key planning positions, the VPAA&R had to attract several research-oriented deans to fill vacating positions and he had to add an associate vice-president for research development (AVPR-Development). The university had the traditional associate vice-president for research administration (AVPR-Administration) who served also as the director of the Office of Research Services. The AVPR-Administration performed most of the routine administrative functions associated with grant application reviews, fiscal accountability, and compliance procedures. The AVPR-Development coordinated the university research planning functions, introduced research development systems, chaired university task forces for special university research developments, assisted in the development and administration of organized research units, and provided liaison with the university partners.

There was a mandate for reorganizing the university to have a research-development orientation. Your authors were hired because they were expected to implement that mandate. The faculty senate (1979) and the administration were not satisfied with the existing university orientation, organization and the quality of service in the extant offices. Darling (1981) intended to upgrade these services by adding another associate vice-president for research (Development) and a dean of the graduate school as new staff positions necessary to advance the visions of developing Texas Tech

University into a research university. This required developing the graduate and research programs of the university and organizing supporting services to give them a development orientation, rather than an administration orientation.

At numerous planning session from 1981-1984, the academic council members and faculty continually expressed the desire to have the reputation and resources of the flagship universities in Texas and neighboring states. The results of a "Faculty Senate Survey" (1979) and an "Office of Research Services Survey" showed clearly that the faculty were concerned about obtaining more research support and improving the image of the institution and the climate for research development. These desires and concerns were translated into the first agenda item, transforming Texas Tech University into one the four state of Texas major research universities. Other agenda items were formulated from faculty needs and a thorough environmental scan conducted by the research planning team in 1984-85.

The Appointment of Development-Oriented Individuals to Planning Teams

Research development officers have certain characteristics that support the planning function. The success of any strategic plan depends on the university's ability to locate the proper architects of the future and to encourage them to serve on the planning teams. Convincing the best thinkers to serve on planning teams is not easy as most researchers believe that university committee or planning-team service is a poor use of time. Yet, it is their fresh ideas that are needed and that must be incorporated into the plan. Research-development people seem to have accurate crystal balls. The trick is to find them and to get them to share what they see.

It has been the authors' experience that the executive planners cannot always rely on the traditional administrators to do planning and development work. Initially, the senior members of the administration must determine who the architects of the plan will be and invite them to serve in positions of planning responsibility. The selection of the leaders of the planning is the most critical part of the strategic planning process. If the right people are appointed, the process will function in a relatively smooth fashion and the plan will provide the necessary guidelines for future research development. If the wrong people are appointed, the process can be a disaster and typically practical plans will not emerge.

The team leaders must appoint persons who have the vision, drive, organizational ability, and interpersonal skills to hold together teams that design the blueprints for the university's future. In doing so, the leaders themselves must reflect two prerequisites for successful administrative leadership—the creation of attention on future directions by sharing their own and others' visions and the communication of the meaning of those visions.

MODELING THE STRATEGIC-PLANNING PROCESS

When The VPAA&R planning team started its planning activities, they carefully selected a model that would show on one page the major development thrusts to those needing an institutional view. They adopted the "change cube," a model designed to facilitate the adoption of innovations by many cooperating agencies. It allowed them to show graphically how to organize a myriad of research-development activities under a complex of sponsors and performers.

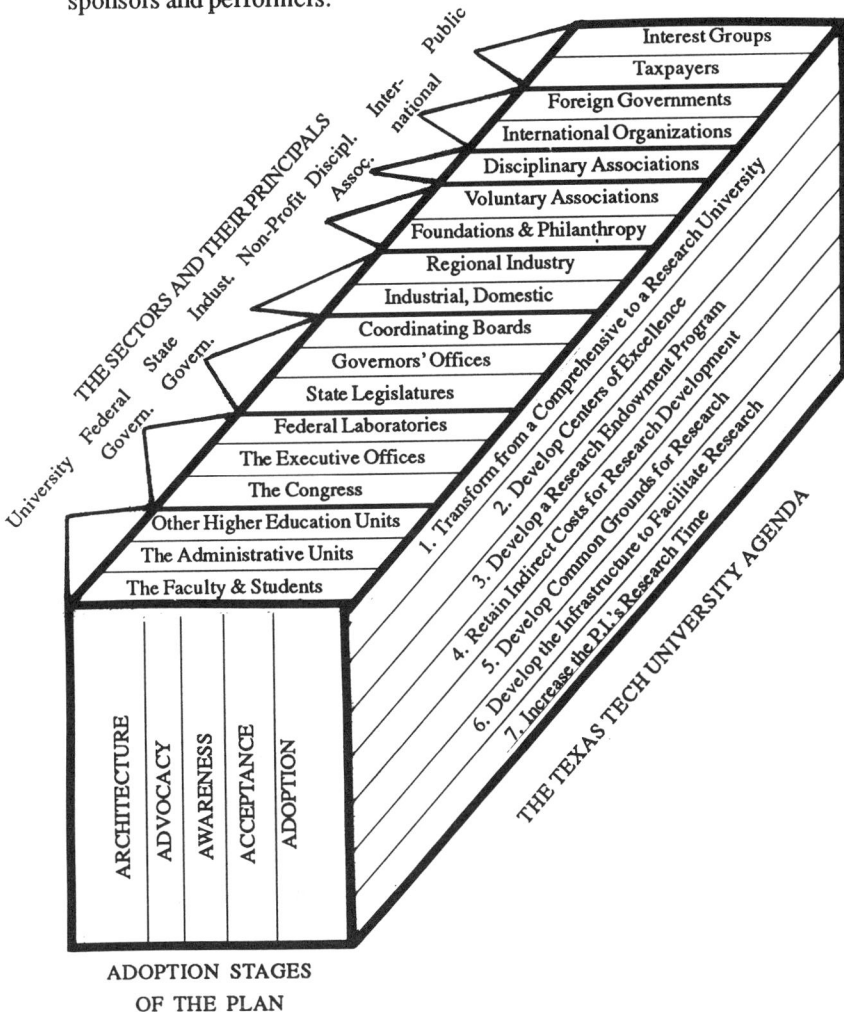

Figure 6.3. The Change Cube: A Model for the Strategic Planning Process.

The first priority on our agenda called for the transformation of an institution from a comprehensive university into a research university. It was critical to keep a large number of constituencies aware of the general changes the institution was planning and to gain their acceptance of these plans. The authors' previous experiences with the change cube indicated that it was the model that best fit Texas Tech's current needs for major changes.

The academic council's chairman, Darling (1979, 1981) and the research council's chairman, Hensley (1966, 1968, 1981) had used the change cube very successfully on previous occasions in the planning and implementation of several large, innovative programs involving conglomerates of national and state agencies, higher-education institutions, labor organizations, and industry.

A generic model for implementation of research strategic-planning is shown in Figure 6.3. Note that there are three dimensions to the model: 1) the sectors and their principals in the planning process, 2) the broad items of the agenda, and 3) the five stages in the planning process. This model guided several years of strategic planning that was initiated from the office of the vice-president for academic affairs and research at Texas Tech University.

The Adoption Stages of the Plan

The front face of the cube provides a diagram for the adoption stages of the strategic plan for university research. The authors have based their planning on gaining the voluntary adoption of a plan by the principals associated with the plan. The authors have found that they gained considerably better adoption of their plans when they followed the sequence of steps.

First, the architect for the plan must be found. Research planning requires a principal investigator (PI) to develop research ideas or research-development administrators who will plan to improve the research climate and infrastructure to advance research.

Second, an advocate for the plan must be found. Someone must champion the plan with the principals in the enterprise.

Third, all of the relevant principals must be made aware of the plan. If the principals are not aware of the plan, they can not accept or reject or modify the plan.

Fourth, all of the relevant principals should be made aware of the benefits and consequences of accepting the plan. Accepting the plan does not mean that the principals support the plan. It means they feel the plan is attainable if the terms and conditions are met.

Fifth, all of the relevant principals should be made aware of the incentives for their adopting the plan. Adoption means that the principals support and adopt the plan by implementing the objectives of the plan and contributing their share of resources to achieving mutual goals.

Innovations are introduced into our society through these five stages. Plans are innovations; consequently, plans should be adopted more readily if the adoption process shown in the change cube is followed.

Creating a Broad Institutional Agenda

The worth of any strategic plan is judged from its agenda. The agenda of the strategic plan carries the viewers far into the future and away from their home bases. It must be prepared with extreme care for it sets the direction of the institution for decades. The leadership of the institution must listen carefully to the various constituencies to determine the critical needs facing the institution and to weigh suggested solutions. The agenda should address major issues and major changes in the institution.

A Development Agenda for Texas Tech University

Strategic planning was selected as the means for developing Texas Tech University into a research university. The members of the research planning team were the architects and strong advocates for transforming Texas Tech from a comprehensive university serving mostly undergraduates into a research university serving professional schools and a much larger graduate school with a research-oriented faculty and student body. The transformation was to be achieved within a decade by following two five-year plans.

In the early eighties, taxes on crude oil, the major revenue source for Texas higher education, was at an all-time high. State and federal support for research was the highest ever. The research administration team provided the faculty with a steady stream of information on research opportunities and provided the president, board, and deans with institutional plans for developing research programs and facilities at Texas Tech. The board of regents and the faculty endorsed the administration's vision of Texas Tech becoming a research university. To accomplish this major purpose the following goals were agreed upon within the president's council and the academic council.

1. To develop Texas Tech University from one of 37 comprehensive universities into one of the four State of Texas major research universities.
2. To develop at Texas Tech University a series of Organized Research Units and Graduate Education Programs, which would be recognized internationally as Centers of Excellence for advanced training and research.
3. To develop a substantial research endowment to support the research and creative activities of faculty and students.
4. To retain for local use the recovered indirect costs which were currently being appropriated by the State and reallocated through the General Appropriation.

5. To develop Common grounds within the Texas Tech influence sphere for the purpose of creating cooperative research and training programs with industry and local communities.
6. To establish the infrastructure and institutional climate necessary to facilitate the research efforts of faculty, students, and sponsors.
7. To increase the amount of research time available to the principal investigator and other researcher by reducing the administrative burdens and instructional loads.

The Research Sectors and their Planning Principals

Strategic planning requires an early identification of the structure of the research enterprise, the sectors, and the principals to be involved. The top face of the change cube shows what the research planning team considered to be the generic names of the sectors and principals involved in planning for university research. This should appear in the first-generation plan so all can see immediately the performers and sponsors of research. As we saw in the Killoren impact model in Chapter 1, the following eight sectors and their principals should be considered in strategic planning for university research: university sector, federal-government sector, state-government sector, industrial sector, nonprofit sector, disciplinary associations, international sector, and public sector.

In the mid-1980s, the research planning team targeted the eight sectors and their principals shown in Figure 6.3 for involvement in Texas Tech's strategic planning. This chapter deals mostly with how the authors planned with the principals in each sector.

Within each sector there are principals who somewhat guide planning activities within the sector. Note, we use the terms somewhat guides planning activities to call attention to the fact that although this chapter has for explanatory purposes ordered the sectors and principals within the sector there is no real hierarchy that is followed. In the university sector, ideas arise everywhere. Sometimes ideas were sparked by an agenda item— most of the time they are not. The university community is composed of very independent, extremely intelligent persons. The thoughts, plans, and development activities of these independent scholars and administrators cannot be governed according to the nice theoretical models we have produced. The models explain. They do not control. At best the vice-presidents can gather information that fits into a strategy and identify emergent agenda items so others may begin cooperative development. Trying to control the development of ideas and plans within a rigid hierarchy defeats the purpose of a research university—unfettered inquiry. Inquiry must be encouraged by administrators, not directed by them. Attempts to dictate plans from the top down and to put all academicians under a single plan will meet with great resistance. The best an administrator can hope for is to identify groups of researchers with common interests and then provide the administrative support they need. The persuasive power of the administrator in helping diversely motivated people to cooperate on research development is the sine qua non in strategic planning for university research.

It was very important for Texas Tech to know what other universities were planning for research development and what they were currently doing. First, in our environmental scan of other institutions we had to know the intentions of the two major research universities in Texas: The University of Texas (UT) and Texas A&M University (A&M). Their systems were so large and powerful and their investigators so influential that they dominated the state research policy making. Second, we needed to know the research development planning of other institutions so we could either avoid duplication of program development or look for ways of cooperating with them.

The TTU planning committee (1986, 23-24) noted that:

> Texas Tech University competes nationally with 94 public and 62 private universities for faculty, research grants, and to a lesser extent, students. Also competing nationwide for faculty and students are 1,856 four-year and 1,270 two-year institutions.

> Within the state, TTU competes with 37 other public senior colleges and universities for students, faculty, funding, and research projects. The only schools which have a distinct advantage over TTU are the University of Texas at Austin and Texas A&M University. Their basic advantages are threefold:(1) they have constitutional status, (2) they have the Permanent University Fund and the flexibility inherent to it, and (3) each has benefited from the symbiotic relationship between them. The only advantage any other public university might have is proximity to a larger population base , such as the University of Houston.

> In order for TTU to become a university of the first rank, innovative leadership and faculty dedication are necessary. Innovative leadership will be required to:

> a. Obtain resources to foster excellence;

> b. Develop a mechanism to foster or reward interdisciplinary research efforts; and

> c. To identify ideas or research that could be used as the springboard to bring TTU into the first rank of research universities.

In this jumble of activities, knowing the roles of the principals in the different sectors becomes very important to the architects of research planning for communication lines between the university sector principals and the principals in the other sectors must be established. Without communication the adoption strategy cannot be put into place. And, without identifying the principals in the sectors, cooperative long-term research plans cannot be developed. The academic administrative hierarchy that existed at Texas Tech during most of the eighties contained the following principals and illustrates a rather typical university administration at that time: board of regents, president, vice-presidents, deans, department chairs, and investigators. We will examine the roles of these principals through a series of administrator and faculty vignettes.

In addition to the order of the aforementioned academic positions, there were a number of directors of organized research units (ORUs) that operated independently, but under the oversight of one of the administrators in the hierarchy. These ORUs were incredibly independent of the academic administrative hierarchy because they were formed and governed by groups of research fellows who came together voluntarily to do research work. They stayed together as long as there was mutual benefit and autonomy of thought. The ORUs had very different functions and purposes from the academic hierarchy. They had to operate independently. There was always tension between the ORU directors and the academic administrative hierarchy. Sometimes, the issues of governance and development were of such a nature that open conflict erupted. It was a sign of administrative genius to be able to keep that conflict to a minimum while developing a particular research effort.

Key Roles in University Planning

Where does strategic planning start in the university sector? Who starts it? It is difficult to determine exactly when it started at Texas Tech and who started it. However, once started, it continued as part of institutional self-studies, cooperative plans with sponsors, and formal university strategic plans.

Certainly, in the early eighties and before, there was a tremendous mass of research plans and research activity that needed to be ordered under a general plan for cooperative development. The vice-presidents for research developed a number of systems that brought some order to the activities and plans. We expected much of the detailed planning to occur outside of our plans and systems. That is as it should be. Operational planning and development occur through many people planning with one another on- and off-campus. There was no way that university unit planning could be directed from a central office and it was never our intent to have all planning orchestrated by the vice-president and his associates. We did develop philosophy, policy, and systems and partnerships for strategic planning and we placed research information on computers so it could be managed easily. Also, we initiated many planning meetings where research was discussed for the first time in terms of a strategic outlook and where cooperative development with many partners was emphasized repeatedly.

Most importantly, we initiated a number of university research development systems designed to promote research on campus and to let the research principals and public know what research was being conducted at Texas Tech and what our strategic plans were.

The first steps toward formal strategic planning were taken when Vice President for Academic Affairs Darling in 1982 directed the members of the academic council to prepare long-term development plans for each college, school, and organized research unit in the university. The planning called for Texas Tech and its constituencies perceiving the institution as a research university, for identifying existing and new centers of research and graduate education excellence and for presenting plans for upgrading and expanding research and graduate programs that had the potential to gain national recognition. The unit plans for the nine colleges and schools and the major centers and institutes reporting to the VPAA were prepared during the early eighties and published as the *1984 Institutional Self-Study*.

The TTU Planning Committee (1986):

> The Planning Committee worked to develop a strategic planning perspective to complement the planning effort already in effect at the departmental, college and vice presidential levels. It was never intended that the Planning Committee should establish a plan for each department, but that it should look at the goals pertinent to the Central Administration. This information would be passed on to the departments to provide some "Top Down" perspective for their planning efforts. Much of the information used was based on the 1984 Institutional Self-Study and the preliminary data gathered for the Capital Campaign.

We believed that we had to know personally the principals because they were the people who had the research ideas, who would do the work, and who could best do the institutional planning at their appropriate levels. Consequently, we did considerable walking around the campus to visit with investigators in their laboratories and offices and a lot of traveling to sponsors headquarters to determine their standing and to begin talks about partnerships. Later, deans, department heads, and principal investigators prepared the formal strategic, tactical, and operational plans necessary to achieve mutual long-term goals. Also, the vice-presidents for research did a lot of reacting to requests from principals to assist them with specific plans that were well developed before they came to our offices. We believe the best role that the vice-presidents can perform is listening carefully to the plans of others and then providing pertinent suggestions for eliminating voids in the plan and encouraging the planner to continue good work.

Most administrative units in the university were considered in strategic planning. The board of regents, the president's office, the vice-president's offices, the colleges, the academic departments, the organized research units, the development office, finance and administration, the library, legal affairs, news and publications, public affairs, and student affairs are administrative units that were considered for their ability to advance the research goals of the university. Also, many of these administrative units have responsibility for reviewing certain aspects of research. Consequently, planning must be achieved within the guidelines established by the several administrative units on campus.

For example, the Office of Research Services and the Office of Development had an extensive set of policies and procedures that were followed in planning and developing research projects or units. Moreover, the advisory groups such as the faculty senate, the student groups, and the support associations were brought into the planning process by initially including one of their members on the planning teams. These liaison members returned to their constituency groups and involved their fellows in the planning.

THE OFFICE OF RESEARCH SERVICES (ORS)

During the administrative period being discussed, the Office of Research Services was designated as the centerpiece in Texas Tech's strategic planning for research.

The office had been established in the mid-1960s to administer federally-sponsored projects, and until 1983, its activities had been limited to the administration of sponsored projects. The VPAA&R wanted the office to provide a strong development thrust and to coordinate strategic planning for research for the University. In 1984, he created two new, separate positions—the dean of the Graduate School and the associate vice-president for research-development (AVPR-Development).

These new positions were vital to his charge of rapidly developing graduate education and research as they would devote their respective efforts to developing graduate education and research. Moreover, he felt that to properly cultivate all aspects of the research efforts two very different approaches were required and two associate vice-presidents for research were needed. In his mind, both the aggressive development and the proper administration for research could not be handled by a single senior officer. He was convinced that day-to-day administrative duties would, by their demands for immediate solutions to operational problems, crowd out the development activities. In an attempt to install a development focus at Texas Tech, he split a full-time position into two half-time positions. He then had to find two research administrators who wanted to teach half-time and administer research half-time. He found two individuals who each had a long history of funded research and who liked the proposed combination of activities. He appointed them to administer and develop research on the Texas Tech campus. The AVPR-Development liked the arrangement because his colleague and he were out of the office frequently and someone had to be available on a day-to-day basis to tend the shop. Also, he liked the flexibility it provided for continuing his teaching and conducting his own research. For him, it was the ideal research-development structure. The VPAA&R coordinated the activities by suggesting that each associate should be familiar with and capable of doing the other's work and by having frequent meetings with his associate vice-presidents to discuss problems and issues. After these discussions of the problem or issue, which were viewed as planning and evaluation sessions, someone was given responsibility for solving the problem or studying the issue.

This new arrangement of having an associate vice-president for research-development involved in institutional-wide research development puzzled many of the traditionalists on campus whose thinking was limited only to "project development." They did not see the need to involve the central administration in the development of research. Despite numerous planning sessions and explanations of the assumptions behind this administrative arrangement in the university, many faculty and deans never saw the value of such a structure and rejected the idea of the central administration being actively involved in planning. The authors recognized this resistance and attributed it to a "project mentality," which had dominated the Texas Tech research administration for two decades. It is often very difficult to get the faculty and college administrators to accept new orientations and new administrative structures.

The reorganization for a development orientation relied on the following positions in the Office of Research Services. The Office of Research Services was administered by the AVPR-Administration, who was also the director of the Office of Research Services. John Kice, an outstanding research chemist, teacher, and administrator served as director. William Schultz, the assistant director of ORS was responsible for the daily operations of the office. Clara McNamara served as the general secretary and assisted principal investigators with their budget preparation and grant management. Mary Ann Seaman served as the secretary to the AVPR-Development and was responsible for proposal processing and organization of program development materials. Shirlene Hagler was the research information specialist. Two student workers provided clerical assistance.

The Office of Research Services (ORS) was involved in the strategic planning process because it reviewed and processed all sponsored project proposals submitted to outside agencies. The planning process for research subventions has several planning steps. The classical sponsored research proposal was generated by a principal investigator who submitted a research proposal to a funding agency after it was reviewed and approved by a department head, an associate dean for research, and an associate vice-president for research. Copies of the proposal were filed in each office that approved the proposal. Ostensibly, a proposal review may seem to be more of an administrative check than a planning function. More careful study of the process in an institution dedicated to strategic planning reveals that every data element is entered into the development system and that the proposal routing check is an excellent way of assuring that the institution makes serious commitments to a line of research by committing at the departmental level to certain amounts of release-time for the PI, matching funds for new equipment and travel, laboratory space and support for research assistants.

At the dean's level, the associate dean, after discussing the proposal, may suggest a joint proposal with a co-investigator from another department, provide developmental travel expenses, match travel funds for delivering paper presentations, and incorporate the proposal into a capabilities statement that will be compared with an industrial organization's "laundry list" for additional funding.

The AVPR-Development established in ORS a standardized format for gathering and reporting grant and contract information. Shirlene Hagler, information specialist, with the help of a graduate student from the computer science department created the computer programs necessary to sort massive amounts of grant-related information. This information was sorted for the institution as a whole and then directed to college officers, department heads and to individual faculty depending upon their research interests. Also, Hagler constructed a computerized system for the reporting of proposal submissions and awards. Summary and detailed reports were distributed monthly to all departments and investigators depending on their standing requests for information. Much of the information related to grant opportunities and institutional grant information was placed on the university research information system and could be accessed by anyone with a terminal connected to the system. Every college and many departments had such terminals.

The "Annual Report of the Activities of the Office of Research Services" became a valuable tool in planning as it provided a very complete, historical analysis of level of proposal submissions, number of awards per year, and total dollar value of sponsored projects for the last two decades.

VPAA&R spent a considerable amount of time researching critical issues and drafting policy and procedures that would facilitate the conduct and planning for research. During 1982-83 the staff of ORS and William Schultz, assistant director of ORS, produced and published the *Sponsored Projects Administration Notebook* (SPAN). This loose-leaf volume provided faculty and staff for the first time with a single source book for practical and planning information on all aspects of sponsored projects— proposal planning and development, proposal submission and agency reviews, negotiation of awards, and administration and management of grants and contracts by a principal investigator once an award was received.

In 1984, the AVPR-Development initiated a total systems approach (TSA) to planning and administration of grants and contracts. This system was thoroughly described previously in Chapter 5. It is mentioned again because the philosophy and technology associated with TSA to strategic planning were vital to managing the very large number of activities associated with research development and administration and because a number of existing systems were integrated and revised to support the emphasis being placed on research and graduate education development. The specifics of strategic planning for research related to the AVPR-Development is explained in more detail later.

The administrative experiment of placing an associate vice-president for research-development in a proposal processing and grants administration office has considerable merit as the development and administrative functions are inextricably linked. Also, the creation of separate senior level offices was advantageous to the associate vice-presidents for it allowed them to be away from campus large amounts of time without the fear that campus activities were not being represented in a timely manner by a senior-level administrator who had a well-established reputation as a researcher. The beauty of this system resided in the fact that faculty and outside partners did not have to plan around a single vice-president's schedule. Some vice-president was usually available for meetings and for immediate decision making. Planning and administrative operations moved very rapidly with the dual associate vice-presidents. Most importantly, cooperative, long-term planning had a champion who concentrated on research development, not administration. This results in substantial increases in proposal submissions, grant and contract awards, and research expenditures, cooperative agreements, and investigator satisfaction justified the reorganization for a development orientation in the Office of Research Services.

THE COMMUNITY OF SCHOLARS

The faculty and students at Texas Tech were the source of most research ideas and it was their vision of what could be that had to be communicated by the university leadership to sponsors and performers alike. It should be kept in mind that leadership at Texas Tech University was not synonymous with administrator. Our research leaders came from the faculty researchers who were in-and-out of the administration in the university, in-and-out of committee chairs within their disciplines, and on-and-off advisory councils to sponsors. The established leadership positions in the university rotated frequently among academicians.

Our researchers did not like serving on committees, especially planning committees. Jay Conover, (1989) Horn Professor and distinguished statistician, in warning junior faculty members of the dangers of encroachment on individual research time advised faculty to be stingy in allocating their time to committee service. Although Professor Conover's advice was sound advice to the individual, it was never heeded by the authors because they wanted the best minds in the university to bear on institutional problems; consequently, they turned to the best thinkers and asked them to serve in critical planning posts.

Our leaders were people with visions—they had plans for achieving what others cannot see. In tracing the history of the cyclotron (Chapter 3), the importance of E. O. Lawrence's ideas to the planning for bigger and better accelerators at the University of California was shown. Although there are few people with Lawrence's genius and vision, we felt that each faculty member should be involved in planning for the optimum development of their discipline and institution. Many research administrators are so convinced of the power of faculty ideas that they believe "It (research) doesn't require a plan—just a strong research faculty." While we value faculty ideas as highly as anyone, the authors believe the development of the ideas of the faculty can be facilitated by the strategic planning process.

The Primacy of the Principal Investigator

At the center of the university sector are the principal investigators who are the primary architects of our future because they are the ones who generate the new ideas that advance humankind. In this section, we will consider the primacy of the principal investigator by looking at the contributions of the faculty and students in conducting research. In the research university the emphasis has shifted from developing the student to developing the principal investigator. This is a radical change that is not often discussed, but is absolutely essential as the main revenue stream of the research university depends on the principal investigator, not on student fees. In fact, more and more the training of the student depends upon the ability of the faculty to obtain grants that will support graduate and undergraduate student training and research.

Making a case for the primacy of the principal investigator can be accomplished by supplying a chart of accounts for a university's research and noting that each account has to have a principal investigator who conceived the project and presently administers it. Although several hundred projects worth many millions of dollars present a compelling case for the value of the PI to the university, they can not show the special human characteristics of the investigator. And, this, above all else, is what makes a researcher and distinguishes the principal investigator from the rest of mankind. Consequently, the authors have chosen to explore in some depth the role of the investigator. To stress the value of the PI, they have presented vignettes to elucidate the unique qualities of this most valuable academic role.

At the university, students, faculty and administrative officers are interacting continually in research planning. In the planning process the principal investigator performs the seminal work. For this reason, they are more important than the president, vice-presidents, and deans who weld great administrative power through control of resources and administrative positions.

Principal investigators dominate the research universities by producing new solutions to mankind's problems. They are uniquely trained individuals who can first ask the right questions and next conceive the right answers. Although they may put forth a new theory this morning, that plan may have been years in the making. Research administrators must help the public understand the rare talents of the researcher and the tremendous investment of thought and training that is part of every successful investigator. Productive scholars hold the first rank in research universities because they are the people who develop the research ideas, who do the conceptual work, who have the appropriate disciplinary contacts and who can best do the institutional planning at their appropriate levels. They are the thinkers—the intellectual capital of the institution—an expanding asset for humanity.

Although they are at the lowest level of university administrative hierarchy, they enjoy an intellectual and esthetic preeminence over administrators and teaching colleagues because they can conduct research—the most intellectually difficult task in the university. Because they find joy in research, the difficulty and the importance of their work is frequently masked to the novice or the outsider. They make original thinking appear easy, it is not. Few can do it.

In the research university, their primacy is acknowledged and rewarded. The entire institution is dedicated to serving the PI because their intellectual output creates the major revenue stream for their institution and their products form the base for our advanced technological society.

At Texas Tech University, in the mid-1980s, many faculty through peer recognition of their work had established themselves as leaders in their field. They had been involved in research planning long before we asked them to put forth their plans for developing research at Texas Tech. We asked the university researchers to look to the future and plan the next research advancements by preparing long-range plans for their unit, not just project proposals. Prior to the introduction of strategic planning, independent faculty plans advanced the university significantly in the direction set by outstanding researchers.

Knox Jones' ideas for the development of a museum division devoted to the study of systematics, evolution, and natural history of mammals and his work as graduate dean and vice-president for research show the primacy of the principal investigator in a research university, and these achievements demonstrate the importance of placing outstanding researchers in key administrative roles. Texas Tech University supports a multimillion dollar museum with a Natural Science Research Laboratory that is dedicated to mammalian biology. This museum has an international reputation for being the center for research on taxonomy, distribution, biogeography, and ecology of mammals, and for its thousands of museum specimens and outstanding collection of frozen tissue for experimental studies. It took a great many people to build such a museum, but it was the ideas of Knox Jones and his leadership that made Texas Tech's research reputation as a center of excellence for the study of small mammals.

He conceived the plans for building the museum's Natural Science Research Laboratory, his work started extraordinary mammal collections, and his grants-writing ability brought in hundreds of thousands of dollars to take graduate assistants and colleagues into the field to collect and study mammals. His building of academic and research programs, editorship of scientific journals, and teaching of esoteric research technologies have received world acclaim for decades, but it was the potency of his ideas and his insistence on standards of excellence that attract to him a steady stream of graduate students, international scholars for post-doctoral study, and distinguished research associates.

Magne Kristiansen ideas for the development of a pulsed-power laboratory were clearly set forth in proposals that to the general public seemed as wild as a Flash Gordon comic strip, but his scientific papers were taken very seriously by key members of congress and the scientific professions. His plans now form a major component for the nation's strategic defense initiatives. Although there is considerable security guarding some of Kristiansen's conceptual work and technology, the physics and electrical engineering research societies acknowledge his fundamental theories and the Department of Defense relies on his continuing work and the research of his proteges for the control of space and the defense of the nation. He is the mentor for a generation of physicists, engineers, and mathematicians who are exploring ways of collecting and transmitting billions and billions of volts of electrical power.

David Koeppe's pioneering ideas for creating stress-resistant plants surfaced repeatedly in the department of plant and soil science plans and his research reports lead the way to creating on the Texas Tech campus a world class research program for the nation.

Kathleen Hennessy's productive mind created numerous plans for advancing expert systems, computer visual inspection of microchips, electronic document interchange, and gamma nets in neural net interconnections, which started a steady flow of industrial scientists to campus to see her pilot programs.

Rod Preston's ideas for designing the TTU Feed Mill, Feedlot Pilot Facilities, and the Burnett Center for Beef Cattle Research and Teaching to aid in advanced studies of beef cattle nutrition were advocated and promoted early by the College of Agricultural Sciences and the Cattle Raisers Association and supported later by the university administration. Preston's seminal ideas on body composition and anabolic agents in beef cattle and sheep and his synthetically produced hormones appeared first in the most prestigious scientific journals. His pioneering work formed the base for hundreds of additional projects and thousands of technical reports. His original work and follow-up studies by others were picked up by commercial magazines and the popular press. Each of our exemplars' ideas were incorporated into the planning of the university.

The aforementioned investigators created many individual plans that they had to develop aggressively on a campus that was in transition from a teaching institution to a research university. Many times their ideas were not supported by their colleagues as such ideas were too far ahead of the times. However, when looking over the long term, it appears most of their plans developed reasonably well as their organized research units are now supported quite well by long-term commitments from the university and major sponsors.

It is important for the research administrator to understand that principal investigators, in a nonresearch climate perform research at great personal sacrifice and additional effort, are misfits. In a teaching institution or in an emerging research university, the teaching-oriented faculty, which are preponderate, will not only oppose the ideas of researchers, they will attack the character of the PI and denigrate their work because the researcher threatens their established way of life. Formally, research administrators may change the mission statement of the institution and the goals of the units, redirect funds to the research functions, write philosophy statements supportive of research, and install an incentive system that rewards research efforts. Informally, the resisters to research form an institutional climate hostile to the researcher. Research exemplars are absolutely vital to the implementation of any strategic plan for university research for they change the climate for research. In the process, the researcher suffers all the abuses that accrue from the enmity of distrust and human jealousy. The normal work and the normal accomplishments of the principal investigators pose a threat to all who are unwilling or incapable of matching the productivity standards of a good researcher. The resisters, who are not spending their time doing research, manipulate the systems and by innuendo and direct falsities try to force out the researcher. Only the most dedicated researchers remain in this climate because fighting colleagues is unproductive and debilitating. Those that stay do so because they have personal goals that keep them on target and because they steadily attract the superior students, loyal patrons, and research-oriented associates. Individually, they build research programs. Collectively, they change the climate of the institution.

The aforementioned investigators were selected for study because they were outstanding research planners. Modern research requires that the principal investigator has a number of research skills and personal qualifications. Our exemplars exhibited the following characteristics.

1. Intellectual brilliance in asking the right questions and in finding the right answers.
2. Dedication to the work of the discipline.
3. A satisfaction from writing about their findings.
4. Long-term knowledge contributions to a discipline.
5. Ability to organize the critical mass of students and colleagues into organized research units that could go beyond the capabilities of the single investigator.
6. Sustained an active research career for more than a quarter-century.
7. Relied heavily on outside grants to support their research.
8. Early in their career, they found their niche in their discipline and from that vantage point provided leadership to the entire discipline and their university.
9. Their scholarly interests emerged early in life and they were doing research before they entered graduate school.
10. Outstanding teachers who see the preparation of bright graduate students as a major responsibility.

Each of our model researchers exhibited these general characteristics. Individual vignettes will provide a personal example of how certain characteristics were developed by a particular researcher.

The Development of a Scholar

Visitors to Texas Tech University are impressed by TTU's museum. Its vast expanse consists of several components: the main museum buildings, the Moody Planetarium, the Ranching Heritage Center, the Lubbock Lake Site and National Landmark, the Natural Science Research Laboratory (NSRL), the Val Verde County Research Site, and the Cotton Heritage Center. The size of this sprawling complex of educational, cultural, and research facilities and the beauty of the collections awe the casual visitor. The visitor sees eight temporary and twelve permanent exhibition galleries dedicated to the social and natural sciences and the visual arts. The Ranching Heritage Center, an outdoor exhibit, displays through its collection of thirty-one original pioneer buildings, hundreds of authentic tools, and preserved collections of transportation means the history of southwest ranching.

The Lubbock Lake Site and National Archaeological Landmark contains a complete cultural sequence from Clovis (12,000 years ago) through historic times. Two research libraries and a 90-acre natural history research site preserve an enormous collection of materials for scholars of the Southwest. The Natural Science Research Laboratory affords research opportunities in herpetology, mammalogy, medical zoology, ornithology, and vertebrate paleontology. Unfortunately, visitors do not learn of the dedication of certain living investigators who planned and built the giant facilities, the unique collections, and the current displays by forming partnerships with philanthropists, the state, the National Geographic Society, and the National Science Foundation.

For example, Knox Jones is a prime contributor to the collections, to designing and developing the facilities, and to publishing original findings. Somewhere in the Museum, models of the principal investigators should be on display for it is their creative ideas that built the Museum. Unfortunately, museums discuss only the prime items in their collections and the major contributors to the endowments, forgetting the PIs who laboriously collected and developed the facilities. PIs are uncommon people who are as fascinating as their collections. Principal investigator accomplishments should be used to inspire young people toward emulation of their scholarship. The principal investigators are the chief treasure of the Museum for they are an appreciating resource. It takes many years to develop a scholar of the first rank.

Principal investigator Jones' life can help us understand the unique value of the scholar. Knox's biography illustrates his early interest in animals and their habitats. His school transcripts reveal that he was educated in the public schools of Lincoln, Nebraska and that he excelled scholastically. When asked, "Why did you decide to be a zoologist?" He recalls that when he was eight or nine years old he spent much of his spare time collecting butterflies. Before his teens, although his parents encouraged him to think about a career as a medical doctor, he knew he wanted to know about animals and spent a lot of time "hanging around" the Nebraska State Museum. "Hanging around" and the shortage of men during World War II led to his being hired at fourteen to help dig fossils. As a high school student he excelled academically and athletically. When he was nineteen and twenty he had summertime jobs trapping rodents for the State Game Commission.

In 1951, he graduated from the University of Nebraska with a B.S. Degree majoring in zoology, minoring in geology and history. Research conducted as an undergraduate resulted in twelve scientific publications. He earned an M.A. Degree at University of Kansas in 1953. His active military hitch (1953-55) was served as an army officer in Korea where he was assigned to a research team investigating the causes of hemorrhagic fever. Hemorrhagic fever is caused by mites carried by rodents. Again, Knox, a mammalogist, was collecting and classifying the mammals of Korea. What could have been two years of dreary military routine, turned into a mammalogists ideal field project. While in Korea he assembled the largest collection of Korean mammals and shipped them back to the Smithsonian Institution for their collection. Later, for six years of army reserve duty assignments to Walter Reed Hospital, he worked on the Korean mammal collection at the Smithsonian. In 1962, he was awarded the Ph.D. with a major in zoology and a minor in paleontology from the University of Kansas.

His post-doctoral professional and administrative experience at the University of Kansas shows the initial stage for the making of a world-class natural historian and it demonstrates the importance of the PI's work to advancing the reputation of a particular university. In 1962, Jones was appointed assistant professor of zoology and assistant curator of mammals at the Museum of Natural History, the University of Kansas. His diligent work in advancing the mammal collections, prodigious publication record, and leadership in advancing systematic and evolutionary biology at the University of Kansas lead to his promotion to associate professor and associate curator in 1965. Continued work collecting mammals in the American tropics and on the central plains of North America, leadership in the graduate council as the representative for the biological and medical sciences, and chairman of the University of Kansas Senate Committee on Scholarly Publications earned him advancement to professor and curator in 1968. In 1967, he was promoted to associate director of the Museum of Natural History.

The primacy of the principal investigator to the advancement of a professional field is recognized in every discipline. Colleges and universities organize faculty and students along disciplinary lines. The knowledge content of a discipline is composed of thousands of individual research contributions from principal investigators. Scholars organize the individual investigator contributions into monographs and textbooks. Teachers transmit the disciplinary knowledge to students. Students graduate and use that knowledge in practice.

The value of a principal investigator is judged partially by his or her research contributions to a discipline. Knox Jones' 341 scientific publications, including 13 books authored or edited, and numerous scientific papers delivered at scientific and educational conferences give him a place of honor in the field of biology. He is acknowledged by his peers to be an outstanding basic researcher. There are hundreds of biologists and libraries that have standing requests for his publications. Text book writers are sure to include the biological principles of systematics contributed by principal investigator Jones. Ecologists of the great plains routinely use the findings of his research. Daily, his colleagues from around the world call or write him asking his advice on matters dealing with knowledge of mammals. On campus and among his associates he is teasingly referred to as "batman." It is an appropriate title because much of his work has dealt with the biology and natural history of bats, the only mammals that have developed true flight. He is known by biologists throughout the world as the leading authority on bats. The following major contributions, which he jointly authored or edited, are among those that made him preeminent in the field of mammalogy: *Orders and Families of Mammals of the World* (Wiley, 1984), *Pleistocene and Recent Environments of the Central Great Plans* (Kansas, 1970), *Mammals of the Northern Great Plains* (Nebraska, 1983), *Guide to Mammals of the Plains States* (Nebraska, 1985), *Handbook of Mammals of the North-Central States* (Minnesota, 1988), *Readings in Mammalogy* (Kansas, 1976), and a three-volume treatise on the evolutionarily unique bats of tropical American family Phyllostomatidae (Texas Tech Press, 1976-1979).

This huge contribution of biological knowledge was the result of Knox Jones carefully planning his work, setting definite research goals, and working sixty or more hours a week on advancing his discipline through teaching and research. To the external world scholars seem to have a very easy life. True, their work is usually a labor of love, but it is not easy. The successful scholar is absorbed in his work. The intellectual problems and the imperatives of the discipline are always running through the mind of the researcher.

One of your authors on several occasions has waited for Knox to come back to the campus from one of his hundreds of weekend field trips. Although now over sixty years old, this eminent scholar continues his forays into the field, trapping hundreds of rodents and bats, personally skinning specimens and later cataloging them for future scientific study by himself, colleagues, and especially graduate students. Physically the work is long and hard. I watched him and his graduate students lug cases of odoriferous specimens from jeeps into the museum and I have interrupted his work at night and on weekends. I have never seen him idle and his workdays are very long. Always after exhausting field trips, he taught his classes, made his committee meetings, and had time for colleagues. The point we are making with the Knox Jones vignette and others is research is work, hard work, enjoyable work, that is conducted by highly trained persons with dedicated minds. Knox is one of those rare individuals who labor at asking questions for mankind, seeking answers, and preserving that knowledge for the present and future generations. Despite all of this work, he has never lost his humanity.

It is important in examining this person to know that he is a charming and witty companion, he enjoys his family, he relishes the cultural events of the city, and seems to manage rather well sponsorship of several organizations and extracurricular activities.

He is an international resource. Yearly, he edits nearly one hundred articles and proposals from his colleagues. We will call attention to the fact that by Knox's bringing the editorship of the *Journal of Mammalogy* to Texas Tech and by the continuing efforts of Clyde Jones, another very respected mammalogist in the NSRL, who was also Managing Editor of the journal, there emanates from the NSRL a tremendous disciplinary undercurrent of publication activity. This current of disciplinary knowledge brings to Texas Tech University the latest scientific findings from all quarters of the planet and it creates in the mind of the receivers throughout the world recognition of Texas Tech as a center for excellence in the study of mammals. Also, Knox served as the president of the American Society of Mammalogists adding considerable immediate and residual prestige to his home institution.

In 1971, Professor Jones came to Texas Tech University as dean of the Graduate School and was appointed professor of biological sciences. In 1974, he was made concurrently vice-president for research and graduate studies, a position he held for a decade. The vice-president for research is the most important research-administration position on a campus because those individuals have responsibility for all university research operations and they lead the campus planning for research. During his administrative tenure, he helped advance research and graduate studies at the Texas Tech in many areas. Unlike many administrators, he chose to actively continue his teaching and research duties. We have selected Professor Jones to show the primacy of the principal investigator in the conduct of research and to show how that research experience influenced his planning and administration of research.

If the principal investigator is the sine qua non in the conduct of research, would not a person trained professionally to be an administrator be the best type of individual to be a research administrator? The answer is no. Would not a nonresearcher administrator be best for senior level administrative jobs? Again, the answer is no. The primary function of research administration is research, not administration. Some argue that it is better to hire experienced administrators to do the planning and the administrative chores of the university, thus leaving the PI spending their time on research. There is merit to the idea that the PI should be freed from routine administrative duties, but there is no replacing research experience in institutional decision making.

The authors believe that only principal investigators have the intellectual power, university and research experience, and the respect of the research fraternity to ask the right questions, to make the right decisions, and the intellectual power to defend the right decisions regarding university research. In Chapter 5, the tremendous power of research administrators from their positions in the university hierarchy was discussed from the point of view of how best to technically organize the university and its partners. In this chapter, we want to look at the orientation of individuals and to show the importance of actual research experience in research administration. Remember that research administrators control huge resources, they decide on all research issues, they are research advocates, and they must place their imprimatur on all planning involving university research. Compromise the principle of positioning competent, experienced, researchers in authority in research offices results in discounting the value of research, ignoring the research operations, and replacing research development questions with regulatory concerns. Always, in the mind of the authors, in a research university, a senior principal investigator, who keeps one foot in the active research arena, should be making the operating decisions concerning the conduct of university research that are not reserved for the PI.

Yes, experienced administrators without research experience should be hired to handle the paperwork, to manage installed research systems, and to implement researcher designed plans. On the other hand, experienced researchers should be placed in senior positions where they can guide philosophy and set policy for the advantage of the researcher. Individuals who are or who have been researchers have a personal understanding of the problems of research and that personal understanding usually leads them to right decisions in operating problems. The nonresearcher administrator should never be allowed to delay development activities or override a principal investigator's operating decisions. Unfortunately, there are several institutions that have placed bureaucrats in key research administration positions for expediency. Ultimately, those expedient appointments come back to haunt the institution because the nonresearcher never really understands research and the researcher; consequently, they delay making decisions and when they do make decisions, they are usually the wrong decisions. Research planning, policy making, and key operating decisions can not be left to bureaucrats.

It is one thing to say that principal investigator experience is essential to research planning and administration, it is quite another to prove it. There are no great masses of empirical evidence to support this belief because universities seldom admit their bad experiences with inept administrators. Nevertheless, principal investigators know with certainty when they have a good administrator or a bad one. Invariably, in the discussion of good and bad research administrators, specific individuals and their policies will be mentioned. We will not present specific names of poor administrators, but we will contrast the nonresearcher model with Vice-President Jones because the subject is difficult to discuss without using polar extremes.

Knox Jones stands at the positive pole. He serves as an exemplar for the research administrator who was and who wants to remain a researcher and scholar when they are appointed to key university administrative positions. At the negative pole is the nonresearcher administrator.

Jones came to research administration after conducting dozens of his own research projects, directing many graduate student projects, and helping colleagues as a co-investigator. His experiences as a curator were an asset to Texas Tech University, but it was his having been and continuing to be a researcher that made Jones most valuable. Having a research background and a development orientation made him an excellent research administrator who made the right choices on research policy matters for a comprehensive university at a turning point in its history. He understood the importance of research and graduate education and guided resources in that direction.

In research administration, there is no substitute for research experience. We will note that Knox possesses and uses excellent interpersonal skills, that he has extraordinary organizational abilities, and that he knows many of the principals in the research enterprise. However, his greatest power for getting things accomplished rests on his understanding of the doing of research and the delivery of bona fide graduate education, on his willingness to take-on the bureaucracy when administrative policy and procedures hinder the principal investigator's work and on his leadership in advocating new research programs.

Research administrators are in the business of moving research forward. In the university setting, it requires individuals who understand how to develop supporting facilities and facilitative policies for the researcher. Research administrators who are experienced researchers are the best administrators to fill key administrative positions in the universities. Knox Jone's record confirms this belief.

Vice-President Jones planned for and/or helped implement the following supporting research facilities and activities, to name some: Natural Science Research Laboratory at the Texas Tech University Museum, Texas Tech University Press, Institute for Child and Family Studies, Texas Tech's Comparative Literature Symposium, and exchange programs with several foreign universities.

Each of these central activities facilitated the work of Texas Tech's researchers and advanced the reputation of the institution. The aforementioned activities were chosen to indicate some breadth in the development plans of an administrator, who is a scientific researcher. It shows that the researcher's past experience can help in the planning and development of other areas as well. Truly, this man's knowledge of the development process carried over to areas outside of his scientific specialty.

Knox, in his role as the senior research administrator and graduate school dean, championed the formulation of policies that facilitated the work of researchers, both faculty and graduate students, and assured the rights of both.

Once more, research experience is the telling ingredient for success in policy formulation. It is very difficult to quarrel with a person who is doing more than is being asked of others. Vice-President Jones took the lead in reforming and developing the following transforming policies at TTU.

1. Complete reorganization of the graduate faculty, with the concurrent establishment of meaningful criteria for appointment and continuance.
2. Instituted periodical in-depth reviews of all graduate programs at Texas Tech University to ensure adequacy of faculty, equipment, library holding, space and students.
3. Increased by more than two-fold the graduate programs at TTU, especially at the doctoral level.
4. Developed an incentive program whereby special funding was attached to departments and programs heavily involved in sponsored research.
5. Assisted in developing publications exchange programs at the Texas Tech Library, using publications of the newly established Texas Tech Press.
6. Enlarged the Office of Research Services (research administration) and established the position of director, later associate vice-president for research.
7. Established a popular graduate faculty-graduate student summer research program in which students were supported for joint faculty-student investigations.
8. Developed outstanding graduate student instruction awards to recognize those students who contributed in an exceptional way to the teaching mission of departments and programs.

In the early eighties, Jones requested that his associate vice-president, Arnold Gulley form a committee of researchers to study the measurement of research productivity at Texas Tech. The need for such a study had arisen from the increasingly important role that research was playing in a comprehensive university with a strong instructional orientation. Existing information on research suffered from the lack of comparability in form and in time period of measurements. Reports were unwieldily, defied summarization and were of suspicious quality. The committee for the measurement of research productivity (1981) recommended replacing the term "research" with the more comprehensive term "creative activities" to recognize explicitly those faculty contributions that result in the creation of new works in the arts, artistic design, and literary accomplishments. And, it provided guidelines for a systematic approach to the collection of research productivity measurements.

Vice-President Jones adopted the recommendations from his fellow researchers and implemented the following procedures, which laid the foundation for gathering useful information for decision making and research planning.

> Each department chairman, director, or area coordinator will compile the information requested in the proposed format. In addition, a summary and remarks interpreting the creative activity within the unit will be attached. Included should be goals and objectives related to research, and an evaluation of the kind and quality of creative output. Remarks concerning any special impediments to research faced by the department or area also may be included.
>
> The report will be examined by the appropriate dean who will attach his/her evaluation of the units's creative productivity. This evaluation should be based upon comparisons with corresponding units in other universities.
>
> The report, the chairman's summary and remarks, and the dean's evaluation will be forwarded to the Vice-President for Academic Affairs and Vice President for Research. These documents will serve to provide information about research productivity and will facilitate the university's decision-making process.

Earlier we mentioned that Jones had authored over three hundred articles and thirteen books in three decades. Most of his career, he has collected and classified rodents and bats rather than investigating the larger or economically more important species that are of current public interest. Although these small mammals do not receive great media attention, the Jones' articles and monographs create a valuable spectrum of biological knowledge that is used repeatedly by a wide variety of practitioners, such as physicians, military strategists, and agricultural scientists. This biological knowledge was the result of extensive field work and comparative investigations by principal-investigator Jones using the NSRL's vast mammal collection. At the beginning of all this work was the creative mind of Knox Jones, principal investigator and the primary thinker in a large research team.

Although the investigations of Knox Jones are classified as basic biological research, they have great social utility because the public needs to know more about small mammals, which frequently are considered to be pests or are important from a medical viewpoint. The mice, ground squirrels, and gophers of the Great Plains create many nuisance and economic problems for farmers and ranchers. Several rodents in Korea carry the mites that cause hemorrhagic fever that incapacitated and killed our troops. The mice of the southwest region carry bubonic plague; rabbits carry Lyme's disease. Bats, the night fliers, because they are known to carry rabies, and some species lap blood, are the subject of Dracula-type myths and are usually abhorred by the public. The medical community has an intense interest in knowing the species carriers and distribution of potential vectors of disease such as Lyme's disease. Regardless of their immediate social benefit, it is important to science that small mammals are maintained in collections, which serve as a valuable resource for comparative studies, for historical reference, and for future investigations. If these reference collections were not maintained it is doubtful that discoveries such as the effects of DDT on predatory birds would have ever been made.

Biologists have a great interest in the small mammals because their short life spans make them excellent models for the study of basic biological phenomena. Like many systematists, Jones based his research on classical methods involving the collection and preservation of animals from specific geographical areas. The classical systematists performs the following functions:

1. Collects specimens for future study, gathering specific data as to their habitats and their associates in the process.
2. Catalogs and classifies the specimens according to acceptable current phylogenetic classification.
3. Tests current concepts by careful study of morphological traits, both among species and higher taxonomic categories, but also within species groups in order to document intraspecies variation and thus evolutionary trends.
4. Describes the changing distribution patterns of animals and the effects of the environment on them.

Jones and his colleagues accumulate specimens that are valuable in differentiating subtle characteristics of species that superficially appear to be the same. Some differences between species can be discerned only genetically from studies at the cellular or molecular levels, or by careful analysis of skeletal and dental morphology. Knox and his fellow mammalogists have shown repeatedly that this information is vital in the recognition and understanding of the biological species. Thorough analysis of this fundamental knowledge permits Jones and his fellow scientists to draw assumptions about the survival rates of the species or populations as a whole under certain conditions as well as direction and rates of evolution. Perhaps of more importance, it leads to the detection of environmental changes and their effects on small mammals that then allows some very educated guesses about what may happen to other species, including humans, where the changes can not be detected in such short periods.

Early in his career Knox collected thousands of mammals and published over a hundred articles dealing with the mammals of the New World. Mid-career, he specialized in collecting and classifying the mammals of the tropics. His team of research associates and four or five graduate students spent six years collecting mammals in southern Mexico and Nicaragua to assist the United States Army with an important research thrust. The army-university partnership was mutually beneficial because the army paid for the research and learned about the animals and their ecoparasites that were of concern for tropic military strategy and the university benefited through adding thousands of specimens to its collection and opportunities for numerous dissertations and thesis projects.

When he came to TTU he started the Natural Science Research Laboratory at the Museum, which established a reputation for biological scholarship in systematics research. The NSRL is composed of the following scientists and associates.

Knox Jones, mammalogist and biogeographer, acts as principal investigator for numerous projects focused mostly on biodiversity studies of small mammals. He also serves as editor for the Museum's publication series, *Occasional Papers, Special Publications,* and *Museology*; as editor of the *Texas Journal of Science*; as editor for reviews for the *Journal of Mammalogy*.

Dilford Carter, mammalogists and comparative morphologist, acts as a principal investigator for the study of Yugoslavian mammals.

Clyde Jones, mammalogists and natural historian, acts as principal investigator for several long-term projects and as managing editor of the *Journal of Mammalogy*.

Robert Baker, mammalogist interested principally in cellular and molecular systematics, acts a principal investigator for numerous grants involving chromosome marking and DNA analysis as well as serving as director of the NSRL.

Stephen Williams, collection manager for the NSRL, acts as research associate and oversees the classical preservation of specimens and the preparation of frozen tissue samples and the storing of them in an Ultra-Cold freezer in the Museum laboratory.

Michael Willig, biometrician and evolutionary biologist, measures and records a vast array of data associated with specimens of mammals in the NSRL collection and advises others as to appropriate statistical treatment of data.

Many other biologists are associated from time-to-time with programs at the NSRL, joining certain development teams and serving as project associates when appropriate. These include faculty from the Biological Sciences, Museum Science, the Colleges of Agriculture and Engineering, and the Texas Tech University Health Sciences Center.

In addition to the established professional staff at NSRL there are at any given time several post-doctoral students pursuing some project work and a dozen or so graduate students working on dissertations, theses, and independent research projects.

Principal investigators, such as Knox Jones, not only conceive the fundamental questions for basic research, they must also manage the research activities of large research groups such as the aforementioned. Their research skills must be constantly undated and they must be highly aware of the work of their colleagues and students.

During his administrative career, principal investigator Jones stayed close to home and focused his attention on the bats of North America. In recent years, his attention has been given to the environment and now, he is mapping the biodiversity in the North Rosillas Mountains, a recent addition to Big Bend National Park. A review of his vitae shows a widening range of synthesizing monographs and books that deal with the distribution and taxonomy of the mammals in North, Central, and South America, the Antillean region, northeastern Asia, and the Balkans. Titles of some of his major works were listed earlier. His current work is concentrated on the Great Plains and adjacent Southwest, and he has recently published guides and handbooks of mammals of the Plain States and North-Central States. A handbook on the South-Central States is in preparation.

The quality of his work is highly regarded by his peers. He is the only person to have received both the Jackson and the Merriam awards from the American Society of Mammalogists, the most prestigious awards in the field of mammalogy.

On campus, the primacy of this investigator's seminal thought is acknowledged by hundreds of students who have asked him to serve on their theses and dissertation committees, by dozens of faculty who have asked for his help on specific projects, and by the administration who continuously placed him on committees where his creativity could direct institutional efforts toward educational excellence and research.

Supporting Pioneering Investigators

A word about research pioneers in general. Research pioneers are essential to universities because their travels oftentimes show the way to a rich new field of inquiry. Exploring new ground is part of the primacy of the principal investigator, but few academicians like leaving the comfort of an established discipline and traditional ways of doing things. Pioneers are a couple of standard deviations from the mean investigator. Their backgrounds, temperament, and questing minds entice them outside established academic boundaries. They deserve special study for they are the most misunderstood of investigators. One description of such visionaries is that they are not only the first to see the light at the end of the tunnel, but they can also envision the green fields and the rich landscape beyond. They need special supporting services because they do not wait for institutional approval of their activities. They move into an area, doing things their way, and later research support personnel have to follow them to tidy up the entire area. Support persons often complain about such cleanup efforts, but that is what they are paid for. Research support personnel would not have jobs without pioneers and research would be appreciably slowed without the maverick trail blazers. It is the job of the vice-president for research to identify pioneers and help them develop successful research programs.

Earlier the point was made that principal investigators are the intellectual capital of the university. That capital is quite varied. Professor Knox Jones, a mammalogist; was discussed as an example of the classical principal investigator who started his basic research career early in life by collecting butterflies in the shadows of the Nebraska State Museum and continued his line of inquiry by collecting mammals and studying the changing distribution patterns of animals and the effects of the environment on them. Animal systematists are natural scientists; their work fits readily into the academic tradition and it is easily subsumed under established divisions of biology.

Kathleen Hennessey will be discussed because she is an academic pioneer who has developed her career on production research and information technology innovation. She exhibits all the sterling characteristics of the principal investigator, but her brilliant and extremely active mind frequently carries her away from the herd and leaves her musing about problems she finds on new ground.

The authors have a strong suspicion that the character and development-orientation of many investigators were formed very early in life. Kathleen Hennessey's early childhood experiences support this speculation. Kathleen, like the other investigators in this series of vignettes, started researching questions at an early age. Her independence was developed in the wilderness of Alaska where she was raised among mining engineers and Eskimos who prized independent problem solving. She attributes her inquisitiveness to her father, a mining engineer, and her mother, an amateur archaeologist and poet. Kathleen accompanied her mother on digs when she was nine years old. Very early she was given jobs for the mining operations that required her to measure and record things in a methodical way.

During the long arctic winters, she and her siblings acquired much of their formal education by correspondence through the Calvert School, which requires independent thought; lessons were individually graded and returned from Baltimore. Their informal education was equally valuable as it taught them to problem solve with resources at hand in an uncomfortable and dangerous environment.

She grew up among Eskimos whose Stanford-Benet scores usually exceeded 120. Playing with Eskimo children in the wilderness taught her to respect others' expertise and to judge the quality of ideas outside her own realm on their merit for practical solutions rather than for the pat academic response. She feels that a gold mining camp provided an enriched learning environment because she learned to expect failure and to gain success by trying a different approach the second time. Their cabin or tent was frequently filled with men drawing plans for heavy equipment, testing ore, and plotting mining operations. Problems had to be understood and solved on the spot in the remote wilderness without outside help.

Like all good investigators, Kathleen Hennessey asks the right questions, but in a variety of fields in which she is not currently teaching or practicing. Then she transfers complex theories of knowledge and innovative technologies to the problems of the field. She has created during the last three decades some fundamental theories and generic computer programs that allow her and her teams to come up with amazingly efficient solutions to long standing industrial problems by creating new computer technologies to replace manual labor. Her theories and technologies also allow her to create extraordinary computer-produced models of complex phenomena.

When she started creating these theories and technologies for representation and processing of knowledge, computer science research and education were just starting and were attached to mathematics, science and/or engineering departments. Systems analysis and design were not regarded by mathematicians and scientists as basic research and engineers were more interested in applied research problems associated with computer hardware. Yes, rigorous representation of knowledge was essential to the semi-conductor industry, but it was not winning the academic prizes that went to crystal growing, cutting, and etching for computer chips. Exploring the theoretical aspects of computeraided design as representation of knowledge in an electrical engineering department was not as respectable as problems of electron transport and storage in boron oxide and silicon crystals.

Like other PIs Professor Hennessey works countless hours and her work is acknowledged by the few experts in her field as being superlative. Graduate students consider her to be outstanding. She has eighteen graduate students working in her laboratories and a long list of others waiting to be invited to serve on one of her investigative teams. Industrialists come to her laboratories for a peek at what she has coming down the pike and she is a privileged guest in IBM, Sun, Xerox, Boeing and Texas Instruments' research laboratories. She received the largest Texas advanced technology grants awarded to the university in 1987 and 1989 and the second largest grant awarded by the Texas advanced technology research program. Kathleen has multiple sponsors for her laboratories. She owns more intellectual property—patents and software copyrights—than any other person in the college. Despite prodigious productivity, accolades from industry and state and national recognition, her direct manner and aggressive development of her projects unsettles colleagues and administrators.

One can judge this PI with orthodox measures, but it is her development of unorthodox solutions that has given her the reputation of being a far-out innovator and enhances her value to the university. She is acknowledged to be passing the competition in the international race for developing superiority in computer technology. She was recently chosen to represent the United States at a Paris conference on international interchange of multimedia documents. Kathleen and colleagues recently designed new computer programs that quickly and accurately evaluate computer chips for circuit defects. The main benefits of this new technology lies in two areas.

The reduction of labor costs associated with computer chip inspection. Until recently, computer chips coming off the manufacturing lines were randomly sampled and examined manually through a microscope. The evaluation of one silicon wafer, which contains several hundred chips—could take a human inspector as much as an hour to analyze for defects. With the technological theory conceived by Hennessey and her students, and the development of the computer technology by her teams, one wafer can be evaluated with much more accuracy in only a few minutes. Although Kathleen has been building a theory of knowledge and testing it for more than a decade, it is in the area of automated visual inspection of computer chips, that her theories have proven their worth.

The improvement of the quality of computer chips by the detection of flaws in chips. By converting the computer-aided and design files used to produce the photo mask from which chips are produced into a grammar, defects can be identified in the same way programming errors are flagged by a Fortran or C compiler. The computer is thus able to detect possible defects based on its knowledge of what a flawless chip should be. For instance, the inspecting computer knows that the wafer should contain a network of tiny, unbroken lines with specific configurations. If the evaluated wafer does not match the standard, the system marks the image with a small red circle to indicate the component and location of the defect.

The inspection system is based on ideas originated by one of Kathleen's students who was denied admission to the computer science doctoral program. In typical pioneer fashion, she found support for him and helped get him admitted to another program. Their six-year collaboration produced over a million dollars in research funding, more than a quarter million worth of gifts of equipment and facilities from top companies such as General Signal and Xerox, six patent applications and fourteen software copyrights. Because the computer science graduate curriculum could not be adjusted to allow her to teach knowledge-based theories, she transferred

to the Business College's information systems program where she is director of the Institute for Studies of Organizational Automation and its
knowledge-based systems research laboratory. She also coordinates two
graduate interdisciplinary studies programs in health computing and
knowledge-based systems.

Her research efforts extend to other fields, such as image analysis of thin
sections of rock to determine oil and water carrying capacity, development
of techniques to interchange documents on open system networks, and
analysis of medical texts and doctors' notes for common patterns of key
words. Another task is modelling of knowledge for secondary mathematics
curricula.

Her former students play leading roles in the information industry, such
as Hewlett-Packard's international network accounts manager, Hyundai's
senior industrial electronics laboratory manager, and coordinator of the
University of Missouri-Kansas City's telecommunications research
laboratory. Where some seek the comfort and security of established
knowledge, pioneers like Kathleen become restless and frustrated unless
they are probing the edges of the unknown. This makes both types of
academicians uncomfortable, but it is an essential tension for progress in
research.

The Principal Investigators Role in Developing World-Class Research Facilities

Rodney L. Preston, distinguished researcher and teacher and holder of
the Thornton Chair in Animal Science, is the third principal investigator
that is considered for their personal preparation to be a researcher and then
for their role in the research university.

Rod Preston was born in Denver and reared on a farm near Arvada,
Colorado during WWII. During his secondary school education, he
developed a strong interest in the biological sciences, while his performance of the usual farm chores gave him a practical knowledge of a wide
range of farm animals. He studied vocational agriculture and showed
animals in the junior division of the state and National Western Stock
Show.

In 1949, he enrolled in the animal nutrition program at Colorado State
University (CSU). His early interest was dairy science and he worked part-
time in the CSU Dairy. While working in the dairy, he became a good
friend to a grad assistant who he helped with research on animal nutrition.
In 1951 he was awarded the Roy M. Green Memorial Scholarship. His undergraduate research experience established a specific interest in animal
nutrition. In 1953 he received the B.S. degree in animal nutrition with high
distinction from CSU.

He transferred to Iowa State University for his graduate work because he was attracted to their strong programs in animal nutrition and veterinary physiology. While at Iowa State, he narrowed his research interests to endocrinology and the role of hormones in the growth of animals. He earned the Masters and Ph.D degrees in animal nutrition and veterinary physiology from Iowa State University in 1955 and 1957.

He has served on the animal science faculty at the University of Missouri and The Ohio State University and was chairman of the animal science department at Washington State University. He was named outstanding junior faculty member at the University of Missouri in 1964, was awarded an NIH special fellowship for research studies in the Netherlands in 1964-65. He was elected to membership in the following honor and science societies: Alpha Zeta, Gamma Sigma Delta, Phi Kappa Phi, and Sigma Xi. He has received numerous awards for his research from his peers and was honored by Texas Tech University as the Barne E. Rushing Research Award winner in 1990. He is a long-standing member of the American Society of Animal Science, American Institute of Nutrition, Society for Experimental Biology and Medicine, and the Plains Nutrition Council. He was editor for the applied section of the *Journal of Animal Science* and is a past-president of the American Society of Animal Science. He currently serves on the National Academy of Science-National Research Council Committee on Animal Nutrition.

The reader will note the similarities between the research characteristics of Knox Jones and Rod Preston. Both have outstanding publication records, both direct large organized research centers, both have served as editors of journals, both have been honored by their peers, and both have an extensive list of grant awards. However, there are some points of contrast between the two researchers that are occasioned by their fields of investigation. Knox's research was supported mostly by the government and the university as there was little commercial interest in bats and rodents. Rod's research on the other hand gained great commercial interest and support. To a large extent, commercial applications of the basic research of Rod Preston and his associates motivates much of the farm and state government support that built the Burnett Center for Beef Cattle Research and Teaching facilities and concomitant programs at Texas Tech University. Although Preston has been awarded a number of government grants for his basic research, much more support has come from the U.S. Brewers Association, the National Feed Ingredients Association, and the National Grain Sorghum Producers Association and from a long list of pharmaceutical companies such as Syntex Inc., Hoechst-Roussel, Hoffmann-La Roche, Inc., Smith Kline Beecham, Eli Lilly and Company etc. It is his many connections with industry and his understanding of the cattle raisers thought processes and the consumer market that makes Rod an exemplar for this book. Also, Preston's prestige as a basic researcher attracts graduate students and international visiting scientists who have an interest in researching and developing cattle nutrition, growth, and management concepts. And, it is his prestige and the department's planning that obtains the large amount of commercial and state funds essential to supporting the world's outstanding research center on beef cattle and feed lot operations.

Preston's ability to understand the needs of students for research topics that will advance their careers, the thought processes of commercial people, and the imperatives of the discipline allow us to see how student, faculty, university and commercial interests can be melded to form a symbiotic relationship that advances the strategic interests of all. It is the plans of the principal investigator that holds these divergent interests together and that facilitates the individual interests of many under the general umbrella of an ORU. The planning and administrative activities for an ORU takes the PI out of the laboratory and into commercial offices. Integrating student demands for basic research and teaching guidance, and commercial needs under the Burnett Center goals requires strategic planning.

Your authors recognized the special nature of graduate education and took the position that the faculty, especially proven researchers, would work very closely with graduate and undergraduate students in planning and conducting research that would advance the department's program aims, the principal investigator's goals and the student's career objectives. We believe that the primary purpose of graduate education is to teach students to conduct research. Departmental research should be directed toward advancing basic research using faculty and student ideas. John Dewey's thesis that students learn by doing is most appropriate when research modes of inquiry are to be learned. In planning any center of graduate excellence, the foremost consideration must be that graduate students learn research by doing research. We examine Rodney Preston's career because it demonstrates the value of the principal investigator planning strategically with students and it provides some insights into the training of an investigator who substantially expanded a professional mode of inquiry and who developed personal research techniques to the point that students want to work with him to learn his techniques.

Most importantly, we have seen in Preston, the characteristic's of the modern researcher that require the scholar to plan strategically and to work from a center of excellence that brings together students, faculty, and sponsors.

Traditionally, teacher-student planning for research has been at the heart of graduate education. In the research university everyone is expected to do research. Students, who elect to attend a research university, plan for admittance long before they apply. They anticipate conducting research from the time they enter the institution until they leave it. For example, we have seen Dr. Preston's early research orientation continue through today. Now, the decades of research intelligence and his enthusiasm are transmitted to his graduate students. His reputation as a biochemist interested in male hormones to stimulate the growth of cattle has attracted many students who have then moved into academic positions throughout the United States. Deana Hancock contacted Dr. Preston in 1984 with the hope that he would agree to direct her work and help her to become competitive in the field of biotechnology. While working with Professor Preston she performed many experiments on ruminants. Her work on the mechanisms of estrogen action that elicits the anabolic response observed in ruminants attracted national attention and won for her the first Eli Lilly Post-Doctorate Fellowship to do research at the Eli Lilly, Greenfield Agriculture Research Center. Later, she was appointed to the Purdue University faculty.

Students are attracted to an institution by the quality of its programs. They enter a graduate program to improve themselves. Reciprocally, the institution expects the student to build the image of the institution. The final quality of student research depend upon the quality of the graduate program, the capabilities of the thesis advisor, and the student's thoughts and preparation. Therefore, without good researchers working from a center for excellence and brilliant students challenging each other, there will be no graduate program—only counterfeit courses falsely carrying a graduate number.

In addition to the attraction of working with one of the best animal scientists in the world, students are also impressed with the capabilities of the research centers where they will work. Preston (1985) in his technical reports on beef research describes the superlative facilities and services offered by the Burnett Center for Beef Cattle Research and Instruction. Brochures and technical reports prepared by the Department of Animal Sciences attract students as they describe the advantages of research facilities at Texas Tech. Their information materials note that the development facilities of the computer-controlled feed mill and the state-of-the-art experimental cattle feedlot cost Texas Tech University $4.3 million to build. Preston and his colleagues discuss with graduate students the potential of using the unique features of the pilot facility, which contains a three-level, computer-operated, dust-controlled, mixing plant that automatically premixes many different diet formulations requiring high accuracy and precision weighing. The student learns that they can set diet formulations for their experimental cattle and send those via belt to the experimental feedlot. The feedlot was designed to maximize experimental flexibility, to give proper control, and to provide sufficient replication. The faculty let the potential students know that daily they will have opportunities to work in the Burnett Feedlot and Feed Mill and to conduct their research in the best facilities in the world. This is quite an enticement to students wanting to be associated with the number-one research facility in their area of study. This one-of-a-kind facility provides 1) uniform conditions across the entire feedlot; 2) 114, eight-headed pens with partially slotted floors and 8, thirty-two head conventional pens with dirt floors—a sufficient number of pens to provide adequate replication of experimental treatments; 3) accuracy in weighing feeds and microingredients, mixing of diets, and delivery of diets to pens; 4) speed in delivering mixed diets to the feed bunks; 5) ease of handling cattle during experimental procedures and accuracy in weighing experimental animals; and 6) efficient use of land, minimizing mud problems and providing ease of cattle waste removal, with potential for research on cattle waste.

Preston and colleagues determined that the general outcome of the Burnett Center is to improve the economic status of beef production in Texas and to develop basic knowledge for use in beef production. The hundreds of specific results from individual contracts with pharmaceutical companies, feed and cattle associations, and meat packers are the individual outcomes of this pilot facility. Training graduate students in the science of beef cattle research is another important outcome of a pilot plant such as the Burnett Center that requires considerable teacher-student planning of specific objectives by Preston and this colleagues.

In developing a graduate program, the teacher-researcher should be considered first as they must have the knowledge of the discipline, the research ideas, and the skills to practice a particular mode of inquiry. Among the faculty of the institution, the researchers with excellent reputations such as Preston attract the serious graduate students for these students want the best training possible. The research-development orientation of the graduate advisor is the key to exemplary training.

Understanding the roles of the principals in graduate education is important to strategic planning for research. First, the graduate dean accepts or rejects all students according to general standards. That starts a plan between the institution and the student. Secondly, the faculty member accepts or rejects a student's request to serve as the director of their research work. The former activity is part of an institutional routine, the later is a very personal commitment that requires mutual acceptance.

Strategic planning between the teacher and student begins with the student approaching a professor to determine if they have mutual research interests and if the professor will accept the student for graduate study. The student understands that the relationship that develops between the faculty member and the student is a very special one. If the student is accepted, the faculty member plans to devote a great amount of time to coaching individually the student. The student plans to follow the master. When their interests do not coincide, the professor will send the student to another professor who seems to match better the student's interests. Finding and keeping a mentor, requires that the student meets the standards of the faculty member and lives by the ethics of the profession. Before the professor accepts the student, the faculty member will determine the career ambitions and the research objectives of the student through informal talks in his office, strolling across the campus and looking over an ORU such as the Burnett Center. If the student seems to have the potential for doing graduate work, if the proposed research matches the research goals of the professor, if a personality match occurs, and if the professor has the time to devote himself to a two to four year mentoring process with the student, the student is accepted as one of professor's graduate students.

The following student theses titles fit under the goals of the Burnett Center: "Mechanism of Estrogen Action Which Elicits the Anabolic Response Observed in Ruminants," "Estimating the Extracellular Water Component of Total Body Water in Beef Cattle Using Sodium Thiosulfate," "Addition of an Enzyme Combination or Gibberellic Acid to Sorghum Grain for Feedlot Cattle," "Effect of Protein Source and Level on Performance of Feedlot Cattle," "Evaluation of Energy Status in Beef Cows," and "Physiological Factors Associated with Compensatory Growth in Beef Cattle."

One sees in the above list the co-mingling of student career objectives and faculty research orientations with commercial interests that is necessary to develop a center of research excellence.

Once a student is accepted the student learns to be a research partner and plans to contribute to their profession. The student contribution is extremely valuable to the university and to the discipline for it must advance of the knowledge of the discipline. For example, the graduate student research dealing with the effect of protein source and level on performance of feedlot cattle and the mechanism of estrogen action that elicits the anabolic response observed in ruminants have immediate commercial significance for cattle raisers. At the Burnett Center students learn to be a contributor as well as a taker from the resources of the discipline and the university. This is a critical transformation in attitude. If it does not occur, the student will not be successful in attaining a graduate degree.

Graduate education is the development of research partnerships between teachers and students. At the Burnett Center, both parties must benefit from the research relationship. The student can expect to be taught a mode of inquiry, to learn how to do research, and to be guided by the researcher. In return, Preston and colleagues associated with the Burnett Center can expect to gain a great deal of routine work from the student and new insights into animal nutrition, growth, and metabolism.

In this beginning collegial relationship, ideas will be developed mutually. There will be times when Preston and other instructors will have the student working on the faculty member's sponsored project. There will be other times that the faculty member will give his best thoughts to the student's project. At the end, it is difficult to say that the research results belong to only one person. The rewards, as was the work, must be fairly distributed. There is a fairness ethic in research that calls for the person who originally conceived the solution to a problem to have the right of first authorship. Others who contributed intellectually to the project are given secondary authorship on publications. The teacher-student research partnership is no different. There is an equality of intellect that governs graduate education. When students work on a faculty member's research project, they can expect to be included as an author only if they have contributed to the formulation of a solution. Data gathering is routine work. Instrument repair is routine work. Analysis of data and invention of new instruments are research. Researchers must plan with the student to assure that the student meets the obligations for being a research partner and that the student receives fair treatment. Planning helps assure fair treatment of both parties. In fact, it is indispensable for a good long-term working relationship.

Theses and dissertations are the original investigations of the student. They therefore have primary authorship of the work. The student owns that piece of intellectual property. However, there is the expectation that several publications may gtow out of the data gathered for the thesis. In this case, fairness calls for the student to include their advisors as secondary authors on outgrowth publications that are mutually developed.

The research tradition has teachers and students dealing with research concepts and planning research projects in every graduate course. Most graduate programs have as their beginning courses research seminars that are devoted to helping the students prepare their research strategy and presentation of results for their career development. Early in the graduate program, the student with a research orientation picks a research area and the student's advisors plan with the student the coursework and independent studies that will advance the research capabilities of the student. Ultimately, the faculty must assure the graduate school that the student has demonstrated a mastery of the techniques of research, a thorough understanding of the subject matter and its background, and a high degree of skill in organizing and presenting the materials. The research should make a significant contribution of new information to a subject or substantial reevaluation of existing knowledge, presented in a scholarly style.

Teacher-Student Planning

To illustrate how teacher-student planning occurred at Texas Tech, the strategy used by Hensley in the late eighties will be discussed. Graduate students were encouraged to enroll in EDHE 5001-Proposal Writing because in that course, their research goals would be developed during their first semester of graduate work. The purpose of the course was to assist the student prepare a research proposal. The student was required to prepare the following progressively more difficult research planning manuscripts:

A Decision Element— a one-page document that listed the purposes, processes, benefits, consequences, budget, and quantitative measures associated with the student's research.

A Prospectus—a twenty or more page document that briefly described the student's contemplated work.

A Proposal—a manuscript of more than fifty pages that described in some detail the proposed work and a timetable for completing it.

This research development process forced the student to begin to think about a possible thesis or dissertation project and to begin to plan with faculty for the conduct of that research. Frequently, these projects extended from two to five years and resulted in significant research being contributed to the discipline.

The work of Don Foreman, graduate student, and the NSF orthotic project staff illustrates the type of teacher-student planning that occurs within departmental environs. In 1986, Foreman an advisee of Reavis enrolled in Hensley's EDHE 5001-Proposal Writing course. Foreman, a teacher in the Lubbock State School for Handicapped Children, wanted to conduct research to advance knowledge of the severely and profoundly handicapped child.

During that same year, Richard Dudek, Donna Reavis, and Hensley were co-investigators on a NSF project developing a number of orthotic devices for disabled children. Reavis planned to use teachers in her Special Education programs to identify severely handicapped children who were in need of custom designed assistive devices. The NSF project staff brought together Reavis' thirty Special Education graduate students and Dudek's twenty-five engineering students in Hensley's proposal-writing class for the purpose of designing biotechnological devices for handicapped children. That multidisciplinary class learned from the instructors and each other how to determine student needs for orthotic devices, how to write research proposals, how to create a graphic design for a customized assistive device for these children, and how to field test the devices. During the weekly three-hour meetings of the class, the project staff and students discussed the design feasibility, materials utilization, and the testing protocols for the individual devices. Each engineering student had selected from a list of needed devices a project to develop. They teamed-up with a Special Education teacher and one of the NSF project staff to form a research planning team that visited the handicapped students in the public schools. Later the teams designed, fabricated, and tested orthotic devices under the supervision of the NSF project staff in the biocybernetics and the engineering laboratories. The PIs liked this strategy of coordinated effort because it allowed them to initiate annually from the biocybernetics laboratory about two dozen projects that were usually funded by the NSF and the Texas Rehabilitation Commission. The Special Education graduate students and the engineering students thought the orthotics projects were the most valuable education experiences in their academic careers. The public school officials and parents were ecstatic about these activities.

Don Foreman, a kind and gentle man with a bent for applied research, was one of Reavis's older students (over forty years of age). He became the principal investigator in a dramatic piece of applied research and development that has tremendous basic research possibilities.

For his research project, Don Foreman wanted to find a better way of communicating with a severely handicapped young adult under his care. The client was Terry, a nineteen-year-old teenager who had profound scoliosis and was severely spasmatic. Terry had no control over malformed limbs and he could not control the muscles in his head or body. All of his body functions were cared for by others. With the exception of Foreman, people around Terry were unable to communicate with him. Foreman was convinced that although Terry had an uncontrolable body, he had a bright mind and a wonderful sense of humor. The difficulty was that the messages from the brain became garbled and uncontrolled before they could be uttered. Don was the only one who believed that he was in touch with Terry's mind. They would communicate very crudely by a simple system of Terry's winking and Don's saying options until they hit on what Terry thought. The research problem for Foreman was to find a way of getting Terry's imprisoned thoughts out to others. Something that had not been accomplished in nineteen years of internment in a state hospital and something that was thought impossible by most of the experienced professional staff.

The solution, which took several months to conceive and design and three years to build and test, was the development of an eye-tracking device (ETD) for the handicapped and linking it to a computer-generated communication and synthetic voice system for severely and profoundly handicapped children. The problem was extremely difficult, most of the professionals when looking at all of the technological problems and the professional diagnosis thought the task was probably not possible. Don

Foreman, on the other hand, was convinced that Terry was bright, despite the psychometricians testing and pronouncements. He convinced the first team of designers Bobby Hudgens, Greg Hatfield, and Reese Wright that they could collectively design and fabricate the planned system before they graduated and he helped the second team of Ka Lam, William Chio, and Chow Ming Wong to persevere in refining the system until it worked perfectly. Michael Parten and Eddie Arrant of the Department of Electrical Engineering and Oliver D. Hensley and Donna Reavis of the College of Education spent three years supervising these students in various laboratories and in the field.

The new, complex, communication system was intended to help Terry interact with the outside world—to express his needs, to show his feelings, and to learn. With all the physical problems Terry had, the team felt an eye-tracking device was probably the best solution to his communication problems. This project was started by Foreman's team one in the fall semester of 1987. After one-and-a-half years of testing various devices, they established the basic plans for the entire synthetic speech communications system, such as the method to track the position of the eye, the method to capture and to digitize the picture of the eye, and the choice of the voice synthesizer. They designed, constructed and tested a prototype. It worked now and then, but it showed that they were on the right track. The second team of researchers refined the technology by replacing first generation models with improved components and by improving interfacing devices.

To design a truly reliable system, the second team had to develop new techniques for tracking a spot on Terry's eye. This was the critical technological component in the synthetic speech communications system built for Terry. This undeveloped technology created by the Foreman teams opened up a whole new area of basic research related to communicating with the severely and profoundly disabled child. Foreman's research publications on the success of Terry and the EDT are causing the field of Special Education and educational psychologists to rethink their theories on the intelligence of severely and profoundly handicapped children. Moreover, Foreman's conclusions and recommendation are leading the development of new ways of testing these children.

This account will mention only a few of the many ancillary benefits resulting from the orthoptic project team's investigation. First, there is the continuing improvement in Terry from the Hawthorne effect. People outside the school now pay attention to him. They ask him about the assistive devices and about life in general and he can respond intelligently. Student created technology had transformed a forgotten ward of the state into a person.

Student research ideas in a research environment and a small amount of seed money from an NSF grant started this long-term project and convinced the Texas Rehabilitation Commission, the public schools, and Texas Tech University to plan together and to pool their financial and human resources to develop more systems for the benefit of other children.

In the final analysis, the research of a number of students and the tenacity of a good graduate student freed the thoughts of a single individual and opened the gate to a new field of scientific investigation.

DESIGNING THE DEPARTMENTAL STRATEGIC PLAN FOR RESEARCH

As we recall from Chapter 5, departmental plans should be reassessed periodically to determine the congruence between the current work and the purposes of the unit. Two Texas Tech academic departments will be discussed to show examples of substantive changes in the unit goals.

Earlier in looking at the primacy of the principal investigator, we discussed the vast expanse of the Texas Tech University Museum, the excellence of its organized research units, and the contributions of its researchers. In this section, the need for reassessment of the departmental purpose statements to keep them relevant to the needs of the constituencies being served and to have them reflect the current and anticipated work of the department is explained. The narrowed goals of the Museum demonstrate the need to review goals to reflect anticipated work. The Department of Plant and Soil Sciences illustrates the expansion of departmental goals to meet the changing needs of the agricultural community of the High Plains.

Museology

The concept for the Museum of Texas Tech University was put forth in 1929 by community and regional leaders and generally endorsed by the academic community. The organization's original purpose was "the comprehensive study of arid and semi-arid lands worldwide." The intent of the original purpose was to collect natural and cultural objects from arid lands throughout the world and to create comprehensive collections for scientific study and public display.

In the early 1980s, museum faculty and university administrators pointed out the enormity of the undertaking associated with the original goal and the current inability of the University and its partners, the West Texas Museum Association and Ranching Heritage Association, to properly house, finance, and maintain proper care of information and artifacts from arid and semi-arid lands worldwide. Moreover, the existing work of the staff and the collections did not match the original purpose statement. Most of the Museum's large collections were formed from the contributions of West Texans and the field-generated natural science and archaeological items collected by members of the Museum staff, their associates and Tech students. In a half-century Texans were very generous in transferring the ownership of thirty-three authentic historic structures, in assigning financially valuable personal collections of period furnishings, clothing and textiles, and in donating extensive related materials to the Ranching Heritage Center. This superlative core facility located on a fourteen-acre site provided a place where the story of ranching in the Southwest is told by authentic objects that stimulate the viewer to step momentarily into previous worlds. West Texans targeted bequests, dedicated endowments, made special purchases, volunteered work, and provided legislative support that dictated a Southwest ranching theme. Their interests preserved the art, ethnographic materials and historical objects of this region. In reality for five decades, the TTU Museum was preserving the heritage and the mammals of the Southwest in several sites and libraries.

The Museum planning committees analyzed the past work of the Museum, considered several scenarios and recommended that the Museum's goal statement should include only the natural history, heritage, and climate of the southwestern United States and the cultures and natural environments which influenced the development of this area and Texas. Narrowing the goals allowed museum personnel to reorient their collections and to clarify the immediate and future needs of collection development and directed financial support for the proper storage and care of items. The previous orientation was too widely dispersed and could include any variety of materials for future incorporation into Museum collections. Now, the Museum's research, education, and collection activities are much more focussed. All potential acquisitions must be evaluated in terms of the new goals of the Museum and the revised mission of Texas Tech University as a research university. Concentration of resources on the Southwest should build stronger collections and enhance the research capabilities of this organized research unit.

Gary Edson (1989), director of the Museum, in speaking directly on changing the goals to guide the long-term development of the Museum noted:

> To enhance the dissemination of information, museums must be clear about what they propose to do. While it is appropriate to address the responsibility of representing all people, it may not be possible to be all things to all people. It is important to remember that museums are not ends unto themselves; they are the means in the service of humankind and cultural evolution. To accomplish this mission, museums must, on one hand, excite people as well as inform them and, on the other expand the cultural and scientific knowledge base through research and publication. . . . Good

museums attract, entertain, and arouse curiosity which leads to questioning and thus promotes learning. They are educational institutions that are set up and kept in motion for the benefit of a defined constituency. . . .

He concluded the Museum's philosophy on its new goals by stating:

The pieces are in place to construct the springboard for propelling the Museum into the twenty-first century with the same visionary enthusiasm with which it was created. The challenge is great but the rewards are greater.

Department heads have tremendous responsibilities for working with professional associations and support groups to foster their research programs. Accreditation by professional associations is very important to a department's instruction and research programs. In 1982, Robert Moore planned for the Museum to be accredited by the American Association of Museums. Clyde Jones initiated a museum accreditation plan in 1983, which was endorsed and given a high priority in the university plan. After years of self-study and planning on virtually every aspect of the Museums operations and after another year of on-site visitations by teams of experienced museum professionals, the Museum was accredited by the American Association of Museums (AAM) in 1990. The Museum director, Edson (1990) who had devoted hundreds of days of planning to the accreditation process immediately thanked the Museum's many supporters for their help after the accreditation was made and noted:

We can be proud of our achievement, but it is equally important to keep things in the correct perspective. Accreditation confirms that we are doing some things right. . . . Accreditation, no matter how rigorous, is entry level success. It is a starting point from which growth is essential.

Department heads provide a very valuable liaison functions between the department and its professional associations and support associations. In the case of the Museum, Director Edson had to represent the Texas Tech University Museum at the American Association of Museums (AAM) and the Texas Association of Museums (TAM) annual meetings and periodically he had to host annual meeting for these associations. Hosting such a meeting requires considerable planning among member institutions and it requires the director to ready host facilities for inspection by association members so the Museum can impress the entire state or national museum community. This is image building. It should be part of every department's strategic planning.

Planning and building a research division requires years of leadership from department heads. The planning activities never end. For example, the Lubbock Lake Site was uncovered in an archaeological dig in 1939. Texas Tech's researchers unearthed evidence of continual human habitation at the Lubbock Lake Site for at least 11,000 years. This very important site had to be preserved for scientific study and eventually opened to the public. The Museum purchased the three hundred-acre site and began the systematic scientific exploitation of the Late Holocene sediments and soils (the last 4,000 years) through survey and intensive exploration techniques. After fifty years of discovery and planning for first rate facilities, the Nash Center was built in 1989. Director Edson and Eileen Johnson, coordinator of the Anthropology Division, had to plan this 4000 square foot facility built to museum-quality specifications for climate control, and for very exacting specifications to provide wet, dry, and chemical space for the processing and cataloging of archaeological and other earth sciences materials. This center was planned to be used as the staging ground for far-ranging southern plains research of the Museum that will initiate a twenty-year plan for surveys and testing of 5,000 acres centering on upland playas lakes. Little is known about the functions of these lakes although of the few playa sites excavated, most have been significant Early Man sites. The Lubbock Lake Land Quaternary Research Center will be the center for expanding rings of exploration by Johnson and her fellow researchers who plan to discover more about aboriginal use of the playas.

Planning for the public opening of the Lubbock Lake State Archaeological and National Historic Landmark required years of planning and the raising of millions of dollars from local organizations, the Texas Parks and Wildlife Department, and federal agencies. If required the establishment of a separate nonprofit Landmark Foundation and extensive fund raising activities. The public opening required planning for a variety of events—some open to the public and others by invitation. Edson had to plan for a separate $300,000-plus fund-raiser to pay for replicas of ancient animal inhabitants at the site, for the professional meetings of two dozen visiting distinguished international scholars contemplating joint projects with the research center's staff, and for ground-breaker ceremonies with the center's partners the Texas Parks and Wildlife Department and the City of Lubbock.

At Texas Tech University many departments have support associations that work to advance particular programs or departmental divisions. Involving these support associations in the strategic planning for the department's research efforts is vital to the long-term success of any departmental plan. The Department of Museum Science in the College of Arts and Sciences has support associations for each of its major research divisions. The West Texas Museum Association (WTMA) started in 1929 with only sixty-nine members who pledged to donate their time, monies, and energies to the advancement of a museum for the Lubbock region that would be the keeper of the treasures from arid and semiarid lands. Sixty years later, the membership grew to number more than 1,750 paying members and their donations to the collections of the TTU Museum exceed 1.5

million items. The WTMA elects its own officers and conducts its affairs independently from the University; yet, there is such a close partnership between the TTU Museum and WTMA that neither could function well without the other. They have had mutual goals and plans for over six decades.

The department head must maintain a very close liaison with the support associations and involve them in all department plans. This requires hours of work on designing operating, tactical, and strategic plans with the support association officers and planning committees.

As one would expect from a sixty-year-old organization, the Museum has the support network and planning system firmly in place—the director must keep it well maintained. This is accomplished by Director Edson and his staff officers meeting monthly with the several support associations, they must solicit the best ideas from executive committees and the boards of overseers for the strategic plans of the Museum and they must help them adopt the new goals of the Museum into association by-laws. The department head must guide the tactical and operational plans of the support associations, or future events will go awry. Narrowing of the Museum's purpose required the restructuring of committees, a redirection of image building activities, and a shifted emphasis in fund raising. The Director must help with the long-term plans for Golden Spur Awards, Ranch Day, and Livestock Day to assure that the several committee plans and all the details are satisfactory to make these annual events, which bring thousands of people from throughout the nation to the Museum, even better than their most successful programs of the past years.

For example, Edson had to work closely with several, presidents of the West Texas Museum Association over a five-year period in planning and fund raising for the development of a new Pre-Columbian Gallery and renovation of several older galleries. In 1989, he and the WTMA officers planned for a year of celebration that included in the main museum an updating of the Lubbock Gallery used to depict the history of this West Texas community from before 1900 to 1950, the opening of a new theater funded by the Junior League, and the starting of construction for a Costumes and History Gallery that will focus on the pioneering period of the South Plains prior to the twentieth century, and the renovation of the Hall of Early Texas Cultures to more accurately represent the American Indian cultures of the Llano Estacado.

Planning activities for one week included a Wednesday appreciation brunch-tea for WTMA officers and staff; an opening dedication of the Pre-Columbian Gallery followed by a Thursday night at the Museum musical party; a Friday afternoon trustees's reception and festive party in the evening at the Museum's main gallery for several hundred of the general

public; and an exciting kite fly for families on Saturday morning. Each of
these activities was a fund raising effort that involved the museum staff in
planning with key donors for the long-term support of specific collections
associated with the Pre-Columbian research plan. No proposals were written at the parties and receptions, but the seeds for future research support
were planted and verbal commitments to existing research thrusts were obtained in casual conversations. These parties afforded Gary Edson and
staff the opportunity to acknowledge the Museum's appreciation of the
WTMA for years of past planning and millions of dollars of support and to
present the vision for the future development of the Museum. Although the
aforementioned activities ostensibly appear rather frivolous and unas-
sociated with formal planning, they are essential planning activities that
were adroitly handled by a very capable research administrator, who is
known in the arts community as a pioneer for art.

Again, the primacy of the creative artist-researcher is evident in the success of these multiple planning-recognition efforts. A professional research administrator or the president of the university could have stood-in
for Edson at all the planning activities, but they would not have had the
creative, competent energies of a real artist and museology researcher.
There would have been no credibility in plans offered and no excitement in
the planning-recognition events. Nonresearchers can only shadow real
development activities—they are not effective planners and developers.
Planning for organized research units must be done by competent, active
researchers who are acknowledged leaders in their field. Successful planning at the departmental level and in organized research units can not occur
without them.

Plant and Soil Science

Another department that changed its goals substantially was the Department of Plant and Soil Science. This department changed its goals because
the economic conditions for farming the Great Plains had changed radically in a decade and the department had to modify its goals to meet the
changed needs of the region.

For over fifty years, Texas Tech University had served the agriculture
community of the Great Plains and Texas by aiming its research at and
teaching its agriculture students how to produce more wheat, cotton, corn,
sorghum, and vegetables through traditional irrigation methods. Teaching
how to produce more crops from traditional irrigation was appropriate.
That plan had been a success for this semiarid region because it served as a
model for successful semiarid farming through irrigation practices made
possible by cheap fuel and vast stores of supplemental water. In the 1970s
fuel prices rose dramatically and the water level of the Ogallala aquifer

dropped appreciably. Great Plains farms could not stay in business with traditional farming techniques. They needed help. The Department of Plant and Soil Sciences changed their research, instruction, and service goals to meet these new needs.

The leadership of David Koeppe was vital in making this change as his research orientation and his development skills were crucial to redirecting the efforts of the faculty and students in the Department of Plant and Soil Sciences. Koeppe's success points out the importance of the leadership of the department head to strategic planning for research.

Again, the primacy of the PI to strategic planning for research must be noted. David Koeppe, an outstanding plant geneticist, was known for his development of tissue culture biotechnology to improve plant varieties for optimal growth. Dave was internationally recognized for his pioneering work in identifying genetic markers linked to plant root disease and plant cold hardiness. His basic research work was applied to developing improved onion varieties resistant to pink-root rot and to cold stresses in semi-arid regions. He also conducted environmental screening for disease tolerant hybrids to obtain onion bulbs with a marketable appearance. Koeppe possessed all of the good characteristics—outstanding publication record, grantsmanship, and graduate teaching record—of the principal investigator identified earlier.

We are looking at David Koeppe because he was an exemplary department head for strategic planning for research. Department heads acting at the foundation level for university administration must plan for the development of the department's graduate and undergraduate programs, for its organized research units, and for the career development of the faculty using internal and external resources. David Koeppe's, tenure as chairman of the Department of Plant and Soil Sciences was marked by his focussing attention on the departments' research goals of integrating instruction, service, and research activities to expand our understanding of how to profitably produce crops while conserving soil, water, and energy and while preserving the environmental resources of the area.

He recognized prior to the energy crunch that the expense of traditional irrigation methods coupled with diminished water reserves in the Ogallala aquifer would present serious challenges to area farmers. This challenge set in motion the reassessment of the goals of the Department of Plant and Soil Sciences. In the eighties, Koeppe (1986) challenged continuously the University and the region with the following thought:

> If Great Plains agriculture is to thrive in the twenty-first century, we must find the means to acknowledge yet overcome the temperature extremes and water scarcities that threaten semiarid agriculture. We must respond to the challenge of semiarid production through innovative agricultural research programs that will help foster the land and the needs of the people for centuries to come.

Over a period of years, Koeppe proposed long-term solutions for farming in semiarid regions. The department integrated his and the proposals of many other faculty into their strategic planning.

In planning and conducting research in his department, Koeppe sustained an effort to bring together planning teams of geneticists, soil scientists, agronomists, biochemists, entomologists, crop physiologists, weed scientists and engineers to advance the research programs of the department. He lead in planning the Plant Stress and Water Conservation Research Program by personally supplying many new ideas and bringing in the best minds in the country to work on departmental innovations. To guide their departmental work, he and the faculty established the following five major goals and attendant research divisions: to identify and create stress-resistant germplasm pools through genetics and plant breeding; to establish new and varied farm management systems to conserve water; to examine plant functions in relationship to light, atmosphere, water, and temperature; to develop ways to measure water use-efficiency in relationship to the soil, the atmosphere, and plant growth; and to improve ways to apply pesticides and control crop pests.

There are several ways that Koeppe and other department heads plan with the faculty to develop the department's research program.

Chairman to Faculty Planning

At Tech, the "Faculty Annual Report" asks for the faculty member to report the percentage of time budgeted to teaching, research, service, and administration. The annual report also asks for measures of scholarship, research, professional productivity and the faculty members goals for scholarly improvement for the next year. The problem for the department head is to plan with the faculty member for the allocation of their time and departmental resources to the goals of the department.

Usually, within a department there are research funds that come from the state, release-time for research (from 25-50% for the average faculty member's instructional load for nine months), and departmental organized research monies. Koeppe using the "Faculty Annual Report" helped the faculty member lay out a strategy for career development according to the ideas of the faculty member, to the operating plans and resources of the department, to the aims and priorities of the department, and within the policy of the college and university.

This strategy began with recruitment of faculty and continued through retirement. Recruitment is extremely important to strategic research planning and departmental development. Koeppe was very able in this regard. He recruited Howard M. Taylor, Rockwell Professor and plant physiologist known for his work on manipulating root systems to reduce drought stress and Henry Nguyen, NSF presidential young investigator award winner noted for his biochemical analysis of seeds to determine the reproductive characteristics of various populations.

Koeppe aggressively recruited the best agricultural scientists expert in tissue culture biotechnology to define cotton somatic embryogenesis to expand the stress-resistant cotton germplasm pool. The Genetics and Plant Breeding Research Division of the Plant and Soil Sciences research program formulated plans for a system for consistently regenerating cotton plants from several strains of cotton tissue. Options for applying this system to the regeneration of cotton plants from cell lines resistant to particular stress factors was a major component in their strategy.

In a department strategy, promotion and tenure reviews are highly visible milestones that help measure the success of the program. Junior faculty and staff in the Department of Plant and Soil Sciences were helped with starter grants and teamed with senior scientists to obtain federal and state research funds to support their research in targeted areas. Later, they coauthored articles with their mentors.

If the faculty members need more money to conduct their proposed research than was available within the department, Koeppe would suggest going to external sources for funds (i.e., college or university organized research funds and federal or state funds). Frequently, he knew someone in an agency or industry that might be interested in supporting the faculty's ideas. As the department head, he introduced the researcher to the potential sponsor with a telephone call or letter of introduction. The process in this type of planning may take ten minutes or several years depending on the urgency to do the work and the rapport with the program officer. In a very low-keyed manner, the department head jointly planned with the researcher the long-term work of the researcher. Through persuasion, resource allocation, and incentive systems, the department head guides the faculty member in a particular direction. This too is part of strategic planning.

Strategic planning requires by the department head a sustained advocacy of the strengths of the department. The advocacy role of the department chair is seen in the following statement by Koeppe (1986,1).

> The strength of our research program grows out of our emphasis on specifically defined areas of expertise and on our involvement in a number of cooperative research investigations with scientists at New Mexico State University, Los Alamos National Laboratories, the University of Arizona, the University of California, Riverside, and the Texas Agricultural Experiment Station, and the USDA-Agricultural Research Service.
>
> Our scientists are becoming worldwide leaders in their fields, placing us in a position to compete for significant funding and to participate in significant breakthroughs that advance the production efficiency of plants under semiarid conditions.

The timeliness of our research is extremely important, not only for the agricultural future of the Southwest and Great Plains of the United States, but for the agricultural future of the Third World. Our investigations promise sustenance for us all.

After this general introduction of departmental strengths, Koeppe praised the individual talents of more than two dozen of his researchers.

Colleague-to-Colleague Planning for Departmental Research

The architects for departmental projects are usually students or faculty who do not need much funding to develop their research ideas. Collegial influence in planning typically is very informal. The original research plans are usually expressed verbally to colleagues at coffee breaks, in chance encounters in the hall, in brain storming sessions, and in development seminars. Faculty usually begin with, "What do you think about this. . . ." Colleagues add to the investigator's concept, suggest different approaches, demolish the idea, point-out related literature, offer to be a co-investigator, and adjust their own work according to the staked claim of their colleague. No paper is generated at this stage of development. A researcher should at this point evaluate the idea to see if it is worthy of wider dissemination. If so, they should continue the thought or modify it in light of colleagues comments. In any case, many colleagues in the college now are aware of a new idea and numerous good development opportunities may appear. This identity awareness of a possible solution to a disciplinary problem is valuable to the advancement of the department and to the discipline because on campus it allows colleagues to direct interested students to faculty members who could direct the student's thesis work. Also, the idea is now in the disciplinary network. The network will ultimately link researchers doing similar work.

On the Texas Tech Campus, one of the best climates for colleague-to-colleague research development exists in the Agricultural Engineering Department, in the College of Engineering. John Borrelli, the department chair, worked assiduously at creating the climate for collaborative work and at promoting the strategic goals of the department by developing joint research projects among his faculty. The authors were very impressed with Borrelli's plans for the long-term improvement of ag engineering research. The faculty were most pleased with Borrelli's balanced recruitment of a very bright and energetic young graduate from the University of Illinois and a seasoned researcher from the University of Missouri. Borrelli's own research and his pairing of faculty with these two new faculty revitalized the department's undergraduate, graduate and research programs. His attention to hiring the very best faculty that were available demonstrates at the departmental level the importance of paying attention to positioning architects for departmental planning and to selecting people with a research-development orientation.

Colleague-to-colleague planning can be seen in the collaborative research efforts of Clifford B. Fedler and James M. Gregory. Fedler and Gregory, in 1985, both had a need to explain granular flow to their classes. Existing models and theories to predict the flow of granular material through orifices were material-specific. Consequently, no scientific principle could be taught to undergraduate students. Instead several relationships for grains and food materials flowing through different types of bins and orifices had to be taught.

What was needed was a general model that would explain the flow phenomena for all granular materials. Collaboration began in September of 1985 when Cliff asked Jim, his senior colleague, if he knew about existing information in the literature. Gregory responded that he was having the same difficulty. Rather than accepting the deficient models into their teaching routine, they decided to research the phenomena themselves. It took them two or three hours of thinking and several cups of coffee before they had conceptualized a new model that promised to explain generically the flow for all noncohesive granular materials. After two months of thinking and trying different equations, making a thorough search of the literature and finding data that could be used in the Gregory-Fedler Granular-Flow Model (G-F Model), Fedler and Gregory verified their mathematical algorithm. Their next phase of research was to test the Gregory-Fedler Equation in the G-F Model using various materials to provide the empirical evidence of the power of the Model to predict actual operating conditions.

With Borrelli, they spent much time planning strategically how to develop this critical piece of basic engineering research and how that research could advance the long-term goals of the department while furthering current technology. The Gregory-Fedler equation for granular flow was recognized immediately by the departmental faculty as a major step forward in the discipline and fellow academicians incorporated the G-F Model into their research and teaching plans.

In 1986, Gregory and Fedler presented a paper, "Equation Describing Granular Flow Through Circular Orifices," Paper No. SWR-86-003, at the Southwest Region Meeting of the American Society of Agricultural Engineers (ASAE). This theoretical paper generated considerable controversy as the G-F Model and its underlying assumptions were a radical departure from currently accepted practice of teaching material-specific relationships that had dominated the discipline for three-quarters of a century. Despite some isolated, sharp criticisms of the theory, the peer review of their paper was generally very positive. Initial submission of a theoretical paper to a national scientific journal was turned down by reviewers because the G-F Model conflicted too much with the information based on material-specific models. They revised the paper to emphasize that the G-F Model, which was based on the physical, scientific principles of balancing forces, gave much more accurate predictions when using computer simulation techniques and provided a generalized model that was appropriate for teaching. The revised theoretical article was ultimately accepted after they had published several empirical studies.

The G-F Model created quite a stir in the professional ranks, shortly after the Southwest meeting, two empirical studies by themselves and students confirmed their equation and theory. Later in the year, the paper was selected as being one of the top-ten ASAE papers in 1986. The G-F Model and his pioneering work on biogas from biomass in developing countries lead to Fedler being nominated and receiving the 1986 Halliburton Outstanding Researcher Award. The College of Engineering faculty were quite proud of Fedler, who at thirty years of age seemed to be the youngest person to have received this honor.

It is interesting to note that in five years the collaborative planning of the faculty lead to more than twenty funded projects that brought into the university several hundred thousand dollars from federal and state agencies and from industrial sponsors. This money supported more graduate students, which increased money from the state general education appropriations to the University. It is sufficient at this point to note the long-list of grant titles and publications developed from the initial basic research of Gregory and Fedler. Also, it is instructive to note that twelve other faculty and several graduate students collaborated with these instructors on more than a dozen refereed publications and a larger number of paper presentations.

The ideas and grantsmanship abilities of Fedler attracted the attention of the dean who gave him the major responsibilities for coordinating and preparing the Lubbock Texas proposal for the Texas superconducting supercollider discussed in earlier chapters. That responsibility placed Fedler in a leadership position that had him planning with dozens of engineers and scientists on campus and throughout the state.

Lately, Gregory and Fedler have teamed with Hensley in developing models for upgrading engineering education and in establishing CUES (the Coalition for Upgrading Educational Strategies). This coalition of individuals from more than twenty institutions in the Southwest has concentrated its attention on bringing undergraduate research into the science and engineering programs of cooperating institutions and in functionally structuring knowledge for its efficient dissemination.

This collaborative research was based on their planning assumptions that the new starting points for the next generation of educational and research innovations will be coalitions of mutually committed people working with restructured organizations to meet the educational needs of conventional and nonconventional students and to respond to the nation's demands for a more sophisticated science and advanced technology. This work, which is partially supported by the National Science Foundation, promises to have far-reaching positive consequences for all engineering and science programs. If the initial successes continue, the models developed at Texas Tech and tested throughout the Southwest may be adopted throughout the country.

Fedler's latest work has captured international attention. In 1987, he developed the idea on growing algae for fish food in West Texas. The project began with interest from an individual and member of the Lubbock Board of City Development (BCD) in raising shrimp in West Texas. Not laughing at the far-fetched ideas, as did most others, Fedler conducted library and field research that indicated that it was possible. His first grant applications were routinely rejected due to the "abnormal" ideas that were inconsistent with current modes of thinking.

With assistance from the BCD member, Fedler and colleagues from across the campus started to publicize the idea to generate local interest. He also approached the Texas Department of Agriculture (TDA) for moral support and funding. In the meantime through colleague-to-colleague discussions, Fedler added several new members to the research team. Each member had an expertise in one of the numerous facets of the research leading to the production of algae. The algae will be used as a fish food, human food additive, and as a raw material from which high-value products can be extracted. Organic dyes that can be extracted from algae have a current market value of more than $2,000 per kilogram.

With the help of Nick Parker, an expert in algae growth systems from the Department of Range and Wildlife Management, Fedler received grants from the Department of Commerce and local government and industry for pilot work. It took three years of cooperative planning to gain the initial support for a rather wild idea. Now, the idea is better accepted within the state and is being supported financially from the TDA to begin developing growth units. The new ideas for growing algae have attracted international attention to the point that team members have been invited to Europe and Asia to discuss the possibilities of implementing their growing systems there.

The purpose of this glimpse of faculty members' planning activities is to show the expanding influence of collaborative efforts that started with two individuals, who brought into their planning several members of a department, who expanded their work to include other colleagues within the college, who graduated to intercollegiate cooperation on several different projects, and who are now boldly leading inter-institutional developments. All of this activity in five years. Department chair and senior colleague, Borrelli's planning and support was constantly a factor in developing a climate where research could thrive. And, once again, we see that the center of research activities is the bright minds with a common purpose and that the successful approach to long-term development is strategic planning. The present success of this unit was modelled five years ago. They are currently modelling their future successes in the second generation of strategic planning. Similar types of planning activities occurred around other brilliant investigators in other units throughout the campus.

PLANNING AT THE COLLEGE LEVEL

The philosophy of placing responsibility for planning at points of competency requires that deans and division heads organize their schools and offices for planning. The vice-president for academic affairs and research involved nine deans in strategic planning for research related to their particular fields of responsibility.

Deans are key principals in the development process as much of the medium and small scale research development occurs within college boundaries. For purposes of explaining the process of strategic planning at the collegiate level, the College of Agricultural Sciences will receive particular attention because the current dean, Samuel E. Curl, was exceptionally competent in planning and implementing research developments for that college.

The Research Development Emphasis of the Dean

The authors want to list several reasons for the College of Agricultural Sciences being very successful in their strategic planning for research.

1. The dean established through his philosophy, policy statements, and administrative decisions a climate to foster research in the college and an expectation that the faculty would perform research that would gain external support and international recognition.
2. The dean organized his office in the early eighties to reflect a development orientation toward advancing agricultural sciences and at the end of the decade he had retained the same staff. The retention of outstanding administrators and innovative faculty gave the college continuity in the planning process that is absolutely essential in the development of large projects and organized research units.
3. He started by selecting development-oriented individuals who had earned excellent reputations as teachers and researchers and who could add to the planning process. The following staffing shows the commitment of this dean to advancing research development: associate dean for industry relations, assistant dean for academic and

      student affairs, associate dean for research and agricultural operations, and associate dean for development.

4. Note that three of the four staff members have development functions as their major responsibilities. It takes an administrative focus and a strong personal commitment to research development to rapidly advance a college. Dean Curl provided both.

5. Most important to the smooth operation of strategic planning process in the college was the formation of college planning teams. This dean understood that the development of centers and institutes had reached a level of complexity that a single faculty member could not develop an ORU alone; and the importance of appointing development-oriented faculty, administrators, and affiliates to agriculture-focussed planning teams to produce agriculture related plans and to carryout certain research operations.

Development Goals

The Goals of the College were to advance significantly: 1) the recruiting of distinguished faculty for research and instruction in targeted areas; 2) the permanent endowment fund of the college; 3) the development of ORU centers (Center for Beef Cattle Research and Instruction, Institute for Plant Stress Research, Agricultural Finance Institute, The Institute for Fisheries and Wildlife Research); 4) The Outreach Program of the College; 5) Several existing laboratories through extensive renovations; 6) New research Facilities at the Experimental Ranch near Justiceburg and the Experimental Farms on campus and at New Deal; and 7) External Funding for Annual Research Operations.

The Influence Paths at the Collegiate Level

The research development process at the collegiate level has at least three levels of influence paths that were thoroughly established by the College of Agricultural Sciences. The first level of influence will be referred to as the chief executive level. In the university sector this level includes the coordinating board members, regents, president, vice-presidents, and deans. In the federal and state sectors all elected officials and agency heads are included. In the industrial and nonprofit sectors, corporate presidents and members of the board of directors are included.

The second level of influence paths are walked by the staff members of the executive officers. The staff level includes the associate vice-presidents, associate deans, agency division officers, congressional staff heads, state science and technology officers, and division heads in industry.

The third level of influence paths are traveled by technical people. The technical level in the university sector includes the faculty and other disciplinary authorities. Agency program officers, congressional technical staff, coordinating board technicians, and industrial laboratory heads are included in this level.

Paths are made by walking. The power to influence principals in the research development process come from all levels. Most of the time, research development originates at the technical level. Principal investigators send prospectuses and proposals into agency program officers who look for work that matches their interests and priorities. On very large developments—centers and institutes—deans frequently will initiate contacts and hold first-round meetings with appropriate congressmen, industrial leaders, and foundation trustees. Once the dean has obtained a general agreement for a long-term development, the project is usually turned over to staff members who spend many, many hours in communicating with other staff and technical personnel to assure that the plan meets the needs of a region and that it is technically sound. Some of the large center developments at Texas Tech University have taken thousands of people hours to develop and over a decade to build after a decision was made by the Board of Regents to support a center or institute on campus.

The dean of the College of Agricultural Sciences made very effective use of his staff and faculty by forming at an early stage of research, college planning teams that included staff and technical personnel. These teams would develop all the decision elements, prospectuses, technical proposals, plans, and background information for speeches, testimonies and reports that were necessary for chief executive advocacy roles. The technical staff played major roles in second-round meetings and subsequent sessions for after general acceptance of broad ideas by chief executives in the sponsoring agencies, the sponsors wanted to talk about technical problems that the dean and his office staff were not competent technically to address. The dean was always present and he diligently worked at getting other chief executives to critical meetings when executive approvals were necessary to obtain certain long-term partnership commitments. Consequently, the dean relied very heavily on his planning teams for splendidly formulated plans while he handled adroitly the politics of the occasion.

A primary strategy of the College of Agricultural Sciences was to promote the development of research by establishing endowed chairs and professorships that would advance the college while serving the needs of the state, region, and nation. It was the college's intent to secure new research grants and attract top-notch students to the college by appointing the following nationally recognized scholars to research professorships. The college established four endowed chairs and recruited four distinguished agricultural scientists to fill them. These renowned scholars have over the years more than fulfilled the college expectations and have certainly justified initial investments in their areas of research.

The dean's advisory committee was a fundamental element in the Dean's strategy to build the college's permanent endowment fund. Dean Curl invited eighteen agricultural leaders to serve as industry consultants to the college. These extremely influential community leaders were bank presidents, officers in the High Plains Research Foundation, chairman of the Texas Agricultural Forum, editors of farm journals, state conservationists, chairpersons of committees of the Texas and Southwestern Cattle Raisers Association and the Texas Cattle Feeders Association, distinguished ranchers, and very successful farmers and agribusinessmen.

The dean made it known to his advisory committee that the college was increasingly dependent upon the private sector for program support, particularly for that extra measure of funding required to develop programs of excellence. The dean's advisory committee planned with the dean and faculty to sponsor Ag Olympics, 4-H events, fair exhibits, and joint projects that in the beginning inspired confidence in the faculty and students and finally paid rich dividends to the college in the form of large gifts. The large increases in total permanent endowments in the middle and late eighties were the result of early eighties plans that came from the close ties of the administrative staff and faculty with specific people in the agricultural industry.

The dean's planning teams were very conscientious in formulating and implementing strategies for the development of ORUs. The dean planned closely with the executive officers of the university and the board of regents to establish several centers of excellence in agriculture. This process will be explained more fully in the section related to developing organized research units.

The dean and his staff conceived and used the outreach program of the college to convey information about the college to a wide range of constituencies and to gather information about their needs and development plans. In 1985, the college presented over twenty-five workshops, conferences, and short courses for the general public. They published *Milestones*, an annual report on research development, and periodically disseminated research bulletins and newsletters, as well as sponsoring contests and special activities for various agricultural groups in the region. The message of the college representatives to their partners was the College of Agricultural Sciences would work with the agricultural community in efforts to expand and deepen its abilities to serve agricultural industry both scientifically and educationally.

They employed their research development staff, faculty, alumni and friends in strategies to build the college's fund for excellence, which supported scholarships, improvements in academic programs, the purchase of new laboratory equipment, and faculty development. The college used this fund and specific endowments to advance its goal of assuming a significant position of national influence in agricultural research.

The vice-president for academic affairs and research and associate vice-president for research were invited frequently to participate with the college's faculty and affiliates in planning activities. They observed that the dean and his staff members later invited the college affiliates and planning team members to special events and publicly thanked them for contributing to the pioneering efforts of the college and for expanding its visions. Administrators and faculty made it a point to stress the college's continual effort to merit their partners support by offering targeted research and services to the agriculture community of Texas and the nation as a whole. In their development publications (*Landmarks* and *Milestones*) and at local and regional conferences the college made a sustained effort to acknowledge formally its benefactors and to mention their contributions to its planning efforts and their support for projects. This strategy was very successful for over the years individuals, companies, foundations, and agricultural organizations continually helped in developing plans for advancement and repeatedly contributed substantially to the annual financial support of specific programs.

The dean's office implemented a strategy for faculty research development that rested on upgrading promotion and tenure standards and provided salary incentives for faculty who performed research in an exceptionally able fashion. The College of Agriculture helped the authors test and install several innovative university systems at the college level.

The dean's conscious efforts to include the research agenda in his regular meetings with the academic council, with his department heads, and with faculty took the vision of the college into every quarter of the university community.

Other deans and other colleges used strategic planning for research with varying degrees of success. The authors appreciated the dean's style and the College of Agricultural Sciences attitude toward the planning process because

1. They kept the university administration informed and involved in the college plans.
2. They were most cooperative in getting college faculty and administrators to serve on university planning teams.
3. They followed through on planning commitments in a timely manner. Schools that did not have dedicated administrative development staff and planning teams could not meet the deadline requirements that are omnipresent in research development activities.
4. The college administration listened to ideas of the faculty and helped them develop their visions of the future.

5. The official plans of the college were realistic and were built on areas where the college had a long established record of achievements and a critical mass of investigators and support personnel. They started small and built on success. They formed their plans around several brilliant minds and built on existing operations.

6. They were willing to use their own money in entrepreneurial activities; consequently, they received a fair share in University matching funds. In times of State reductions of funds, they didn't waste their time whining about inadequate state financial support, they went after other monies. They set their goals and did not waver.

7. They were willing to explore multidisciplinary arrangements. They always were major contributors in any intercollegiate endeavor.

8. Most importantly, when they received the development money, they delivered what they said they would do and more. Through delivering on their proposals, they established credibility and were considered reliable partners.

A Decade of Planning and Development
to Establish a Major ORU

The authors have analyzed several testimonies and reports from Texas Tech University to congress to give the reader some idea of the complexity associated with the development of an ORU that is aimed at solving a critical national agriculture problem. They rely very heavily on Dean Sam Curl's (1986a) testimony to the Agriculture, Rural Development and related Agencies Subcommittee of the U.S. Senate Appropriations Committee to show the amount of planning necessary to develop a major ORU on a university campus.

The planning teams technical activity for the development of the Plant Stress Laboratory, the Cooperative Research Program in Plant Stress and Water Conservation, and the TTU Institute for Plant Stress Research, was coordinated by the associate dean for Research and Agricultural operations. The college planning teams consisted of the dean, three associate deans, all department heads from the College of Agriculture, several department heads and faculty from other colleges, representatives from other universities, and representatives from agriculture affiliates. Prior to the dean's testimony and submission of supplementary reports, the associate dean spent long hours with congressional staff members determining the types of questions and the depth of the answers that would be wanted during their particular round of planning. The planning team then prepared a comprehensive report from which the dean's staff selected pertinent information for inclusion in a verbal presentation.

At the beginning of his testimonies, the dean expressed his appreciation for the opportunity to testify before the Committee on behalf of urgently needed research in the area of plant stress and water conservation. Next, he reviewed the status of the established joint research developed by Texas Tech University, the USDA-ARS, and the Texas Agricultural Experiment

Station. Remembering previous testimony, he again called the following politically sensitive problems to the senator's attention:

1. The Southern Great Plains is one of the most developed and productive agricultural regions of the United States. A great percentage of the water presently used to support this agriculture comes from the vast Ogallala aquifer a rapidly declining an virtually non-rechargeable groundwater reservoir (This unseen, underground lake covers an area larger than the Great Lakes of the United States.)

2. Estimates of the future life of the water supply from this formation vary, but all agree that it is not limitless. Many wells in the southern part of the formation are already going dry.

3. With the rapidly escalating cost of traditional energy sources, the costs required to lift the water for irrigation has become prohibitive in a number of areas.

The dean then supplied, in capsule form, the College of Agricultural Sciences' solution of developing genetically improved crop varieties possessing more efficient stress tolerance and improved water use mechanisms, and for the development of cultural practices for maximizing water use efficiency. He mentioned that the cooperative research program focuses on these urgent needs of the Southern Great Plains. He referenced previous documents to show the wide cooperation among the universities, state and federal agencies, and farmers in the Southwest Consortium, which he represented when addressing the research aspects of the plan.

At this point, he officially submitted to the committee a written statement that provided an in-depth progress report of the research planning and program activities to date for the congressional record. This record and past testimony presented a comprehensive assessment of the problem and a set of precise recommendations for what TTU and their partners proposed as the most cost-effective federal-state-university cooperative research strategy for dealing with the complex agricultural problems facing the Southern Great Plains and other semiarid regions of the nation.

The authors must point out that the 1986 testimony was only one meeting in a continuing dialog with the United States senators and representatives that had started in the mid-seventies. Planning really started in the mid-seventies when the Tech faculty made their representatives aware of the problems. Texas Tech proposed to the federal government a partnership for developing a national plant stress research facility and a basic research program to develop plants tolerant of the climatic stresses in semiarid lands. In 1977, congress appropriated $100,000 to initiate a feasibility study (Senate Document 59) to determine the most appropriate program and location for the Plant Stress and Water Conservation Laboratory. That study was presented to congress in March of 1978. In fiscal year 1979, congress appropriated $800,000 to initiate planning for the research program and proposed facility in cooperation with Texas Tech University. In fiscal year

1983, congress appropriated $500,000 to complete planning for the laboratory. The research program plan and the architectural plans and specifications for the laboratory were completed in 1985 and a cooperative USDA-ARS research unit was placed in temporary space on the Texas Tech campus at a Texas Agricultural Experiment Station north of the campus.

In fiscal year 1980, congress appropriated $200,000 to initiate basic research on the problems of plant stress. In fiscal year 1981, congress appropriated $400,000, $450,000 in FY 1982, $750,000 in 1984, $900,000 for FY 1985, and $1,150,0000 in FY 1986 for basic research projects.

The establishment of the Institute for Plant Stress Research, the initiation of the Southwest Consortium, and the early results of the basic research conducted by the faculty gave great credibility to the college planning as the dean advocated the placement of the Plant Stress Laboratory and the Basic Research Program at the top of the senate's priority list for developing agriculture. He pointed out that the TTU proposal for the development of stress resistant plants and water conservation is not a program dealing with a single crop or a problem of local proportions. He made sure that the senators did not miss the fact that the facility and program represent a comprehensive investment in the future that could help to avert an economic disaster throughout large portions of over six states wherein a large and very significant portion of our present agricultural productive capacity is found.

At this early time, this key facility and the pilot programs were being recognized as a national center for excellence in plant stress and water conservation research. A strong planning and technical development program had been established with the USDA-ARS Plant Gene Expression Center in California. Dean Curl provided further evidence of the stature of this program by citing 1) receipt of a competitive grant of $400,000 of state funding from the Texas Advanced Technology Research Program, and 2) charter membership in the newly created Southwest Consortium on Plant Genetics and Water Resources Research. This research consortium included as charter members Texas Tech University, New Mexico State University, the University of California at Riverside, the University of Arizona, and the Los Alamos National Laboratory. (A request for $500,000 FY 1987 funding for the consortium was made in earlier testimony.)

In the strategic plan, the congress was asked to increase the level of funding for the cooperative research program in plant stress and water conservation at Lubbock, now in its seventh year by more than $1 million over the budget allocation for fiscal year 1986. This new appropriation would bring the total research program funding by the federal government to $2,150,000. The dean also asked the committee to authorize funding in the amount of $24 million to construct the proposed Plant Stress and Water

Conservation Laboratory, as planned, on the site made available for lease to the U.S Department of Agriculture by the Board of Regents of Texas Tech University.

The dean always closed out his testimony with a sincere thank you for past support and continuing interest in this extremely important and timely research program and an offer to respond to specific questions.

The questioning session at testimonies was a very important part of the planning process because new concerns could be identified which had not surfaced in earlier planning sessions with the congressional staff. The dean then had to respond to those concerns by pointing to a section in the strategic plan that addressed those concerns, or if the plan did not address the senators' questions, he had to give assurance to the committee that TTU would make changes in the plans to meet the concerns of specific senators.

Similar planning for the development of state supported agriculture research occurred in the state impact area. The same planning process took place for the simultaneous development of several organized research units within the College of Agricultural Sciences.

The dean's planning team for the Burnett Center for Beef Cattle Research and Instruction called on his associate deans, department heads and faculty throughout the University. Members of the dean's advisory committee and the affiliates of the Burnett Center were particularly valuable in planning the world's largest and most modern feedmill and feedlot research facility. The College of Agriculture Science planned the Burnett Center for Beef Cattle Research and Instruction on the following facts.

1. Beef cattle are the most important livestock commodity in the agricultural economy of Texas.
2. The High Plains of Texas is the center of the American cattle feeding industry, accounting for almost one-quarter of the nation's supply of fed beef.
3. The fed beef have the potential of being a significant export thus helping the United States reduce the mounting trade deficit.
4. In the early eighties, over five million steers were fed annually on the High Plains. The cattle feeding industry alone is estimated to generate a revenue of over $3.5 billion.
5. Feed manufacturing plants and meat packing plants of this region contribute a significant part to the total Texas economy and the nation.
6. Feed is a major expense in the production of beef cattle. Cattle fed on the High Plains consume over six million tons of processed grain annually.
7. Cattle are ruminant animals capable of converting fibrous feeds and urea that humans cannot utilize as food into beef, which is a high quality protein consumed by humans.
8. Meat consumers are influenced by health-related issues and many pay attention to fat intake. Health conscious consumers and dieters are purchasing lean beef although it may be more variable in tenderness.

The College of Agricultural Sciences considered all of these economic factors in making the decision to establish a center of excellence related to the production of fed beef cattle. Although the Department of Animal Sciences had been studying the efficiency factors of raising beef through conventional research, the faculty recognized that new technologies must be developed and applied to feedlot operations if major advances in the economic efficiency of cattle feeding were to be achieved.

In the early eighties, the college planned a new $4.3 million computer controlled feedmill and state-of-the-art experimental feedlot to be built on the Texas Tech University Experimental Farm at New Deal. The Department of Animal Sciences (1983) proposal aimed to achieve the following purposes.

The Burnett Center should seek to apply new technology to on-going research programs at Texas Tech with a basic objective to improve the economic status of beef production in Texas and to develop basic knowledge for use in beef production.

They planned that the feedmill complex would consist of two adjoining primary building. One research feedmill designed for delivery of completely-mixed, all-concentrate diets, built in 1976, needed some renovation. A new three-level, computer-operated, dust controlled, mixing plant was to be constructed in the mid-eighties. The new facility would provide fully automated premixes and batch-mixes to serve the research feedlot. These facilities were designed to provide maximum flexibility in delivering different diet formulations to animals in the feedlot. We should note that the college was building on a well-recognized research program and that part of the planned research facilities already existed. These factors made it much easier to involve faculty and sponsors in research planning and to obtain a commitment of financial support for the development of the Burnett Center and associated research positions.

ESTABLISHING A CLIMATE FAVORABLE TO RESEARCH

The vice-president's (VP) role as a planner is critical to the development of a favorable climate for research in a university. It should be abundantly clear to the reader that your authors believe that the principal investigator is the primary person in the research enterprise. They also believe that it is the role of the vice-presidents for research to be the architects of plans to develop the institution, to advocate their and other's plans, and to work toward establishing an awareness, acceptance and adoption of the agenda of university by the institution and its constituencies. Research administrators must develop a place where research can flourish. Simultaneously, they must work diligently at aiding the principal investigator in planning future research and at developing the infrastructure of the institution for planning and the conduct of the research.

Establishing a climate favorable to research requires the VP to advocate the research capabilities of the institution to a large number of constituencies and then coordinate their development activities. The VP for research is the champion of research on the campus and its coordinator. They must have in their mind a good knowledge of all the major research that is going on. Whereas the PIs develop projects, the VPs should be constantly developing new supportive services for research. That keeps the VP on the edge of institutional advancements. In the same fashion that the PI needs state-of-the-art instrumentation, the VP must develop the planning infrastructure and the state-of-the-art institutional services for the researcher. This is the VP's responsibility and they must lead in introducing institutional change. To do this they first must understand and be dedicated to the academy. Then, they must have visions of what research can do to advance academic ideals. They must have the wisdom to select the best development plans for the institution and the guts to stay with those plans until they come to fruition.

Sharing Visions

This section describes the role of two vice-presidents for research at Texas Tech University during the 1980s. Their primary planning role was sharing visions among individuals. They were listeners and advocates. They encouraged the principal investigators, deans, and presidents to generate ideas to advance their units. They listened to the individual's vision and then they attempted to favorably place these ideas before sponsors. They kept an open door for people wanting to develop new ideas. The vice-president had weekly staff meetings to discuss with specific academic leaders their plans for research development. And, they visited the laboratories and field stations to discuss PI problems and to listen to PI plans. They went with the PIs, deans, and directors to Austin, Washington, and industry offices to provide senior level advocacy for the development of a PI's project or a director's organized research unit. Mostly, they encouraged people with ideas to develop those ideas.

They were readers and writers. Part of each day was reserved to read plans for developing an individual's research thrusts. They read the plans of department chairs, deans, and sponsors. They tried with their staff to coordinate and disseminate this information in a way that people with mutual interests could come together. To develop a favorable climate in the University, they had to write many position papers, policies, and procedures and to design numerous plans to develop research on campus. These papers were thoughtful responses to what they had heard and read. Their writing had the purpose of placing the ideas of others before sponsors and gaining acceptance of these new ideas.

The VPs chaired key committees where they established a climate for developing new ideas to advance the university. The academic council and the research council were two of the most effective planning bodies. They established ad hoc committees for every critical issue as the work of a university proceeds only through its committees. They appointed many planning committees for the development of specific work. In turn, they served on many committees where they represented the research interests of the university.

They lead by example. They continued their own teaching and research. This was an important role as the researchers on campus felt that their research administrators were first faculty members and secondly administrators. Staying inside the principal investigator community allowed VPs to have credibility in research and academic matters.

Developing a Supportive Environment for TTU Research

The VPs spoke at many service club dinners to gain local acceptance of Tech's research plans. To do this effectively, the AVPR-Development had to create a slide show of Texas Tech investigators performing research in their laboratories and field studies. This presentation became known as the dog-and-pony-show and its three sets of slides were constantly being borrowed by some university member.

They addressed local and state civic groups on particular items of civic interest. This required the production of many special reports and the arrangement for faculty to testify on the technical aspects of a subject. In these instances the VPs prepared the way for the technical presentation and then supported the experts.

They worked with professional associations and industrial affiliates in advancing common interests. The VPs sometimes initiated but mostly facilitated the exchange of personnel and joint planning. This was a very time consuming activity that developed a support environment for TTU research. Time invested in forming partnerships paid handsome benefits when strong industrial and professional support was needed in Austin or Washington.

They responded to the needs of the institution, state and federal bureaucracies. And conversely, it was often necessary for the senior level research administrator to break open for an investigator a log jam in an administrative department. Unfortunately, vice-presidents are sometimes more effective in dealing with the bureaucracy than PIs. When it was necessary for the VPs to use the power of their position to move things expeditiously, they exercised that power judiciously.

Gaining Acceptance of the Agenda of the Strategic Plan

In the summer of 1984, Darling and Hensley were concerned that Texas Tech University was not perceived by its own faculty and throughout the state as being in the same academic class as the University of Texas and Texas A&M University. President Cavazos and the board of regents wanted Texas Tech to be an institution of the first rank. The vice-presidents for research assumed that for Texas Tech to be an institution of the first rank, it must be perceived as being a research university. When that occurred, Texas Tech would be in the same league with UT and A&M for they considered themselves to be research universities. Consequently, the major item on our agenda was to change Texas Tech's mission and to project an image of its being a research university. This required many speeches to off-campus audiences and hundreds of chats with individuals on the importance of Texas Tech being a research university.

Planning with Individuals

Making individuals aware of Texas Tech's research capabilities was part of our planning mode. Individually, we had very serious talks with administrators, faculty, and the public about Texas Tech becoming a research university and about its current research capabilities, which were more than respectable. The researchers were supportive of this direction, but there was considerable opposition to this goal by teaching-oriented individuals who did not agree with the assumptions and the vice-presidents' orientation. In these personal discussions, we learned a great deal about the strengths and weaknesses of the institution. This information was then incorporated into the institution's strategic planning. We had hundreds of private conversations in which our agenda was always clear—Texas Tech was to be a research university.

Planning with Councils

The academic and research councils were essential elements in the vice-presidents planning mode as their members represented the major units on campus. Members were very influential and they were responsible for developing their units. Philosophically, the councils were in agreement generally with Texas Tech becoming a research university. However, the deans and associate deans did not like the central administration taking such an aggressive stand on the matter, did not like the centralization of power that was occurring with the development emphasis, felt that the pace of change was too rapid, and that it was being imposed rather than welling-up from the grassroots. These were honest opinions, but they did not change the VPs course or pace.

The vice-presidents followed the model for the strategic planning process shown in Figure 6.3. That model brought about a very rapid approval in the council for faculty plans. Planning university research developments at the vice-president's level usually followed a five step protocol.

1. Deans, staff members, and the faculty senate representative placed a plan on the academic council agenda.
2. The plan was usually distributed prior to the academic council meetings. With research plans, the associate VPs had the research council review the plan prior to its submission to the academic council. The AVPR-Development introduced into the academic council only research council approved plans. This facilitated discussion and approval by the academic council. Seldom was a research council recommendation overturned by the academic council.
3. The plans were discussed in the academic council. Council members were urged to discuss the plans with their constituencies and to be ready to vote on the plan at an established future date.
4. The council's recommendations were considered and usually incorporated into the plan.
5. The vice-president implemented the plan when he had authority to do so or when the plan required a higher review, he advocated the plan in the president's council or before the board of regents.

This five step protocol allowed the university to review and recommend a vast number of research plans, policies and procedures in a very short period of time. The input of the academic council members into the planning process was invaluable. They held the academic power, they were extraordinarily good administrators, and they had a plethora of good ideas. Although they represented diverse interests and competed fiercely for institution resources, the academic council, as a whole, could be relied upon for sound institutional advice. The adoption of any plan required their acceptance and advocacy. Generally, the planning activities of this group were successful. The development activities of individual deans and staff member have been explained earlier.

The weekly staff meetings were excellent planning sessions. For example, on August 24, 1984 the vice-president met with his staff to plan for the following research developments: 1) The Texas Tech research development system, 2) Law School's plan for development of centers of excellence, 3) researcher reimbursement on travel that exceed state allowances, 4) College of Education's plan for a Hispanic education symposium, and 5) development of a strategic plan for a research park at Texas Tech.

This meeting is an example of the first stages of strategic planning and its overlap with operational and tactical planning. The Texas Tech research development system, which is explained in Chapter 5, was outlined at that meeting. Byron Fullerton, dean of the Law School explained the current development initiatives of the Law School. He discussed the lack of external funding for various Law School functions and activities, which he attributed to the relative youth of the school with its yet small number of alumni. Dean Fullerton plans included the development of medical-law conferences, gerontology law center, journal on the legal implications of genetic engineering and biotechnology, and the West Texas Law Center. Byron was looking for money to support the aforementioned areas and wanted more institutional money for faculty summer research and research assistants. Follow-up work helped develop these initiatives. Dean Ishler of the College of Education explained "The Quest for Excellence In The Education of Hispanics: Developing a Plan for Action." This project developed very well. Herman Garcia and the president became very involved in this project, which attracted national attention. The initiatives of the deans were recorded on program development status charts and the research development staff helped deans and faculty with the development of plans and with the liaison between possible sponsors. Darling asked Kice to prepare a strategy to solve the reimbursement problems. Darling assigned Hensley the responsibility for preparing an environmental scan and several possible scenarios for the development of a research park at Texas Tech before April 1, 1985. A great number of ideas and views were interchanged at these meetings, but before the meeting ended, someone was given responsibility for solving the problem or developing a plan of action.

Advancing Texas Tech from a Comprehensive University to a Research University

The roles of vice-presidents for research depends largely upon their personalities and orientations and the institutions' traditions and purposes for placing them in its administrative structure.

In the early 1980s, President Lauro Cavazos was looking for senior-level administrators who would help him develop Texas Tech University into one of the state's premier institutions. President Cavazos' was development, not maintenance oriented. He saw Texas Tech greatly expanding its operations and sphere of influence. Cavazos' and Darling's advancement orientations and goals matched. Darling was hired in 1981 to lead the academic community and Hensley was invited two years later to serve at an associate vice-president concentrating on research development and strategic planning for research.

When the authors interviewed for their respective positions they discussed their roles as champions of research, their plans for developing Texas Tech's research, and their administrative philosophy with all the participants in the search process and in their addresses to the general faculty. Their stress on research development and their advocacy of using strategic planning to develop Texas Tech into a research university created controversy among academicians before they arrived on campus. The traditional emphasis had been on undergraduate teaching and planning was usually centered on individual proposal preparation; therefore, many faculty resisted the new orientation and the deans resented the centralized control that strategic planning seemed to imply. Conversely, most researchers supported the vice-president's agenda and philosophy.

Moreover, in the early eighties, throughout the university there was great ambiguity about the mission of Texas Tech. Although there were a large number of individuals doing research, most of the faculty had been employed primarily as teachers, not as researchers. Many of the university community wanted to continue Texas Tech as a comprehensive university with an equal balance among undergraduate education, graduate education, service, and research.

Most faculty and administrators expressed their desire to be associated with an institution of the first rank. Despite their desire to be associated with an internationally recognized university, they could not agree on how they would excel in individual units in order to achieve that reputation. Your authors called for individual units to focus their resources on an area of excellence and to view Texas Tech as a research university. We advocated the following:

1. Develop strategies to acquire additional resources to support research and graduate education.
2. Identify in each department and ORU their niche for superlative scholarship and develop strategies to achieve eminence in the field, and
3. Concentrate on attracting the best research-oriented faculty and students to their units.

The authors made it clear that if Texas Tech was to survive as one of the top Texas universities it would have to change its mission and its orientation. They maintained that Texas Tech could best serve Texas, the Great Plains, and the nation by changing its mission from a comprehensive university to a research university and by concentrating institutional resources on developing graduate and research programs. The authors had a vision of Texas Tech becoming a nationally recognized research university and they espoused a development philosophy from their initial visits to the campus until they resigned their positions. Research and graduate program development was their overriding intent and strategic planning was their major mechanism for developing research.

In addition to following the formal planning processes and the technology described in Chapter 5, the authors constantly exercised their personal influence and senior positions to advance the research development agenda in daily operations. They consciously worked at reassessing the administrative activities of Texas Tech University with the intent of influencing changes in its: purpose, people, philosophy, planning, policy, procedures, programs and projects, and practice.

John Darling, Chairperson of the purpose committee of TTU institutional self-study of 1984 started the process of changing the purpose of the institution by having the purpose committee and the academic council re-assess the Mission Statement of the university and the public image of Texas Tech. Vice President Darling understood the importance of preparing the university for a change in purpose. Consequently, he requested being appointed as the chairman for the purpose committee. Leadership of the purpose committee was a critical role in strategic planning for once the new purpose was in place supportive philosophy, policy, procedures, people and programs would follow.

The *Report to the Southern Association of Colleges and Schools, Spring of 1984* thoroughly traced the evolution of Texas Tech's purpose and made the recommendations that would lead the board of regents to adopt a purpose statement indicating that Texas Tech was a research university. The purpose committee pointed out that:

> As the institution has developed, its purpose has broadened to include in a real sense research and public service. . . . Texas Tech has not yet achieved its purpose to an optimum degree, nor will it because of the changing nature of this purpose. It is encased in an evolving role consistent with its designation as one of the four major publically supported comprehensive universities in Texas; and indeed the conclusion seems apparent that Texas Tech University is emerging as a leading educational institution regionally, nationally, and internationally. To help fulfill this emerging role during the coming decade, Texas Tech should address itself to many purpose-related objectives, including the following:
>
> The university should continue its emphasis on expanding and strengthening its research thrust. As a result, additional attention must be given to securing the necessary support for this effort from all available sources. This emphasis should occur not only within the framework of the traditional academic units of the university but also should include efforts across organizational lines from an interdisciplinary perspective. TTU purpose committee (1984,26)

The VPAA&R and the purpose committee stressed in academic council meetings and recommended in the institutional self-study that:

Texas Tech has developed rapidly as a graduate institution, and it is significant that a great deal of curriculum development is occurring at the graduate level. . . . Mindful of the limitation of resources, the institution should screen and select programs for development in which it has a comparative advantage, and in which it can facilitate the optimum use of available resources.

The university should make a major effort in resource procurement. A planned program for the development of support from a variety of bases to supplement existing sources of revenue is in the planning stage. This plan should be developed and carried out. TTU Purpose Committee (1984,26-27)

Projecting a New Image

Texas Tech University was the most prestigious higher education institution in West Texas, but it was not seen as one of the nations' distinguished research institutions. Southwest conference athletics gave Texas Tech a large following of loyal Red Raider fans in four states. Texas Tech football and basketball teams were sometimes ranked in the top-twenty teams of the nation and were frequently listed in the top-fifty teams. The authors wanted Texas Tech to be perceived as being in the same academic and research league as the University of Texas and Texas A&M University. This required changing the mission statement of Texas Tech to reflect its present interest in research and its future purpose of being one of the nations' research universities.

Changing the image and mission of Texas Tech required the VPAA&R and AVPR-Development to use every opportunity to communicate the research capabilities of Texas Tech to the university and general communities. Internally, they worked with the faculty and the board of regents to influence them to accept the following mission statement. "Texas Tech University is a research university dedicated to serving the education and research needs of its constituencies." Before the 1984 self-study was released over 150 people had been involved in the planning process and had generally endorsed the proposed change in the formal purpose statement for Texas Tech.

The authors prepared in 1984, a slide presentation that started with the statement that Texas Tech University is a research university. The first slide was followed by forty to fifty slides of Texas Tech's research. This presentation had three copies that were used by Texas Tech faculty and administration when they made presentations to hundreds of groups in Texas and the nation. Brochures were prepared that explained the new mission and research plans of Texas Tech. These information sources stressed the fact that Texas Tech was a research university and that Texas Tech was the institution in West Texas and the surrounding region where sophisticated science and elegant education were being developed. The point was made that this advanced science, technology, and education were dependent upon Texas Tech's research orientation.

Many of the teaching-oriented faculty and regents were not ready to project Texas Tech's image as being a research university. In the early 1980 the Legislature continued to think of Texas Tech as being a comprehensive university that they had established when they converted it from Texas Technological College to Texas Tech University in 1969. The Board of Regents in 1980 established Texas Tech's official purpose in the following statement.

> Purpose. The role of Texas Tech University is that of a multipurpose state university with a range of program offerings which provide the opportunity for a liberal education for all students and for professional training at the undergraduate and graduate levels. In addition, the university recognizes the value of the university's participation in community service and the significance of scholarly research leading to effective dissemination of knowledge. (Texas Tech University *Catalog* 1982)

For the authors, the above statement was too general for directing a university that wanted to advance research and graduate education very rapidly. They worked to change the image of Texas Tech on campus and throughout the state. In the early eighties, there was much talk by legislators for the need to totally reorganize higher education to make it more responsive to the economic needs of the State. The vice presidents for research prepared several critical position papers and gave important testimonies to select committees and to legislative committees on the value that a research university would have for West Texas and the Great Plains region. After a half-decade of intensive advocacy by many Texas Tech leaders and supporters, the Texas State Legislature in a general reorganization of Texas higher education set Texas Tech's status as a research university with the following mission statement:

Emerging National Research Universities

> Shall be a comprehensive graduate research university offering an array of undergraduate, master's, doctoral and special professional degrees. Emphasis will be on excellence in teaching and research. Research endeavors benefitting the academic strength of the institution and the economic strength of the State of Texas shall be conducted with emphasis on maintaining momentum as an emerging national research university. Funding for research shall be from private sources, competitively acquired sources, and appropriated public funding.

The following institutions were placed in this tier: North Texas State University, Texas Tech University, University of Texas at Dallas (upper-level serving Dallas-Fort Worth Metroplex), and University of Houston/University Park (Sage 1987)

Unfortunately, this accurate classification by the Texas select committee on higher education did not include Texas Tech in the same category with UT & A&M, but it did a great deal to dampen criticism of the internal effort to transform Texas Tech into a research university. The passage of HB 2181 made Texas Tech a "de jure" research university. The vice-presidents' next jobs were to create the climate that would keep Texas Tech de facto a research university.

Your authors believe that without a strategy and the sustained advocacy for Texas Tech being a research university, Texas Tech would have been classified as a comprehensive university by the Texas legislature and that this would have severely retarded its research development and constrained its research service to Texas and the nation. Texas Tech's strategic planning in the early eighties strongly influenced its change in purpose, which was recognized by the legislature in 1987. Moreover, the first-generation strategic plans presently exert a strong influence on the direction of the institution and promise to continue that influence for sometime into the future.

A Local Strategic Planning Conference Advanced Texas Tech from a Comprehensive University to a Research University

The vice-presidents for research must be prepared to make modification in their roles as the institution and the external environment changes rapidly, but they should not change requisite goals. The development of a strategic planning conference to advance research shows how changes in the internal and external environment may affect their roles but keep the institution on track.

Hensley (1984) suggested to Darling "We could, if the president deems it advisable, conduct a working conference for strategic planning to advance science and technology in Texas (500+ key state and national leaders) that would input through 'working papers' Texas Tech's interests into the governor's strategy." In a subsequent meeting the AVPR-Development and the VPAA&R proposed to President Cavazos that Texas Tech host a Texas science and technology council meeting in the early part of 1985 for the purpose of demonstrating to the state that Texas Tech was a research university and a major player in the development of science and technology. They also discussed the organization of an annual research development conference that was to attract a large number of current and potential sponsors to the Texas Tech campus to plan strategically and to form new partnerships. This strategy had worked exceedingly well for the authors at Southern Illinois University-Carbondale in the late seventies and early eighties. At Texas Tech, the planning for the first conference was to focus on the development of advanced technology programs as that was the overriding interest in Texas in the mid-eighties.

The president agreed with the proposal and agreed to address the research council in the early part of 1985. On January 16, 1985, the president presented to the research council a progress report on the Texas science and technology council and endorsed the concept of Texas Tech hosting a working conference for developing science and advanced technology in Texas. He placed vice-presidents Darling and Hensley in charge of developing such a conference and asked the research council members to serve as the major planners. He suggested it might be held in the fall of 1985. Hensley suggested that the research council and their faculty should consider the following broad goals for the conference with the intent of improving the research image of Texas Tech University and to advance specific research programs:

1. To publicize key research programs and principal investigators in order to develop in the public an awareness of the unique research capabilities of Texas Tech and to convince them that Texas Tech was one of the state's four major research universities.

2. To invite key business, industrial, and governmental leaders to serve on the college planning teams for the development of specific strategies aimed at developing Texas Tech's research programs and for forming partnerships to develop "hot" advanced technologies that could improve the economy of Texas.

3. To invite the governor and legislators to campus to assist in planning for Texas Tech becoming one of the state's research universities, in obtaining their commitment to the long-term development of TTU's centers of excellence, and in solidifying support for Texas Tech's "special line-item research programs."

4. To invite the public into the university for an evening open house to see the quality of Texas Tech's research programs and to improve their understanding of the contributions of the research university to their community.

5. To invite state and federal science and technology program officers to the conference to obtain their assistance in developing Texas Tech's and the state of Texas strategic plans.

Chairman Hensley asked the research council to return to their colleges and to plan with their faculty ways that their departments and ORUs could contribute to a two-day planning conference focussed on developing research partnerships for their major research efforts. These partnerships were to meet the needs of the state, nation, and region.

Initially, there was quite a clamor over focussing on advanced technology and on bringing industry representatives and politicians onto the campus as partners. A number of the research council members felt that the emphasis should not be on advanced technology as that stress detracted from the comprehensive nature of Texas Tech and created the image of Texas Tech being a vocational training school. All of the arguments associated with the basic-applied research issues were aired. Several groups felt that too much attention and resources were being given to industrial research needs, thus detracting from the undergraduate programs. Some deans and faculty did not want to be part of a university effort and advocated performing some similar type of activity in a decentralized manner.

It took the vice-presidents several months to prepare the campus for the conference to be held in the fall of 1985. In May of 1985, there was general agreement in the academic and research councils to holding a research conference at Texas Tech in the fall of 1985. That did not come to fruition as three factors caused the conference to be delayed for almost two years.

On campus, the president and board of regents had been embroiled with the academic side of the university in a long and acrimonious controversy over the revision of the Texas Tech tenure policy. Also, the president's running battle with certain members of the faculty senate and some research center heads caused the faculty to decisively vote no confidence in the president. In Austin, due to dramatic shortfalls in state revenue, legislators were surfacing plans to cut severely the higher education appropriation by 15% to 20% for 1986 and were promising more draconian cuts for the next biennium. Within the Texas Tech academic administration, leadership changed dramatically when Vice President Darling resigned in July of 1985 and was replaced by Donald Haragan in August. Haragan had a different agenda and a different administrative orientation from Darling. By September, the president suggested placing the conference on hold. Associate Vice President Hensley continued to advocate the conference by bringing up the topic at every opportunity, but the state budget cuts, financial exigency policies, and the "tenure flap" pushed the conference off the academic council agenda for more than a year.

For several months, Vice President Haragan (August, 1985) devoted most of his energies to the hard decisions on cutbacks to be made during the year, to the problems associated with the tenure study committee, and to the reorganization of the university. Governor Mark White (February 1986) asked for a plan to be instituted by agency heads by March 1 to effect a 13% reduction of general revenue appropriation for the current year and in anticipation of a 13% reduction for the next fiscal year. Hiring employees and salaries were frozen, travel was curtailed drastically, and other economies were affected. Campus morale was at a low ebb.

Hensley in late March 1985 again discussed the conference with Vice President Haragan and his fellow staff members who were looking for faculty morale boosters. Haragan felt the idea was worth trying and asked the AVPR-Development to develop it. In April of 1986, Hensley met with the Board of City Development, the city council and the governor's staff. Governor Mark White liked the idea and agreed to be the luncheon speaker. In May a "Proposal to Hold a A Working Conference for Developing Advanced Technology in Texas: Strengthening the Government/Industry/Education Partnership, September 26 and 27, 1986 at Texas Tech University." and the tentative program were approved by the president and key town people. In July of 1986 the Texas legislature started special sessions, which promised to run into the fall. The Governor's staff wanted to postpone the conference until the early part of 1987. The university complied.

In September of 1986, the conference was again placed on the academic council's agenda. After two months of debate, Vice President Haragan felt the concept with a change in emphasis and a change in title could be implemented. AVPR Hensley was to organize the conference and to find the external $30,000 to finance it. VP Haragan would morally support the concept, but could not during budget cutbacks find the money for such an endeavor.

The Lubbock community financially supported the conference, which brought the general population onto the campus to see research in action, not athletics nor recitals. The AVPR-Development had worked very closely with members of the city council, the Lubbock Board of Community Development and the Chamber of Commerce to convince them that Texas Tech's research meant economic prosperity for the city and region. The advanced technology concept appealed to the business entrepreneurs of the area. Private citizens were very willing to finance the government-industry-university partnership idea. The conference was a small amount to finance. Moreover, the mayor and the president were interested in declaring a Texas Tech appreciation day. The two ideas were merged and a new plan for a Texas Tech appreciation day and a research day and open house were approved by the academic council.

Governor Mark White lost the gubernatorial election to William Clements. Changing governors and keeping the plan intact were relatively easy because members of the board of regents were close friends with the new governor and they persuaded him to participate in the research day and Texas Tech appreciation dinner. Key legislators, many of the chief executive officers in Texas and the governor came to Lubbock to participate in the planning of our research programs. At the Texas Tech appreciation dinner, Governor Clements (1987) unveiled his higher education plan and his economic revitalization plan. His first hand knowledge of the local support for Texas Tech and his viewing of especially prepared video tapes of Texas Tech's research helped him to see Texas Tech as a vital research arm in the state's efforts for economic revitalization, not just a teaching institution. Thereafter, Texas Tech was mentioned my the governor and his staff as one of the state's research institutions and a major element in his economic revitalization plans. The conference with its 1,000 plus participants, state media coverage, and a long-series of newspaper feature articles more than any other single event established Texas Tech as a research university in the minds of the citizens of Texas. The conducting of tours through research laboratories, the staging of field demonstrations, the observation of pilot plants in operation, and the viewing of a series of thirty-two video tapes showing the research of major centers and institutes lead to a sincere appreciation for Texas Tech as a research institution. Although the authors see February 27, 1987 as the day Texas Tech was accepted as a research university, the planning for this acceptance started years earlier in the executive team's planning meetings. It took hundreds of hours for the AVPR-Development to arrange for the leaders of the State of Texas to pay attention for a whole day to the research achievement of Texas Tech.

The synergy of the event had long-lasting positive consequences. The materials prepared for the open house and the proposals developed during this time convinced many sceptics that Texas Tech was indeed a research university. The faculty left the Texas Tech appreciation dinner feeling that the City of Lubbock, local industry, and the state government were very supportive of them. In turn, the town's people were convinced that Texas Tech was a major resource to their region and the state. The date for the official designation of Texas Tech as a research university was on June 19, 1987 when the governor signed HB 2181 into law. That law placed Texas Tech in Tier Two as an emerging national research university, a fair classification, although originally we had planned to be included with the University of Texas and Texas A&M University.

Recruiting and Retaining the Best Researchers

Fundamental to our intent to develop Texas Tech into a research university was our plan of attracting and retaining the best research-oriented people to Texas Tech. Influencing the recruitment of research faculty was a major effort for the vice-president and his associates. The vice-president was intent on attracting the best faculty to Texas Tech. It was his philosophy to seek the "superstar" or an emergent "superstar." Also, sizable salary increments and the best of institutional resources were given to retain leading researchers. The recruiting and retention philosophy included the belief that the cost for the best is worth more than the cost of the average faculty member as the grants and contracts of distinguished faculty and their attraction of superior graduate students will more than offset their salary differentials. This personnel philosophy does help in the recruiting and retention of researchers, it does not help the morale of faculty who are not productive researchers.

Deans and department heads felt that inclusion of the VPAA&R or one of his associates with their enthusiasm for research development was a positive tool in recruiting research-oriented faculty. One of the authors was usually included in the interview schedule for all administrator and key faculty candidates. In these interviews, the vice-presidents stressed the research mission of Texas Tech and pointed out the research capabilities of Texas Tech. Although these interviews were very time consuming, they gave us an opportunity to know the research interests of new faculty, to begin early planning for research developments, and to convince candidates that their research would be supported immediately and in the future by the central administration.

Also, new policy and systems for granting tenure and promotions was installed in 1982. Again, the VPAA&R and his staff made extensive reviews of all candidates for promotion or tenure. Those that did not meet a high standard for research performance were not granted promotion nor tenured. The policy stressing research productivity and rigorous reviews over a five-year period significantly influenced faculty research productivity and upgraded the standards for faculty graduate education and research performance in most colleges. The VPAA&R practice of interviewing faculty and administrator candidates discouraged nonresearchers from applying for tenure-track positions. Similarly, deans quit sending forward recommendations for faculty with poor research records for promotion and tenure as they knew low-level performing faculty petitions would be denied at the VP level.

We worked with the existing faculty by conducting faculty convocations and by taking the research staff to every college to discuss research opportunities. The VPAA&R introduced in 1983 a plan for faculty administrative internships. The purpose of the faculty internship was faculty development by assisting promising young faculty to acquire administrative experience in university higher administrative offices. In 1984, Reed Richardson was assigned to the office of the vice-president for research. During the next two years Richardson was actively involved in the planning of university research. He produced for the university special plans for improving animal resources and facilities on campus and prepared *Grantsmanship Information: Guidelines, Outlines, Checklists and Indices of Sponsored Project Funding—College of Agricultural Science, Texas Tech University* (May 1, 1985). Reed's guidelines contained several sections such as the "progress planning charts" and "checklists and worksheets" that greatly aided the planning process in the colleges and in the research services office. One of the major tasks of the AVPR-Development was to work with faculty to help them develop their ideas into projects and programs. The AVPR-Development visited most of the research laboratories and support facilities to observe first hand the condition of facilities and the type of research being conducted. At these on-site visits, the AVPR-Development encouraged the investigators to start their strategic planning for their unit. Many of the outlines for the strategic plans of an ORU were conceived at these on-site visits. Later, the faculty would come to the office of research development to receive additional help in planning programs and projects.

The AVPR-Development conducted a number of proposal writing seminars for faculty and classes for graduate students and post doctorates on proposal writing. These seminars and classes were very successful in helping the faculty develop their ideas into formal proposals which were then sent to potential sponsors. Over 40 percent of first-time submissions achieved some funding support. The funding rate increased to 65% for seminar participants revising according to reviewer comments and making a second submission. Very informal, but extremely thorough proposal critiques and analyses of reviewer comments from the AVPR-Development were quite valuable to beginning and to some experienced investigators.

Changing the Institution Philosophy Statement

Beginning in the early eighties and throughout the decade, we constantly worked with deans and faculty to develop an institutional philosophy that reflected a research development emphasis and supported the items in the agenda of the strategic plan for research. The first item on Texas Tech's agenda was "to develop Texas Tech from one of more than thirty-seven comprehensive universities into one of the four State of Texas major research universities." The authors kept this agenda item always in front of the principals in the planning process. They spent much time advocating a research development philosophy and writing statements to advance that mission.

Many research philosophy statements were written and discussed during the eighties. The institution's thinking on research philosophy evolved into the following statement, which was generally accepted in the late eighties, but not officially adopt by the University at this writing.

THE RESEARCH PHILOSOPHY OF TEXAS TECH UNIVERSITY

Texas Tech University, designated by the State of Texas and recognized by the Federal government as one of the nation's select research universities, accepts the responsibilities of conducting research that will advance its academic strengths, the economic development of Texas, and the well-being of the Nation and humanity. Texas Tech University is a comprehensive graduate research university offering an array of undergraduate, master's, doctoral and special professional degrees. The faculty and students of Texas Tech University are committed to advancing its international reputation as a center for excellence in research and education. Scholarship is fostered by the following philosophical principles and commitments essential for the practice of unfettered inquiry:

1. The University supports and values a full spectrum of research activities. The word "research" in this context embodies a comprehensive range of creative undertakings. Such projects may be traditional or innovative, *funded or unfunded*, and include basic and applied investigations in the sciences and technology, development, production research, and technology transfer, scholarly inquiry in the humanities, and original contributions in the fine arts and performing arts. Research produc-

tivity may be defined by various disciplines *but it is not synonymous with the receipt of extramural funding*. The rare and valuable intellectual gifts required to accomplish these missions are supported by the University through its commitment to develop and maintain many centers of excellence in research.

2. Research is problem-driven, and may cut across disciplinary boundaries. New disciplinary and interdisciplinary organizational structures have evolved, and will continue to evolve, to respond to the current and future needs of our faculty.

3. As a steward of knowledge for humankind, the university is ideologically and financially committed to supporting all scholarly functions, including research—the practice essential in scholarship.

4. The continuous and rigorous affirmation of academic freedom and independent scholarship at Texas Tech University sustains its scholars and their work toward excellence in research. The University encourages independent scholarship, the sine qua non of academic life.

5. As one of the nation's leading research institutions, Texas Tech University proudly acknowledges its responsibility to expand the frontiers of knowledge. The University is grateful to patrons of its programs in art, humanities, sciences and engineering who have made it possible for faculty and students to uplift the human spirit and improve human conditions. Dedicated researchers are invited to join its faculty and students in their search for knowledge and their service to humanity. Hensley (May 1990)

The content of the aforementioned statement was strongly influenced by the senior research administrators suggesting a plan for formulating the statement, selecting a widely representative group of researchers to help in the drafting of the statement, and then advocating that statement throughout the university. After years of discussing the merits of being a research university, the above statement was still too research-oriented to suit several groups on campus and it had to be adamantly defended by Hensley as late as May of 1990. The attacks on the content of the statement came not from researchers, who strongly supported the philosophy, but from nonresearchers who could not grasp the concept of what the researcher does or what a research university should be. The critics were very shrill in predicting the demise of the undergraduate program and the decline in scholarship donations if the university adopted and published such a statement.

Academic Programs Are the Foundation for the Higher Education Enterprise

The vice-president's role is critical in planning new academic programs. Because strategic planning is about making choices for the long-term, it is vital to the development of new programs to acquire endorsements and commitment of resources from the academic vice-president. New programs should be developed continuously and existing programs should be reviewed periodically for revitalization or termination. Program assessment and development requires opinions and options from people outside their program field. The vice-president focuses his attention on academic program development for that is the mechanism for degree production and a major revenue source. Therefore, the vice-president, who has oversight of all programs, is an excellent person to assist in the advancement of programs and projects, especially those that are multidisciplinary. Through reading environmental scans, requests for proposals from sponsoring agencies, and unit scenarios for program development; the vice-president is alerted to many opportunities for forming partnerships to develop some new training or research program or to modify existing programs to meet some emergent need. The vice-president and his staff cannot chase every opportunity for program development is very expensive. Also, it can lead an institution into long-term obligations that cannot be supported at a later time.

Despite these drawbacks, there are select opportunities that should be explored and if they meet the following tests for institutional benefit, they should be developed: 1) the development complements the mission of the institution and goals of the proposing unit; 2) the development will provide a comparative advantage over competitors; 3) a sponsor commits to long-term program support; and 4) the development can maximize the use of available resources.

In the seventies and eighties, Vice-President Darling spent several weeks each year developing international contacts and sister-institution partnerships in Europe, Africa, Asia, South America, and the Pacific Rim Counties. He saw international education and research support from foreign countries as a major source of future revenue for Texas Tech University. Several faculty and student exchange programs and the Agency for International Development training programs for third-world countries were developed under his active leadership. Also, his AVPR-Development had a standing interest in international research program development.

More important when considering personalities in the planning process, Jacque S. Behrens, director for Student International Programs, became very important as she initiated one of the largest program development efforts in Texas Tech's history. Behrens was eager to learn how to write proposals and to be involved in academic strategic planning. When she joined the vice-president for academic affairs and research planning teams, she brought with her a great many intangible assets for international program development. She knew most of the key people in the area of international education, had traveled widely, and had hundreds of former-student friends in Texas Tech Alumni Clubs around the world. Being the consummate home entertainer and having a genuine interest in the welfare for foreign students on our campus, she had earned a deep affection from these students, to the point that they frequently communicated with her.

Attracting international students fit into the VPAA&R's strategy for academic and research program development. In West Texas, oil drilling and production were in a serious downturn during the middle eighties, this reduced production boded ill for our petroleum- and agriculture-related programs because students would not enter programs that lead to a tight job market. As a consequence of the oil downturn and moderate oil prices, your authors saw a diminution of student enrollment in engineering, agriculture, and business. Therefore, the authors were eager to attract foreign students into Texas Tech petroleum- and agriculture-related programs with the hope these programs could survive on a high percentage of foreign students until the West Texas oil production revived and domestic students returned to engineering, business, agriculture and geology programs. How the Malaysian-TCIE-TTU engineering program and the MARA training programs were developed should provide some insight into the pressure that accompanies a response to an RFP that matches a priority item in the strategic plan agenda.

Our planning with the MARA Foundation, the Malaysian Ministry of Education, and several Texas universities and colleges serves as an example of joint ventures working well for all partners. Excerpts from Hensley's (1986) "A Chronology of Major Events in Developing the Malaysian/TCIE/TTU Engineering Program" and the Malaysian Project shows the efforts of several principals in planning international education programs.

On June 4, 1985, the MARA Foundation issued an open announcement of opportunities for world class universities to train Malaysian students in Malaysia.

June 14, 1985, Joe Neal of University of Texas and Jacque Behrens discussed the possibility of the Texas Consortium on International Education (TCIE) submitting a Letter of Inquiry to MARA.

June 27, 1985 Neal and Behrens discussed with VPs, deans, and faculty the general endorsements and existing training occurring in Malaysia.

June 28, 1985 Habibah, director of MARA (She controlled a very large petro-dollar annual budget) and Sahol, deputy director of MARA, invited TCIE representatives to visit Shah Alam for discussion of possible education programs.

June 29, 1985, Neal requested of Vice-President Darling the assignment of TTU academic personnel to go with Behrens, Tom Hoemeke, and him to Malaysia to discuss mutual interests.

June 29, 1985, Vice-President Darling asks Associate Vice-President Hensley to go with the TCIE representatives and to develop for TTU a project if there appears to be substantial benefits for TTU.

June 30, 1985, Vice-President Darling and staff meet to discuss opportunities. Colleges of Engineering, Agriculture, and Business are to be given priority for development. Hensley is to design the strategic plan and develop it project-by-project with the MARA Foundation and the Malaysian government representatives. Great rush in getting visas approved and travel plans set.

July 2, 1985, Behrens, Neal, Hoemeke, and Hensley leave for Malaysia to discuss with the ministry of education and the MARA Foundation the very detailed objectives, procedures, budgets, and evaluation 1) for the TCIE project, and 2) for a long-range TTU cooperative institutional development of the MARA Institut Teknologi.

July 4-6, 1985, Director Habibah and Deputy Director Sahol show the TCIE representatives Malaysia. Much discussion of higher education problems among the Malaysian and TCIE representatives. General discussion, cordial visiting, and sight seeing with no agreement on goals, procedures, evaluation, and scope, continues for two days. On the third day, Hensley suggested that the planning teams closet themselves with a computer and prepare a long-term plan for the MARA Foundation and TTU and a operating plan for a first-year project for TCIE with Texas Tech as the prime contractor. The project was to start January 1990 to meet demands of Director Habibah to place a large number of students immediately in a new Shah Alam Centre.

July 7-8, 1985. After two eighteen-hour writing sessions, Sahol and Hensley produced a mutually acceptable draft proposal and a strategic plan with the following broad goals:

1. Beginning January 1, 1986 to train annually from 200 to 800 Malaysian students at the TCIE Center at Shah Alam, Malaysia. TTU is to be the prime contractor in offering introductory university-level courses (freshman and sophomore levels) following the standard curriculum of TTU that could lead center-trained students to admittance to the junior year in Engineering, Architecture, and Computer Science at Texas Tech or other engineering schools.
2. To provide placement services for students completing the two-year programs so that they may continue work toward baccalaureate degrees. And, to provide the special dormitory and advisory services necessary for the physical care and intellectual guidance of 200 to 800 Malaysian students while in Texas.
3. Beginning January 1, 1986 to develop the Institut Teknologi MARA as a sister institution to Texas Tech University. (a) This objective called for the Institut Teknologi MARA faculty (many had only BA or MA Degrees) to obtain doctorates from Texas Tech University. Support for 25 faculty to obtain advanced degrees in science and engineering was established. (b) Cooperative Research Development. Annually, 10 senior level TTU faculty were to visit Malaysia for the purpose of assisting the Malaysian faculty develop education and research centers applied to the problems of Malaysia. (c) Ten post-doctoral students from the Institut Teknologi MARA were to study at TTU in their respective disciplines for the purpose of developing their research competencies and for transferring educational technology.

Sahol and Hensley composed a general letter of intent, a MARA request for a proposal, a plan for development, and a preliminary TTU proposal. The TCIE and the MARA planning teams spent a number of days advocating to Malaysian officials the adoption of a detailed proposal that explained the operating procedures for the project goals. After three days of face-to-face negotiations and making many changes according to the demands of the Malaysian bureaucracy, the TCIE and MARA planning teams met with the minister of education and gained from him approval of the grand plan with the proviso that final acceptance of detailed and exact proposals would be contingent upon the usual approval on both sides. Five million dollars were appropriated immediately for the MARA-TTU Plan for 1986. Adoption of the plan on the Malaysian side was relatively easy.

On return to the United States, Hensley, AVPR-Development learned that Vice-President Darling had resigned his position. That was bad news. In the interregnum, without a strong advocate in the vice-president's position, Associate Vice-President Hensley could not muster the power to gain approval of the plan in a timely fashion and the grand plan was dramatically modified and the scope of the projects greatly reduced. The magnitude of the plan frightened a Texas Tech bureaucracy that was accustomed to dealing in thousands of dollars for short periods, not millions of dollars for long periods. The shrill voices of doom created enough dissonance within the university that the interim vice-president delayed submitting the general plan to the president in a timely fashion. The Malaysian planning team tired of answering interminal questions from petty administrators took their money and the first objectives of the plan to other Texas schools where favorable commitments were obtained. When the new vice-president assumed office the original plan was not salvageable. In dallying, Texas Tech lost the leadership role and the sister institution development plan was never seriously studied at Texas Tech. In protest over the resistance on the TTU campus, Hensley resigned his position on the TCIE planning team because he could not support the modified plan. Ultimately, a TCIE Shah Alam Center was established with Texas Tech faculty operating the center. Unfortunately, TTU relinquished the prime contractor's role and submitted only a $2.7 million proposal to subcontract for one-fifth of the TCIE students to be trained at Texas Tech.

A great deal of time and ego goes into program planning. Intense, concentrated thought and extraordinary personal commitment is essential for successful planning. Half-baked ideas and half-hearted efforts are never satisfying to strategic thinkers. Total commitment on the part of the developer to the grand purpose is required. Even then, adoption is not assured. Obtaining acceptance of a vision by many constituencies is quite difficult. For the architect of a plan, rejection of a well-developed idea is not just another day at the office, it is an ego bruising process that is difficult to mask. Hensley and the Malaysian planning process illustrate this point.

From June 29, 1985 to January 1, 1986, the AVPR-Development spent 108.5 hours in planning sessions with Malaysian officials, 162.5 hours in planning sessions with Texas Tech personnel, and many unaccounted hours in deep thought on the next generation of tactical planning. He had a tremendous personal stake in the outcomes as his ideas and proposal writing experience dominated the grand plan. He spent several thousand dollars of scarce travel and development resources, which were later reimbursed by TCIE. From the university perspective, the project plans were implemented successfully by Larry Masten of TTU. From the architect's perspective, the withering of the long-term plan for the cooperative development of graduate education and research was a lost opportunity to place Texas Tech in a position in Southeast Asia from which it could develop future education and research. His ego suffered because he could not overcome the reactionary forces on his home campus and could not gain adoption of a plan approved by a sponsor. Rejection on his own campus of the long-term plan was a personal defeat tied closely to campus politics and to administrative power struggles. The award of subcontracts to Texas Tech provided no personal consolation. However, once he determined that his administrative superiors were not going to commit to the grand plan in a timely fashion, he moped about rejection for one afternoon, punched the body bag the following morning to purge frustrations and aggressions, and ran several miles in the afternoon to sort ideas for a new plan, The next day, he put his efforts elsewhere.

Planning for the Development of Common Grounds

From July through September of 1984, the vice-presidents for research met frequently with the president to discuss the building of a research endowment that would support a number of centers of excellence on the Texas Tech campus and to plan the creation of a Texas Tech University research mall (research park). During the fall of 1984, Texas Tech research and development personnel held many planning meetings to discuss developing a $20 million TTU research endowment and the common grounds for government-industry-university research. It was the president's strategy to create over a decade a $60 million university research endowment. It was our intent to create in each center of excellence, smaller ($500,000-$1,000,000) endowments to support endowed chairs and professorships, which would be incorporated into of the president's plan. These centers of excellence and their regional extensions would be strategically placed to serve the needs of West Texas. They would create very visible signs that Texas Tech was a research university and would show the positive impact of specific Texas Tech research centers on the region. The first phase of this strategy called for research malls to be established immediately in Lubbock. Hensley (November 3, 1984) advocated that:

> The purpose of a university park is to provide a common ground where the
> university faculty and their various constituencies can come together for instruction

and research services which are not easily conducted on nor appropriate for the main campus. The development of the university park rests on the assumption that the university and its partners will construct several specialized malls leading from the central campus into undeveloped areas. The concept of the university park can be understood by assuming the park is laid out in the fashion of a wheel. The central campus of the university and the Health Sciences Center with its beautiful grounds is the hub and the malls are the spokes of the wheel. In practice, the park layout will not be as perfect as Figure 1 depicts, but the model conveys in a simple way a very complex development undertaking that occurs in an incremental fashion.

In the fall of 1983, AVPR Hensley visited with Donald Hart and Ned E. Huffman of Research Triangle Park to study their modes of organization and operation. He spent some time at the Stanford Industrial Park and talked at length with Kay Tamaribuchi of MIT about the problems of industrial liaison. He talked with Mark Money and studied his work on a model for the establishment of university-related research parks within a framework of selected management principles. Notes from these visits and other information on research parks were loaned to the president, faculty, and administration from the Office of Research Services. After several lengthy discussions, the president agreed with the vice-presidents that a university park might be needed, but he was reluctant to commit any institutional resources to develop the common ground until the fundamental questions of the establishment of a research park was thoroughly discussed by the faculty and community. He felt is was necessary to first start his enterprise campaign and then turn the university's attention to the research park. Also, he stressed that a research mall is a new idea for West Texas that would encounter considerable resistance from the faculty who would see this as a diversion of resources from existing efforts and from existing civic groups who would see industrial park development as their prerogative. On the other hand, he acknowledged that there was a number of higher-education organizations and their constituencies that expected Texas Tech to take the lead in developing industry-university partnerships. Although the vice-presidents used their best arguments, the president was not convinced that the development of a research park was appropriate for Texas Tech at that time. However, he was willing to start strategic planning on the development of common ground if certain conditions were met. He instructed his staff that before such a complex enterprise as that proposed by the vice presidents for research could be endorsed by him, they would have to answer several fundamental questions in very specific terms.

He asked the following questions.

1. Is there at this time a valid need for a university park with a research mall in West Texas?
2. Does Texas Tech have the charge and capabilities to develop such an enterprise?

3. What are the benefits of a research mall to Texas Tech?
4. Are there successful examples of development of a common ground for cooperative research elsewhere?
5. How does Texas Tech manage the complexity of change associated with the development of a research mall and a university park?
6. Can Texas Tech obtain an institutional commitment to developing a research mall in a seasonal manner?
7. Can a research mall jeopardize existing areas in the university or damage its reputation?
8. How can Texas Tech administer cooperative research?
9. What are the means of financing a research park?

The president wanted these questions thoroughly discussed with faculty and community leaders before he would commit institutional resources to developing the strategy. He instructed the vice-presidents for research to provide specific answers to the aforementioned questions and to not let the research park interfere with his plans for the enterprise campaign. We agreed with all of his stipulations and began a series of planning meetings with the principals in the various research sectors.

Cavazos (November 3, 1984) created, on the advice of the vice-president's council, the Texas Tech University and Health Sciences Center Development Council. Associate Vice-President Hensley was asked to serve on that council representing the research interests of the university. John Anderson, director of the Office of Development, was asked to chair the development council. Its primary purpose was to coordinate all contacts with the private sector that were instigated by university personnel and support groups. Initially, this broad charge posed some problems for some academicians. After a number of ground rules for development were established, the Development Office and the Office of Research Services worked jointly on a number of specific development plans and campaigns. John Anderson's and John Bradford's planning and work were quite valuable in developing the supportive environment for research at Texas Tech and they continually supported the idea of centers of excellence in a research mall. How this coordination occurred and how strategic planning for the research endowment was developed is explained in the section of this chapter on "Formulating the Strategic Plan for the Development Office."

During September and October the president and the vice-presidents discussed with key board members the possibilities of developing several joint ventures with industry and the advantages of Texas Tech having a research park. In November the board of regents accepted the idea and established a committee on research parks. For several months, the vice-presidents and deans worked with the committee on site location and financing arrangements. It was generally agreed among the steering committee members that particular joint ventures were to be located on a central axis of the mall or on the periphery of Lubbock.

On October 5, 1984, the VPAA&R asked the AVPR-Development to head a committee to draft a strategic plan for a research park. The associate vice-presidents and the associate deans for research were to develop the plan. Each division on campus was asked to submit their ideas on how they could benefit and contribute to such a park.

The AVPR-Development held a series of research development meetings with faculty groups for the purpose of helping them plan for: 1) a nuclear magnetic resonance center for imaging of humans and animals, 2) a Continuing Education center and hotel for restaurant, hotel and institutional management, 3) a viticulture center and enology program, 4) a plant stress laboratory, 5) a feed lot and beef cattle research center, 6) a biotechnology center, 7) a disaster research center, 8) a pulsed power center, and 9) a center for International Urban Studies.

All of these plans and several more had considerable promise for obtaining long-term government and industrial support. All had the potential of becoming centers of excellence for their investigators were doing outstanding basic and applied research and they were development oriented. Unfortunately, facilities were not available on campus for these centers. Therefore, the AVPR-Development proposal for developing on a common ground research facilities that were financed by industrial partners and city bonds was enthusiastically endorsed by the research community. This rather ambitious plan was to locate joint-venture research centers in the vacant two-hundred acres between the medical school and the Methodist and St. Mary's Medical Complex and on the periphery of Lubbock.

To develop the critical mass of industrial partners to maintain a research park, the Research Development Office created in 1984 the "Industry-University Development Opportunities Announcement," which collected information from the organized research units on campus and placed that information in a standardized announcement that was then sent to targeted businesses and research organizations. Announcements were distributed on a very broad spectrum of research activities ranging from cattle feedlot activities to star-war technology. This effort elicited a number of inquiries into specific work and lead to particular sponsorships. More importantly, its success encouraged many principal investigators to begin developing industrial partnership instead of relying solely on government support. Moreover, individual deans and department heads began to produce a series of brochures and annual reports that extolled the research capabilities of their units. Acceptance of this strategy by the faculty and industry was most encouraging to the university administration.

The AVPR-Development also prepared a slide presentation and a brochure that provided an abstract of the research projects that offered a high potential for commercialization. They also listed Texas Tech's organized research units. The slide program and brochures were presented to a number of technology transfer meetings that were held in the eighties. At these meetings sponsored by the Advanced Technology Development Institute, the Fantus Company, Aladdin Industries, Inc., and other technology transfer associations, a great deal of information was exchanged between industry and university representatives. There were a number of contacts that were made at the technology transfer meetings that developed into fruitful partnerships. Industrial representatives from Texas Instruments (August 24, 1984), William Reed Company (December 7, 1984), WIPCO (September 19, 1984), Marriott, and other companies came to campus to help our researchers with their strategic planning and provided immediate funding for a number of cooperative works. Investigators such as Richardson (April 19, 1985) and Hatfield (June 27, 1985) found these meetings with industry representatives to be very informative and productive in planning long-term research developments within the government-industry-university framework. Technology transfer meetings in these early days of the industry-university partnership period advanced research somewhat by the initial contacts made by the vice-presidents, but the vast majority of the industrial contacts were made by the individual faculty members and administrators such as those made by William Marcy (August 1984) and Director Mike Mezack (July 2, 1984) through their professional associations and their private consulting.

The vice-presidents performed the role of university liaison officers with industry and developed in the public an awareness that Texas Tech had a great amount of commercially exploitable research and that Texas Tech was eager to explore possibilities for industry-university partnerships. That was a valuable pioneering role at Texas Tech in the eighties as many of the faculty on the campus did not want to see these partnerships developed. The same types of resistance to industry-university partnerships that were discussed in earlier chapters had to be overcome at Texas Tech. Our strategy was to advocate the partnership from our positions in the central administration and to financially support fledgling partnerships in the ORUs and by PIs. It was also our plan to establish an Industrial Liaison Program modelled after MIT's program.

Budget considerations never allowed Texas Tech to hire an industrial liaison officer for the university.

Dean Haley (January 24, 1983) worked very closely with Vice-President Darling for two years in planning the Laboratory Facility for Restaurant, Hotel, and Institutional Management (RHIM). She and the other deans handled most of their industrial liaison functions on a college-by-college basis, but informed and called into planning service the vice-presidents as needed. They preferred that arrangement and your authors were never able to convince them of the value of a central development effort for industrial liaison.

The vice-presidents wrote and encouraged the deans to write feature articles on different aspects of the industry-university partnership for local newspapers and they appeared on local television with slide presentations of existing centers and plans for the future. They prepared a number of video tapes on specific research projects that were used on occasion by community groups and more often by the ORU directors and deans.

When the draft academic plan for development of specific centers in a university park and research mall was finished, VPAA&R Darling (April 12, 1985) informed the university that

> The Vice President for Academic Affairs has asked the Office of Research Services to develop a draft copy of a strategic plan for the development of a University Park and Research Mall for Texas Tech University. The preliminary materials associated with this plan have been gathered from the respective offices on the campus and placed in an overall plan. This information is available for your review and input prior to formal submission to the Board of Regents in May. You are encouraged to read this document and to comment on its appropriateness for your college.

Many of the plans formulated for the research mall were developed into centers of excellence and are described elsewhere in this chapter. The strategic plan for the research park contained the outlines for the development of many of Texas Tech's organized research units. It was a most impressive document because the directors of the ORUs had prepared realistic research plans based on past accomplishment and the pledges of their partners for specific support.

The deans provided several lists of companies that they and their faculty talked with about locating an office or laboratory in the Texas Tech research park. ORU directors such as Marcy obtained the several pledges such as the following one from Varian manager, Sam Barlow (September 13, 1984), "I did submit a trip report to my management recommending that Varian SEG participate in the Engineering Research center and specifically the SMART LAB. I have recommended that Varian's involvement at this stage be as an industry sponsor, ($10,000-$20,000), and to designate an individual to serve on the University/Industry Advisory Board."

Several local groups had their own ideas of what the park should be and were very enthusiastic about its development. Westar, a group of realtors, business, and civic leaders, was most supportive of the efforts to develop the park. Croslin (April 16, 1985) noted:

> The creation of a Texas Tech Industrial Park would be a nucleus to bring high technology industries to Lubbock.
>
> We understand that the development of an industrial park is a major project which should not be taken lightly or singly by Texas Tech university. We at Westar wish to confirm that considerable community support already exists to cooperate with Texas Tech University in any way possible and acceptable in creating the industrial park.

John Logan, (April 9, 1986) president of the Lubbock Chamber of Commerce and member of the Board of City Development noted:

> The Lubbock Chamber of Commerce enthusiastically endorses the proposed development of a university Research Park.
>
> This organization has long been involved in community industrial and economic development activities and is fully aware of the importance and need for developments such as the university Research Park. We pledge to you our support of the project and would hope that we have an opportunity to work with you in the development of this much needed facility.

The board of regents' research park steering committee in the spring of 1985 had several hearings with the university and Health Sciences Center staff to hear reports from the deans and vice-presidents who collectively had several million dollars in pledges for specific joint ventures. By April of 1985 there was great enthusiasm for the concept because there were several excellent plans and letters of understanding for specific developments with industry pledging specific amounts of long-term support.

President Cavazos (April 22, 1985) noted:

> The April 16th meeting of the Research Park Steering Committee was very productive. In response to the direction from Mr. Birdwell, we are now to develop: (1) a preliminary land use plan for the property east and west of the Health Sciences Center, and (2) a strategy for funding the development of the project facilities. No Texas Tech dollars are to be expended for this development.
>
> Dr. Payne is to take the lead in coordinating the planning, and he will work closely with Dr. Darling and Dr. Richards to appoint appropriate individuals to this project. In addition to the land use plan and the financial plan, I would like for you to include ideas on how this entire project will be managed and how the research park facility will be operated.
>
> I expect a report to be ready for preliminary review by July 15, 1985.

The president's change in leadership to start the financial development of a very large urban development project was a change in emphasis and a change in mode of development. This change was a logical progression for a president who wanted enormous, rapid growth, but it was the beginning of failure for the research park because it reversed totally our strategy for building on small increments of success in areas that where already prepared to accept centers of excellence with certain modifications. This change was five to ten years premature. We had no record of success to justify building a multimillion dollar infrastructure before we had actual operating joint ventures.

Despite the vice-presidents' sincere support of this next level of development the change in scope and focus created great resentment on the academic side. Operationally, the VPAA&R could not maintain an ordered plan for development. This new development philosophy did not set well with the associate vice-president for research as it completely reversed his policy for having the staff of each center of excellence show a track record of cooperative research and a long-term plan and pledges for self-financing before they planned for facilities development. The vice-presidents for research had planned on initially placing two centers of excellence that had enough pledges to justify renovation of an existing industrial building on the East Campus and on building a Hotel Continuing Education center adjacent to the Medical School and Lubbock General Hospital. Marriott had pledged to do this. This change in strategy hastened the resignation of the VPAA&R and started the erosion of the influence of the AVPR-Development.

Vice-President for Finance and Administration, Eugene E. Payne (June 20, 1985) provided an "Outline for a Feasibility Study for the Texas Tech Research Park" and noted it would probably cost between $200,000 and $300,000 for a marketing plan, financial, plan, land use, and physical model. The first development of a land tract of 30 to 100 acres would cost between $1 to $3 million. Payne suggested the use of a study team from the Urban Land Institute, Washington, D.C. that "will put together a study team which will guide the institution and the visit the institution and work with the staff to develop a feasibility study for $70,000." Vice-President Payne felt that it was important to have a realistic master plan for the development of the entire research park. And, he stated the time period from the beginning of a feasibility study to the first construction is normally three years if there are no delays.

Hensley at the aforementioned meeting "expressed concern that there be adequate involvement by the academic administration and faculty in the development of the plans for the research park. TTU academicians should be involved in the plans and should direct the planning of the research facilities, not outside consultants. He felt Payne's cost estimates were too high for the beginning development of an incremental strategy."

Darling expressed concern "that we do not attempt to model Texas Tech after any one specific school. We need to consider our unique needs and strengths. The research park should be developed incrementally. We have some thrusts which are going now, especially in engineering and agriculture. We should move forward on those as soon as possible. We have some thrusts going now with the hotel and conference centers. We should move forward on these immediately without waiting for a long external study. He warned that the plan could be studied to death by external consultants and we should use our own people for future planning and existing plans as a point of departure."

Dean Haley expressed concern that the hotel conference center move forward and that the needs of the hotel, restaurant, and institutional management academic program be fully considered.

The subcommittee felt that it was important for the board of regents to either approve or disapprove the hotel-conference center. If disapproved, the project should be dropped; if approved, TTU was to proceed on the development of an RFP that would be released to a number of firms for the development of the facility. It was agreed that Williams and Bray should proceed expeditiously to develop a land use plan. It was agreed that the plan should include the use of the East Campus. They were to coordinate their efforts with Westar and the city.

Hensley (July 17, 1985) in a memorandum to Gene Payne noted:

> First, your proposal to issue separate RFPs for specific project development is excellent. I believe that the deans will want to aggressively develop joint ventures for their respective areas of concern.
>
> Dean Somerville and Dean Haley seem eager to start on their respective projects. Mason seems to be most eager to move. Our problem is to assure the success of Texas Tech's initial efforts as an early failure can scuttle the entire program. Success will require more internal organization and firmer sponsor commitment for short and long-term support than is now present.
>
> As I indicated earlier, the RFP should include a number of elements related to long-term support and project management if they are to have any chance of success. Some way must be found to assure the timely (administrative) reaction to both college initiators of projects and their sponsors. Also, the university will need guidelines for proposals that address the issues of (1) project organization, (2) immediate and short term goals by the colleges and sponsors, (3) capital development for laboratory facilities, (4) intellectual and property rights, and (5) self-financing strategies of laboratories.

The board of regents (July 26, 1984) listened to the subcommittee status report on: 1) land use plan, 2) educational conference center, 3) research park, and 4) feasibility study. They authorized the administration to develop a request for a proposal to secure bids for the private funding and development of an educational conference center provided that there are adequate regental controls on design, construction, and use. The contract award was to be made by the board of regents.

The board of regents steering committee (August 2, 1985) reported:

> that there would be positive benefits derived from the development of a commercially funded research facility directly related to the College of Engineering. There may also be benefits from the development of private research facilities in the area of medicine, chemistry, biology and agriculture.

They felt it would now be appropriate to address the question: Is the development of a privately funded research park economically feasible?

A month earlier John Darling had resigned. The academic side was in disarray. In the interregnum, the research park was renamed the Texas Tech University Advanced Technology Park. A new research park RFP committee was formed consisting of Haragan, Somerville, Hensley, Blair, Goodin, and Payne. On August 30, 1985 a meeting was called and extensive discussion was held on the steps to take in the development of the research park and an RFP. Dean Somerville suggested a radical change of course. He suggested that it would be better at this time to broaden the research base of the institution rather than charging ahead on the development of the research park. And he proposed forming the Center for Applied Research and Engineering (CARE) and the Texas Tech University Research Foundation in its place. Hensley adamantly opposed the Somerville proposal as being an administrative burden that would retard Texas Tech's research growth rather than advancing it. With the exception of Hensley, all committee members concurred with the Somerville proposal. It was obvious that Hensley was not inclined to support the new direction and he was not invited to subsequent meetings. Without Darling and Hensley leading the charge, the research park concept died and the university developed under the leadership of Mason Somerville a research foundation instead.

The power struggles that always arise in development deserve mention here because they contribute in many ways to the abortion of very good plans. While the vice-presidents were working with a large number of faculty, administrators, and civic leaders to develop the research park, a covert agenda by a faculty and administrator faction determined to remove the president and his supporters and to give more power to the academic side was being actively pursued. This covert agenda was omnipresent and it side tracked the development of the research mall and delayed other strategic plan agenda items.

Recall that earlier, the authors had mentioned the TTU Faculty Senate Survey (1983) on "The Research Atmosphere at Texas Tech University" that showed that a number of the faculty were saying they could not perform research on the Texas Tech campus because the climate for research was not facilitative. That same faction continued complaining about central research administration despite the significant improvements that were made.

Also there were a sizable number of faculty and administrators who were strongly opposed to the president and his "usurpation of faculty perogatives." This faction was constantly working in opposition to the president. Any idea or project that could be construed to be an advancement of the president's ideas or an increase in the power of the "East Wing" (the East

Wing was where the president and his staff were located) was opposed and the faction surfaced a different plan. We will not describe the gory details of the personal battles between the president and certain members of the faction, but we will say that the nonresearch matters such as the "tenure flap," the "residue of resentment" from the firing of certain department heads, and the "personality clashes" created a heavy burden on the vice-presidents for research because we were part of the "East Wing." Consequently, any idea we put forth was opposed automatically by the faction. The deans correctly analyzed the situation and proceeded very cautiously. Some administrators covertly encouraged the president-faction clashes to advance their personal power. It was not a pleasant situation to be in, but research needed to be developed and administered and that was our role in fair weather and foul.

In addition to the president-faction clashes, the AVPR-Development philosophically clashed constantly with the Dean of the College of Engineering who championed the development of a Texas Tech Research Foundation as an option to the Office of Research Development in the university. Hensley opposed this "administrative solution" as being an expedient solution that would not make lasting university or state reforms and would divert monies and effort from actual research to support another level of bureaucracy. The personality clashes between AVPR-Development and the Dean of College of Engineering were constant. Both had aggressive personalities and their administrative philosophies were at opposite poles. Although this personality clash was very minor in comparison to the president-faction clashes, it was certainly another factor detrimental to research development harmony. On the positive side, their arguments galvanized support for certain opposing scenarios and factions.

Despite the failure to establish a research mall, the strategic planning and its development efforts greatly advanced the Joint Ventures on the campus and established common grounds on the East Campus and in other locations in the Lubbock area. It significantly improved industry-sponsored cooperative research funding. More importantly, it made most people on campus think first about research and their long-term contributions to building partnerships for academic excellence at Texas Tech University. It was not a waste of time for it raised the goals of many on campus and lead them into new areas of exploration.

As we mentioned earlier in this book, a great deal of the strategic planner's effort is spent in gathering and then making others aware of new information and its potential impact on the institution. The development of policy for the recovery and use of indirect costs shows the information gathering efforts of the vice presidents and their use of that information to promote the fourth item of the university's research development agenda.

The Vice Presidents for Research came from a state where the universities were allowed to retain their earned indirect costs. The Texas laws requiring the return of indirect costs to the State for re-budgeting was perceived by them as a severe handicap in developing research on the Texas Tech campus. Most of the faculty were convinced that the State should allow the state universities to retain their recovered indirect costs. Unfortunately, most were also convinced that the State legislature was not going to change its policy of placing a state levy on recovered indirect costs. Hensley (November 3, 1984) believed that a concerted effort by all the state schools could succeed and suggested that the president should through the Texas Science and Technology Council recommend the changing of the State law to allow universities to retain their earned indirect costs. AVPR-Development in December 14 of 1984 reported the results of a telephone survey of eight universities in neighboring states to determine their policy on retention of indirect costs. The study revealed that the sampled institutions retained all or some of their earned indirect costs. Five institutions retained all of their indirect costs and three retained part of their earned indirect costs according to legislature determinations. The president used this information in State councils and with legislators to help them see the need of Texas universities for recovery and retention of indirect costs. Hensley (March 4, 1985) in discussing the economic benefits states derive from higher education research and development with the Texas House of Representatives, Committee on Science and Technology, brought to their attention the need of the universities to maintain their infrastructure through reclamation of their indirect costs.

Working from his position on the Organized Research Formula Study Committee of the Coordinating Board Texas College and University System, the AVPR-Development urged the Committee to recommend to Commissioner Ashworth that the Coordinating Board should advocate to the Legislature the retention of indirect costs by the universities. Retention of reimbursed indirect costs would change the practice of including these reimbursements as a part of "Other Educational and General Income" (thereby separating indirect costs from the institutional appropriations by the Legislature). The Organized Research Committee (November 13, 1985) presented a "Pay-Out" analysis for their strategy and made a recommendation for institutional retention of earned indirect costs to the Commissioner who appeared to misunderstood the recommendation. In any case, he declined to support the Committee recommendation at that time, but suggested presenting the Committee's analysis and recommendations to the Council of Presidents who could then recommend it to the next Legislature. The "Pay-Out" Analysis of the Committee attracted considerable interest by the Austin law firm of Jones, Day, Reavis, and Pogue who were planning to push legislation on indirect cost reimbursement during the next session. After two years of a concerted effort by the presidents, influential citizens, and the vice presidents putting indirect-cost studies before many state legislators, the Select Committee, and commissions; the Texas House of Representatives (May 19, 1987) passed H.B. 2181, which changed the Higher Education Code to allow each institution to retain any funds received from a funding entity designated for paying overhead expenses of conducting research. This was a good example of university administrators planning with state legislators and others to change detrimental policy and then having the Legislature approve the suggested changes. This change fit into the State's strategic planning as it provided incentives for universities to bring more federal and industrial support into the State.

Once the money was returned, the problem was how to distribute it. The AVPR-Development, as a member of one of the TTU Strategic Planning Committee, (May 23, 1987) after several weeks of planning meetings, recommended designating the returned overhead for the development of research and the improvement of graduate education. The Committee recommended establishing the following programs using 40 percent of the returned indirect costs.

1. A *University Research Grants Program* to assist individual researchers by supporting their start-up research from a university fund supported by indirect cost reclamation.

2. A *Special Programs Development Fund* to assist existing graduate programs and organized research units in the development of a particular new thrust. Sizable grants $10,000 to $50,000 would be made to ORU or graduate programs that developed a plan for significant improvements in their centers. This was to help develop centers of excellence.

3. A *Matching Grants Program* to graduate programs and ORU's for the development of equipment, program support personnel, and graduate fellowships when the initiating unit can show a significant amount of *outside* funding to make the match.

4. A *Regional Research Development Program* to expand cooperative research work with the teaching universities and community colleges. Texas Tech would fund 25 percent of a joint research project that would propose to solve a regional problem. The local government and industry would supply the other 75 percent. This program had the purpose of extending Texas Tech's sphere of influence through regional development. This strategy took Texas Tech out of Lubbock and into Amarillo, El Paso, Odessa, Wichita Falls, and

Plainview. It also had the advantage of leveraging three dollars of local support for every one dollar Texas Tech put up. Unfortunately, prior to this plan the university had make no statement of support for regional research development and had committed no funds to a strategy that promised to keep Texas Tech among the first tier research universities of the State.

This plan created such a controversy over how indirect costs should be distributed on campus that Hensley (1987) conducted a "Survey of University Use of Indirect Costs" to provide factual information about overhead recovery. Hensley (March 28, 1988) published for the first time a realistic picture of the recovery and use of university indirect costs. He found that the A-21 Model has a negative influence on the conduct of science in American universities because it fails to consider the following factors in its determination of indirect costs.

1. The unrecovered indirect-costs of universities.
2. The state's levy on university recovered indirect costs.
3. The discounting of university indirect-cost rates.
4. The setting of low indirect-cost rates by sponsors.
5. The institutional diversion of recovered indirect-costs from the research infrastructure of the institution.

This information proved to be very helpful in strategic planning as it provided a more realistic set of facts and assumptions for using indirect costs to build the university research infrastructure.

DEVELOPING THE INFRASTRUCTURE TO FACILITATE RESEARCH AT TTU

In Chapter 5, we stressed the importance of positioning the architects of the future. Here, we want to stress the importance of linking the right people because it is the network of research-oriented people that forms the infrastructure for strategic planning within the research enterprise. In thinking about developing the infrastructure of the university, it is imperative to consider how to link the right university people with key people in other sectors and how to transfer critical information among them.

The infrastructure of the research enterprise does depend on equipment, facilities, and systems, but it is also very dependent upon the personal networking of individuals who serve on essential committees. The institution must have many partners and these partners must be requisitely positioned and research-development oriented. Remember, the research enterprise is an association of colleagues. Their councils, committees, professional associations, and commissions do the strategic planning. It is the vice-president's role to assure that individuals, committees, and councils are linked properly. The vice-president must see how the needs and resources of the research enterprise are connected under the purposes of the university and they must provide the commitment necessary to keep the particular development moving through all of the relevant principals and their organizations.

Developing the Proper Campus Linkage

In an earlier section, we discussed working with the academic and research councils. In this section devoted to developing the infrastructure, it bears repeating that the deans and the associate deans for research are the prime contacts for strategic planning within the college. Also, they are the people who are invaluable when the university needs input, review and support for a plan.

In 1984, the research council and the Office of Research Services had a tradition of being administration-maintenance oriented. They met monthly to discuss the administration of projects. The AVPR-Development changed the administration orientation to development orientation by placing on the research council's agenda every research development item that was being considered by the central administration. This lengthened the research council meetings, but it brought a debate and a vote to development items needing endorsement or discussion from this group. The AVPR-Development asked that all research development business be conducted around papers. He asked the principals to distribute position papers or plans several days prior to the meeting. Oral debate was limited to a reasonable time and the research council members were encouraged to write and disseminate dissenting opinions. Votes in the research council were postponed until the topic had been thoroughly discussed in the colleges. The debates over new issues were often wild and wooley, even for West Texas.

The AVPR-Development found that the members of the research council were usually the most informed persons about research planning in the college. Consequently, he frequently called on them for information and advice. Conversely, he was contacted often on special planning activities.

The vice-president developed a number of planning protocols and close working relationships with the associate deans and deans that permitted the rapid drafting of research plans by people who were very busy and who resisted frequent meetings. University research plans were usually started by the vice-president forming an ad hoc committee to develop papers that addressed a particular issue. Usually, the AVPR-Development invited two or three associate deans to serve on a committee with five or six of the faculty with experience on the issue. This ad hoc committee drafted a position paper or plan. The position paper when finished by the ad hoc committee was widely disseminated and discussed by the committee members on their home turf and then forwarded to the research council, which then debated the issue and approved or amended the committee's recommendations. The research council's recommendations were forwarded to the academic council, which also debated the issue and amended the research council's recommendations. The vice-president took their recommendations and drafted academic policy, standing operating procedures, and plans that had to be reviewed by several groups on campus before the policy or plan was adopted by the university. This may seem a lengthy process, it is. And, it is necessary for it builds in the academic community a high degree of awareness of the issues and acceptance and support for a particular plan.

The majority of planning went through the associate deans for research. However, there were times when the head of an ORU or a PI came directly to the vice-presidents with requests for assistance. When that happened they were graciously received and given a proper hearing. They were asked to prepare a short paper or a prospectus and to address the research council at their next meeting if they so desired.

Some deans tried to control planning by attempting to have it develop along an administrative chain of command in the same fashion that routine purchasing or travel are handled. Planning is different from the administration of the routine business. It must be handled differently. The vice-presidents discouraged such bureaucratic thinking as it is totally unsuited for the academy. The university is a vast reservoir of walking and book-bound knowledge. Faculty must have unencumbered access to it. Administrators should be people who point out how one can do something or point the way to someone who has a resources that can help develop another's ideas. Administrators are not arbiters of the value of ideas. They may allocate their resources according to their unit goals, but they may not try to prevent an idea from developing. Control of ideas is where the great tension lies between faculty and administration. Administrators may not control ideas. They may allocate resources, appoint committees and interpret policy and law, but they may not control the faculty's ideas.

Now and then an administrator or a support person forgets that the university is a forum where all people have the right to exchange ideas. When they forget, they should be reminded that they are the servants of the people and their reputations as good stewards rests on their always keeping the forum open and the ideas flowing. Research administrators have the responsibility of designing research development systems and then encouraging people to go beyond existing systems. The personal networking on campus facilitates the development of innovative ideas and complex planning. Good stewardship demands that the personal networking be nurtured.

The research council meetings allowed people within the university to quickly obtain an indication of the difficulty of developing a particular plan for the associate deans and directors knew what the climate for research was in various departments and they knew how to connect people to accomplish the plan. The research vice-president's role is to know who the "gatekeepers" are in the various units and how to encourage them to open their areas for innovative plans.

Long-term planning that advanced the research agenda of the university occurred also on the administrative side of the Office of Research Services. Kice (October 1, 1984) outlined in very specific terms what was being contemplated in terms of changes in the program of research incentive awards in order to focus TTU's very limited discretionary monies on the development of research centers of excellence in a more organized fashion. He asked the research council to consider and approve a new set of policies that required proposers to "show evidence of the building of additional research excellence in established areas of departmental strength or, alternatively, does it make a convincing case for the support of new thrusts designed to meet emerging disciplinary imperatives or social and industrial needs." The new policy required departments to plan long-term for the annual spending of $10,000-$20,000 of funds from the Tech research incentives program. Strickland (October 5, 1984) noted "Input from department chairmen on the revised incentive program for research were solicited prior to the October 3, 1984 research council meeting . . . Responses were reasonably uniform and generally were opposed to the change although it was noted that such a plan would allow funds to be awarded in larger amounts and provide more accountability for the use of funds." Hensley (October 15, 1984) advocated the revised policy and noted to the council: "While (the Strickland plan) is a justified maintenance approach, it does not promote our current priorities of developing Centers of Excellence. Also, it does not provide assurance of prior faculty involvement in research planning which the faculty repeatedly asked for." The research council narrowly approved the new recommendations in November of 1984.

Such exchanges were frequent. Many deans and department heads did not like having to provide assurance of faculty input into planning and they certainly did not like the accountability features. However, such changes were necessary to give the faculty more of a say in the planning and spending of university research funds and to assure that deans and department heads were accountable for university research monies. By the way, accountability is not limited to expenditures matching budgets. It is about the ability of the administrator to make the wise choice of allocation of resources for the long term. Administrators must be held accountable for their decisions.

Prior to 1984, there was no standardization for reporting on research activity. This led to some very creative reporting and poor planning information. Hensley (March 20, 1985) with the help of the research council created a set of guidelines designed to produce an array of descriptive indices that were considered as standard measures of the current conditions and that helped show trends for sponsored activities in units. In the early years of the Office of Research Services standardizing reports and accounting procedures, some deans and associate deans adopted, but did not accept, centralized reporting according to the ORS Guidelines. Later, most acknowledged the value of the centralized planning, services, and reporting. Winer (September 27, 1988), associate dean for research, College of Arts and Sciences commented:

> I forwarded to Arts & Sciences department chair-person information such as the attached report (which is the end-of-year summary), all based on information your office has provided me. I know that the Office of Research Services provides this information to the university community in a variety of ways, so this is simply one more way to try to get the message across. . . . I very much appreciate the information you share with all of us through your monthly and quarterly reports and through the research council meetings. Even more, I very much appreciate the help everyone in your office has given me in the almost thirteen months I have served as associate dean. Let me take this opportunity to say, officially, "Thank you!"

After two years of the research management information system being in place and after considerable joint planning, most of the associate deans would have echoed Dean Winer's appreciation of centralized systems and reports. They were a major component in the research infrastructure. However, it was the linkage of the people in ORS with the staffs in the several dean's offices and with other research support personnel that built an efficient network of people who knew how to acquire and process information and most importantly, who knew how to make decisions that facilitated research.

Darling (October 24, 1984) had to instruct deans, department heads, and an associate vice-president that they had to honor faculty "released time" when the faculty member bought out their teaching time with sponsored research grant monies. In some instances, faculty were obtaining grant monies to support their research time and department heads were not reducing their teaching time. The faculty complained about the department head's exploitation and the vice-president had to issue a policy that assured that faculty were actually given their "released time." Also, the central administration and deans had to return "faculty position money" earned from such released time to the earning unit. Sound policy on these and many other issues helped establish an infrastructure that supported individuals and units that were doing research. It is the role of the vice presidents for research to assure that the deans and their subordinates do not usurp the prerogatives and resources of faculty and students. Time is of course a valuable resource. Where it is spent is the prerogative of the faculty based on who buys their time. Despite university and Office of Management and Budget statements to the contrary, the university does not own 100% of the faculty's time. Universities buy from the faculty quality teaching, service, and research for reasonable periods, perhaps the forty hour work-week guides decisions on dedication of faculty time and effort. Vice-presidents must assure the fairness ethic in this regard or the infrastructure for research will decay.

The associate vice-president invited members of the faculty senate research committee to serve on the research council and in turn he attended at their invitation many of their meetings. The information supplied by ad hoc committees, such as the Faculty Senate, Research Support Study Special Committee (1988), greatly aided the university administration in assessing the state of faculty research support. Their questionnaire administered in the spring of 1988 provided the faculty's perception of the appropriateness and the functioning efficiency of systems for allowing release time for faculty research, travel, computing support, and technical and stenographic support. It rated support for graduate assistance, administrative structures, and accounting and personnel systems. Contacts with the members of the senate research committee formed valuable relationships and gave the central administration an approach to the faculty that was not available through administrative channels.

Darling in 1982 established retreats to the TTU Junction Center where the academic council and others were invited to plan the future research developments of the university for the last decades of the twentieth century. These meeting laid out an operating plan for the next year and established long-term goals for the academic side of the university. Haragan (August 27, 1987) used the academic council retreat to produce a planning document called "Texas Tech University in the Twenty-First Century." This background report guided study and discussion on campus for the next several years.

The vice-president's role in planning required a continual interaction with the Texas Tech Board of Regents on routine matters and on strategic planning. In August Vice-President Haragan asked his associate vice-presidents to provide to the regents a status report on research at Texas Tech. Hensley (August 11, 1987) approached the board of regents in the following manner:

Vice President Haragan suggested that I should make available to you information regarding new State research programs and changing law contained in H.B. 2181. Since I am not sure of the level of data and the detail of information that you would like from me, I have prepared three documents, which I will be pleased to discuss with you.

The first is a one-page *Executive Summary* providing the essential elements of the four new State research programs, the provisions of H.B. 2181 for research development, and the implications of this law for Tech.

The second is a two-page "Listing of Texas Tech University Research Development Issues, Present Status, and Selected Options Brought About by H.B. 2181."

The third document is a several-page report, *Background Information Regarding the Impact of H.B. 2181 on Research Development at Texas Tech University*, which provides in some detail secondary information that is related to statutory and social changes addressed in new state programs and changing public expectations.

In the papers and during the lengthy discussion, the AVPR-Development, strongly advocated the following: 1) An institutional policy statement supporting the legislative charge for Texas Tech to be a research university. 2) Expand Texas Tech's sphere of influence and direct service area by establishing TTU research and education centers throughout West Texas. 3) Focus new resources on university research development for centers of excellence. 4) Create an institutional environment that facilitates multidisciplinary research and organized research units. 5) Develop government-industry-university partnerships and commongrounds. 6) Initiate a new round of strategic planning for university research development. 7) Reassess the complementarity of research and graduate education for supportive program development in both functional areas. 8) Use the returned indirect costs to develop and maintain university research.

The vision and the goals of the vice-president were basically the same as those he had advocated to them three years earlier. However, facilitative legislation had created much of what had been planned in 1984 and vast amounts of new monies were now available. The new challenge for Texas Tech was competing for those monies and directing them toward further developing Texas Tech into a research university.

In addition to such formal presentations, the vice-presidents informally chatted with individual board members about these issues at luncheons, teas, and cocktail parties. The research committee of the board was a staunch supporter of the proposed research developments and created the policy necessary to effect change. Having a supportive board is an essential part of the research infrastructure. It takes a lot of time and effort on the part of the research community to develop that support.

Developing the Infrastructure for the Federal Partnership

Earlier in this chapter, the research services of the university were described. The services by the administrative personnel in the Office of

Research Services are an essential component for developing a university infrastructure that facilitates the federal-government-university partnership. Research support personnel are the people who formally connect faculty ideas with federal programs. Without them there would be no central exchange point. This office is a critical transfer point for ideas and dollars. It was the AVPR-Administration's role to provide the linkage in these routine, but essential transactions.

The role of the AVPR-Development was to work on solving the generic problems of the federal-government-university partnership. This required his knowing policy analysts and program planners in the federal research agencies and knowing how to obtain their assistance in planning for university research. In performing this role he worked through the Society of Research Administrators and National Council of University Research Administrators. The SRA national and regional meetings provided a series of research symposia that looked at the critical issues of the research enterprise. The most knowledgeable people in the government, university, and other sectors were invited to share their ideas about a specific problem of the research enterprise.

These connections allowed the research administrators to work collectively on problems of bureaucratic accretions that were burdening researchers. Since World War II the increasing time it takes to comply with federal regulations has progressively eroded the researcher-time of the investigators. This was a difficulty that Hensley and Lang addressed in 1984 in the first volume of the SRA series and later Norris (June 30, 1988), Hensley, and other Texas university research administrators addressed from the Texas Consortium and from the federal demonstration project (FDP). The FDP had as its objective the reduction of federal paperwork and elimination of direct agency approval for changes in sponsored research projects performed by universities. Also, Hensley (May 22, 1985) testified to congress on the significance of research support personnel to university research and their impact on research policy. In each of these cases, the federal government made plans to follow many of the recommendations of the university groups, thus improving the infrastructure for research on the university campus. In this instance the vice-president assumes the role of researcher in studying university research operations, in identifying the serious deficiencies in the partnership, and in planning for long-term solutions with the federal bureaucracy. This is a new role that has been assumed by few research administrator; nevertheless, it ultimately facilitates research in the federal-government-university partnership. The serious study of the research university and the research phenomena is an important role of the vice-president that should be performed more often.

Developing the Infrastructure for State Partnerships

The vice-presidents for research served on more than a dozen state commissions, coordinating committees, and study groups. As members of these commissions they influenced the long-term planning of the state. For example, the AVPR-Development served as the liaison officer for the Texas Natural Fiber & Food Protein Commission (NFFPC), which was funded by the Texas legislature. The liaison officer met semiannually with the industry advisory committee to monitor the progress of the research programs being funded through the NFFPC. The mandate for NFFPC is utilization research; to find new ways to make money by processing cotton, peanuts, oilseeds, mohair, wool, etc. Texas Tech's Textile Research Center (TRC) provided a wide range of fiber and textile testing services to fiber producers. More importantly, TRC pioneered new weaving and spinning techniques and invented new textiles by blending fibers. The legislature was very interested in the work of NFFPC and the Textile Research Center as their research had resulted in several textile factories locating in Texas.

For four years, the AVPR-Development provided senior level support to TRC Director James Parker who provided progress reports on the contracts that TRC had with the NFFPC. These research contracts with NFFPC and their affiliates were quite large and necessary to the TRC strategic plans. In February of 1988, the AVPR-Development received a telephone call from a very concerned Carl Cox, executive director of the commission, who needed help in an upcoming review by the Texas senate sunset commission. Director Cox was very anxious about mounting opposition to the NFFPC from certain political aspirants. Their rhetoric was capturing the public's attention and the rather dry research reports from NFFPC was not convincing legislators to testify in behalf of the NFFPC. Several telephone conversations with Director Cox convinced the vice-president of the gravity of the situation and motivated him to leap-frog the opposition by preparing a comprehensive report of NFFPC activities entitled, "Natural Fiber & Food Protein Commission An American Model that Challenges MITE." The NFFPC commissioners were most impressed with the report and asked Hensley to testify to the senate sunset commission and to use the report as the foundation for their justification of continuation.

After four years of listening and reading about the achievements of the NFFPC, which were truly remarkable, Hensley (April 24, 1988) was able to summarize their achievements in terms of economic payoffs that the opposition politicians had not seen before. As an academician, he had credibility and his testimony that the NFFPC operations should serve as a model for the entire nation to revitalize a faltering economy shocked the opposition. After several questions from the opposition, the very aggressive advocacy for the NFFPC by the vice-president and his cost-benefit analysis stopped the attack and the opposition started studying trend analyses that they had to support as good Texans and Americans. After the hearings were concluded, the NFFPC commissioner said that the report and the AVPR-Development's testimony turned the sunset commission from a discontinuance to a continuance recommendation. Although the executive director was too laudatory in his comments and the commissioners overly gracious, the point of recalling their remarks is to show the goodwill that was established by the study and testimony. Moreover, the public saw a plethora of concrete benefits growing from their tax dollars and the government-industry-university cooperation. The study was an aggressive response to a call from a partner needing academic skills. It cost Texas Tech over a week of the vice-president's time, a couple of weeks of a graduate assistants time, plane fare, and publication costs. The commissioners and Carl Cox did not forget the study and the network of Texas Tech research supporters was strengthened.

It is the vice-presidents role to work closely with the president in drafting recommendations for legislation that will advance research in the state sector. Hensley and Kice (October 24, 1984) informed the vice-president staff's that

> Extra compensation for academic-year work on "private" grants and contracts and a faculty overload policy, especially for faculty doing industry sponsored research should be allowed at Texas Tech, but existing state law seemed to prevent extra compensation for research although extra compensation was allowed for "teaching" overload. They also reminded the staff that "currently research and technology transfer activities were not recognized by the legislature as legitimate university activities.

These state restrictions severely hampered our development of industrial partnerships and needed to be addressed. Vice-President Darling discussed the issues with the president and Mike Sanders who agreed that it was a matter that could be best approached through the Texas Science and Technology Council and the Council of University Presidents. President Cavazos and Sanders worked with several legislators and the councils in obtaining support for a liberalization of the state's rules on faculty academic workloads. In March of 1985 Senator Edwards (1985) introduced SB 1051, which allowed institutions to

> recognize that research, technology transfer, and professional development are important elements of faculty academic workloads by giving appropriate weight to research, technology transfer, and professional development activities when determining the standards for faculty academic workload. An institution may give those activities more, less, or the same weight as classroom teaching.

Another important part of the Texas Tech strategy to develop its infrastructure was to obtain significantly more money from the State to support its centers of excellence. These centers of excellence were to be located in a research mall and university park and supported by a government-industry-university partnership. Hensley (November 3, 1984) gave to President Cavazos plans entitled "The Position of Texas Tech University in the Strategic Plan for the Development of Science and Technology in Texas" and extensive background materials related to the long-term goals of the university. Cavazos (November 11, 1984) found that the plans and materials provided by the AVPR-Development were exactly what was needed to make his committee meeting with the Texas Science and Technology Council go well. It was important in developing our research infrastructure to have our state representatives very knowledgeable about research issues and to have them acknowledged as leaders in the state organizations. A president does not have the time to do the background study for each research issue that they are required to address. Consequently, the AVPR-Development must supply him and other key executive officers with position papers, background information, and the details of plans that fit into his vision of the institution in the next decades. And, they must brief these people face-to-face on the critical points of the issue and the essential terms for extended agreements. Having senior staff who deal primarily with the research issues and long-term planning is an essential part of the research university infrastructure.

The research council members were very concerned about the advancement of graduate education and research at Texas Tech. In November they developed with Hensley (January 9, 1985) a position paper on the "The Indivisibility of Graduate Education and Research." The president used this paper in formulating a set of recommendations from the Science and Technology Council. It was the intent of the paper to promote Texas Tech University as one of the state's centers of graduate education and research. The president's influence on the Texas S&T Council and other state committees allowed the university to input its goals into the state strategic plans. Many of Texas Tech's faculty ideas were to find their way into state planning recommendations. Conversely, the president was very good about sending the minutes and plans of his state meetings to his vice-presidents who disseminated relevant information to their staff and faculty. The president was an important link between state and campus strategic planning.

The vice-president for academic affairs and research played a vital role in establishing the infrastructure for research in the state offices. Darling (July 11, 1985) worked with the commissioner of higher education, to draft the guidelines of the advanced technology research program. The Texas Tech faculty were very concerned about the state procedures for submitting proposals to the Texas advanced technology research program. Darling in June of 1985 surveyed the faculty through the deans to determine fair treatment of all in the forthcoming state competition. The faculty recommendations were forwarded to Kenneth Ashworth, commissioner of higher education, who used the ideas in the new guidelines.

Developing the Infrastructure to Support
Research Development in the Industrial Sector

Because your authors did a good deal of writing and speaking on the advantages of the government-industry-university partnership, they were invited to serve on national committees and to participate in meetings related to that partnership. Governor Dukakis (1987) and James Ebert, chairman of the roundtable, invited the AVPR-Development and thirty-four other scientists, administrators, and policy makers to participate in a workshop on "State Government Strategies for Self-Assessment of Science and Technology Programs for Economic Development." The workshop held in Washington, April 8 & 9 was sponsored by the Government-University-Industry Research Roundtable, the National Governor's Association, and the National Research Council. The purpose of the workshop was to provide a setting where state government representatives can come together with university and industry officials to examine methods for assessing the performance of state science and technology programs at universities that assist industry or are parts of collaborative efforts with industry. Participation in this and other such workshops was a first step in a continuing process of collaboration among the National Academy and state government officials. Once the participants shared views and worked together in seeking to understand better the objectives and operating assumption of the state programs, they formed a network of individuals that frequently exchanged information from their work perspectives. Your authors found the connections with other participants and the steady flow of information to be quite valuable. In return, they over the years delivered several studies to the sponsoring agencies and helped their fellow participants.

Developing the Infrastructure to Support Research
Development in the International Sector

For many years, Texas Tech University has been actively conducting research in several areas of the world. The International Center for Arid and Semi-Arid Land Studies (ICASALS) had a large number of research fellows whose international interests ranged widely from the agriculture of arid lands to urban development. In the early eighties Texas Tech was conducting several research and training projects in foreign countries and was very interested in attracting foreign students to the Lubbock Campus, especially graduate students.

In the 1970s through directing several large Agency for International Development (AID) Projects, your authors had established a personal network for international development that was working rather well in attracting large groups of students to our universities for advanced professional training. The VPAA&R in 1982 brought that network to Texas Tech. In 1982, the VPAA&R visited China and Japan and established for Texas Tech a number of cooperative agreements with sister-institutions for the exchange of faculty and students and the development of cooperative research.

A previous section dealt with how the VPAA&R asked the AVPR-Development to put together a Malaysian higher-education planning team to plan with the Malaysian government and the MARA Foundation a strategy for the development of the Malaysian higher-education system. As explained earlier, these plans resulted in the creation of cooperative agreements that established the following elements of the research infrastructure: 1) the Texas Consortium for International Development, 2) a TTU pre-professional program in Shah Alam, Malaysia, 3) a TTU program for professional education of Malaysian students on the TTU and cooperating campuses, 4) an exchange of faculty, 5) a system for cooperative development of science, engineering, business, and agricultural programs, and 6) a cooperative research program.

The Malaysian Project was a major part of the TTU strategic plan for developing the university infrastructure for research at Texas Tech. The TTU planning team spent several months planning the long-term (10 years) development of Malaysian-Texas consortium higher-education partnership. The planning time was well spent because it resulted in a multimillion dollar contract with the MARA Foundation, it afforded our faculty an excellent opportunity to gain international education experience and to carry on research in a foreign country, it brought hundreds of Malaysian students to our campuses, and it established a number of strong personal friendships and professional collaborations that have lead to many other significant project developments. This seminal project in Malaysia based our faculty and institution strategically in Southeast Asia.

Similar planning occurred for other international developments in China, Japan, Africa, South America, Turkey, and Saudi Arabia. The China strategy is explained more fully under the AVPR-Development section of this chapter. Idris Traylor, director of ICASALS and Behrens were continually planning with faculty and students for future developments. Director Traylor spent a great deal of time abroad and on campus arranging collaborative academic efforts. He was an essential element in the infrastructure of the institution. His vast network of friends and colleagues carried ideas into practice. Idris was enormously valuable to our research efforts. Each of ICASALS's developments further built the foundations for the faculty and students to do research in foreign countries. A research university must have agreements with several sister institutions to do cooperative work and they must have a continual exchange of scholars.

James Jonish's and George Peng's (ICASAL Staff and Fellows) planning for Fullbright-Hayes fellowships for TTU faculty bears special mention here because this continuing effort placed dozens of Texas Tech faculty for a summer or an academic year in a foreign country to conduct cooperative research. Jim's planning and research development efforts to place large teams of faculty in a particular country for focussed study were brilliant and sustained. Many faculty and students benefited immensely from his plans to develop cooperative research on arid lands. The AVPR-Development owes Jim and George a considerable debt for conceiving the original plan that helped him gain Fullbright support for his scholarly efforts in China in 1988. Many other TTU faculty owe Jim Jonish and George Peng similar debts for establishing a long-term plan for research development in China and other countries with large expanses of arid and semiarid land.

FORMULATING THE STRATEGIC PLAN
FOR THE DEVELOPMENT OFFICE

Prior to 1982, Texas Tech had received modest gifts and some large endowments for scholarships, distinguished chairs, and buildings through random and uncoordinated efforts. Sometimes those efforts placed colleges and individual faculty members within the university in competitive positions within a particular foundation or corporation. In some instances, local donors and state corporations complained to the president of the duplicative and uncoordinated fund raising efforts and requested an organized approach from the university.

In the seventies, the development office lacked a strategic plan and its staff performed their operations without standardization from very cramped quarters in a dingy suite located in the business wing of the Administration Building. There was literally no place in the old development office where the development officers could plan with donors. A strategic plan, private offices, uniform policies and procedures across campus, computerized files, and support personnel for professional development officers are essential to any successful and efficient operation that involves intensive planning with the donors from the nonprofit sector. It was apparent to the executive officers of the university that a development strategy, new facilities, and new staff were desperately needed for the Development Office.

The planning process for university advancement and the organizational structure of the development office changed dramatically with the appointment of John Bradford as vice-president for development in 1983. Bradford, who had served successfully as the dean of the College of Engineering for almost two decades, knew most and had strong friendships with many of the chief executive officers in Texas. In addition, he had definite ideas about the development process and how a development office should be structured and operated. In less than a year, John Bradford completely reorganized Texas Tech's development activities and established modern efficient operating systems in appropriately furnished quarters. The ability to transform the development services and to change its image overnight rested on the research-development orientation and persuasive personality of John Bradford.

President Cavazos' appointment of John Bradford as vice-president for development was welcomed by the research community for it meant they had another advocate for research in a senior administrative position. Bradford's research and administrative career indicated that he understood what had to be done to develop research. The research community was not disappointed in his planning for research and in his restructuring of the development program. His dedication to research and his administrative acumen advanced research development funds on the Texas Tech campus rapidly and significantly. Bradford development-orientation and his belief in the payoff for strategic planning originated in his conceiving and implementing a strategy for the College of Engineering (COE) developing a corp of elite engineers who would support engineering research at Texas Tech. In 1965, as dean of the College of Engineering, Bradford established the distinguished engineers program at Texas Tech. The COE started this program to recognize the accomplishments of Texas Tech graduates and to create an elite group of alumni who later would be in corporate positions and would be personally able to advance the college in many ways.

Each year the college selected former Texas Tech engineering students who had distinguished themselves by extraordinary professional achievements and who had made significant contributions outside their professional responsibilities. Bradford (1984) recalled that it took over a decade for most of the "distinguished engineers" to become chief executives in large corporations. And, it took thirteen years before any large gifts were given to the college by distinguished engineers. However, between the thirteenth and eighteenth year of the program, the distinguished engineers accounted for more than $8 million given to the college. That high level of financial giving from that elite group of engineers continues to increase.

The distinguished engineers program is a perfect example of putting a strategy into place and sticking with it until it has achieved its purpose. Bradford maintains the dollar amount is a poor indicator of the effectiveness of the program. He likes to point to the enhancement of the college's and the university's reputation by its distinguished graduates, the many specific research projects awarded from companies employing the alumni, and the scholarships, the summer employment and cooperative programs that came from the engineering faculty working with their alumni.

The Planning Process for the Development Office

Early in 1983, Vice-President for Development Bradford recommended to the president's executive council, the board of regents and his development council the acceptance of a strategic plan designed to accomplish the following objectives.

To develop principles and procedures for the conduct of a university-wide development of programs, including: 1) the organizational restructuring necessary for conducting several new development programs and establishing related lines of communications and responsibilities; and 2) the adoption of a generally acceptable timetable for the implementation of the strategy.

To describe the role of the following principals in the development process and to establish standing operating procedures for development work under the new plan: 1) academic planning and participation, which the president and Bradford saw as essential to the ultimate success of the strategy, was to be coordinated through the Development Office. 2) Identification and research on prospective donors were to be handled by both academicians and development officers depending on an appropriate approach to the donor. All requests to visit potential donors were to be channeled through the development office. This was a particularly thorny problem that required a great deal of campus planning as prior to 1982 faculty and administrators pursued donors at will. 3) Goal-setting by the principals. This required a great amount of Development Office leadership to establish realistic goals in the university units. 4) Cultivation and involvement of prospective donors and the selection of university and external leaders for specific development programs was to be coordinated through the Development Office. 5) Formation of distinct development phases for different programs and campaigns was to be planned by the members of the Development Council, and 6) establishing an annual giving program that was separate from the capital campaign.

To determine the main elements of the current programs supporting the development strategy and plan for the communication of their place in advancing the university.

To establish a plan for prospect cultivation and prospect clearance procedures from the Development Office.

To plan and recommend a series of budgets related to the programs included in the strategic development plan.

To plan for new quarters and services that were commensurate with the expectations of the university for the Development Office.

Planning and Changing the Policies for Development

Vice-President Bradford became the architect for several key documents that guided strategic planning for development on the Texas Tech Campus. The Development Offices' *Policies and Procedures Manual for Institutional Development* provided the guidelines to implement the board of regents' intent to have a centralized service, which was to be primarily responsible for all programs and activities relating to the development of private sector support for the university and its components. The board gave the authority for the final approval of all internal plans, programs, activities, and procedures for raising private sector funds to the president who delegated that authority to the vice-president for development.

This new policy gave the Office of Development the oversight responsibility for all planning and for the coordination of the programs and activities of all groups and organizations affiliated with Texas Tech that relied on private sector support. This brought about a radical change in practice. University policies were not liked by many deans, department heads, faculty, and heads of many of the support groups who had been operating according to their own entrepreneurial bent. The president and his executive council were rightfully blamed for the board policy. The intent of the board and the Development Office policies manual was resisted by some key campus figures, who continually complained of more bureaucratic control. Some resistors were persons, who had their own development activities in operation and didn't want to report their activities to a central university authority. Criticism of the Development Office came from persons who had always relied on state appropriations and who saw no benefit accruing to a state university from the private sector.

The resistance was handled very well by Vice-President Bradford and his staff who continually worked with unit heads to make them aware of the services provided by the Development Office. They helped the unit heads to develop their own plans for enhancing the unit image and supporting research and graduate studies with private funds. Some of these unit plans were excellent and the return on unit planning was extraordinary. The authors can trace much of the success of unit advancement plans to the Development Office's strategy for upgrading unit advancement efforts. Again, to demonstrate the importance of personalities to strategic planning, the authors have to mention Bradford's personal, successful, development activities and research experience, which he shared in formal and informal ways with unit heads. He was a reservoir of development information and his availability to help in unit planning was a tremendous asset. Centralization of planning and operational authority for development was in the authors' opinion an unpopular, but necessary stratagem for the present phase of university advancement and certainly, the success of the development strategy could not have been achieved without it.

The *Policies Manual* set the development philosophy on campus. Its main motivation was the encouragement of private sector financial support from alumni, students, faculty-staff, parents, corporations, foundations, associations, and friends. Private gifts were seen as having power far beyond their face value. The plan required applying private support selectively to specific areas of the academic and research programs with the objective of making an immediate—sometimes dramatic—difference in the university's ability to achieve academic and research excellence and superiority.

The Development Office operated on the assumptions that excellence in research and education is established by endowment levels that reflect carefully identified needs within the university. The entire campus reviewed President Cavazos' recommended guidelines for endowment levels in 1981 and 1982. After considerable bickering over levels and exceptions for existing standards within certain units, the board of regents (1983) set the following endowment levels for most unit plans: 1,000,000—endowed chair; 500,000—endowed professorship; 200,000—endowed fellowship; 100,000—endowment for research and development programs; 50,000—endowed lectureships; 35,000—regental scholarship; 25,000—presidential scholarship; 20,000—dean's scholarship; 10,000—departmental scholarship; 5,000—designated scholarship.

The academic community and the major supporters of Texas Tech were brought into the planning for the standards for each of aforementioned categories. These endowment levels and attendant standards were to guide planning of endowed academic positions until the turn of the century when they would be reviewed.

The propensity for the vice-president for development for strategic planning is seen in his *Capital Campaign Plan 1983*. Bradford (1983) introduced the plan by saying

> The present plan presents a general design for the successful conduct of a campaign for Texas Tech University and the Texas Tech University Health Sciences Center. The campaign will consist of three main phases, of which the first—Advanced/Major Gifts—is most important. Together with supplementary or "satellite" plans for each phase, this campaign plan will comprise the master blueprint for all operations of the university's development from 1983 through 1990.

Although this classic plan is much too lengthy for reproduction, the capital campaign timetable is mentioned to call attention to a specific plan in the Development Office that raised more than $60 million for capital improvements in a three year period. That plan and the process required to develop it greatly increased the sophistication of planning on campus. The monies obtained from that program raised many programs from mediocre to good programs and advanced good programs into centers for excellence.

The process of planning the capital campaign at Texas Tech illustrates the increasing complexity of planning for research in major universities. Bradford suggested to the president that he appoint Fred Bucy, a "distinguished Texas Tech engineer," the president and chief executive officer of Texas Instruments, and member of the Texas Tech Board of Regents as the national chairman of the enterprise Campaign. Bucy, President Cavazos, and the development staff spent hundreds of hours planning with alumni chapters their development strategies. They personally visited local chapters and assisted with individual development efforts. These pioneering efforts of the early eighties established the model and a base of good will for the successful operations of today.

Executive Director of the Development Office, John Anderson and the Research Development Office created a Texas Tech data file of several hundred businesses that it wanted to approach for matching gifts to further research. This data file was obtained by using data from national directories and from the specific directions of faculty who had developed inside contacts with corporate officers. The matching gifts file was used by faculty and development officers to send announcements of industrial opportunities and to send letter of inquiry to heads of nonprofit organizations and corporations. Matching gift data was helpful in allowing the various colleges to design their strategy and then to compare it with the other colleges' matching gift plans.

John Bradford held monthly planning sessions with deans, senior administrators, and key community leaders to help them keep-up with the strategy for building the matching gift program and to improve communication with their corporate sponsors. Prior to Bradford's introduction of these special planning sessions, there had been considerable confusion on campus as to who should approach corporate officers for matching gifts and under what circumstances. These issues were discussed thoroughly in Development Office sponsored breakfasts and special meetings. Out of these special meeting came a set of understandings that evolved into plans and guidelines on how companies providing matching gifts would be approached and how they should be given recognition for their contributions.

Part of Brad's planning genius rested on his establishing the right positions in his organization and then finding the right development people to fill these positions. One of the positions established in Texas Tech's Development Office to help in creating the strategy for improving corporate funding for university research was the director of planned giving.

Karen Wilson (1986), the first director of planned giving worked very closely with the board of regents, the Enterprise Campaign National Steering Committee, the Enterprise Campaign Local Steering Committees (Lubbock, Dallas, Amarillo, Midland, Houston, Austin, Fort Worth, San Antonio), the Texas Tech University Foundation and Texas Tech Medical Foundation.

In the first section of this chapter, we wrote about the importance of positioning research-development-oriented persons in requisitely organized structures. The appointment of Karen Wilson as the director of the new Office of Planned Giving demonstrates the value of giving due attention to the first phase of strategic planning. Director Wilson's intelligence, personality, and professional training as an attorney helped her to be very effective in planning with donors to use current tax reform packages to improve their financial position and to advance specific areas of the university and the Health Sciences Center. As an example, she introduced at Texas Tech the Short-Term Charitable Lead Trust, which allowed the donor to create for a term of ten years or less a charitable fund that had several tax advantages for the donor and provided an annual income to the university for the term of the trust. At the end of the trust term the original trust property is returned to the donor. In our scan of the nonprofit impact area, the director of Planned Giving Tax Update stands out as a valuable stratagem. This informative brief was sent to potential donors and university strategists to assist the researcher and the donor in long-term planning for advancing a particular area. Her professional assistance in drafting the Short-Term Charitable Lead Trust and other legal documents was an essential service in the development process.

The Development Office's assistance in unit planning was vital to designing the university's strategic plan. For example, the strategic planning of the College of Business Administration, which became part of the university strategy, was summarized in a document entitled "Preparing a New Generation of Business Achievers." In this special edition of *Texas Tech Business*, a magazine published by the College of Business Administration (COBA), Dean Carl Stem (1985) and the COBA faculty explained why tax-supported business schools must plan for and depend on private funding to achieve excellence. The COBA planners let all college alumni, Texas business, and its many friends and supporters know that Gift income in 1985 contributed 30% of the operational resources of the college. COBA planned to support all of their development program, alumni and external relations activities entirely from gift income. In this document they explained their plan to use 80% of the annual fund and the college endowment income to support students on scholarships and to pay for supportive services. Their strategy relied on 50% of their faculty development and research resources to be derived from gift income. This development planning in COBA significantly advanced their research capabilities and enhanced their image. Other colleges had different strategies, but all were actively involved in strategic planning for the development of private sector partnerships to advance their units. The unit plans formed and tested in the mid-eighties are now incorporated into the operating and tactical plans of the colleges.

The value of people to the strategic planning process is seen in Bradford's appointment of Gary J. McNamara to the position of director of development research. McNamara brought a number of new ideas on how the university should plan for the long-term partnerships with the nonprofit sector. He developed for the first time procedures for working with prospects and worked with individual units in setting their first-generation plans for achieving successful solicitations. Gary was particularly good at determining the place of a particular individual or foundation in the development plans for a department and then bringing in the pledge that would provide long-term support for a specific research thrust. Gary helped William Marcy, director of the SMART lab raise private sector support for development of robots to work in cleanrooms in which microchips are made. He also worked for private-sector support of Feola's work on developing a human blood source from stroma-free hemoglobin solutions (SFHS) extracted from the blood of healthy, commercially plentiful Hereford cattle. The success of the plans for developing the aforementioned individual research projects and many others rested on countless hours of Gary and other development staff discussing with donors the plans of individual principal investigators and listening to the donor's goals for giving to Texas Tech. After this development-research was completed and a commitment made, they then prepared a long-term development agreement for donor support of a specific organized research unit. This work is very dependent on personalities.

The highlighting of the of Development Office's functions and the expertise of its personnel should make the point that planning with partners in the nonprofit sector is very complicated and without them a strategic plan for research will not be accomplished. Bradford's (1985) "Seven Steps to Successful Giving," and his exhortations for doing Homework! Research! Planning! and Cultivation form a framework for a successful strategy for the nonprofit sector.

THE IMPORTANCE OF THE PRESIDENT
IN STRATEGIC PLANNING

Keller (1983,125) has described rather well the importance of the president in strategic planning. Your authors echo his sentiments that

> A president should supply the emotional injections that jolt faculty, students, and
> staff out of their tendencies to coast. He or she needs to hold out visions of poten-
> tialities and worthy objectives that motivate others to perform beyond the ordinary.
> Leadership is the poetic part of the presidency. It sweeps listeners and participants
> up into the nobility of intellectual and artistic adventures and the urgency of thinking
> well and feeling deeply about the critical issues of our time.

We too found that the university planning process was dependent upon
the personal initiatives of the president and upon his approval of major research plans developed at lower levels of the administrative hierarchy.
Lauro F. Cavazos was president of Texas Tech University and Texas Tech
University Health Science Center from 1980 to 1988. He understood the
strategic planning processes very well and used them to project his and
other's visions of what the university could become. He saw Texas Tech
becoming an institution of the first rank.

Person-to-Person Planning

President Cavazos (1985a) was very fond of talking about "Opportunities as far as the eye can see." He liked to stand with visitors on the east-
ern edge of the campus and look to the west. He would tell a dramatic story
of the pioneering spirit of Texas Tech and point out the past developments
that filled the western horizon with Texas Tech buildings. This was his
alma mater and he loved to discuss how the faculty and Texas were building
a first-rate comprehensive research university that is second to none in excellence, beauty, usability, diversity, and spaciousness. He knew every one
of the hundreds of buildings, departments, and organized research units in
that vista. Moreover, he knew the people and the research that was being
conducted there. Although he stressed the importance of research, his role
was much larger and he neglected nothing in his exposition of the achievements of Texas Tech. He was very personable and persuasive when he discussed with groups the opportunities at Texas Tech. He talked with
enthusiasm about the world-renowned Peter Hurd mural in the rotunda of
Texas Tech's Holden Hall and how that famous work captured the spirit of
optimism and willingness of the university to see things with new eyes. He
would stop his sweeping narrative by pointing out on the far northwest
horizon the massive buildings of TTU Health Science Center, which
provides health education for citizens of Texas and patient care for the West
Texas region.

His personally guided tours would end in his office where he would show
his visitors models of future developments and give them specialized
brochures aimed at their interests and Texas Tech's development goals. He
would discuss with them Texas Tech's needs for an enhancement of its state
funding, growth in its private funding, and additional industrial support to

help sustain and build an even greater faculty, to attract even more productive students, to develop new programs, and to construct the facilities necessary to prepare students and the region for the challenges of the twenty-first century. This personal tour was given to hundreds of potential Texas Tech supporters, few left without becoming a participating planning partner and a contributing supporter to Texas Tech.

Informal and Formal Planning Sessions with the President

Within the university, the president devoted a great amount of time and effort to informal planning sessions with faculty and constituency leaders and to formal planning sessions with his executive council and the board of regents.

The authors found he was particularly fond of bringing groups of academicians and administrators into his office for informal planning sessions related to faculty members' ideas for advancing the university or related to a community leader's ideas for a joint venture or a request for research. These informal sessions, which were a critical activity in the planning process, were quite effective in generating items for the university research agenda of the strategic plan. These informal meetings were frequently called by the president after he had received a decision element, a prospectus, or a preliminary proposal describing a research plan that would involve the long-term commitment of major university resources to a particular program.

The principal investigator and their administrative supporters or the community leaders were given a half-hour to an hour to explain the scope of the work, the organization of the ORU, its goals, and the blue-sky plans of the developers. During these meetings the president listened intently for the long-term goals and personal commitments of the principal investigators and their administrators or for the goals of community leaders and their commitments to the venture. He always asked a series of penetrating questions about the impact of the project on various constituencies and he wanted to know how the project would ultimately enhance the institutional reputation and how the developers intended to finance its immediate and long-term operation. If the principal investigators or business leaders were convincing, they were encouraged to put their ideas into formal proposals for projects, centers and institutes or to incorporate the project into formal departmental or ORU plans. At the end of these sessions, he would indicate to the principal investigator which of his executive officers would be responsible for the development of the plan and he would explain to the PI a particular pattern for the development of that project. After the meeting with the president, the vice-president for research would set-up a planning team that would shepherd the fledgling project through the pitfalls of project and program development. The president would receive periodic progress reports about the specific plans and would see the final plan when the proposal was ready for institutional endorsement. Sometimes, this planning process took months to develop a working proposal.

It is easy to show the importance of documents in a paper-trail related to formal planning. It is more difficult to show the value of the informal planning sessions in the research development process as the verbal content of the many meetings is now lost. Despite the lack of documentary evidence, the authors want to make the point that the informal meetings and the early discussions about project feasibility were vitally important to the development of organized research. The president's informal planning sessions were of value to the vice-president for academic affairs and research and his research planning teams because the president gave clear signals as to how he felt about a specific organized research unit in its seminal stage of development. Usually, these chats and sharing of ideas buoyed the spirits of an entrepreneur with a realistic plan, for they often received the president's personal assurance that he would support the development of the outlined work. Invariably, these plans soon found their way into the agenda for the executive council and board of regents planning sessions. Plans approved by these bodies were strongly advocated by the president and some consideration for funding was initiated by him or his staff.

Guiding the University Planning Teams

At times, he personally organized specific university planning teams. Usually, he called on members of his executive council, staff, and members of the board of regents to act as the chair of a planning team. In consultation with his chairperson, he would appoint several faculty and community members to serve on a particular team or committee. He knew what he wanted from the team and spent considerable time with member explaining their role and objectives. Typically, the president's procedures for developing a formal plan consisted of the following steps.

1. Determine the specific needs of a particular constituency.
2. Assign responsibility to his staff for developing plans to meet those specific needs.
3. Issue a set of guidelines for the development process for each plan.
4. Set deadlines for staff development of specific plans.
5. Establish a review process by the principals in the planning operation.
6. Set the agenda for future development

How he established plans has been explained in the preceding section related to the development of the Enterprise Campaign. President Cavazos understood the importance of his leadership in research planning and development activities. He called press conferences for major development activities and introduced the chairperson for the activity and explained to the press the importance of the activity to the long-term goals of the university and its partners. The press announcement provided a general awareness of the new programs being launched from the president's office. His personal magnetism came across on television and created great respect for him in West Texas.

The Influence Paths of the President

Presidents are very interested in maintaining university support from a large number of constituencies. Lauro Cavazos, president of Texas Tech University and Texas Tech Health Science Center, was no exception. The West Texas Community, the state, and national agencies frequently used the president as the first point of contact for planning involving the university. The president responded often as a good neighbor and partner by offering to lend assistance in mutual planning. This meant that once the president made a commitment to a joint venture a faculty member had to be found and asked to do the planning and research. Despite the fact that TTU had a MIS system that listed faculty capabilities and interests, the task of convincing a faculty member to perform a service for a community or an interest group is difficult even when the faculty is paid handsomely for the work and most often they were expected to do the planning and development work gratuitously. Faculty are extremely independent in choosing research topics. (This is as it should be for allowing decision-making at points of competency and for preserving academic freedom.) Business people and community leaders oftentimes, incorrectly assume that a university president has the same control over the faculty that a plant manager has over hourly employees. Consequently, they have a false sense of expectation of what the president can actually do and they often make unreasonable demands for university services. Despite the local communities' inflated expectations of what he could do, President Cavazos was exceptionally good at bringing community leaders together with academicians for joint planning.

His close working relationship with the presidents of chambers of commerce and local business leaders resulted in Texas Tech conducting economic trends and community impact studies that set the groundwork for Texas Tech University gathering data about the interaction between the university and its communities. Cavazos and Stafford (1981) approved joint planning for university and community economic development that demanded very broad investigations that served as a basis for evaluating the extant economic situation and for developing future plans. Analysts from the Office of Planning, under the direction of Professors Rouse and Jonish of the Department of Economics, studied personnel and financial data gathered in the university and surrounding communities that resulted in an historical and current analysis of the economic impact of the university on the surrounding communities.

The Design Process for the 1982 Campus Master Plan

President Cavazos (1982a) gave Bray, director of planning the responsibility for the development of a new comprehensive campus master plan. The president insisted that "This Campus Master Plan is to be based upon a careful study of actual needs at the university." He felt that certain steps in the planning process were so important that he prescribed that the planning effort should be guided by the following principles:

1. A detailed five-year plan should be developed, as required by the Coordinating Board; however, we should also have a general plan through the year 1999.
2. The plan should provide for improvement in pedestrian flow, vehicle traffic, and parking.
3. The plan should provide for preserving the traditional and unique features of the Texas Tech campus.
4. A planning process should be used which is based upon sound enrollment projections and objective space formulas for each departmental area. Space formulas, or standards, should be used to determine the actual needs for both academic and nonacademic departments. The planning process should also include an "appeals" process for equitable consideration of nonformula needs that might be required by departments.

The president was also insistent that Bray devise a calendar for development of specific plans, which could then be reviewed by the principals in the planning process.

In 1983, the president appointed the Texas Tech University Planning Committee for the purpose of developing a strategic plan for Texas Tech University. This planning committee, widely representative of the university community, included representatives from the Office of the Vice-President for Academic Affairs, Office of Development, engineering, housing and food services, sciences, fine arts, business, economics, and the director of planning, Robert Bray.

In December of 1984, the Texas Tech University Planning Committee released their first document, *Strategic Decision Area—Part I Definition of Basic Philosophy and Value*. Part I of the strategic plan was debated in the faculty senate, in the academic council and in the colleges. The committee members heard testimony on a large number of issues and reviewed recommendations from the senate and other organizations. In June of 1986, the committee published *A Strategic Plan Phase I* consisting of the following parts.

Part I—Strategic Decision Areas: Definition of Basic Philosophy and
    Values
Part IIA—Executive Summary of Environmental Scan
Part IIB—Environmental Scan
Part III—Goals for the Next Three Biennia.

This 120 page document first determined what decisions had already
been made concerning the mission and role of Texas Tech University.
Secondly, it provided the environmental scan to see how the future might
affect the university, and third the committee recommended goals for the
future. The goals were framed in biennia to more closely correlate with the
existing tactical planning that was responsive to legislative demands. It
was the intent of the president, the planning committee and the planning office staff that the information in the strategic plan would be useful to individual departments in their planning. The president's office delivered
valuable help in all planning efforts by providing personal leadership, data,
data analysis, and training in specific planning techniques. The TTU Planning Committee (1986, 91-92) in assessing Texas Tech University in the
competitive research environment drew the following implications.

> Texas Tech University simply does not have the financial resources to compete with
> the top ranked public research universities. However, TTU has all the pieces in place to
> move into the first rank if there were a breakthrough in the interdisciplinary approach to
> research, or if two or three good new ideas developed at TTU were to catch hold.
>
> The role of TTU in the West Texas area is that of a flagship institution. It is the only
> school with doctoral and special professional programs. It is the only West Texas institu-
> tion listed in the top 125 research universities by amount of research expenditures. It has
> broad undergraduate and graduate curricula that are not seriously challenged by any
> other institution within 300 miles. More people from the West Texas region attend TTU
> than any other institution.
>
> In order for TTU to become a university of the first rank, innovative leadership and
> faculty dedication are necessary.
>
> Innovative leadership will be required to: obtain resources to foster excellence;
> develop a mechanism to foster or reward interdisciplinary research efforts; and to iden-
> tify the ideas or research that could be used as the springboard to bring TTU into the first
> rank of research universities.
>
> The state will not fund a push for excellence in West Texas, especially if it is perceived
> as a loss of funds in another part of the state. Dedication on the part of faculty is needed to
> continue moving the institution forward and to maintain a position where, if resources
> and opportunities become available, TTU can emerge as a top-ranking institution.

Liaison with State Planners

The president was very effective as a state higher-education leader. In
positioning his architects for strategic planning, the president employed
Mike Sanders, an attorney, who had an abundance of Texas political savvy
as the director of public affairs. Director Sanders spent much of his time in

Austin, the Texas state capital, serving as the legislative liaison for Texas Tech and he kept the university informed of the Texas legislative plans, the governor's initiatives, new coordinating board policies, and select committee mandates. More importantly, he was the person who gained acceptance of the academic and research plans that had to be approved by the legislature or a state agency.

In June of 1984, Texas Governor, Mark White, created through Executive Order MW-24 the Texas Science and Technology Council. The Governor appointed President Cavazos and twenty-eight other distinguished citizens to research, develop, and report to the governor the means available to the State of Texas to become a national leader in science and technology development.

Later in the year, Texas Science and Technology Council Chairman, Mike Waterman created four study committees and appointed the following chairmen: Research— Hans Mark, chancellor, University of Texas System; Education—Lauro Cavazos, president of Texas Tech University and Health Sciences Center; Technology Development and Transfer—Bob Kirk, CEO of LTV; and Legislation and Policy—Henry Cisneros, mayor, City of San Antonio. President Cavazos' key role on the Texas Science and Technology Council allowed him to provide a strong influence on the plans of the S&T Council, and in turn, the council's plans became part of Texas Tech's environmental scan materials and were incorporated into our scenarios for option considerations.

At the request of the president, the AVPR-Development lead a planning team that prepared an environmental scan, several scenarios and options, and a series of recommendations for research development that became a plan for "The Position of Texas Tech University in the Strategic Plan for the Development of Science and Technology in Texas." Hensley (November 3, 1984) supplied these plans and 340 pages of background information that addressed in considerable detail the following factors:

1. The indivisibility of graduate education and research and the need for the State of Texas to increase support for graduate programs that would attract world-class investigators and superior graduate students to the research universities of Texas.

2. The many connections between university research and graduate education and the progression of technological innovation from basic research to the production lines of Texas industries. The need for Texas to fund significant foundation programs to support basic research, applied research, development efforts, production research, and technology innovation.

3. The linkage between state support for graduate education, basic research and federal grants for research, and graduate student stipends. The benefits to the universities and to the State of Texas if the legislature would allow the universities of the state to retain their indirect costs to aid in the development of undergraduate and graduate research was shown by anecdotal accounts of success in other states.

4. The success of states such as North Carolina, California, and Massachusetts in using their education facilities to develop government-industry-university partnerships for attracting industry to their states. The vice-president for academic affairs and research's position papers noted that Texas needed to make a clear, continuing commitment to providing a firm foundation of support for departmental research and graduate education.

5. The paper, "The Position of TTU in the Strategic Plan for the Development of Science and Technology in Texas," stressed the necessity for the State of Texas to assist the research universities in developing research common grounds (research park) where graduate students, professional scientists, engineers, and technicians could meet to conduct the sophisticated science, advanced technology and elegant education that is possible only on research common grounds. It discussed ways of maintaining the research infrastructure and developing research park plans.

President Cavazos, a very convincing public speaker, used his position as chair of the Texas S&T Council's education committee to advocate the adoption of elegant education, advanced technology, and sophisticated science plans of Texas Tech University into the Texas science and technology strategic planning. Cavazos (November 11, 1984) found that the material provided by the vice-president was exactly the background information and plan needed to make his committee meeting go well.

President Cavazos monitored at the state level new opportunities for research funding. When the State of Texas introduced its Advanced Technology Program he immediately informed his executive council of the state initiatives and its deadlines. Cavazos (1985a) distributed a memorandum to key academic officers informing them that the just passed appropriations bill contained provision for $35 million to be appropriated to the coordinating board "for distribution to certain eligible institutions of higher education to further advanced technological research and instruction." He started immediate planning by requesting

Texas Tech to be in the forefront with proposals for use of this money. While we are waiting for the Coordinating Board's guideline we should make the most of the time and get our ideas together for proposal so that we can react immediately to the guidelines and

put ourselves in position for strong consideration. I ask that you give this your prompt attention.

   Additionally, I am asking the Vice-President for Academic Affairs and Research to establish a suitable coordinating group within the Academic Council to facilitate the early
compilation of proposals and to ensure a thorough interchange of information and joint
action as necessary on proposal ideas.

Through the efforts of Mike Sanders the university community had
known for over a year that such a bill was being drafted and that it had a
high probability of being passed. The vice-president for academic affairs
and research and his staff had prepared the academic community for the
possibility that the legislature would establish a program that would enhance the state's economic recovery by focussing resources on universities
and industries jointly developing advanced technology projects.

   The associate vice-president for research-development had followed
very closely the drafting of the bill and had made specific recommendations to members of the state legislature for certain provisions of the bill.
During the drafting of the bill, the AVPR-Development had discussed with
the research council the economic recovery motivation for the bill and emphasized that the selection criterion for projects would weigh the projects
potential to contribute to the development of knowledge and instruction in
advanced and emerging technologies that hold substantial promise of great
benefit to the people of Texas. Also, the research council knew that the
money would be awarded through a competitive program rather than to the
general support of on-going research at eligible institutions. This meant
that TTU faculty would be competing with faculty from the other major research universities in the State. The associate vice-president urged the
faculty to link their established research interests with an industrial concern that might want to carry the laboratory innovation into commercialization. He felt that conceptually sound proposals supported by industry
would enhance the faculty members chances of being funded. This
strategy proved to be correct. It was no great insight on the part of the associate VP because he was only acknowledging the history of such
programs in Ohio and Pennsylvania, which the Texas legislators saw as
successful models. As we discussed earlier in this chapter, the associate VP
for research suggested that the university should hold a two-day planning
conference to bring industry leaders onto the campus for a period of intense
planning for advanced technology. The president immediately picked-up
the idea and started planning with local and state representatives for the
conference. Throughout its long development, the president was very supportive of the idea and urged its implementation. Although the university
needed to be planning with industry, many faculty sneered at the thought of
doing development work and resented the president's urging them to work

with industry. The establishment of the Advanced Technology Research Program was the perfect entree for the reconsideration of joint planning with industry.

Developing Private Sector Funding

Lauro Cavazos, a graduate of Texas Tech, saw his university taking giant steps toward its education and research goals through the legislature adopting plans for building the basic components of a sound public institution and for the private sector providing supplementary funds that would advance Texas Tech toward national recognition as a center for scholarly inquiry. Early in his presidency he saw the importance of a large endowment to the university. He determined that his major focus would rest on dramatically increasing the endowment base of the university and the Health Sciences Center. His motto was "Education for tomorrow's world." And, his major strategy was the development of the Enterprise Campaign, which was designed to attract large, private-sector contributions to Texas Tech for research. He designed and implemented the strategy exceedingly well—the campaign exceeded its goals. But, most importantly, it jolted faculty and alumni into thinking differently about Texas Tech and how it was to be supported.

Cavazos (1982) in making his environmental scan recognized that state sources of support were becoming scarcer and more difficult to acquire. He always pointed out to his many constituencies that shortfalls in oil, gas and agriculture production had forced serious cutbacks in legislative appropriations for Texas Tech. He acknowledged that faculty were improving in their ability to acquire research grants, but he stressed that such funds did not address the long-term research development problems and, eventually, the ability of Texas Tech to meet its mission as a research university. He emphasized that the shortfall in state appropriations came at a time when the social expectations for education were at their highest, that an increasingly technological society demands not only highly-trained professionals, but researchers capable of providing leadership in an advanced technological society, and that science and technology in the early eighties was demanding ever more expensive equipment and facilities. He stressed the need for Texans joining with Texas Tech to provide the elegant education, sophisticated science, and the advanced technology that would allow Texas to diversify its economy and to attract high tech industry to West Texas.

In his many meetings with the public, he gave specific examples of the highly complex and vitally important research requirements of certain faculty for state-of-the-art facilities and equipment. He appealed to Texans to not allow Texas Tech to fall behind in any area as the economic competition is too keen to allow other areas to get a step ahead. He liked to appeal to the competitive nature of Texas Tech supporters. He would usually end his speeches by urging Texans to join with Texas Tech in planning for the achievement of a specific challenge in a series of goals that would advance Texas Tech toward its quest for national recognition as a center for excellence in learning and research experiences. He was very successful in convincing the private sector supporters that individuals, foundations, and corporations would have to build a giant endowment to support a nationally recognized research university.

On the campus he told the faculty that they could build Texas Tech into a truly great public university by forming multiple partnerships with the private sector. At convocations and in departmental chats, he encouraged the faculty to seek private sector support as supplemental to legislative funding. He worked closely with certain deans and investigators to bring private sector support to develop advanced facilities and programs of excellence that did indeed attract superior faculty and students. He constantly took the position with the faculty and regents that for Texas Tech to take its place in the community of great universities, it had to establish a great endowment. He worked on the following assumptions: 1) major endowments come primarily from the private sector; 2) they are largely a product of the professional and personal accomplishments of alumni; and 3) they undergird public financial assistance.

With these assumptions in mind, he convinced the board of regents, through many personal meetings in their offices, tours of the specific facilities on campus, and by advocating his staff's specific plans at board and committee meetings, that they should adopt the following goals for the Enterprise Campaign: Funds for Endowment—43,000,000; Academic Enrichment—20,000,000 (to provide endowed chairs, professorships, lectureships, and to allow faculty to strengthen their credentials); Student Assistance—18,000,000 (to assist prospective undergraduates and graduate students, provide endowed fellowships and scholarships, attract students of the highest ability); Research and Venture Projects—5,000,000 (provide endowment for a fund to underwrite promising ventures and research projects which have great potential but which have not yet attracted outside funding); Major Capital Equipment Acquisition—7,000,000 (to expand equipment inventories in critical disciplines); Funds for Construction and Renovation—7,500,000 (to expand and build critical facilities); Annual Giving Programs—2,500,000 (to increase unrestricted funds available to support the work of support associations; Grand Total—$60,000,000.

The president had suggested the Enterprise Campaign in the early eighties and it took him and his staff several years in working with regents, faculty, students, and the general public to build the acceptance necessary to launch such a ambitious plan for Texas Tech. Vice-Presidents Bradford,

Darling, and Payne prepared for the president in the early eighties a series of plans that coincided perfectly with the aforementioned goals. These plans were then used by President Cavazos (1986a) and J. Fred Bucy, Jr. regent and chairman of the Enterprise Campaign Steering Committee, in the mid-eighties to project the "University's dream of becoming a nationally-recognized institution with a reputation for excellence" and to challenge pace-setter donors to set high standards for the Enterprise Campaign. The funds arrived in the mid-eighties. The momentum of this large effort continued as annual giving grew greatly.

Most importantly, President Cavazos had "supplied the emotional injections that jolted faculty, students, staff, and alumni out of their tendencies to coast." His planning meetings with the faculty senate, academic council, and board of regents were lively and sometimes fiesty affairs. During the formative periods not everyone agreed with the first-generation plans, wild debates accompanied the presentation of draft models. These debates simmered for months and the arguments over goals and means continued long after the campaigns were over. During these tumultuous times the president "hung tough" and did not compromise the new research orientation and a higher set of academic standards. Ultimately, the overriding agenda item, of developing Texas Tech University into a research university noted for its scholarly excellence, was achieved.

All of President Cavazos' visions were not accepted by the university and West Texas, but on the balance, his many plans jolted the university up to a higher level of teaching and research and his vision greatly improved the foundations for developing research. Texas Tech was transformed during Lauro Cavazos tenure. That advancement followed his vision. His personal magnetism swept Texas and the research-oriented faculty into participating with him in the nobility of planning intellectual, artistic, and institutional adventures. Until he departed from Texas Tech in August 1988 to accept President Ronald Reagan's invitation to be the nation's Secretary of Education, he lead the faculty and West Texas in thinking well about themselves, in feeling deeply about the critical issues of the eighties, and in planning their mutual destiny.

WORKS CITED

Barlow, Sam. September 13, 1984. Letter to Dr. William Marcy TTU from Varian (Semiconductor Equipment Group) supporting the University/Industry Joint Ventures and the SMART LAB.

Bolton, Robert and Dorothy G. Bolton. 1984. *Social Style/Management Style.* New York: American Management Association.

Bradford, John R. 1983. *Capital Campaign Plan.* Lubbock, Texas: Texas Tech University and Texas Tech University Health Sciences Center.

————. 1983. *Policies and Procedures Manual for Institutional Development.* Lubbock, TX.: Office of Development Texas Tech University and Texas Tech University Health Sciences Center.

————. 1984. "Distinguished Engineers Program," Meeting of the Members of the Development Council on December 3, 1984. Lubbock, Texas: Development Office, TTU.

————. 1985. "Seven Steps To Successful Giving," Lubbock, Texas: Development Office, TTU.

Cavazos, Lauro F. November 21,1980. *Letter to Dr. Kenneth Ashworth.* Lubbock, Texas: Texas Tech Univerity

————. Lee Stafford. 1981a. Letter to the Business Community from Tech and the Lubbock Chamber of Commerce requesting planning assistance. Lubbock, Texas: Texas Tech University. July 20, 1981.

————. 1982a. Memorandum to Bob Bray, Director of Planning. Subject Campus Master Plan. Lubbock, Texas: Texas Tech University. June 18, 1982.

————. November 3, 1984. Letter to members of the Development Council explaining its formation and asking them to serve.

————. November 12, 1984. Memo to Dr. Hensley thanking him for the planning materials supplied earlier.

————. January 16, 1985. "A Progress Report on the Texas Science and Technology Council" delivered to the TTU Research Council.

————. 1985a. "Opportunities As Far As The Eye Can See."*The Enterprise Campaign.* Lubbock, Texas: Texas Tech University. Spring 1985.

————. April 22, 1985. Memorandum to Drs. Darling, Payne and Richards on the Subject: Research Park Development.

College of Agricultural Sciences. 1985. *Milestones.* Lubbock, TX. Author, Texas Tech University.

Committee for the Measurement of Research Productivity. 1981. *Report of the Committee for the Measurement of Research Productivity.* Committee Members: Eric Bolen, Stephen C. Hora, Harley Oberhelman, Robert O'Reilly, Betty Street, and John Walkup. Lubbock, TX: College of Business Administration, TTU.

Conover, William J. January 23, 1990. Research Seminar on Developing A Research Program.

Coordinating Board Texas College and University System . October 24, 1980. *Long-Range Plan for Texas Higher Education.* Austin, Texas

Croslin, Lloyd Jr. April 16, 1985. Letter to Lauro Cavazos from Westar supporting the University/Industry Joint Ventures and the TTU Industrial Park.

Curl, Samuel E. 1986a. Verbal Testimony presented before the Agriculture, Rural Development and related Agencies Subcommittee of th U.S. Senate Appropriations Committee on behalf of the Plant Stess and Water Conservation Research Program, Washington, D.C. May 6, 1986.

Darling, John R., H. El Said, O. D. Hensley, and H. Wilson. 1979. "An Evaluation of the Egyptian Middle Management Education Program, Technical Report #3. Contract No AID NE-C-1546." Cairo, Egypt.

————. October 5, 1984. Instructions to Dr. Hensley to develop a plan for the Establishment of Research Malls and Common Grounds

————. October 24, 1984. "Release of Faculty from Teaching Duties When Assigned to a Research Grant." Vice President Order to Deans and Staff.

————. April 12, 1985. "Strategic Plan for the Development of a University Park" Memo to TTU Deans

————. July 11, 1985. "Letter to Ken Ashworth with Recommendations for Advanced Technology Research Program Guidelines."

————. and Hensley O. D., 1986 "Social Styles As A Key to Managing Up in University Research Administration." Journal of the Society of Research Administrators. Vol. XVII, No. 3. pp.41-54.

Dukakis, Michael S. and Ebert, J. February 26, 1987. Letter of Invitation to O. Hensley to Participate in the Government-University-Industry Research Roundtable. Washington,D.C.:National Academy of Science.

Dudek, Richard, Hensley, O. and Reavis D., 1987. Proposal for Developing Orthotic Devices to NSF for $94,000. Contract No, NSF EET-8802907

Edson, Gary. 1989 *Muse News*, Newsletter of the Museum of Texas Tech University. Spring 1989. pp.2-3.

Edson, Gary. 1990 "Directly Speaking." *Muse News*, Newsletter of the Museum of Texas Tech University. Spring 1990. pp.2-3.

Edwards, Chet Senator, 1985. Texas Senate Bill 1051 "Relating to the Requirement that an Institution of Higher Education Adopt Rules Regarding Faculty Workloads." Austin, TX: March 8, 1985.

Enderle, John D. 1989. *National Science Foundation 1989 Engineering Senior Design Projects to Aid the Disabled.* Fargo, ND: NDSW Press.

————. Faculty Senate, Special Committee Research Support Study. August 24, 1988. Texas Tech University

Gregory, J. M. and Fedler C.B., 1986 "Equation Describing Granular Flow Through Circular Orifices." Paper No. SWR-86-003, Electrical Power and Process, presented at the ASAE Southwest Region Meeting, Baton Rouge, LA. April.

Fedler, C. B., R.A.Hartwig, D.L. Day and M.P.Steinberg. 1985. "Biogas from Biomass in Developing Countries." Paper for the International Symposium on Sustainable Development of Natural Resources in the Third World. Ohio state University, Columbus, OH. October

Haley, Bess. (January 24, 1983). Memorandum to Vice President Darling on Laboratory Facility for Restaurant, Hotel and Institutional Management. (RHIM)

Haragan, Donald R. August 20, 1985. "Academic Council Minutes, Meeting #16."

————. August 27, 1987. "Texas Tech University in the Twenty-First Century." A Background Report for Study and Discussion at the Academic Council Retreat Junction Texas:

Hatfield, Lynn L. June 27, 1985. Letter to Oliver Hensley from the TTU Department of Physics relaying Rockwell International's interest in supporting the University/Industry Joint Ventures and the TTU Research Park.

Hensley, Oliver D. 1968. "A Study of Factors Related to the Acceptance and Adoption of a Cooperative Supplementary Educational Service Center." Unpublished dissertation, Southern Illinois University, Carbondale, Il. February 1968.

————. 1969. "Project TURNS: Transforming and Utilizing Non-Segregated Schools for Demonstration Schools." A project funded by USOE to coordinate school desegregation plans in Arkansas, Louisiana, and Mississippi from 1968-75. Northeast Louisiana University was the Grantee Institution.

————. and John R. Darling. 1981. *Strategies for Development: A Working Conference for Exploring Government/Industry/Labor/Education Partnerships.* Southern Illinois University, Carbondale, Il., Office of Research and Projects, October 26-27, 1981.

————. November 3, 1984. "The Position of Texas Tech University in the Strategic Plan for the Development of Science and Technology in Texas." A comprehensive research plan that was prepared by the Associate Vice President for Research, TTU.

———. S. Lang. 1984. *Comments on Circular A-21, SRA Monograph #1*. Chicago: Society of Research Administrators.

———. November 12, 1984. "Review of the Graduate School Planning Statement." sent to the Vice President for Academic Affairs and Research.

———. December 14, 1984. "The Retention of Indirect Costs by the Western Mountain State Universities." A Telephone Survey of eight universities in states neighboring Texas.

———. December 21, 1984. "The Position of TTU in the Strategic Plan for the Development of Science and Technology in Texas," Memo to John Darling.

———. January 9, 1985. "The Indivisibility of Graduate Education and Research." a Position Paper from the Research Council TTU.

———. January 30, 1985. "Guidelines for the Development of Organized Research Units." a proposal for a TTU Research Policy.

———. March 4, 1985. Testimony to the Texas House of Representatives, Committee on Science and Technology on "Higher Education: The Benefits of Research and Development." Austin, Texas.

———. March 20, 1985. "Development of Indices to Describe the Condition and Comparative Status of Institutional/Departmental Sponsored Program Activity." A Policy for Standard Measures of Sponsored Activity.

———. July 17, 1985. A Memorandum to Eugene Payne Vice President for Finance and Administration, TTU regarding the TTU Research Park.

———. J. Behrens, and L. Masten. October 15, 1985. *Malaysian Project*. A proposal to the MARA Foundation for $2,700,000 for the Shah Alam Centre Cooperative Program. Contract MU107.

———. February 12, 1986. "A Chronology of Major Events in Developing the Malaysian/TCIE/TTU Engineering Program." A Final Report to the Academic Council and the Research Council of Texas Tech University.

———. Editor, 1986. *The Identification, Classification, and Analysis of University Research Support Personnel*. Lubbock, TX: Texas Tech University Press.

———. 1987 . "A Survey of University Use of Indirect Costs." Lubbock, Texas: TTU, Office of Research Services

———. August 11, 1987. "A Status Report on Research Development at Texas Tech University." delivered to the TTU Board of Regents at their monthly meeting.

———. March 28, 1988. "The Reclamation and Use of University Indirect Costs" Lubbock, Texas: TTU, Center for Excellence in Education.

———. April 24, 1988. "Natural Fiber & Food Protein Commission An American Model that Challenges MITE." Testimony to the Texas Senate Sunset Commission on the Continuation of the Natural Fiber and Food Protein Commission, Austin, Texas.

———. Editor, 1988. *The Classification of Research*. Lubbock, TX: Texas Tech University Press.

———. May 1990. "The Research Philosophy of Texas Tech University" A paper prepared by a Planning Committee of the Research Council. Lubbock, Texas: TTU Office of Research Services.

Jonish, James E. and Robert L. Rouse. 1982. *Texas Tech University: Economic Trends and Community Impact*. Lubbock, Texas: Texas Tech University, August 1982.

Kice, John. October 1, 1984. "Draft Plan for Revised "Research Incentive" Awards Program." Memo and Draft Plan to Texas Tech University Research Council Members.

Koepppe, David E. 1986. *Research Report: Department of Plant & Soil Science.* Lubbock, TX.: College of Agricultural Sciences, Texas Tech University.

———. 1986 "Interim Progress Report, Biotechnology Applied to the Agricultural Areas of Plant Breeding, Gentics and Propagation." Lubbock, TX.: Department of Plant and Soil Sciences, Texas Tech University August 1986

Logan, John A. April 9, 1984. Letter to Oliver Hensley from the Chamber of Commerce supporting the University/Industry Joint Ventures and the TTU Research Park.

Marcy, William M. August 1984. The SMART LAB Planning Conference of 1984, College of Engineering, TTU

McCartney, David L. 1989. "HSC Receives Eye Research Grant." *Lubbock Avalance-Journal*, Thursday, June 22, 1989, A-3.

Mezack, Michael. July 2, 1984. *A Proposal for A Continuing Education Center and Hotel for TTU.*

Milestones 1985. Lubbock, TX: College of Agricultural Sciences, Texas Tech University

Norris, Julie. June 30, 1988. "Federal Demonstration Project, Phase II. Organizational Meeting" at the Coordinating Board Offices, Austin, Texas.

Organized Research Formula Study Committee, Coordinating Board Texas College and university System. November 13, 1985. "Recommendations of the Organized Research Formula Study Committee." William D. Lasher, Chairman.

Payne, Eugene E. June 20, 1985. "Outline for a Feasibility Study for the Tech Research Park." and Minutes of Subcommitee of the Research Park Steeering Committee. Office of the Vice President for Finance and Administration, TTU.

———. September 4, 1985. Research Park RFP Committee Meeting at Texas Tech University.

Preston, Rodney, and McCroskey J., 1985. *Beef Research Report 1985.* Agricultural Sciences Technical Report No. T-5-183, Department of Animal Sciences, Texas Tech University.

Richardson, C. Reed. 1985. *Grantsmanship Information: Guidelines, Outlines, Checklists and Indices of Sponsored Project Funding—College of Agricultural Science, Texas Tech University.* Lubbock, Texas: Texas Tech University, May 1, 1985.

———. April 19, 1985. Letter to O. Hensley of TTU providing a progress report on development of Industry/University Partnerships

Somerville, Mason H. August 30, 1985. Comments at the Research Park RFP Committee Meeting. TTU. Hensley's Minutes of Meeting.

———. September 4, 1985. Proposed Plan to Develop the Texas Tech University Advanced Technology Park

Southern Association of Colleges and Schools. 1989. *Resource Manual on Institutional Effectiveness.* Atlanta, GA: The Commission on Colleges of the Southern Association of Colleges and Schools

Strickland, James H. October 5, 1984. "Revised Incentive Program for Research." Memo from the Office of the Dean of Engineering, TTU to John Kice, Office of Research Services.

Texas A&M University. 1989. *Undergraduate Catalog 1989-1990 No. 112.* January 1989. 17, 1. 11

Texas Instruments. September 12, 1984. Letter to Dr. William M. Marcy of TTU in support of the University/Industry Joint Ventures and the SMART LAB.

Texas Tech University. 1984. *Bulletin of Texas Tech University, Undergraduate Catalog 1984-85.* LX, 3. January 1984. 8.

———. 1984. *Institutional Self-Study*, a Report to the Southern Association of Colleges and Schools. Lubbock, Texas: Author, Spring 1984.

————. 1985. *The Enterprise Campaign.* Lubbock, TX.: Texas Tech University. Spring 1985.

Texas Tech University Board of Regents. November 1984. Appointment of a Research Park Steering Committee. November 1984 Board Meeting.

————. Steering Committee for a Research Park. (1985, July 26) "Subcommittee Status Report from Eugene Payne to President Lauro Cavazos." Lubbock TX.: Texas Tech University

Texas Tech University Board of Regents, Steering Committee for a Research Park. August 2, 1985. "Minutes of the Committee: Approval for the Development of a Request for a Proposal (RFP) for a Research Park"

Texas Tech University Faculty Senate. 1983. "The Research Atmosphere at Texas Tech University." The Survey was made in the 1982-83 academic year.

Texas Tech University Planning Committee. 1984. *Strategic Decision Areas- Part I, Definition of Basic Philosophy and Values.* Lubbock, Texas: Texas Tech University, December 1984.

————. 1986a *A Strategic Plan Phase I.* Lubbock, Texas: Texas Tech University, June 1986.

Texas Tech University Strategic Planning Committee, Subgoal 2, Objective c. May 23, 1987 "The Development of Research and the Improvement of Graduate Education." Lubbock, Texas: Author.

The University of Texas at Austin. 1981. *The Graduate School 1979-1980 and 1980-1981.* Catalogue Number: Part VII, Issue 8109, August 1981. 11.

White, Mark. 1984. Executive Order MW-24, *Texas Science and Technology Council,* Austin, Texas: Office of the Governor, June 21, 1984.

————. February 17, 1986. "Governor's Meeting with State Agency Heads to Set Goals for Financial Constraints Caused by Falling Revenues." Austin, Texas.

William Reed Company. December 7, 1984. Letter to Dr. Vice President Darling of TTU in support of the University/Industry Joint Ventures and the Continuing Education Conference Center.

Wilson, Karen. 1986. *Tax Update.* Lubbock, TX.: Texas Tech Development Office, November 1986.

Winer, Jane L. September 27, 1988. Memorandum to the Office of Research Services regarding Arts & Sciences FY88 Extramural Funding Summary from the College of Arts & Sciences, Texas Tech University.

WIPCO. Wholesale Industrial Plastics Company of Lubbock. September 19, 1984. Letter to Dr. William M. Marcy of TTU in support of the University/Industry Joint Ventures and the SMART LAB.

CHAPTER SEVEN

STRATEGIC ACADEMIC RESEARCH PLANNING IN THE CONGRESS

Harlan L. Watson

I am very pleased to be asked to contribute to the Society of Research Administrators Monograph on Strategic Academic Research Planning. The views that are presented here are my personal and professional views, developed over the course of more than seven years of exposure to and study of science and technology policy as a staff member in the U.S. House of Representatives, and before that, in the U.S. Senate. My comments do not necessarily represent the views of either the Committee on Science, Space, and Technology or any of its individual members.

The title of this presentation, "Strategic Academic Research Planning in the Congress," is somewhat misleading, in that it will not be comprehensive in its discussion of all the parts of Congress that have input to our national science and technology policy, but rather from the more narrow jurisdiction of the House Committee on Science, Space, and Technology.

CONGRESS AND SCIENCE AND TECHNOLOGY POLICY: THE LEGISLATIVE PROCESS

Congress is an institution in which power is widely shared—with multiple points of access and influence—and where important decisions often are made piecemeal and inconsistently. This complexity can be seen in the rather cluttered Figure 7.1, which lists the committees of the U.S. House and the U.S. Senate for the 100th Congress, which began on January 6, 1987. Also listed are the four joint committees whose rosters included members of both the House and Senate. The numerals in parentheses give the numbers of subcommittees and task forces of each committee. As summarized at the bottom of the figure, this Congress has fifty-four committees, 234 subcommittees, one task force, and two panels.

Many of these entities have at least some input into our national science and technology policy. These inputs may be direct, in the form of the authorization or appropriation of funds through the various mission agencies such as the National Institutes of Health or the Departments of Agriculture, Defense, or Energy. These inputs may also be indirect, through the powers of Congress to make laws with regard to the organization of the executive branch, taxes, patents, and so forth, or through general oversight of the executive branch. The Committee on Science, Space, and Technology is highlighted in Figure 7.1 in the list of House committees. This Committee has the most comprehensive view of our national science and technology policy, and my observations will be from this perspective.

In this section, I discuss the legislative process and the role of the Committee on Science, Space, and Technology. In order to provide some background to the way that decisions are made in Congress and how the Committee fits into the larger national context. I then will describe the Science Policy Study that a Task Force of Science and Technology Committee members conducted during the 100th Congress, and which the Committee will be finishing this year. Let us first, however, consider briefly the size and distribution of federal funding for research and development.

Figure 7.1. 100th Congress' Committees (Number of Subcommittees and Task Forces).

HOUSE	SENATE
Agriculture (8)	Agriculture, Nutrition, and Forestry (6)
Appropriations (13)	
Armed Services (8)	Appropriations (13)
Banking, Finance and Urban Affairs (8)	Armed Services (6)
Budget	Banking, Housing and Urban Affairs (4)
District of Columbia (3)	Budget
Education and Labor (8)	Commerce, Science and Transportation (8)
Energy and Commerce (6)	
Foreign Affairs (9)	Energy and Natural Resources (5)
Government Operations (7)	Environment and Public Works (5)
House Administration (6)	Finance (7)
Interior and Insular Affairs (6)	Foreign Relations (7)
Judiciary (7)	Governmental Affairs (5)
Merchant Marine and Fisheries (6)	Judiciary (7)
Post Office and Civil Service (8)	Labor and Human Resources (6)
Public Works and Transportation (6)	Rules and Administration
	Small Business (6)
Rules (2)	Veterans Affairs
Science, Space, and Technology (7)	Ethics
	Indian Affairs
Small Business (6)	Intelligence
Standards of Official Conduct	Aging
Veterans' Affairs (5)	
Ways and Means (5)	

Figure 7.1. Continued.

JOINT

Aging (4)	
Children, Youth and Families	Economic (6)
Hunger	Library
Intelligence (5)	Printing
Narcotics Abuse and Control	Taxation

SUMMARY

51 Committees (27 House, 20 Senate, 4 Joint)

234 Subcommittees (143 House, 85 Senate, 6 Joint)

3 Task Forces (house)

Table 1, reproduced from "Special Analysis J" of the Fiscal Year (FY) 1988 budget request submitted by the president to Congress in early January of 1987, shows that the fiscal year 1987 federal obligations for reseach and development (R&D) are estimated to total $59.5 billion for the conduct of R&D and $1.9 billion for R&D facilities. For FY 1988,the administration has proposed increasing this total to $66.7 billion, including $64.8 billion for the conduct of R&D and $2.0 billion for R&D facilities. This FY 1988 request represents an increase of over $7 billion, or 12%, above the FY 1987 level.

Table 1. Total Federal Funding for Conduct of R&D and Related Facilities (In billions of dollars)

	Obligations			Outlays		
	1986 actual	1987 estimate	1988 estimate	1986 actual	1987 estimate	1988 estimate
Conduct of R&D	52.6	57.6	64.8	51.6	54.6	59.1
R&D facilities	1.6	1.9	2.0	1.6	1.8	1.9
Total	54.2	59.5	66.7	53.1	56.3	61.0

Table 2, also reproduced from "Special Analysis J", lists the twelve agencies of the federal government whose R&D obligations exceed $150 million annually. These twelve agencies fund over 99% of total federal R&D, and the top seven (Departments of Defense, Energy, Health and Human Services, Agriculture, and Commerce, and the National Aeronautics and Space Administration and National Science Foundation) account for over 97% of the obligations for the conduct of R&D by the federal government.

As might be expected, the Department of Defense is, by far, the largest funder of federal R&D, accounting for over 65% of federal R&D obligations this current fiscal year and for over 68% of R&D obligations in fiscal year 1988.

Table 2. Agencies of the Federal Government whose R%D d obligations exceed $150 million.

Interior	378	366	364	386	373	370
Environmental Protection Agency	317	329	346	307	333	352
Commerce	394	397	333	373	375	314
Agency for International Development	211	217	233	95	300	171
Veterans Administration	188	211	214	83	214	209
All other[1]	483	514	463	464	525	463
Total	56,612	57,631	64,771	51,576	54,548	59,108

[1]Includes the Departments of Education, Justice, Labor, Housing and Urban Development and Treasury, the Tennessee Valley Authority, the Smithsonian Institution, the Corps of Engineers, and the Nuclear Regulatory Agency.

Table 3, again from "Special Analysis J", shows obligations and outlays for basic research by major agencies and departments. Here we see a different ranking of funding agencies from that given in Table 2. For Fiscal Year 1987, the major funder of basic research, at approximately $3.36 billion in obligations, is the National Institutes of Health, followed by the National Science Foundation at $1.359 billion, the Department of Energy at $1.084 billion, NASA at $1.069 billion, and the Department of Defense at $858 million.

Table 3. Conduct of Basic Research by Major Departments and Agencies (in millions of dollars)[1]

Department or agency	Obligations			Outlays		
	1986 actual	1987 estimate	1988 estimate	1986 actual	1987 estimate	1988 estimate
Agencies supporting primarily physical sciences and engineering:[2]						
National Science Foundation	1,259	1,359	1,585	1,313	1,310	1,513
Defense-Military functions	921	858	907	845	844	811
Energy	964	1,084	1,133	947	1,087	1,143
National Aeronautics and Space Administration	917	1,069	1,016	932	983	1,002
Interior	129	123	115	135	129	118

Table 3. Continued.

Department or agency	Obligations			Outlays		
	1986 actual	1987 estimate	1988 estimate	1986 actual	1987 estimate	1988 estimate
Commerce	26	24	24	27	23	24
Other Agencies[3]	10	10	9	11	11	10
Subtotal	4,227	4,527	4,788	4,210	4,387	4,620
Agencies supporting primarily life and other sciences:[4]						
Health and Human Services	3,335	3,663	3,712	3,234	3,475	3,579
(National Institutes of Health)	(3,118)	(3,360)	(3,442)	(3,013)	(3,185)	(3,308)
Agriculture	431	454	454	419	440	474
Smithsonian Institution	63	73	78	59	67	72
Environmental Protection Agency	39	38	39	36	39	40
Veterans Administration	15	16	16	15	15	16
Education	11	12	11	8	15	11
Other Agencies[5]	17	16	13	14	15	15
Subtotal	3,909	4,271	4,322	3,786	4,067	4,207
Total	8,137	8,798	9,110	7,996	8,454	8,827

[1] Amounts reported in this table are included in totals for conduct of R&D.

[2] Includes mathematics and computer sciences.

[3] Includes the Corps of Engineers, the Tennessee Valley Authority, and the Department of Transportation.

[4] Includes psychology and social sciences.

[5] Includes the Departments of Labor, Justice, and Treasury, and the Agency for International Development.

Let us consider where the Committee on Science, Space, and Technology fits in. The committee has broad and comprehensive responsibility over the federal government's R&D efforts. Its jurisdiction has grown and evolved over its twenty-seven-year history.

The committee's composition and organizational structure for this 100th Congress are shown in Figure 7.2. The committee is chaired by Congressman Robert A. Roe of New Jersey, and the ranking republican member is Congressman Manuel Lujan, Jr. of New Mexico. The committee has forty-five members from twenty-seven states, and there are seven subcommittees (Investigations and Oversight; National Resources, Agriculture Research, and Environment; Energy Research and Development; Science, Research, and Technology; Space Science and Applications; International Scientific Cooperation; and Transportation, Aviation, and Materials).

100TH CONGRESS MEMBERSHIP AND ORGANIZATION

Chairman: Congressman Robert A. Roe (D-NJ)
Ranking Republican Member: Congressman Manuel Lujan, Jr. (R-NM)
45 Members Representing 27 States

SUBCOMMITTEES
Investigations and Oversight
Natural Resources, Agriculture Research and Environment
Energy Research and Development
Science, Research and Technology
Space Science and Applications
International Scientific Cooperation
Transportation, Aviation and Materials

TASK FORCE
Task Force on Technology Policy

Figure 7.2. Committee on Science, Space, and Technology 100th Congress Membership and Organization.

The committee's responsibilities are summarized in Figure 7.3. It is responsible for all legislation, including budget authorization, concerning the National Science Foundation, the National Bureau of Standards, the National Aeronautics and Space Administration, the Office of Science and Technology Policy, the Office of Technology Assessment, the National Technical Information Service, the Department of Commerce's Office of Productivity, Technology and Innovation, as well as the civilian research and development programs of the Department of Energy, the Environmental Protection Agency, the National Oceanic and Atmospheric Administration, the Department of Transportation, the Federal Emergency Management Agency, the U.S. Geological Survey, and the Bureau of Mines. The committee has jurisdiction over all federal environmental R&D, general scientific research, development, and demonstration, and all federally-owned or -operated nonmilitary energy laboratories. Over and above this legislative jurisdiction, the Science Committee is the only committee in the entire Congress with special oversight functions to review, study, and make recommendations about all laws, programs, and government activities involving federal nonmilitary R&D.

LEGISLATIVE JURISDICTION

National Science Foundation
National Bureau of Standards
National Aeronautics and Space Administration
Office of Science and Technology Policy
Office of Technology Assessment
National Technical Information Service
Office of Productivity, Technology and Innovation
Department of Energy-Civilian R&D Programs
Environmental Protection Agency-R&D Programs
National Oceanic and Atmospheric Administration-R&D Programs
Department of Transportation-R&D Programs
Federal Emergency Management Agency-R&D Programs
U.S. Geological Survey-R&D Programs
Bureau of Mines-R&D Programs

OVERSIGHT FUNCTIONS

[House Rule X.3.(f): "The Committee on Science, Space, and Technology shall have the function of reviewing and studying, on a continuing basis, all laws, programs, and government activities dealing with or involving nonmilitary research and development."]

Figure 7.3. Committee on Science, Space, and Technology Legislative Jurisdiction and Oversight Functions.

Science and technology decisions, like all decisions the Congress must make, are always subject to the competitive reality of the federal budget process. R&D programs must compete with other federal programs for the limited federal dollars available. Those programs that have survived must then compete against each other because there will always be a greater number of worthy programs and projects than there will be funds to implement them.

At all times, Congress is faced with the decision of how to allocate funds for the greatest benefit, and always, in the process, Congress must reconcile differences to arrive at a consensus. When you consider that all members of Congress vote according to their own judgment of national priorities, you begin to see that reaching a consensus is not always an easy task.

Although it may not appear to be initially, the federal research and development budget is an important tool in the determination of national science and technology policy. The process of determining the funding for R&D items in the budget is, in and of itself a designation of policy. Those programs that are funded move the Nation towards objectives believed important to pursue.

THE BUDGET PROCESS: AN IDEALIZED VERSION

The funding of programs starts with agency proposals that are reviewed by the Office of Management and Budget (OMB) and consolidated in the president's budget request to Congress. If the budget process worked as intended, the president's request for each budget account and agency would then be subjected to a three-part congressional review process: authorizations, appropriations, and overall budget resolution. Let us consider each in turn.

To begin, authorization committees with legislative jurisdiction over specific agencies and departments review those budgets and programs. For example, the Science Committee would review the National Science Foundation budget at this time and the budgets of all other agencies that I mentioned that fall within its jurisdiction. These reviews proceed independently in the House and Senate, and the review process carried out by these committees is technically termed an annual authorization. The authorization bill then goes to the House and Senate for consideration. The House and Senate should agree on a compromise version of the bill for signature by the president before the second part of the review, the appropriations process, commences. This is the way the processes are supposed to proceed. In actuality, the two processes often run parallel, or in reverse order.

The second review process, the actual appropriation of funds by the committees on appropriations, is supposed to be guided by what the authorization bill contains. The authorizing committees establish a policy or direction whereas the committees on appropriations permit implementation of the policy by providing funds. What an authorizing committee recommends, however, can be decreased by the appropriations committees.

The third congressional budget review process is to set limits on total federal income and expenditures through an overall budget resolution. Although this is a separate function of the budget review, it is not isolated in sequence or time-frame but instead operates throughout the total process.

Research and development programs are part of what is commonly termed the controllable part of the federal budget, or that portion for which there is no prior legal obligation to commit funds. The Science Committee, with its extensive jurisdiction over R&D, has a significant impact on the spending of these federal funds which comprise a significant percentage of the controllable budget.

As an authorizing committee, the Science Committee determines policy in several ways. The committee can establish a balance between basic and applied research. With the regular process of annual program-by-program reviews, it can support promising programs and track their progress. It can also discontinue less viable programs. Year by year, budget cycle by budget cycle, the committee is able to monitor all research and technology development that falls within its purview. Also, as the committee considers authorizations each year, it must also take into account related issues such as government-industry-university relations, technology transfer, and scientific and technical manpower needs.

The above discussion presents an idealized textbook version of the budget process. In reality, the focus on the deficit in the past few years has greatly reduced the role of the authorizing committees in the budget process. This has been particularly true because the passage of the Balanced Budget and Emergency Deficit Control Act of 1985 (Public Law 99-177), better known as the Gramm-Rudman-Hollings (GRH) Deficit Reduction Act, has complicated the budget process.

SCIENCE POLICY STUDY

In addition to the regular responsibilities associated with the committee's jurisdiction, its Task Force on Science Policy recently completed a two-year review of our nation's science policy, which is expected to be completed by the committee this year, and which I would like to discuss with you. The Task Force, chaired by then committee Chairman Don Fuqua, was engaged in this study from January of 1985 through December of 1986, and planning for the study began in the fall of 1984.

A science policy study of this magnitude has not been undertaken since 1944, when Vannevar Bush, director of Franklin Roosevelt's war-time Office of Scientific Research and Development, was commissioned by the president to conduct an examination of the role of science in America as a highly industrial nation. Bush's report, entitled *Science-The Endless Frontier*, was the basis for a redirection of America's thinking regarding the federal government's role in relation to science.

The Bush report proposed that the federal government take a new role in the post-war years by providing financial support for basic and applied research, chiefly in the nation's universities. The report recommended that the federal government accept responsibilities for promoting the flow of new knowledge in the sciences and engineering, and for the development of scientific talent. One result was the establishment of the National Science Foundation (NSF) in 1950. The specific mandate of the NSF was to promote basic research and science education in the nation. In the same decade, both basic and applied research at the National Institutes of Health were vastly expanded. The Bush report has since served as the basic rationale for the federal government's funding of a diverse and ever-growing research effort that has come to include the social sciences and engineering, as well as the conventional sciences.

Between the Bush study, and the committee's own, there were two congressional reviews of American science policy, both in the mid-Sixties, nearly twenty years ago. Each of these was initiated in part by the Soviet launch of the satellite Sputnik and the challenge that this presented to American science and technology. However, neither of these reviews compares in scope to the committee's current undertaking.

In attempting to define the scope of the study during the fall of 1984, the task force was very much aware of the vast encompassing reach of science and technology policy. At one extreme, it includes the most basic research performed by investigators whose singular goal is to extend the scientific knowledge base, with no practical application in mind. At the other end are the scientists and engineers whose work is directed toward producing a product for the marketplace. The task force agreed at the onset that trying to encompass these two extremes in science and technology, and everything that fell between them, would be an impossible task. It would, in fact, immediately render the inquiry superficial. Therefore, the task force decided that the Science Policy Study should be limited to only those issues that were connected with the federal government's support of basic and applied research.

In December 1984, the task force issued a report, "An Agenda for a Study of Government Science Policy", whose table of contents is reproduced in Figure 7.4. Within the parameters outlined, the task force examined the conditions under which basic and applied research are conducted in the universities, in government laboratories, in independent research institutes, in museums, and in industry. The study also covers both science and engineering education at the graduate and postdoctoral levels.

The task force asked series of critical questions that it hoped would uncover both the strengths and weaknesses in America's science-producing network. In fact, the agenda formulated 139 such questions, including the following being asked about the goals of federal science policy:

What are we as a nation aiming for in providing support for science?

How do our goals for science relate to our other national goals?

Are the goals for science internally consistent?

How does a statement of national goals for science relate to science policy issues, and given a set of goals, what is needed to achieve them?

Have our goals changed, and to what extent do the policies for government support of science, which have evolved over the last forty years apply to the next forty years?

To what extent must changes now be made in those policies to achieve the national objectives and goals?

The committee is optimistic that this study will lead to new insights and about our science needs as a nation. In this process, it is taking into account the changes over the last four decades in order to address the next several decades.

The inquiry has been conducted by inviting a number of witnesses to address the broad questions that are posed in the study agenda and then to comment further as they wish on issues germane to the study.

The distinguished experts that have appeared before us come from diverse research and administrative positions in academia, government, nonprofit institutions, foundations, and private industry. They have brought many different perspectives to the inquiry.

Figure 7.4 Science Policy Study Agenda Contents.

CONTENTS

At this point in the study, the task force has completed its work, and the current plans are to finish the study at the committee level during this year. Figure 7.5 lists the hearings schedule for 1985, and Figure 7.6 lists the hearings schedule for 1986. The task force held sixty-six days of hearings on twenty-four topics, and heard testimony from 233 different individuals, including five Nobel laureates.

1. Goals and Objectives of National Science Policy-February 28; March 7, 21, 28; April 4
2. The Role of the Research Museums-April 17
3. *The Relationship of Industrial Basic and Applied Research to Government Science Policy*-April 23, 24
4. International Cooperation in Big Science: High Energy Physics-April 25
5. The Future of Science-May 2
6. *The Federal Government and the University Research Infrastructure*-May 21, 22; September 5
7. International Cooperation in Science-June 18, 19, 20, 27
8. Science in the Political Process-June 25, 26
9. Scientists and Engineers: Supply and Demand-July 9, 10, 11, 23, 24, 25
10. Impact of the Information Age on Science-September 10, 11, 12
11. The Role of the Behavioral and Social Sciences-September 17, 18, 19
12. Science in the Mission Agencies and the Federal Laboratories -October 2, 3, 4, 22, 23, 24
13. *British Methods of Science Evaluation*-October 30

Figure 7.5. Science Policy Task Force Hearings-1985.

1. Demographics and Manpower-February 19, 20, 27
2. Science and the Regulatory Environment-February 26; March 5, 6
3. Research Funding Mechanisms-March 12, 13, 19, 20
4. Research Project Selection-April 8, 9, 10
5. National Research Funding Levels-April 15, 16
6. Policies for Biomedical Research-April 22, 23, 24
7. Research Funding as an Investment-April 29, 30; May 1
8. The Role of the National Academies-May 6, 7, 8
9. Research and Publication Practices-May 14
10. White House Science Council Panel on the Health of U.S. Colleges and Universities-May 15
11. Scientific Research and University Finances-September 16, 18

Figure 7.6. Science Policy Task Force Hearings-1986.

I might mention that the formal hearings were only the most "visible" part of the study. The task force also commissioned thirteen studies by the Congressional Research Service (CRS) of the Library of Congress, the General Accounting Office (GAO), the Office of Technology Assessment (OTA), and staff listed in Figure 7.7. In addition, the task force members and staff participated in numerous workshops, meetings, and site visits during the course of the study.

The task force had originally intended to complete a draft report of the study during the summer of 1986, hold extensive hearings on this draft in late summer, and issue the final report of the study by the end of October 1986. However, this schedule has slipped and the draft will not be available until later this year.

In closing, I want to mention that in December of last year, the retiring Chairman, Don Fuqua, issued his "Chairman's Report," which detailed his personal observations and recommendations with regard to the study. It is not clear at this time how many of these recommendations will be included in the final report, which must be approved by the committee during this session of Congress.

1. Reader on Expertise in the Political Process (CRS)
2. Nobel Awards as Indicators of National Strength (CRS)
3. International Big Science Facilities (CRS)
4. Bibliography of National Academy Policy Studies and Reports (CRS)
5. Impact on Science of the Information Age (CRS)
6. The Social and Behavioral Sciences (CRS)
7. Science Support by the Department of Defense (CRS)
8. Federal Funding Mechanisms for University Research (GAO)-federal Funding Mechanisms in Support of University Research-Assessing federal Funding Mechanisms for University Research
9. The Regulatory Environment for Science (OTA)
10. History of U.S. Science Policy Since 1945 (Staff)
11. Demographic Trends and the Scientific and Engineering Work Force (OTA)
12. Science Funding as an Investment (OTA)
13. University Finances: Research Revenues and Expenditures (GAO)

Figure 7.7. Science Policy Task Force Commissioned Studies.

CHAPTER EIGHT

STRATEGIC PLANNING
FOR ACADEMIC RESEARCH IN NATIONAL
UNIVERSITY ASSOCIATIONS

Jerold Roschwalb

Thank you Mr. Chairman. I am genuinely pleased to be here with you today. The alternative, you see, would be to sit in Washington at my home waiting for Monday. That is another form of planning though not necessarily strategic—probably best described as a tactical kneejerk. I accepted Dr. Hensley's invitation to participate in this panel because I was certain that I would learn a great deal from my colleagues. The other reason is that I have never participated in a progressive oxymoron.

To assert that there is planning in national university associations is a fact. Do not for a minute believe that our annual meetings happen spontaneously. We also have colleagues like ourselves who set aside a few moments of meditation each morning to think out what lunch they will bring. However, to talk about strategic academic research planning in One Dupont Circle implies an act of will, an optimism, an intensity of religious faith that would escape the best of us.

I should note early on that I will restrict my remarks when I speak of the national university associations solely to the realm of what is covered in the rubric, "federal relations." Although I do not understand the intricacies of the many other activities that go on in our associations, I admit to admiration for those of my colleagues who can balance the books, particularly if this is done legitimately, arrange for parking stickers for the basement garage, a matter inconsequential when compared to its stature on campus, but nevertheless a matter not to be sneezed at.

All sorts of activities are carried out; furniture arrives fairly close to the time announced, walls are painted, dead light bulbs are replaced, usually by live light bulbs, 75% of the elevators work at any given time, the security guards on the ground floor are always cheerful and friendly to all who come in, including the professional pick pockets who ransack the building, and, above all, monthly paychecks arrive on schedule with all the proper deductions and calculations.

Facetious as one might be about these matters, one cannot help but be full of admiration that all of these numbers and facts and details are brought together correctly over time to enable the other activities of the association to go forward. The reason why it is possible for those parts of associations to be involved in strategic planning is that they involve generally rational content over which the association managers have some control.

Federal relations as it affects university interests is more like a novel in progress. Almost anything can change at any time. Characters can be added or removed from the scene. It is a bit like the baseball game that players in the 50s used to engage in hotel lobbies on rainy afternoons. They would be spotted by fans who would give their eye teeth to be able to go home and tell their neighbors that they played cards with the best pitcher in baseball. The essence of the game was that there were no rules. The objective of the game was to fleece the fan.

Now this does not apply precisely to higher education federal relations. There are, after all, rules in the operation of the Congress. But there is one prominent rule taught to me by a staff member. I complained to him bitterly that his boss was out on the Senate floor turning things inside out and causing great consternation for my constituency. He looked at me calmly and said, "Jerry, where does a gorilla sleep?" Puzzled, I answered, "I do not know." He replied, "Wherever the hell he wants to." And lesson taught.

If a new desk is delivered to an office at our association, it is perfectly reasonable to assume that the old desk was inadequate, perhaps too small or beginning to fall apart; hence, the replacement. Or perhaps a new staffer is arriving and we need a new desk. All very simple and reasonable.

Using the context of federal relations, whether they be in the agencies or on the Hill, a different form of reasoning would have to be followed. The Democrats brought in the new desk because the Republicans did the same thing when they were in the Senate majority. The Republicans brought in a desk to show the Democrats that even though they are in the minority, they still have some furniture clout. The desk looks like it was brought in, but it will soon be removed. The desk was not really brought in. It is in a holding pattern brought over from another committee where it has not yet been decided who should get the desk, if anyone.

The desk is really part of a larger furniture scheme and until we get the entire picture, there is nothing intelligent we can say about it. The desk is not a desk. It is a rodent volleyball court that is being used at NIH with experimental mice and has been brought here as evidence of the misuse of animals in research. The desk is a House desk. The Senate does not recognize it as a desk. The desk is a ploy. Its entire object is to distract everyone while the chairman of a subcommittee slips a chair into the pending legislation. The chair is not a ploy. It is intended to distract the chairman so that he cannot slip a chair into the legislation. We cannot discuss the desk any further, since we do not have a rule from the Rules Committee.

Obviously, the above is exaggerated, but only slightly so. What I did not tell you was that all of the items listed regarding the desk have to be thought of simultaneously. It was seven or eight years ago that a House staff member called my boss to report on me. He called me a lunatic and I immediately got a raise.

Most of all, there is nothing wrong with this. This really is the democratic process in a most complex society involving highly sophisticated, generally well-educated, and ambitious human beings. The most important rules are not put down and the most important rules are not that different from those that breed success in any sector of our society. All the planning, strategic or otherwise in the world, will never replace basic courtesy, respect for the complex responsibilities of staff and the burdens they carry in serving the political, philosophical, and personal interests of their principals.

Keeping your word, delivering on what you say, producing hard evidence when it is possible, making life just a little easier for the people responsible for producing legislation, showing support for the chairmen or member who goes out of his way to be helpful. All these add up in the total process.

There is an old saw—you are not to allow your children to watch two things being made; the first is sausage and the second is legislation. They both are messy processes. One would think that it would be virtually impossible to engage in strategic planning for higher education on the federal scene. In fact, it is quite possible, necessary, and a developing reality even though it takes place in a sometimes irrational, always highly emotional, sometimes illogical, very fast changing environment in the passing of legislation and the promulgating of regulations.

A quick note on history. The university community had limited relationships with the federal government prior to the Second World War. A number existed, some of consequence, including those in the world of agriculture, because the federal government has for a century funded most fundamental agricultural research and extension activities. ROTC has existed for some time and to the degree that the federal government had research laboratories in the Department of Defense, at the Bureau of Standards, the Smithsonian Institution, and elsewhere there were natural linkages between colleagues in the various disciplines.

But dollars provide the matrix in which relationships between the federal government and the universities engage, in what has been called partially accurately a symbiotic relationship, and dollars did not flow in large amounts until the 1950s.

Accepting generalizations for what they are, it seems fair to say that the modern era for federal government higher-education relationships was created by the Soviet Union in the autumn of 1957 when Sputnik was hurled into the air and propelled the federal government into major new funding for NSF, the creation of NASA, and the expansion of DOD research efforts. The second phase of this era was the discovery by the citizenry that not only was death as inevitable as taxes, but it could prove as painful and messy and almost interminable. The so-called war on cancer led to a more sensible, organized support for NIH as a whole and possibly the greatest medical event in this century, the acceptance that one could be mentally ill and merely sick and addicted to drugs without being criminal. All these enhanced the relationship between the research institutions and the people of the country represented by their national government.

The problem was and is that these developments did not happen in any organized sequence. There was no logical progression. They happened in the context of national politics and the change from the Johnson to the Nixon Administration, from the Carter to the Reagan Administration had turbulent effects, some sudden decisions, some drawn-out battles, many of which going back twenty years still go on.

To make matters even more interesting, every state university, and, to a certain degree, private universities as well—are dependent upon similarly undependable, incalculable, unpredictable forces. The forces are political and change with different administrations in the governor's office and control over the various houses of the legislature in the various states year by year.

What the states want the universities to become can differ markedly from what the institutions hope to become themselves and can differ again from what the federal government's needs may be at a given moment, only to have all three change, but not in concert with one another. It reminds me of an argumentive friend I knew in school who loved nothing more than a debate and when you got tired of arguing with him and said, "I now see your point, I agree with you," he would respond, "It is too late. I've changed my mind." All this is certainly obvious to you and in fact better known to our audience than to me who has basically learned about it from this audience over the years.

We have been told by our parents with one range of words or another and have tried to communicate to our children a fundamental truth: one of the marks of an adult is the acceptance of reality.

Children are given to exclaim with great justice often, "It is not fair!" But life, we learn, is not like an athletic event. You cannot protest by pulling your team off the field except in a pine box that bears extraordinary definitiveness.

Higher education's dealings with the federal government until about 1970 were amiable. Limited numbers of voices from the academic community were heard in Washington. These very senior and respected university officials were harkened to some degree. Remember, of course, in that period of time, everything was growing. The debate was not on whether there should be a fellowship program in NASA, but what kind of fellowship program. In that environment, it does not take extraordinary lobbying skills or expertise to look pretty good. A combination of forces—the election of Richard Nixon and an administration with a somewhat different philosophy of how the federal government should spend its dollars in the support of students and in the support of research to some degree, changes in the national economy, different kinds of inflation rates, a growing attention to civil justice in our society and, therefore, in our institutions and the need to bring disadvantaged students into the vortex of our small world, coupled with a vastly increasing demand by the nation for new knowledge in all of the scientific and engineering disciplines created the new federal relations that is just about 15 years old and is still very much evolving.

Although research is our territory, I should note that because the federal government provides some funds for half of our student body, about six million students, and that the sum involves many billions of dollars, a very substantial effort in federal relations for student aid programs goes on, and extends across types of institutions including the community colleges, the smaller liberal arts private schools, all public institutions, and the private research universities. I mention this primarily because the people active in this environment frequently are the same people in the large universities who are involved in the research world.

The research world is smaller. Granted that some kind of significant research may be conducted on as many as 225 or so campuses, these institutions have constituted themselves into a RUN, a Research University Network. Not surprisingly, within this network there are those institutions who devote more attention and energy to strategic planning with federal agencies because federal funding is life's blood to them and they probably represent about seventy-five schools or roughly a third of this larger body. They are usually those institutions at the very top of the NSF list of institutions receiving federal support.

Out of the chaotic spontaneity of the fifties and sixties is organized chaos and at times, quite seriously, organized effort in the best federal relations sense of the word. Given its membership, the Association of American Universities very frequently takes the lead in identifying issues, convening interested parties to determine strategies and tactics, and to coordinate efforts. Many of you know Jack Crowley (recently became MIT's Washington Office Director), who has been with that organization for almost fifteen years and is perhaps the most respected of our Washington-based federal relations people who plays a central role in this effort. He has several colleagues who also are greatly talented and highly respected who specialize in different areas such as health, graduate programs, and so on.

It should be noted that information is the currency of Washington and there now exists a range of groups that meet regularly for the purpose of information exchange. Under the coordination of the National Academy of Sciences, a breakfast group meets monthly with representatives from the Physical Society, the Chemical Society, COSSA, NASULGC, AAU, etc.—about eighteen or so participants. The groups keep each other on mailing lists and are connected electronically and that does prove useful.

There is the Ad Hoc Committee to support Medical Research Funding that has been in existence for about seven years, chaired by AAMC's John Sherman who is a pillar of integrity in our community. I was going to say that he may be the most respected person among health staff on the Hill, more accurately he may be the only fully respected person in our crowd. The steering committee consists of about fifteen to twenty representatives of association-based people, faculty-based people, consultants for various learned societies. The group's work is endorsed by about 150 medical research-oriented societies. The group studies the funding needs of NIH and ADAMHA, prepares a professional brochure containing data and arguments and organizes a well-wrought lobbying effort annually.

The beginnings of another such group for NSF, currently chaired by Brady Metheny of the "Delegation" in Massachusetts, consists of similar and sometimes identical people with comparable commitments for that agency. The current impending crisis in NSF funding in the Senate is doing much to make that group gel.

One mechanism put into place about eight or so years ago that has proven to be a boon is the so-called research group that meets every other Friday morning. Participants come from the associations concerned with research issues including ACE, COGR, AAMC, and like associations. Also participating are Washington-based representatives from research intensive universities. At each meeting information is gathered around the table to be evaluated. Notes are taken and published Monday, first by electronic mail to all members of the Research University Network and others in the community concerned with research issues. The document on electronic mail (coupled with mailed text to those unable to get the electronic message) runs four single-space pages each time, approximately, and keeps the entire field aware of what we in Washington think is going on and what we also think may be important.

Periodically, large amounts of paper are sent to our network containing summaries of legislation and analyses of regulations. Several times each year the entire network is invited to Washington where we meet, sometimes on Capitol Hill, if a gracious staff can find a room for us. Guest speakers from the congressional committees give intense summaries of what is taking place and the implications of that. There are innumerable meetings that take place throughout the year on given subject matters. For example, a task force might be put together to deal with some aspect of energy research or the University Research Initiative in the Department of Defense. They meet as often as is deemed useful and always when people come to Washington, it is expected that they will be making their way to their congressional delegation offices to discuss their concerns, provide information of specific value to their campuses, and win hearts and minds.

Testimony is delivered by the research-based associations on all appropriations bills involving research and all authorization bills as they are produced on schedule. Staffs of the associations spend countless hours with indulgent staff members reviewing legislative proposals, offering comments, recommendations, and, when necessary, groveling with great dignity. In short, the mechanics of federal relations activities are pretty well in place. They are ever changing. No one assumes that what we have is perfect. Much of what we have is still experimental.

There are serious problems. We do not have a data base. We do not seem capable of determining how to create a data base. We rarely can tell members of Congress or staff what they really want to have at a given moment and so we fall back on poesy, plenteous rhetoric, and what for academics passes for prayer. We have done remarkably well despite this shortcoming, partly because we are a cheap date. For the price of one B-1 bomber, we could fund NSF so that everyone over the age of eleven would have a research grant. But the country still prefers to pay for people to die more expensively from Alzheimer's disease than to spend as much money as can be absorbed by our research scientists to do research related to that disease as well as so many others.

What is really going for us is the general feeling in the Congress about higher education and especially research. Members of Congress like us, like what our institutions do. Their relationships with institutions are generally positive both in personal experience, in the fact that we are huge employers in their districts, in the fact that their constituents attend our institutions generally happily, and because most of them do know that out of our laboratories comes the superconducting material, the new plastics that allow Shuttles to fly, the vaccines that will prevent AIDS or other such horrors.

Despite the occasional fraud and abuse case, allegation, or reality, despite our inability to provide what sometimes seems imperative in the way of hard facts, we remain the white hats in the eyes of most members of Congress. When we get beat up, it is not as an industry so much as for a specific problem. Funds rarely get cut back for research in a big way. It is just that they do not increase in a big way to the degree that we need them to if the United States is ever to become a superpower.

Well, how does all of this fit together in the context of this meeting on strategic planning? A colleague of mine from the Worcester Institute in Philadelphia quoted Peter Drucker to me the other day along the lines that planning was fine, except that you could not really predict what will happen. Strategic planning's role is to assure that we are ready for anything that might happen in higher education research in federal legislation or regulations.

In fact, there are still instances when we know what is coming and cannot seem to get ourselves together in a way that would assure us dealing with this issue adequately. What I think is fair to say is that the industry has come a very long way.

The fact that we recognize our shortcomings and know to some degree what we need to do in the next period of time is itself an indicator of that and in a great number of instances, considering the volatility of the world we are operating in, I think that we are reaching that point where we can deal with pretty much what happens if it is dealable. As I noted when I began this talk, a very great amount of what we are involved in is beyond the realm of anything human or anything reasonable.

CHAPTER NINE

STRATEGIC STATE PLANNING FOR TECHNOLOGICAL INNOVATION: THE PENNSYLVANIA BEN FRANKLIN PARTNERSHIP

Roger Tellefsen

State governors and legislatures have long accepted economic development as one of the missions that their citizens expect them to pursue. All too often this meant the single-minded effort to recruit industrial facilities from other states using inducements such as tax incentives, low-interest loans, and highway-access improvements. Very opportunistic, and, as the number of political subdivisions working in this type of development increased, collectively self-defeating, state leaders began to realize by the early 1980s that a more balanced approach to economic development was necessary. Perhaps most importantly they began to recognize that economic development was an activity for all their citizens, companies, counties, and colleges. By recognizing the interrelationship between economic development and human resources, environment, energy, infrastructure, business, science, technology, and quality of life, state leaders greatly increased the opportunity to accomplish fundamental, long-term strengthening of the state economy. To focus efforts and get enthusiastic participation required that a strategic plan be formulated, implemented, and progress evaluated. In Pennsylvania, under Governor Dick Thornburgh, that strategic planning process was known as "Choices for Pennsylvanians."

Beginning in 1979 and continuing through September 1981, an extensive effort was undertaken by the State Planning Board to examine the conditions present in Pennsylvania, and the relationship that the state economy had to the regional and the national economy. The board also carefully considered where Pennsylvania's economy could go, given its current endowments and the additional resources that reasonably could be made available. To identify the problems and opportunities, they began at the top of the hierarchy through meetings with industry, government, labor, and academic leaders, and then tested these perceptions through studies and wide solicitation of public comment in meetings throughout the state. They were very aware that in economic development matters government functions as a facilitator and integrator, only rarely as an actual creator of jobs, and then in only the most limited sense. They saw that the private sector, through the choices they make, creates the economic reality that leads to growth. They also found that institutions of higher education could play a more direct role in economic development without doing harm to their traditional mission of research and graduate education.

Out of the "Choices for Pennsylvanians" process came the "Advanced Technology Policies for Pennsylvania." This made advanced technology important to all state agencies, not just one technology department. The four policy objectives were: 1) increase the capital and other financing available to advanced technology industry; 2) provide technical assistance and services; 3) enhance the skills of Pennsylvania's work force; and 4) promote the expansion of markets for advanced technology products.

A close examination of the philosophy underlying these objectives reveals how the strategic planning process resulted in a new approach to the use of technology as an economic development tool. During the 1970s, technology, in the form of assembly factories for computers, instruments, and other "clean" manufacturing facilities, was seen as an alternative to the "dirty" smokestack industry of the past. What the planning process revealed was an underutilization of technology by existing industry, an underutilization that contributed to the relative decline in the fortunes of large sectors of American (and Pennsylvanian) business. By basing the technology initiative on the development and application of technology, rather than the production of high technology products, all of Pennsylvania's existing and new companies could participate in a technology-led economic revitalization. This was a very important distinction for a state with a tradition of manufacturing and a skilled work force.

One underrecognized advantage that Pennsylvania had compared to other states was its higher education sector. With four of the top fifty research universities and a total of 160 degree-granting colleges and universities (second in number only to New York State) located in Pennsylvania, a tremendous human and scientific resource was already in place. However, except for a few outreach programs such as the Cooperative Extension Service in agriculture and the Pennsylvania Technology Assistance Program (PennTAP) in industry, the formal participation by higher education in economic development efforts was quite limited. We found that there was a net outflow of graduates as the lack of job opportunities in Pennsylvania forced graduates to leave for other states; at the same time, there was a great need for an infusion of scientific and technical expertise into large and small Pennsylvania companies. We found that there was an impressive university research capability in a wide range of scientific and technical areas; at the same time, universities and companies were not talking to each other. Thus, as part of the strategic plan to renew the Pennsylvania economy, we enlisted the support of the leaders of both the higher education and business communities for an advanced technology initiative we named the Ben Franklin Partnership.

Several possible models were considered in planning the Pennsylvania program. Some models had a long history, with an accompanying record of performance. Others were newer, with less information about the relationship between structure and performance. The possible models for state R&D efforts at the time were: *Centers of Excellence*—identify a specific technical field in which one or a consortia of higher education institutions excel, or which corresponds to an existing industry need, and fund the people, equipment, and buildings to create an identified basic research center. From an economic development perspective, this model works by spinning off new technologies developed in the laboratory, and encourages the formation of new firms and the attraction of branch operations to the area near the research center. Examples of this model include microelectronics in North Carolina and biotechnology in Massachusetts.

Information Dissemination—facilitate the transfer of technical information from the generator to the user by using computerized data retrieval systems and face-to-face technology transfer agents. From an economic development perspective, this model works by reducing the search costs for new technology that can improve a company's products or manufacturing processes, thus leading to stability and growth of employment and profits. Examples of this model include industrial extension service programs in Ohio, Maryland, Michigan, and Pennsylvania.

Entrepreneurial Education—encourage the start-up and growth of new advanced technology companies by developing entrepreneurial infrastructure such as venture capital sources, law and accounting firms that work with start-up firms, entrepreneurship programs at higher education institutions, and small business development centers. From an economic development perspective, this model works by identifying individuals and companies with high growth potential by virtue of a product or market niche, and connecting them to public and private service providers and funding sources. Examples of this model include small-business development centers funded through the federal small-business administration and entrepreneurship centers in Canadian provinces.

Advanced Technology Consortia—higher education, industry, and government organizations combine to jointly fund research projects, generally of an applied nature. With the majority of the funding connected to identifiable projects with frequent progress milestones, all consortia members have an incentive to participate in the research, and apply the results as they become available. From an economic development perspective, this model works by accelerating the application of technology into industrial products and processes. Examples of this model were few in 1982, but now include Ohio, Michigan, and Pennsylvania.

Pennsylvania chose the consortia model as the best approach to accomplish the revitalization of the state economy. We recognized that the approach required the participation and coordination of a far larger number of people and organizations than other models, but believed that this added to the likelihood for long-term success. We wanted a broad base of support for using technology as an economic development tool, because having worked from the top down to identify problems, we wanted to start from the bottom and work up to implement solutions.

In 1982, legislation was passed and signed establishing the Ben Franklin Partnership in the Department of Commerce. In spite of the large higher-education component of the initiative, the Department of Commerce and not the Department of Education was designated as lead agency. From the beginning it was important that all observers recognize that this was an initiative whose focus was economic development, and that this was not another education institution funding mechanism. The education institutions were to be a vital component of the program, but the outcome measurements of success were not going to be traditional university academic measurements such as degrees granted or papers published.

The Ben Franklin Partnership Board established three goals for the program: 1) maintain and create jobs in new and existing industries through the development and application of new technologies; 2) improve productivity; and 3) diversify the economy.

The objectives were to: 1) establish effective consortium efforts involving the private sector, higher education institutions and government; 2) encourage and strengthen joint research and development efforts; 3) establish and improve education and training programs to enable the workforce to adjust rapidly to changing technologies; 4) provide entrepreneurial assistance to advanced technology firms; and 5) encourage the creation and expansion of new technology enterprises.

Following a competitive review, the board of the Ben Franklin Partnership chose four university consortia to establish four advanced technology centers (ATC).

Advanced Technology Center	Lead University
ATC for Central and Northern PA	Penn State University
ATC for Northeast Tier	Lehigh University
ATC for Southeastern PA	University City Science Center (owned by a consortia of area colleges and universities)
ATC for Western PA	University of Pittsburgh and Carnegie Mellon University

Geographic coverage of the state was established, with each center identifying three or four research areas of emphasis in which their member schools were already proficient, such as computer aided design and manufacturing, advanced sensors, robotics, or advanced materials. The decentralized approach encouraged local initiative to identify critical technologies and to make research connections between industry and academe. Funds from the state were provided based on individual projects developed between an industry sponsor and a university researcher, not on the basis of overall R&D area. Indeed, the most important single factor in deciding whether to fund an individual project was the level of financial commitment to the project by the private-sector sponsor.

The consortia model was also conducive to incorporating an education and training component. This allowed educational institutions to develop new ways of delivering technology training both to their traditional student body and to new corporate sectors that had not yet been served. For example, statistical process control seminars were initially funded by an ATC through a profit-making service provider; later, area community colleges began to provide these courses to firms. In the same manner, entrepreneurial development initiatives were incorporated into the consortia, most dramatically through support for business services in small business incubator facilities.

Of these three program areas, research and development, education and training, and entrepreneurial development, by far the largest component was research and revelopment. Generally over 65% of state funds were devoted to R&D projects.

State funding for the challenge grant program grew from $1 million in FY 82-83, $10 million in FY 83-84, $18 million in FY 84-85, $21.3 million in FY 85-86, to $26.45 million in FY 86-87. Even more impressive than the state commitment was the response generated from the private sector, universities, and others. Although program requirements stipulated that each dollar of state funding be matched with a dollar from nonstate sources, the actual ratio of state to private sector match in FY 86-87 was 2.59, and the ratio of state to all other funding sources was 4.09. The total program budget in that year was $134.7 million, the largest annual state technology program budget in the country.

Over this five-year period, 128 Pennsylvania higher-education institutions participated in the program in various capacities, 2,800 firms were involved, and good research, education, and entrepreneurship results were achieved. The objectives of the program were met and considerable progress made in attaining the overall program goals. Governor Robert P.

Casey inaugurated constancy of purpose that it took to realize the economic development promise of the Research Triangle Park in North Carolina.

Why was the Ben Franklin Partnership for Technological Innovation successful? Foremost, it was a result of effective state strategic planning. The Roman statesman Seneca observed that "If one does not know to which port one is sailing, no wind is favorable." We knew what we wanted, and the program was designed to be flexible enough to incorporate changes in wind direction on the way there.

We knew that we wanted research partnerships, effective two-way exchanges of research between university and company researchers.

Technology development and transfer is much more effective when the generator and receiver are working directly on a problem. The effectiveness drops off when the connection is decoupled in time and import through journal articles or conference presentations. Companies involved in a research partnership have constant access to the information and can apply it in a more timely fashion; the university researchers can publish their discoveries as soon as practical. In the meanwhile, they and their graduate students can work with hard, interesting, real world problems posed by the collaboration with industry.

We knew we wanted private sector participation in funding and personnel. Without private sector funds being devoted to a research proposal, state matching funding was not available. This gave the private sector participants a direct interest in the project, because their money and personnel resources were at stake, and made the academic participants aware of the direct research interests of the company sponsor.

We knew we wanted a decentralized program in order to make the broadest range of Pennsylvanians aware of the benefits of developing and using technology. The consortia approach, with geographic dispersion, best fit the realities present in Pennsylvania. We were fortunate to have the number of fine research universities that we had, and to gain the support of their leaders. We also had a number of locally-oriented business development organizations that rapidly saw merit in the use of technology in the existing businesses. Together, strong regional technology-oriented consortia developed around the ATCs.

We knew we wanted the program to grow incrementally. Over a six-year period, state funding grew from $1 million to $28.5 million. This allowed for manageable growth, and adherence to the goals and objectives of the program. It allowed a track record of results to develop. Too rapid growth would have raised the possibility that the program would have been transformed into a traditional university basic research funding program.

We knew we wanted competition for available funds. Beyond a minimum amount, all state funds to the ATCs were based on competitive factors. Managements of the ATCs became quite entrepreneurial themselves in seeking out companies that had interesting research problems, and in finding research faculty whose work might be useful to Pennsylvania firms.

We knew that the program would be measured for results. In a public program involved in economic development there are certain factors that people look to as an indication of performance. From the start of the program these indicators were collected and used. They were used in regular reports to the legislature and the public. They were used internally to track incremental movements of effort between research thrust areas and broad categories of activity by the ATCs. Many of the quantitative measures (number of new jobs, number of new company research projects, amount of venture capital, number of higher education institutions participating) were used to allocate funds to the ATCs based on performance. More qualitative measures (changes in patent procedures, faculty exchanges, perception of university-industry cooperation by the project participants) were incorporated into the program indirectly.

We knew that we wanted the program to be bipartisan. On philosophic grounds, bipartisanship is appropriate because technology knows no political or geographic bounds. On pragmatic grounds, bipartisanship is appropriate in Pennsylvania because the General Assembly is quite evenly divided. All legislative members were regularly informed about the program, and numerous seminars were constantly being held throughout the state to inform constituents about the program requirements.

Finally, we knew that we had to tell the public about the Ben Franklin Partnership Program. Achieving the goal of an invigorated Pennsylvania economy depended upon their participation. Technology application would lead to a stronger and more resilient economy. Universities and companies, in partnership, were making technical advances that could lead to job growth. All forms of media were used to tell the story: a strategic plan for economic revitalization exists, technology has a big role to play, and every citizen is part of the implementation.

That is one lesson to be drawn by readers of this monograph—That all the strategic planning is for naught if people are not committed to implementation. Examine the reward structures in place for individual and institutional advancement when you calculate the probability of successful implementation of a plan. If the correct incentives are present, you will see real creativity in implementation; if they are absent, even the most charismatic leader will not succeed.

CHAPTER TEN

TEXAS FORMULA SYSTEM FOR PUBLIC SENIOR COLLEGES AND UNIVERSITIES

William A. Webb

The Texas formula system for public senior colleges and universities has become the framework of legislative strategic planning in the State of Texas. Formula functions have allowed the state government to coordinate the development of a functionally diversified higher education system that includes seven classes of higher education institutions. The Texas Higher Education Coordinating Board is responsible for the design and maintenance of the formula system and for coordinating higher education planning and development within the state. Strategic planning for academic research is part of the coordinating board's overall responsibility.

The Fifty-sixth Legislature used formulas for the first time in determining appropriations to public institutions for fiscal years 1960 and 1961. Since 1959, each session of the legislature has relied upon recommendations derived largely through the application of the designated formulas. In 1955 when the Texas Commission on Higher Education was created, one of its statutory responsibilities was to establish formulas to be used in determining the financial requirements of institutions of higher education to aid the legislature in making appropriations. Prior to 1955, appropriations were made more or less by the degree of influence of the boards of regents and the president of each institution rather than on a systematic basis.

In 1965, the Fifty-ninth Legislature replaced the Commission on Higher Education with the Coordinating Board, Texas College and University System. The legislature gave the coordinating board broader powers, increased responsibilities, and greater financial support. The necessary statutory power to continue the formula system was also authorized by the Higher Education Coordinating Act of 1965. Under Section 61.059 of the Texas Education Code, the coordinating board is charged with the responsibility to ". . . devise, establish, periodically review and may revise formulas for the use of the Governor and the Legislative Budget Board in making appropriations recommendations to the Legislature." The formulas designated by the board to be recommended to the governor and the legislature must have two important characteristics: 1) to recommend a level of funding for the colleges and universities and 2) provide for an equitable distribution of funds appropriated by the legislature. These formulas greatly enhanced strategic planning for university research because they

421

removed much of the political maneuvering for funds and they established some degree of certainty to budget planning based on objective information.

Through advisory committees appointed by the commissioner of higher education, the coordinating board reviews, modifies, and designates formulas to be used in the appropriations process. The formula system has evolved slowly over the last thirty years through careful study and testing by the coordinating board study committees, and acceptance by the governor and the legislature. In 1960 five formulas were used in the planning and appropriation processes, in 1968 there were seven, in 1979 the board designated eleven formulas, and in 1986 fourteen formulas were designated to be used in the planning and appropriations processes. During this period of growth and development, the formula system was also modified to accommodate fourteen newly established institutions of higher education. The formula system now serves thirty-seven public senior college and university campuses. Two new formulas are being studied to include funding for allied health and nursing programs for five health science centers. The new formula studies are a mandate from the legislature.

The formula system is not designed to be used as an internal operating budget for each institution. The legislature appropriates operating funds directly to the senior colleges and universities and they have the responsibility for developing their own operating budgets based on their priorities and within the guidelines of the appropriations act.

The legislature adopted a new method of planning and finance for higher education for the 1988-89 biennium. Instead of appropriating an all funds amount to each institution that includes general revenue and other sources of income, only a general revenue appropriation was made to each institution. Another major change is the authorization to institutions to transfer funds among other elements of cost with the exception of faculty salaries. Funds can be transferred into faculty salaries, but general revenue funds appropriated to faculty salaries cannot be transferred to other elements of cost.

The formula study process usually requires over a year of work leading up to the time the coordinating board must designate formulas to be used in the appropriations request process to recommend funding to the governor and the legislature. However, the appropriations bill for the 1988-89 biennium, a most important source of information for committee work was not enacted by the legislature until July 21, 1987. This delay gave the coordinating board a very short time to complete work on recommendations. A directive from the Formula Advisory Committee to the individual study committees advised that the formula were to be studied, but no significant changes were to be made immediately.

The board recommended formulas in January 1988 in preparation for the Seventy-first Legislature, which convened in 1989 to determine appropriations for 1990 and 1991. The formula advisory committee with the assistance of eleven study committees prepared recommendations that the coordinating board considered in 1988. Over 100 people were involved in the study process. In November of 1987 the study committees brought their formula recommendations to the Public Senior College and University Formula Advisory Committee for review and consideration. The Public Senior College and University Advisory Committee then prepared recommendations to be considered by the commissioner. The commissioner presented recommendations and the advisory committee recommendations, if different, to the coordinating board for consideration and adoption.

The most important part of the formula study process is the participation of university representatives and the lay citizens in developing sound recommendations to meet the needs of higher education. The success of the formula system can be attributed to good committee work and because it is an ongoing process that takes place each biennium.

The specific samples of material will explain the function about formula funding for public senior colleges and universities and the responsibilities of the committees in developing formula recommendations for the legislative budget board.

FORMULA RECOMMENDATIONS FOR BIENNIUM APPROPRIATIONS

It is essential in state strategic planning for the legislature to see the distribution of funds according to institutions. This allows them to determine the geographic service being provided within the state. This planning occurs every two years in Texas.

For the 1988-89 biennium the legislature changed the method of finance for higher education and the bill pattern for appropriations. Before, the bill pattern showed appropriations by element of cost and the total appropriation for each university with the method of finance showing the amount of general revenue appropriated and the estimated amount of other educational and general income appropriated.

The new method of finance shows only the total general revenue appropriated to each university. The bill pattern shows only 1) faculty salaries, 2) general administration, 3) student services, 4) utilities, 5) tuition revenue bond retirement funds, and 6) special items that are funded as a part of the total general revenue appropriation. All other elements of cost are to be funded from the total general revenue according to budget decisions made by each university. Additional funds the university has available can be used to supplement the general revenue appropriation.

You will note in the attachments the bases of appropriation for 1988-89 biennium showing the amount of general revenue for each element of cost statewide, used in building the total general revenue appropriation for senior colleges and universities. The legislature actually used the coordinating board's formula recommendations for 1988-89 and funded each element of cost with a specified percentage of general revenue on a statewide basis, not taking into consideration the ability of the individual universities to generate other educational and general income. Before the 1988-89 biennium, appropriation of general revenue depended on the ability of each university to generate other educational and general income. The 1988-89 biennium is a time to observe the impact of the change in the method of finance. For this reason it is important to continue formula recommendations for the 1990-91 biennium as all funds recommendations. This will require the use of estimated other educational and general income for fiscal 1989 that is available from the legislative budget board to form a basis of all funds appropriations to work from in making recommendations for the 1990-91 biennium. If the legislature in 1989 continues with the new method of finance, the legislative budget board staff will then determine statewide ratios for general revenue to be applied to the coordinating board formula recommendations.

The suggested charges to each study committee are based on the all funds method of finance and House Bill 2181. The first priority for each committee is formula recommendations for 1990-91 biennium to be completed by November. These recommendations should be basically fine tuning and updating the formulas. The House Bill 2181 recommendations are for consideration after the formulas, and to be included in the coordinating board appropriation request that will be adopted by the board in July 1988. The formulas are to be considered basic funding and are to be adopted by the board in January 1988.

The following are specific committee charges related to House Bill 2181 and other tasks.

General Administration and Student Services—1) Review current formula and make recommendations for 1990-91 biennium. 2) Study impact of television instruction on funding for general administration and student services.

General Institutional Expense—Review current formula and make recommendations for 1990-91 biennium.

Faculty Salaries—1) Review current formula for salaries and make recommendations for 1990-91 biennium; 2) faculty development formula; 3) educational opportunity services formula; 4) study impact of television instruction on faculty salary formula; 5) initiate planning for incentive funding for academic excellence according to House Bill 2181; 6) study average compensation of faculty at peer institutions nationwide (H.B. 2181).

Departmental Operating Expense—Review current formula for departmental operating expense and make recommendations for 1990-91 biennium.

Instructional Administration—1) Review current formula and make recommendations for 1990-91 biennium, 2) develop plan for allocation of incentive funding, as a percentage of base funding, among the institutions to reward those that have achieved goals set by the board in such areas as minority recruitment, graduation rates, meeting planning goals, and energy conservations, among others (H.B. 2181).

Library—Review current formula and make recommendations for 1990-91 biennium.

Organized Research—House Bill 2181 changed the organized research formula name to research enhancement formula and recommended a basis for the new formula. The committee is to complete the formula development for recommendations for the 1990-91 biennium.

Physical Plant—1) Review current formulas for plant support, custodial services, building maintenance and grounds maintenance and make recommendations for 1990-91 biennium. 2) Development of factor to reduce funding for physical plant at institution that exceed the average square footage in educational and general facilities.

Allied Health Committee—Present formula recommendations when completed for health science centers.

Nursing Committee—Review committee report on formula funding considered by the committee in 1986.

BASES OF LEGISLATIVE APPROPRIATIONS

Texas Higher Education Coordinating Board, Public Senior Colleges and Universities, 1988-89 Biennium. For the 1988-89 biennium, appropriations to the public senior colleges and universities are in a lump-sum amount to each institution and are out of the general revenue fund only.

In arriving at the general revenue appropriation to each institution, amounts were determined for each element of cost and combined. Out of the total appropriations to each institution, separate amounts are shown in the appropriations bill for general administration and student services, faculty salaries, utilities, and special items. Provisions in the bill specify that the amounts shown for faculty salaries are minimum amounts and may be expended for no other purpose, and the amounts specified for the other items shown shall be expended as nearly as practicable for the purposes indicated.

The bases of determining the amounts included in each institution's appropriation for the coordinating board recommended formula elements of cost are shown below. For each of the formula elements, a statewide general revenue amount to be appropriated was determined and divided by the coordinating board recommended formula produced amount. The resulting percentages (multipliers) of the coordinating board recommended formula produced amounts that each institution received are as follows:

	Multiplier		
	Fiscal Year 1988	Fiscal Year 1989	
General Admin. & Stud. Services	.51426	.494465	*$448,000
General Institutional Expense	.553708	.533358	*$154,000
Faculty Salaries	.713614	.751959	
Depart. Operating Expense [1]	.723278	.694848	
Instructional Admin.	.484474	.454814	*$ 94,000
Library	.539772	.519062	*$303,000
Organized Research	.075614	.071704	
Plant Support Services	.381081	.362722	*$115,000
Campus Security	.589285	.566662	*$130,000
Building Maintenance	.595932	.558641	
Custodial Services	.438532	.413593	
Grounds Maintenance	.358131	.342267	
Faculty Development Leaves	(not used)	(not used)	

1. $7,853,360 per year is added at non-PUF institutions after this calculation to replace one-time use of HEAF in their respective methods of financing for the previous biennium.

* minimum amounts to each public senior college and university.

General Revenue Comparison of Legislative Appropriations for the 1988-89 Biennium

All Agencies Of Higher Education

	Appropriated 1988-89		Increase 1988-89 over 1986-87	
	1986-87 Biennium[1]	1988-89 Biennium[5]	Amount	Percent
Public Senior Colleges	$1,718,648,829	$1,940,877,021	$222,228,192	12.9
Public Junior Colleges[2]	849,668,320	827,167,562	−22,500,758	−2.6
Health Related Units[3]	1,140,889,223	1,227,264,343	86,375,120	7.6
All Other Agencies[4]	571,329,491	591,438,292	20,108,801	3.5
TOTAL	$4,280,535,863	$4,586,747,218	$306,211,355	7.2

1. Includes appropriations in H.B. 20 for fiscal year 1986 and S.B. 1 for fiscal year 1987. Does not include salary funds provided according to Article V, Section 95 of the appropriations bill for either year.
2. Amounts in appropriations bill.
3. Includes funds trusteed to the coordinating board for health related purposes, and the Texas A&M University Medical Education Program (95.07 percent of the line-item amount to Texas A&M University included for fiscal 1987).
4. Includes Higher Education Fund, and $17,957,953 appropriated in H.B. 5, Third Called Session, Sixty-Ninth Legislature.
5. Amounts shown reflect a .65 of 1 percent reduction per provisions of Article V, Section 101 in the appropriations bill.

Definitions of the Elements of Institutional costs

The definitions of educational and general functions set out below form a part of a uniform system of reporting for institutions of higher education in Texas as required by Section 22, House Bill 1, Chapter 12, *Acts of the Fifty-ninth Legislature*, Regular Session, 1965. These definitions were officially adopted by the coordinating board on January 24, 1986. The listings of examples are not to be interpreted as necessarily meaning that each institution will have expenditures in all categories, but are intended only as illustrations of the named functions. Excluded from these elements and definitions are student services for which the legislature has authorized fees under Section 54.503. Vernon's Texas Education Code, (S.B. 6, Chapter 12, *Acts of the Fifty-sixth Legislature*, Second Called Session, 1959, p. 99), and all auxiliary enterprise operations and costs related thereto.

428   STRATEGIC PLANNING FOR UNIVERSITY RESEARCH

GENERAL ADMINISTRATION AND STUDENT SERVICES

General Administration (Research Function)

Definition—Salaries, wages, and all other costs for the following functions and activities. Note: Because funds to support the functions performed by governing boards and central administrative offices for certain public senior college and university systems having responsibility for more than one academic institution have historically been separately requested and appropriated, the costs for these boards and offices are excluded from the defined elements.

Government of the institution—The costs incurred on behalf of the governing body in discharging its responsibilities. Example: Governing board.

Executive direction and control—The costs incurred in the executive direction, control and implementation of policies of the governing board and the chief executive officer. Examples: chief executive's office (pesident), chief academic officer's office, chief business officer's office, assistant(s) to the president. Excluded are costs of academic administrative functions defined in "Instructional Administration Expense".

Business and fiscal management—The costs incurred in the attainment of financial goals through proper effective accounting records and procedures and budgetary and cost controls. Examples: Business Office, Fiscal Office, Comptroller's Office, Personnel Services, Purchasing Office, Property and Inventory Control, Internal Audit, Systems and Procedures.

H2 Student Services

Admissions and registration—The costs of administering undergraduate and graduate admission activities, processing and maintenance of student records and reports and the registration of students. Examples: Registrar's Office, Dean of Admissions.

Other Student Services—The costs of administering and coordinating the development and maintenance of the student life program including counseling with students on disciplinary and other nonacademic problems, the guidance of foreign students, student and graduate placement, and student financial aids. Examples: Chief Student Affair's Office, Dean of Men, Dean of Women, Testing and Guidance, Student Life, International Office, Placement, and Student Financial Aids.

GENERAL INSTITUTIONAL EXPENSE

Definition—Expenses of a general nature which benefit the entire institution and are not related solely to any specific department or division. The definition of functions within this element should not be interpreted as implying that each institution should engage in all the activities defined. Included are salaries, wages, and all other costs for the following functions, services, or activities:

1. Public informational activities including bulletins, catalogues, publications, exhibits, and news service.
2. Institutional memberships.
3. Commencement exercises for the graduating classes. Included only are costs of speakers, arrangements, and caps and gowns for guests.
4. Convocations and public lectures.
5. Official functions.
6. Mail services, excluding the cost of postage.
7. Legal fees and expense required to protect the interests of the institution and the state.
8. Development activities (research development).
9. The costs of maintaining and securing records pertaining to sponsored research and alumni of the institution for evaluation of the educational programs of the institution.
10. Telephone central office. Does not include long distance call charges nor cost of telephone instruments. These costs are to be charged to the using departments.
11. The cost of conducting studies for the improvement of the institution.
12. Insurance (other than property and those covered under staff benefits).
13. Other general institutional expense items, except as follows: service department charges (except for mail service and telephone central office) should be allocated to the users, (e.g., stenographic bureaus, central stores, central computer operation costs, printing shops, copy centers, supply centers, microfilm services, etc.); and any item of cost specifically identified within the definition of an element of institutional cost should be included in the cost element and not "general institutional expense."

STAFF BENEFITS

Definition—Premiums or costs toward staff benefits programs for employees. Examples of staff benefits authorized by the legislature are:

1. Staff group insurance premiums,
2. Faculty development leaves,
3. Old age and survivors insurance,
4. Workmen's compensation insurance.

Resident instruction

Definition—Resident instruction includes all functions directly related to teaching, classified as follows.

Faculty Salaries

Definition—Salaries or wages of those engaged in the teaching function, including heads of teaching departments. Included also are laboratory assistants, teaching assistants, teaching fellows and lecturers who are responsible for, or in charge of, a class or class section, or a quiz, drill, or laboratory section. Not included are the salaries or wages of guest lecturers or of student assistants, laboratory assistants, and graders whose duties involve grading, clerical functions, store keeping, and preparations of class or laboratory material or other subordinate functions.

Departmental Operating Expense

Definition—Salaries, wages, supplies, travel, office furniture, equipment, and other operating expense for the operation of instructional departments, other than faculty salaries. Included here are the salaries and wages of guest lecturers and of student assistants, laboratory assistants, and graders whose duties involve grading, clerical functions, store keeping, and preparation of class or laboratory material or experiments or other subordinate functions. Includes teaching equipment customarily assigned to teaching departments and provides for replacement and updating of teaching equipment as well as acquisition of new items. Also includes costs of practice teaching other than faculty salaries, and all direct of prorated computer costs related to resident instructional programs.

Instructional Administration Expense

Definition—Salaries, wages, supplies, travel, equipment, and other operating expense of the offices of academic deans or directors of major teaching department groupings into colleges, schools, or divisions, and the office of the dean or director of graduate studies. Examples of activities include, but are not limited to, the following: instructional budget planning; faculty recruitment, development, assignment, and utilization; curricular expansion and revision; student academic advisement; maintenance of scholastic and admission standards. Not included are the offices of the heads of teaching departments.

Organized Activities Related to Instructional Departments

Definition—All costs of activities or enterprises separately organized and operated in connection with instructional departments primarily for the purpose of giving professional training to students as a necessary part of the educational work of the related departments. Examples of such organized activities are college farms, creameries, poultry processing plants, veterinary hospitals, nursery schools, and home management houses. Does not include cost of practice teaching. Where these activities are not conducted primarily for educational purposes, they should be excluded from the definition of this element of cost.

VOCATIONAL TEACHER TRAINING SUPPLEMENT

Definition—The matching part of salaries, wages, and such other costs as are required to finance the Vocational Teacher Training Program according to provisions of the Texas State Acceptance Act and the Plan of the State Board of Vocational Education for Vocational Teacher Training under the Smith-Hughes and George Barden Acts.

LIBRARY

Definition—Salaries, wages, library materials (examples include books, journals, microforms, audiovisual media, computer-based information, manuscripts, maps, documents and other information sources), binding costs, equipment, and other operating costs of separately organized libraries (including archives).

ORGANIZED RESEARCH

Definition—Salaries, wages, and other costs of separately organized research divisions such as research bureaus, research institutes, and separately budgeted or financed research investigations. Departmental research not separately budgeted or financed and contract research and services are not included.

EXTENSION AND PUBLIC SERVICE

Definition—All costs of activities designed primarily to serve the general public, including correspondence courses, adult study courses, public lectures, radio and television stations, institutes, workshops, demonstrations, package libraries, and similar activities.

PHYSICAL PLANT OPERATION AND MAINTENANCE

Plant Support Services-Operating Expenses

Definition—Salaries, wages, supplies, travel, equipment and other operating expenses to provide physical plant general services, and to carry out the duties of physical plant administration and planning.

Examples of the activities included are: 1) acquisition and repair of general classroom and laboratory furniture (does not include office furniture); 2) central receiving and store of supplies and equipment; 3) safety, including fire, occupational, radiation, health and sanitation safety; 4) garbage and trash disposal—hazardous waste; 5) hauling, moving, and storing; 6) property insurance; 7) truck and automobile expense in general service of the institution; 8) administration of the organizational units of physical plant; and 9) preparation of architectural and engineering plans and specifications for expansion, renovation and rehabilitation of physical plant facilities, excluding fees for new construction.

Campus Security

Definition—Salaries, wages, supplies, travel,equipment, and other operating expenses to carry out the traffic, police, and security services of the institution.

Building Maintenance

Definition—Costs including salaries, wages, supplies, materials, equipment, services, and other expenses, necessary to keep each building in good appearance and usable condition and prevent the building from deteriorating once it has been placed in first class condition for that type and age of building. Does not include auxiliary enterprise buildings. Building maintenance includes minor repairs and alterations, costs of materials, hire of personnel, and other necessary expenses for the repair and/or painting of the following: roofs, exterior walls, foundations, flooring, ceilings, partitions, doors, windows, plaster, structural ironworks, screens, window shades, venetian blinds, plumbing, heating and air-conditioning equipment within or apart of the building, electric wiring, light fixtures, (including the replacement of lamps), washing of all outside window surfaces, built-in shelving, and other related items.

Custodial Services

Definition—Costs including salaries, wages, supplies, materials, equipment, services, and other expenses necessary to keep the buildings in a clean and sanitary condition. Does not include auxiliary enterprise buildings. These services include care of the floors, stairways and landings, and restrooms; cleaning chalkboards, inside of windows, walls, and room furniture and fixtures; assigned dusting, removal of waste paper and refuse and other related duties.

Common operations include: mopping, sweeping, waxing, renovating of floors (sanding and refinishing of floors are excluded); dusting, polishing of furniture and fixtures such as venetian blinds, partitions, pictures, maps, radiators, etc.; cleaning of chalkboards, chalk trays, erasers, and replacement of chalk; washing and dusting of walls, cleaning and disinfecting commodes and urinals, cleaning and washing other fixtures, walls and partitions, and replenishing supplies for restrooms; the emptying and cleaning of waste receptacles, and dusting and cleaning of windows, and other glass surfaces; sweeping and cleaning of entrances, and opening and/or closing buildings, doors, and windows.

Grounds Maintenance

Definition—Costs including salaries, wages, supplies, materials, equipment, services, and other expenses relating to the upkeep of all lands designated as campus proper (improved and unimproved) not occupied by actual buildings, including any court, patio, and/or inner garden or court enclosed by buildings. Grounds Maintenance begins after the site improvements are complete.

Phases of Grounds Maintenance are:
1. Land Improvements: permanent lawns, trees, shrubs, etc.; seasonal flowers, bulbs, etc.
2. Circulation Systems: vehicular—streets and roads (improved and unimproved), parking areas (improved and unimproved), traffic controls-signal lights, signs, and barriers; pedestrian—walks and paths (improved and unimproved).
3. Other Activities: irrigation systems; nonstructural improvements (walls, fences, fountains, campus furniture, etc.); ancillary enterprises (nursery, greenhouse-areas for special academic study).

Utilities

Definition—All costs of purchase, manufacture and delivery of utility services, including: electricity, steam heat, water (hot, cold or chilled), storm sewers, sanitary sewers, compressed air, gas clocks and bells, campus lighting, energy management systems, institutionally owned telephone systems (does not include switchboard operators and commercial telephone service), preventative maintenance, and repairs and minor alterations to production and distribution facilities. Does not include costs of utilities for auxiliary enterprises.

SPECIAL ITEMS-RESEARCH PROJECTS

Definition—The costs of those items which are not included in any of the other elements, or, the costs of those items which are peculiar to the particular institution.

MAJOR REPAIRS AND REHABILITATION OF BUILDINGS AND FACILITIES

Definition—This item includes major repairs, rehabilitation, and renovation of existing buildings and facilities (including repairs and alterations to production and distribution facilities for utilities where such facilities do not primarily serve auxiliary enterprises) including salaries, wages, and costs of materials for such items; but does not include routine, ordinary, annual or periodic maintenance.

FORMULAS DESIGNATED BY COORDINATING BOARD FOR THE PUBLIC SENIOR COLLEGES AND UNIVERSITIES

Coordinating Board, Texas College and University System, January 24, 1986. Recommended formula for general administration and student services. Public Senior Colleges and Universities, 1987-89 Biennium, For Fiscal Year 1988: (Fall Semester 1986 headcount enrollment times the fiscal 1988 rates shown below) plus (7 1/2 percent of sponsored research funds expended during fiscal 1986 times 1.04)

For Fiscal Year 1989: (Fall Semester 1986 headcount enrollment times the fiscal 1989 rates shown below) plus (7 1/2 percent of sponsored research funds expended during fiscal 1986 times 1.04)

For institutions with a Fall Semester headcount enrollment of 4,000 or more use the following rates:

Fall Semester	Rate Per Headcount Enrollment	
Headcount Enrollment	*Fiscal Year 1988*	*Fiscal Year 1989*
First 4,000	$215.26	$223.87
Next 4,000	160.58	167.00
Above 8,000	144.68	150.47

For institutions with a Fall Semester headcount enrollment below 4,000 use the following rates:

Fall Semester	Rate Per Headcount Enrollment	
Headcount Enrollment	*Fiscal Year 1988*	*Fiscal Year 1989*
First 1,000	$478,900 base	$498,100 base
Next 1,500	150.86	156.87
Next 1,500	103.90	108.05

Notes:
 1. If the appropriated rates per headcount for the first 4,000 are different than the recommended rates shown above, the base amounts recommended for each year of the biennium and the below 4,000 headcount rates should be adjusted proportionately.
 2. It is intended that for fiscal year 1989 the amount produced by 7 1/2 percent of Sponsored Research funds expended during fiscal 1986 be increased by the same percentage as the rates per headcount enrollment are increased over fiscal year 1988.

RECOMMENDED FORMULA FOR GENERAL INSTITUTIONAL EXPENSE

Public Senior Colleges and Universities, 1987-89 Biennium. Base period semester credit hours (Summer Session 1986, Fall Semester 1986 and Spring Semester 1987) times the following rates equals dollar request for General Institutional Expense.

	Rates Per Base Period Semester Credit Hour	
Semester Credit Hours	*Fiscal Year 1988*	*Fiscal Year 1989*
First 200,000	$1.37	$1.42
Next 200,000	1.55	1.61
Next 200,000	1.70	1.77
Over 600,000	1.86	1.93

Notes:
 1. Minimum of $169,000 for fiscal year 1988 and $175,800 for fiscal year 1989 unless total semester credit hour productions more than 50,000, in which case the appropriation shall be $169,000 for fiscal year 1988 and $175,800 for fiscal year 1989 plus $.365 in fiscal year 1988 and $.372 in fiscal year 1989 per semester credit hour for all semester credit hours in excess of 50,000 to a maximum of $205,500 in fiscal year 1988 and $213,000 in fiscal year 1989.
 2. If the appropriated rates per semester credit hour are different than the recommended rates shown above, the minimum amounts recommended should be adjusted proportionately.

RECOMMENDED FORMULA FOR FACULTY SALARIES

Public Senior Colleges and Universities, 1987-89 Biennium. Base period semester credit hours (Summer Session 1986, Fall Semester 1986 and Spring Semester 1987) times the following rates equals dollar request for Faculty Salaries.

Fiscal Year 1988
Rates Per Base Period Semester Credit Hour

| | Undergraduate | | | | |
Program	Four-Year Institutions	Upper-Level Institutions	Masters	Special Professional	Doctoral
Liberal Arts	$ 35.12	$ 61.11	$101.47		$345.77
Science	37.57	72.10	168.91		497.89
Fine Arts	67.97	93.09	156.41		501.32
Teacher Education	35.16	37.26	86.57		296.41
Teacher Education-					
Practice Teaching	78.12	78.12			
Agriculture	48.82		140.92		437.96
Engineering	67.77	81.34	179.77		497.89
Home Economics	49.67		120.69		326.63
Law				92.48	
Social Service	53.82	61.88	185.17		345.77
Library Science	36.90	36.90	110.02		345.77
Vocational Training	34.59	34.59			
Physical Training	33.28				
Health Services	106.72	106.72	181.62		551.20
Pharmacy	87.07		185.41		501.32
Business					
Administration	40.95	46.26	114.04		474.89
Optometry				146.17	497.89
Technology	60.69	78.29	177.40		

Fiscal Year 1989

Liberal Arts	$ 38.95	$ 67.77	$112.53		$383.46
Science	41.67	79.96	187.32		552.16
Fine Arts	75.38	103.24	173.46		555.96
Teacher Education	38.99	41.32	96.01		328.72
Teacher Education-					
Practice Teaching	86.64	86.64			
Agriculture	54.14		156.28		485.70
Engineering	75.16	90.21	199.36		552.16
Home Economics	55.08		133.85		362.23
Law				102.56	
Social Service	59.69	68.62	205.35		383.46
Library Service	40.92	40.92	122.01		383.46
Vocational Training	38.36	38.36			
Physical Training	36.91				
Health Services	118.35	118.35	201.42		611.28
Pharmacy	96.56		205.62		555.96
Business					
Administration	45.41	51.30	126.47		526.65
Optometry				162.10	552.16
Technology	67.31	86.82	196.74		

Recommended Formula for
Departmental Operating Expense

Public Senior Colleges and Universities, 1987-89 Biennium. Base period semester credit hours (Summer Session 1986, Fall Semester 1986 and Spring Semester 1987) *times* the following rates *equals* dollar request for Departmental Operating Expense.

Fiscal Year 1988
Rates Per Base Period Semester Credit Hour

Program	Undergraduate	Masters	Special Professional	Doctoral
Liberal Arts	$ 3.59	$13.67		$ 64.29
Science	15.45	51.43		208.27
Fine Arts	15.45	51.43		208.27
Teacher Education (Includes Practice Teaching)	6.45	12.86		51.43
Agriculture	11.62	51.43		208.27
Engineering	23.13	51.43		208.27
Home Economics	9.01	25.73		51.43
Law			13.67	
Social Service	6.45	19.27		51.43
Library Science	7.75	12.86		64.29
Vocational Training	10.26			
Physical Training	6.45			
Health Services	14.39	57.58		233.12
Pharmacy	32.26	51.43		208.27
Business Administration	6.45	25.73		51.43
Optometry			64.81	208.27
Technology	12.19	51.43		
Military Science	6.45			

Notes:
1. If the formula produced amount is less than $654,300 the amount requested shall be 22 percent of Faculty Salaries or the formula produced amount, whichever is greater. The maximum amount that may be requested using the percentage of Faculty Salaries is $654,300.
2. If the appropriated rates per semester credit hour are different than the recommended rates shown above, the $654,300 in Note 1 should be adjusted proportionately.

Fiscal Year 1989
Rates Per Base Period Semester Credit Hour

Program	Undergraduate	Masters	Special Professional	Doctoral
Liberal Arts	$ 3.73	$14.22		$ 66.86
Science	16.07	53.49		216.60
Fine Arts	16.07	53.49		216.60
Teacher Education (Includes				
Practice Teaching	6.71	13.37		53.49
Agriculture	12.08	53.49		216.60
Engineering	24.06	53.49		216.60
Home Economics	9.37	26.76		53.49
Law			14.22	
Social Service	6.71	20.04		53.49
Library Science	8.06	13.37		66.86
Vocational Training	10.67			
Physical Training	6.71			
Health Services	14.97	59.88		242.44
Pharmacy	33.55	53.49		216.60
Business Administration	6.71	26.76		53.49
Optometry			67.40	216.60
Technology	12.68	53.49		
Military Science	6.71			

Notes:
1. If the formula produced amount is less than $680,500 the amount requested shall be
   22 percent of Faculty Salaries or the formula produced amount, whichever is
   greater. The maximum amount that may be requested using the percentage of
   Faculty Salaries is $680,500.
2. If the appropriated rates per semester credit hour are different than the recommended rates shown above, the $680,500 in Note 1 should be adjusted propor-
   tionately.

RECOMMENDED FORMULA
FOR INSTRUCTIONAL ADMINISTRATION

Public Senior Colleges and Universities, 1987-89 Biennium. For Fiscal
Year 1988: .5 times A plus .5 times B, where: A = Computation shown
below; and B = .049 times Faculty Salaries. For Fiscal Year 1989: .05
times Faculty Salaries. The A portion of the formula for fiscal year 1988 is
to be computed as follows: (Part 1 - Part 2) expressed as a percentage times
Faculty Salaries.

Part 1 shall be computed as follows:

5.400 for undergraduate operation plus 0.800 if there is organization for master's level programs; minus 0.800 if there

are doctoral programs and doctoral credit hours produced in the base period exceed 10,000 or minus 0.800 x (doctoral hours/10,000) if the doctoral credit hours produced in the base period are less than 10,000; plus 1.300 if there is organization for special professional programs.

Part 2 contribution is shown below:

Divide undergraduate, graduate, and special professional Base Period Semester Credit hours (Summer Session 1986, Fall Semester 1986 and Spring Semester 1987) by the number of colleges, schools, or divisions in these categories approved by the Coordinating Board as of the Spring Semester of 1987. The results are denoted by USCH, GSCH, SPSCH, their nature as averages being indicated by the bars above the letter symbols. The numbers 21,000 and 3,000 are identified as critical sizes corresponding to these. The part 2 computation is as follows:

Undergraduate: 0.690 + (.000007 x USCH) if USCH exceeds 21,000; .000040 x USCH if not.

plus Graduate: 0.190 - (.000008 x GSCH) if GSCH exceeds 21,000; .000001 x GSCH if not.

plus Special Professional: 0.204 + (-.000002 x SPSCH) if SPSCH exceeds 3,000; .000076 x SPSCH if not.

Note: Minimum of $100,000 unless total fall semester 1986 headcount enrollment is more than 1,000, in which case the appropriation shall be $100,000 plus $50 per fall semester 1986 headcount in excess of 1,000 to a maximum of $150,000.

RECOMMENDED FORMULA FOR LIBRARY

Public Senior Colleges and Universities, 1987-89 Biennium. Base period semester credit hours (Summer Session 1986, Fall Semester 1986 and Spring Semester 1987) times the following rates equals dollar request for Library.

Semester Credit Hours	Rates Per Base Period Semester Credit Hour	
	Fiscal Year *1988*	Fiscal Year *1989*
Undergraduate	$ 4.76	$ 4.95
Masters and Special Professional	9.61	9.99
Law	34.74	36.13
Doctoral	41.13	42.78

Notes:

1. Minimum of $640,500 for fiscal year 1988 and $666,000 for fiscal year 1989 unless total semester credit hour production is below 50,000, in which case the appropriation shall be $320,250 for fiscal year 1988 and $333,000 for fiscal year 1989 *plus* $12.81 for 1988 and $13.32 for 1989 per semester credit hour for all semester credit ours in excess of 25,00 to the minimum of $640,500 for fiscal year 1988 and $666,000 for fiscal year 1989.

2. If the appropriated rates per semester credit hour are different than the recommended rates shown above, the minimum amounts recommended should be adjusted proportionately.

RECOMMENDED FORMULA FOR ORGANIZED RESEARCH

Public Senior Colleges and Universities, 1987-98 Biennium. For Fiscal Year 1988: (.02 times of total Faculty Salaries) plus (.20 times sponsored research funds expended during fiscal year 1986).

For Fiscal Year 1989: [(.02 times Faculty Salaries) a] plus [(.20 times sponsored research funds expended during fiscal year 1986 times I) b], where I is the inflation factor. For fiscal year 1989, the I factor is 1.04. Two factors: (a) Faculty Salaries and (b) Time Sponsored Research.

RECOMMENDED FORMULA FOR PLANT SUPPORT SERVICES

Public Senior Colleges and Universities, 1987-89. For Fiscal Year 1988: (SW x 3.90 x population + .0028 x value of Physical Plant).

For Fiscal Year 1989: (SW x 3.90 x population + .0028 x value of Physical Plant) I; Where the "population" being serviced is equal to (HC + 2 x E); and the "value of the Physical Plant" being maintained is RCB.

Definitions of terms used in the formulas:

SW— is the average hourly earnings for services (adjusted) for January 1986, as shown in the *Survey of Current Business* published by the Bureau of Economic Analysis fo the U.S. Department of Commerce.

HC— is the Fall Semester 1986 headcount enrollment.

E— is the number of active employees as of October 31, 1986, for whom the institution is required to make a contribution under Article 3.50 of the Texas Insurance Code.

RCB— is the replacement cost of buildings as calculated in the formula for Building Maintenance. For fiscal year 1988, include the replacement cost of buildings which will be completed and carried on the books for the institution as of August 31, 1987. For fiscal year 1989, include the replacement cost of buildings which will be completed and carried on the books of the institution as of August 31, 1988. Building replacement cost shall be determined by applying the factors for the specific classes of construction, as shown on *Markel's Handy Appraisal Chart 1/* to the original construction costs of each educational, general and service building.

I— represents a one-year inflation factor for labor and materials. For fiscal year 1989, this factor is 1.04.

Note: Minimum of $129,300 for fiscal year 1988, and $134,500 for fiscal year 1989. If the appropriated *I* factor is different than the recommended *I* factor shown above, the

minimum amount recommended for 1989 should be adjusted proportionately. *1/*
Published by Markel Appraisal Chart Company, Cincinnati, Ohio as of January and July
each year. Use the January 1986 issue for each budget submission.

RECOMMENDED FORMULA FOR CAMPUS SECURITY

Public Senior Colleges and Universities, 1987-89 Biennium. For Fiscal
Year 1988: $24.81 (HC + E) x C x V.
For Fiscal Year 1989: $25.80 (HC + E) x C x V.
Definitions of terms used in the formula:

HC— is the Fall Semester 1986 headcount enrollment.
   E— is the number of active employees as of October 31, 1986, for whom the institution
  is required to make a contribution under Article 3.50 of the Texas Insurance Code.
   C— is a population factor of institutions located in, or adjoining, large metropolitan
  areas. The value of *C* is according to the following table:

Population	C Value
0 – 50,000	1.00
50,001 – 100,000	1.04
100,001 – 200,000	1.08
200,001 – 300,000	1.12
300,001 – 600,000	1.30
600,001 – 1,000,000	1.40
1,000,001 – 1,500,000	1.50
1,500,001 – and above	1.60

The appropriate population for each institution shall be based on the 1980 report of the
U.S. Bureau of the Census of all incorporated communities (cities and towns) which have
a boundary either enclosing the central campus or within five air miles of the central
campus boundary (as determined by the official county map of the Texas State Highway
Department), including the most reliable data on cities across the Mexican border, where
applicable.

   V— is a property value factor for institutions which have a high value campus (i.e., a
  campus which significantly exceeds the average value per square footage). *V* is
  determined by the following table:

$\dfrac{RCB}{GSF} + \dfrac{TRCB}{TGSF}$	*"V" Value*
0.00 to 1.05	1.00
1.06 to 1.10	1.05
1.11 to 1.15	1.10
1.16 to 1.20	1.15
1.21 to 1.25	1.20
1.26 and up	1.25

RCB— is the August 31, 1987 replacement cost of buildings for the institution as calculated in the Building Maintenance Formula recommended by the Coordinating Board.

GSF— is the gross square feet (outside dimensions) of educational, general and service buildings completed and carried on the books of the institution as of August 31, 1987, as calculated in the Custodial Services Formula recommended by the Coordinating Board.

TRCB— is the total *RCB* for all colleges and universities as of August 31, 1987.

TGSF— is the total *GSF* for all colleges and universities as of August 31, 1987.

Notes:

1. Minimum of $139,600 for fiscal year 1988, and $145,200 for fiscal year 1989.
2. If the appropriated rates of increase for 1988 and 1989 are different than the recommended rates shown above, the minimum amounts recommended should be adjusted proportionately.
3. Prairie View A & M Nursing School at Houston, Texas Woman's University Nursing Schools at Dallas and Houston, Pan American University at Brownsville, East Texas State University at Texarkana, Laredo State University, and the University of Houston-Victoria shall request funding on the basis of need.

RECOMMENDED FORMULA FOR BUILDING MAINTENANCE

Public Senior Colleges and Universities, 1987-89 Biennium. For fiscal year 1988, maintenance cost factors times building replacement costs equals dollar request for Building Maintenance.

For fiscal year 1989, maintenance cost factors times building replacement costs times I equals dollar request for Building Maintenance.

Maintenance cost factors are designated as follows (factors expressed as percentage figures):

	Wood-Frame Construction [1]	Masonry-Wood Construction [2]	Masonry-Concrete Construction [3]
Air Conditioned	1.90	1.45	1.25
Non-Air Conditioned	1.75	1.30	1.10

Building replacement cost shall be determined by applying the factors for the specific classes of construction, as shown on *Markel's Handy Appraisal Chart* [4] to the original construction costs of each educational, general, and service building. Buildings to be included are as follows:

Fiscal Year 1988—Include buildings which will be completed and carried on the books of the institution as of August 31, 1988. The portion of the total 1988 request for Building Maintenance for buildings to be accepted between September 1, 1987 and August 31, 1988, should be clearly shown as subtotal. The portion of the total 1988 request for Building Maintenance on buildings completed between September 1, 1987 and August 31, 1988, should be multiplied by a factor of X/12 where X equals the number of months during fiscal year 1988 that Building Maintenance will be required on such new buildings.

Fiscal Year 1989—Include buildings which will be completed and carried on the books of the institution as of August 31, 1989. The portion of the total 1989 request for Building Maintenance for buildings to be accepted between September 1, 1988 and August 31, 1989, should be clearly shown as a subtotal. The portion of the total 1989 request for Building Maintenance on buildings completed between September 1, 1988 and August 31, 1989, should be multiplied by a factor of X/12 where X equals the number of months during fiscal year 1989 that Building Maintenance will be required on such buildings.

I— represents a one-year inflation factor for labor and materials. For fiscal year 1989, this factor is 1.04.
1. Designated as "Frame" on *Markel's Handy Appraisal Chart.*
2. Designated as "Semi-Fireproof" on *Markel's Handy Appraisal Chart.*
3. Designated as "Fireproof" on *Markel's Handy Appraisal Chart.*
4. Published by Markel Appraisal Chart Company, Cincinnati, Ohio as of January and July each year. Use the January 1986 issue for each budget submission.

RECOMMENDED FORMULA FOR CUSTODIAL SERVICES

Public Senior Colleges and Universities, 1987-89.

For Fiscal Year 1988: $(.75 \times SW) \times \dfrac{GSF}{19,000} \times 2080 \times 1.2$

For Fiscal Year 1989: $(.75 \times SW) \times \dfrac{GSF}{19,000} \times 2080 \times 1.2 \times I$

Definitions of terms used in the formula:

SW— is the average hourly earnings for services (adjusted) for January 1986, as shown in the *Survey of Current Business* published by the Bureau of Economics Analysis of the U.S. Department of Commerce.
I— represents a one-year inflation factor for labor and materials. For fiscal year 1989, this factor is 1.04.
GSF— is gross square feet (outside dimensions) of educational, general and service buildings. For fiscal year 1988, include buildings completed and carried on the books of the institution as of August 31, 1987, *plus* the gross area of such similar buildings completed between September 1, 1987 and August 31, 1988, *times* a factor of X/12 where X equals the number of months during fiscal year 1988 that Custodial Services will be required in such new buildings. The portion of the total 1988 request for Custodial Services for new buildings to be occupied between September 1, 1987 and August 31, 1988, should be clearly shown as a subtotal.

For fiscal year 1989, include buildings completed and carried on the books of the institution as of August 31, 1988, plus the gross area of such similar buildings completed between September 1, 1988 and August 31,

1989, *times* a factor of X/12 where X equals the number of months during fiscal year 1989 that Custodial Services will be required in such new buildings. The portion of the total 1989 request for Custodial Services for new buildings to be occupied between September 1, 1988 and August 31, 1989, should be clearly shown as a subtotal.

Note: For purposes of the Custodial Services formula "educational, general and service buildings" do not include auxiliary enterprise buildings, any buildings not requiring Custodial Services, or any buildings where Custodial Services are performed by persons other than those whose salaries are paid out of funds budgeted for Custodial Services.

RECOMMENDED FORMULA FOR GROUNDS MAINTENANCE

Public Senior Colleges and Universities, 1987-89 Biennium. For Fiscal Year 1988: SW (.70P + 122L + .50HC).

For Fiscal Year 1989: SW (.70P + 122L + .50HC) I.

Definitions of terms used in the formula:

1SW— is the average hourly earnings for services (adjusted) for January, 1986 as shown in the *Survey of Current Business* published by the Bureau of Economic Analysis of the U.S. Department of Commerce.

P— is the total linear feet of perimeter of all campus buildings including academic, office, service, administration, dormitories, etc. For fiscal year 1988, include all buildings which will be completed and carried on the books of the institution as of August 31, 1987. For fiscal year 1989, include all buildings which will be completed and carried on the books of the institution as of August 31, 1988.

L— is the total number of acres of lawns and regularly maintained areas (malls, flower beds, parking lots, sidewalks, streets, etc.). Exclude all buildings and areas covered under Organized Activities (e.g. college farms). For fiscal year 1988, include applicable acres as of August 31, 1987. For fiscal year 1989, include applicable acres as of August 31, 1988.

4HC— is the Fall Semester 1986 headcount enrollment.

I— represents a one-year inflation factor for labor and materials. For fiscal year 1989, this factor is 1.04.

RECOMMENDED FORMULA FOR
FACULTY DEVELOPMENT LEAVES

Public Senior Colleges and Universities, 1987-89 Biennium. For each year of the biennium, 1.25 percent of Faculty Salary appropriations for fiscal year 1986-87. The appropriation should be a nontransferable item with the unencumbered balance reappropriated for the second year of the biennium.

Note: Minimum of $20,000 each year of the biennium.

RECOMMENDED FORMULA FOR
EDUCATIONAL OPPORTUNITY SERVICE

Public Senior Colleges and Universities, 1987-89 Biennium. For each year of the biennium, a minimum of $35,000 plus $50 per Fall 1986 head-count enrollment of each minority student over 200 minority students in enrollment.

Note: Minority students include the racial ethnic categories of Black-Non Hispanic; American Indian or Alaska Native; Asian or Pacific Islander; Hispanics.

LEGISLATIVE APPROPRIATIONS FOR ORGANIZED RESEARCH
Public Senior Colleges and Universities

Fiscal Year	Amount
1979-80	$7,163,386
1980-81	7,163,386
1981-82	8,669,338
1982-83	8,669,338
1983-84	8,999,849
1984-85	9,217,664
1985-86	6,794,872
1986-87	6,478,910[1]
1987-88	4,077,100[2]
1988-89	4,077,071[2]

1. For 1986-87, the total appropriation to each institution in Senate Bill 1 was reduced by 6 percent of the 1986-87 general revenue appropriation in House Bill 20. This resulted in a different all funds percentage cut for each institution. The statewide average cut for the public senior colleges and universities as 4.65 percent. This amount assumes across the Board cuts and applies the 4.65 percent average reduction.
2. Amounts represent general revenue only. Total "all funds" will be projected when data are available.

The previous information shows the framework for the legislative strategic planning for higher education in the State of Texas. This very complex system operates on a series of coordinated activities that rely on fourteen Formula Advisory Committees composed mostly of representatives from Texas Colleges and Universities. The long-term objectives for the development of research in the State of Texas were set by the State Legislature in House Bill 2181. In that bill, the Legislature enacted the recommendations of the Texas Select Committee on Higher Education after the Committee had made a thorough study of state needs and resources for higher education. The Texas Formula System provides a state wide system of definitions, classifications, and planning procedures that allows all who are in the higher education enterprise to work with standardized, objective data and similar assumptions. It it a fundamental finance tool for developing higher education in the State of Texas and it is essential in the development of strategic planning for university research.

The formula system provides base funding for institutions of higher education but does not provide total appropriations in that the legislature funds special items related to research, start up of new programs, access to higher education, and other areas that are not in the formula system.